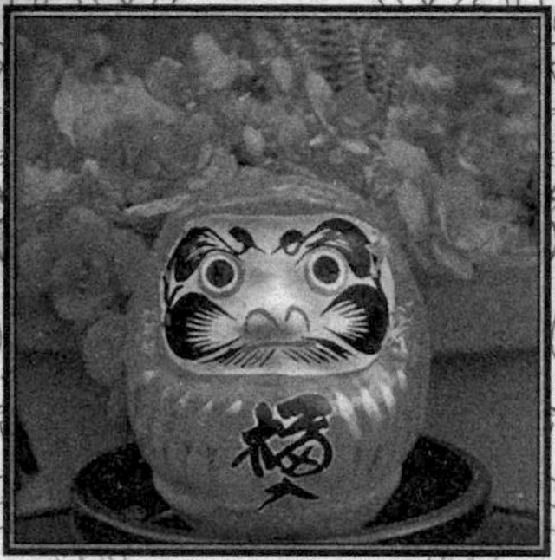
桜

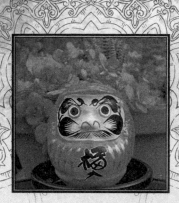

The *Black Clover* anime began airing without incident, so I filled in the right eye on my Daruma! To everyone who's involved with the anime: Thank you very, very, very much!

—*Yūki Tabata, 2017*

YŪKI TABATA
was born in Fukuoka Prefecture and got his big break in the 2011 Shonen Jump Golden Future Cup with his winning entry, *Hungry Joker*. He started the magical fantasy series *Black Clover* in 2015.

BLACK CLOVER
VOLUME 14
SHONEN JUMP Manga Edition

Story and Art by YŪKI TABATA

Translation ✤ TAYLOR ENGEL, HC LANGUAGE SOLUTIONS, INC.

Touch-Up Art & Lettering ✤ ANNALIESE CHRISTMAN

Design ✤ SHAWN CARRICO

Editor ✤ ALEXIS KIRSCH

First published in Japan in 2015 by SHUEISHA Inc., Tokyo.
English translation rights arranged by SHUEISHA Inc.

Printed in the U.S.A.

Published by VIZ Media, LLC
P.O. Box 77010
San Francisco, CA 94107

10 9 8 7 6 5 4 3 2 1
First printing, February 2019

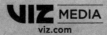

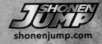

SHONEN JUMP MANGA

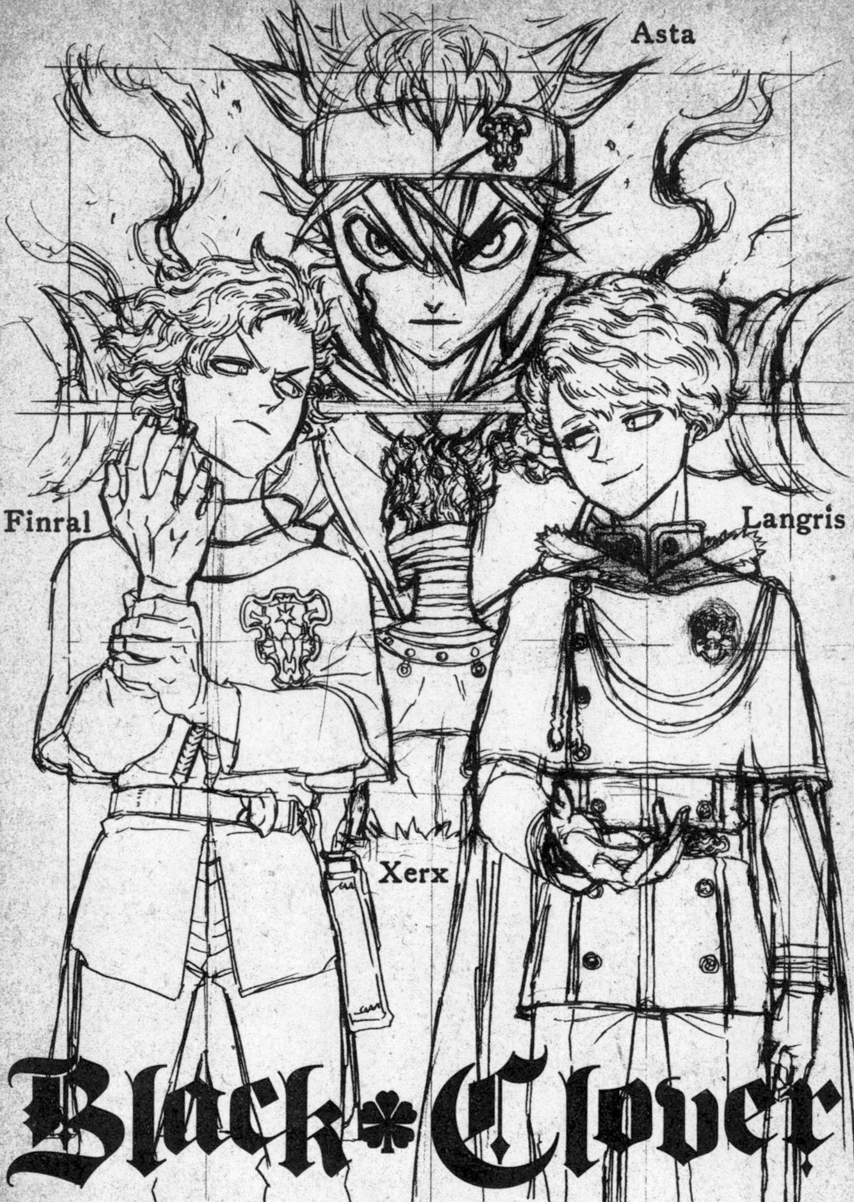
Asta
Finral
Langris
Xerx

Black Clover

YŪKI TABATA

14

GOLD AND BLACK SPARKS

Yuno

Member of:
The Golden Dawn Magic: Wind

Asta's best friend, and a good rival who's also been working to become the Wizard King. He controls Sylph, the spirit of wind.

Asta

 Member of: The Black Bulls
Magic: None (Anti-Magic)

He has no magic, but he's working to become the Wizard King through sheer guts and his well-trained body. He fights with an anti-magic sword.

Mimosa Vermillion

 Member of:
The Golden Dawn
Magic: Plant

Noelle's cousin. She's ladylike and a bit of an airhead, but she can be rude sometimes. She might like Asta...

Noelle Silva

 Member of:
The Black Bulls
Magic: Water

A royal. She feels inferior to her brilliant siblings. Her latent abilities are an unknown quantity.

Finral Roulacase

 Member of:
The Black Bulls
Magic: Spatial

A flirt who immediately chats up any woman he sees. He can't attack, but he has high-level abilities.

Magna Swing

 Member of:
The Black Bulls
Magic: Flame

He has the temperament of a delinquent, but he's quite courageous and does the right thing. Good at taking care of his companions.

Xerx Lugner (?)

Member of: ?
Magic: Ash

A mysterious character who appeared out of nowhere. He seems to have infiltrated the selection test, but his motives are unclear.

Sol Marron

Member of: The Blue Rose Knights
Magic: Earth

Spirited, freewheeling and exceptionally energetic. Adores her captain and calls her "Sis."

Kirsch Vermillion

Member of: The Coral Peacocks
Magic: Cherry Blossom

Mimosa's older brother. A narcissist who just can't get enough of beautiful things. There are rumors that he'll be the next brigade captain.

Langris Vaude

Member of: The Golden Dawn
Magic: Spatial

Finral's younger half brother. He isn't fond of Finral, who folded under the pressure of becoming head of their family.

Alecdora Sandler

Member of: The Golden Dawn
Magic: Sand

Due to his intense adoration for his captain, Vangeance, he sees Yuno as an enemy.

Solid Silva

Member of: The Silver Eagles
Magic: Water

Noelle's older brother. He looks down on Noelle, who became a Black Bull even though she's a royal.

❖ ❖ ❖

STORY

In a world where magic is everything, Asta and Yuno are both found abandoned on the same day at a church in the remote village of Hage. Both dream of becoming the Wizard King, the highest of all mages, and they spend their days working toward that dream.

The year they turn 15, both receive grimoires, magic books that amplify their bearer's magic. They take the entrance exam for the Magic Knights, nine groups of mages under the direct control of the Wizard King. Yuno, whose magic is strong, joins the Golden Dawn, an elite group, while Asta, who has no magic at all, joins the Black Bulls, a group of misfits. With this, the two finally take their first step toward becoming the Wizard King...

In the first round of the Royal Knights Selection Test, Asta and Mimosa fight as a team of three with the cynical Xerx. Xerx ignores teamwork and yanks them around, but they manage to win their way to the next round. After that, the drama continues, and in the final battle of the first round, Yuno and Noelle's team are pitted against Solid's team!

BLACK ❖ CLOVER

CONTENTS

BLACK ✣ CLOVER
14

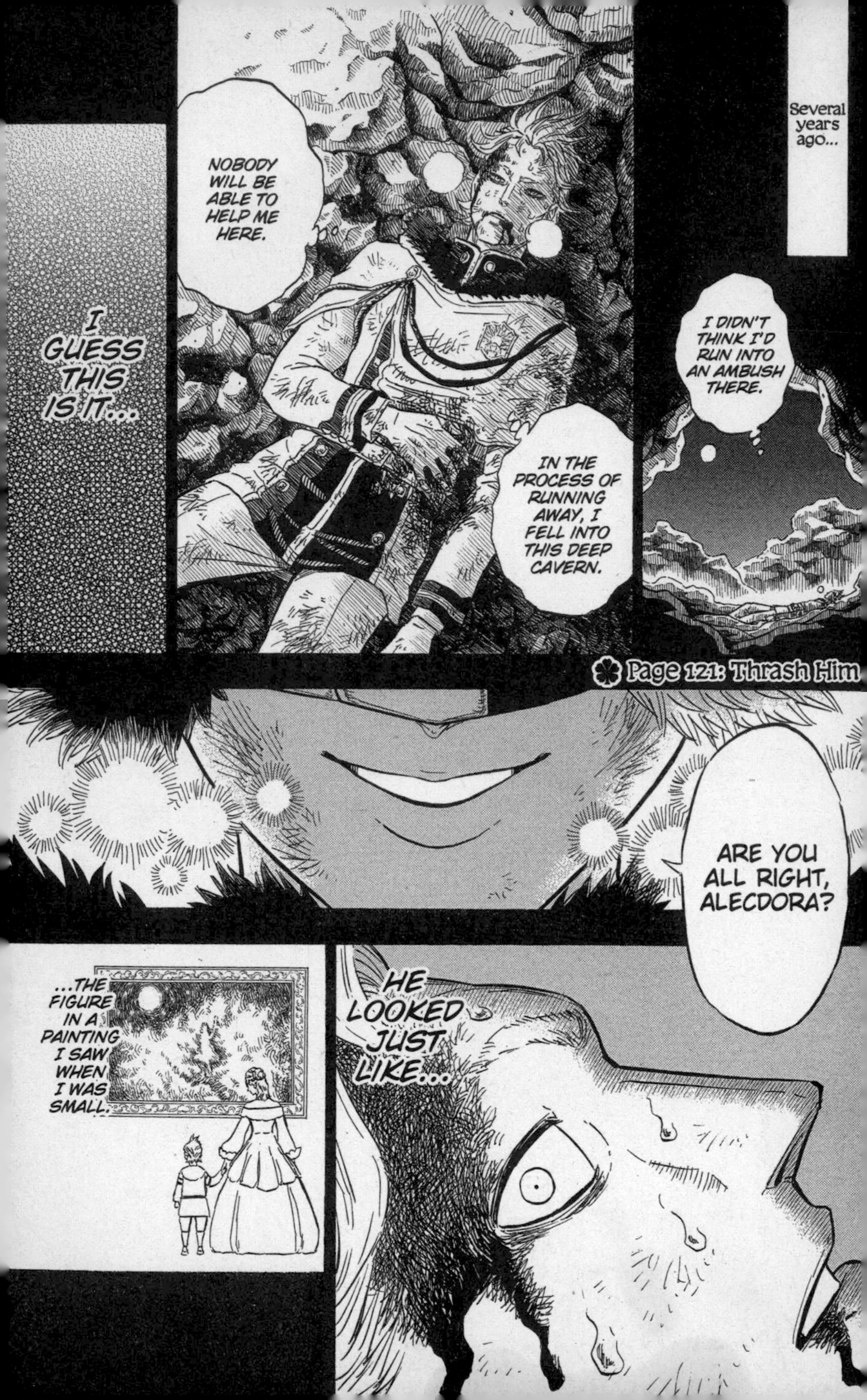
Several years ago...
I DIDN'T THINK I'D RUN INTO AN AMBUSH THERE.
IN THE PROCESS OF RUNNING AWAY, I FELL INTO THIS DEEP CAVERN.
NOBODY WILL BE ABLE TO HELP ME HERE.
I GUESS THIS IS IT...
Page 121: Thrash Him
ARE YOU ALL RIGHT, ALECDORA?
HE LOOKED JUST LIKE...
...THE FIGURE IN A PAINTING I SAW WHEN I WAS SMALL.

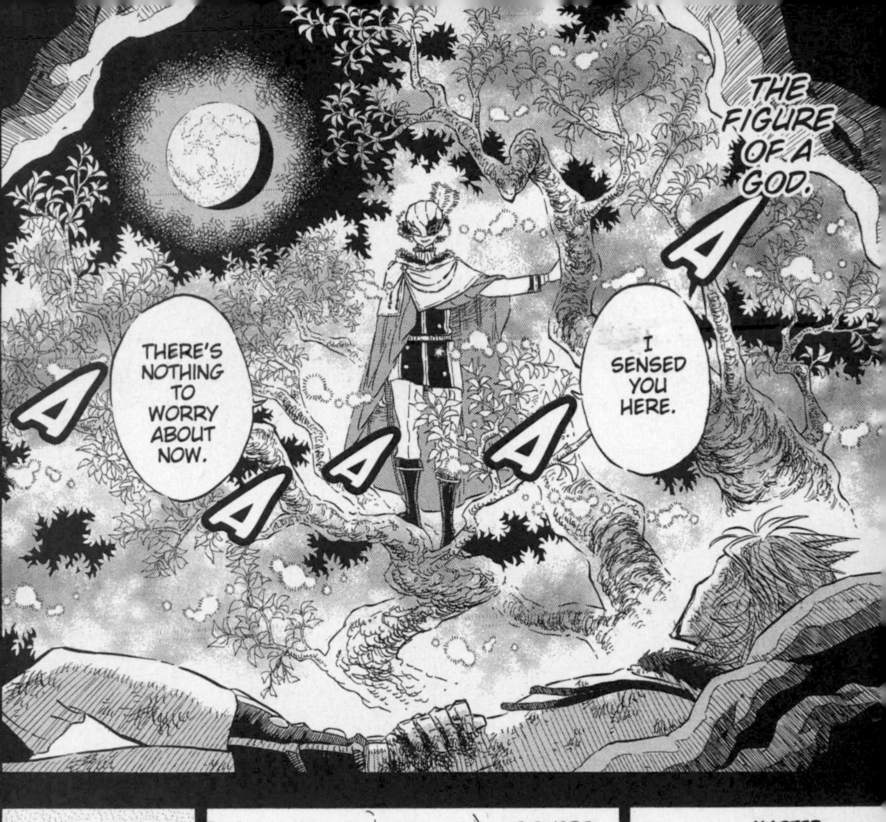
THE FIGURE OF A GOD.
I SENSED YOU HERE.
THERE'S NOTHING TO WORRY ABOUT NOW.
MASTER VANGEANCE HAS SOME OTHER MYSTERIOUS POWER BESIDES MAGIC.
A WARM POWER THAT SEEMS TO CONNECT HIM TO HIS BRIGADE MEMBERS.
I SWORE THAT I'D DEVOTE MY GRIMOIRE TO HIS SERVICE.
I WORKED HARD TO ENSURE THAT THE GOLDEN DAWN WOULD CONTINUE TO BE THE STRONGEST BRIGADE.
WE ARE AN ELITE TEAM OF NOBLES, CHOSEN BY MASTER VANGEANCE!!
HOWEVER, IN OUR MIDST...

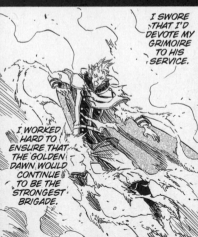

Page 121: Thrash Him

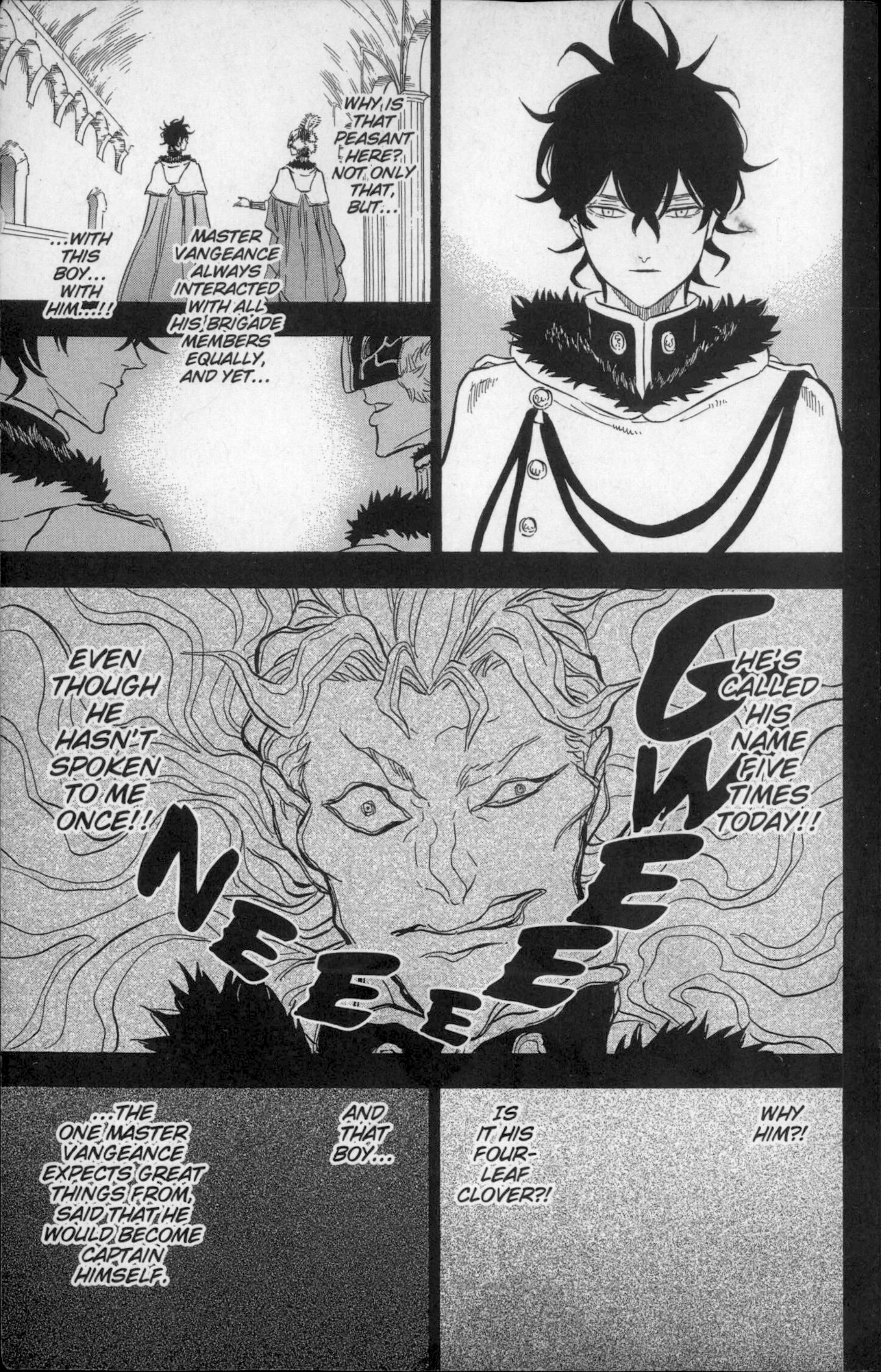
WHY IS THAT PEASANT HERE? NOT ONLY THAT, BUT...
MASTER VANGEANCE ALWAYS INTERACTED WITH ALL HIS BRIGADE MEMBERS EQUALLY, AND YET...
...WITH THIS BOY... WITH HIM...!!
HE'S CALLED HIS NAME FIVE TIMES TODAY!!
GWEEEEEEN
EVEN THOUGH HE HASN'T SPOKEN TO ME ONCE!!
WHY HIM?!
IS IT HIS FOUR-LEAF CLOVER?!
AND THAT BOY...
...THE ONE MASTER VANGEANCE EXPECTS GREAT THINGS FROM, SAID THAT HE WOULD BECOME CAPTAIN HIMSELF.

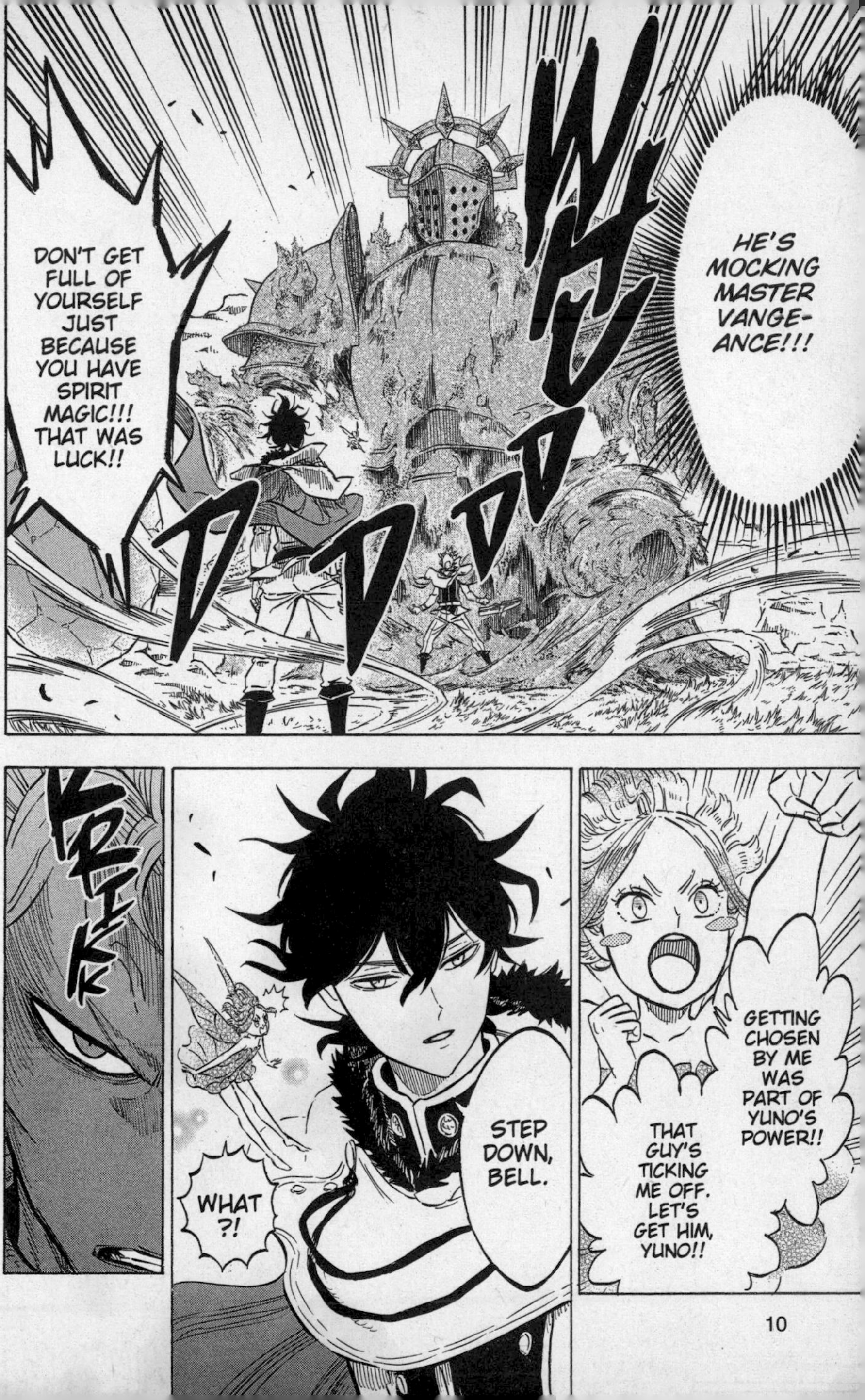
HE'S MOCKING MASTER VANGE-ANCE!!!
DON'T GET FULL OF YOURSELF JUST BECAUSE YOU HAVE SPIRIT MAGIC!!! THAT WAS LUCK!!
GETTING CHOSEN BY ME WAS PART OF YUNO'S POWER!!
THAT GUY'S TICKING ME OFF. LET'S GET HIM, YUNO!!
STEP DOWN, BELL.
WHAT ?!

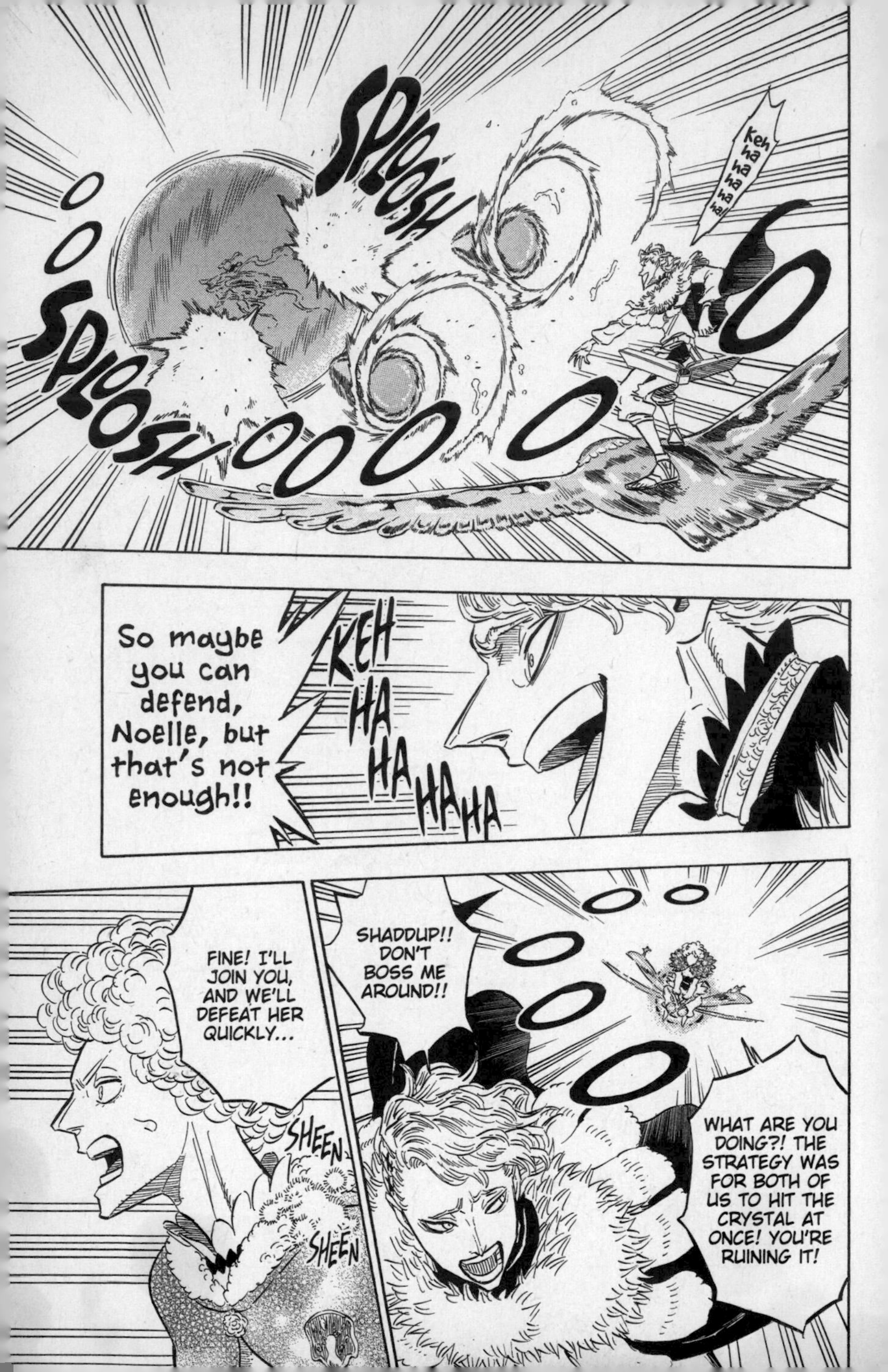
Keh ha ha ha ha ha!
SPLOOSH
OOOOOOOO
SPLOOSH
KEH HA HA HA HA HA
So maybe you can defend, Noelle, but that's not enough!!
OOOOOO
WHAT ARE YOU DOING?! THE STRATEGY WAS FOR BOTH OF US TO HIT THE CRYSTAL AT ONCE! YOU'RE RUINING IT!
SHADDUP!! DON'T BOSS ME AROUND!!
FINE! I'LL JOIN YOU, AND WE'LL DEFEAT HER QUICKLY...
SHEEN
SHEEN

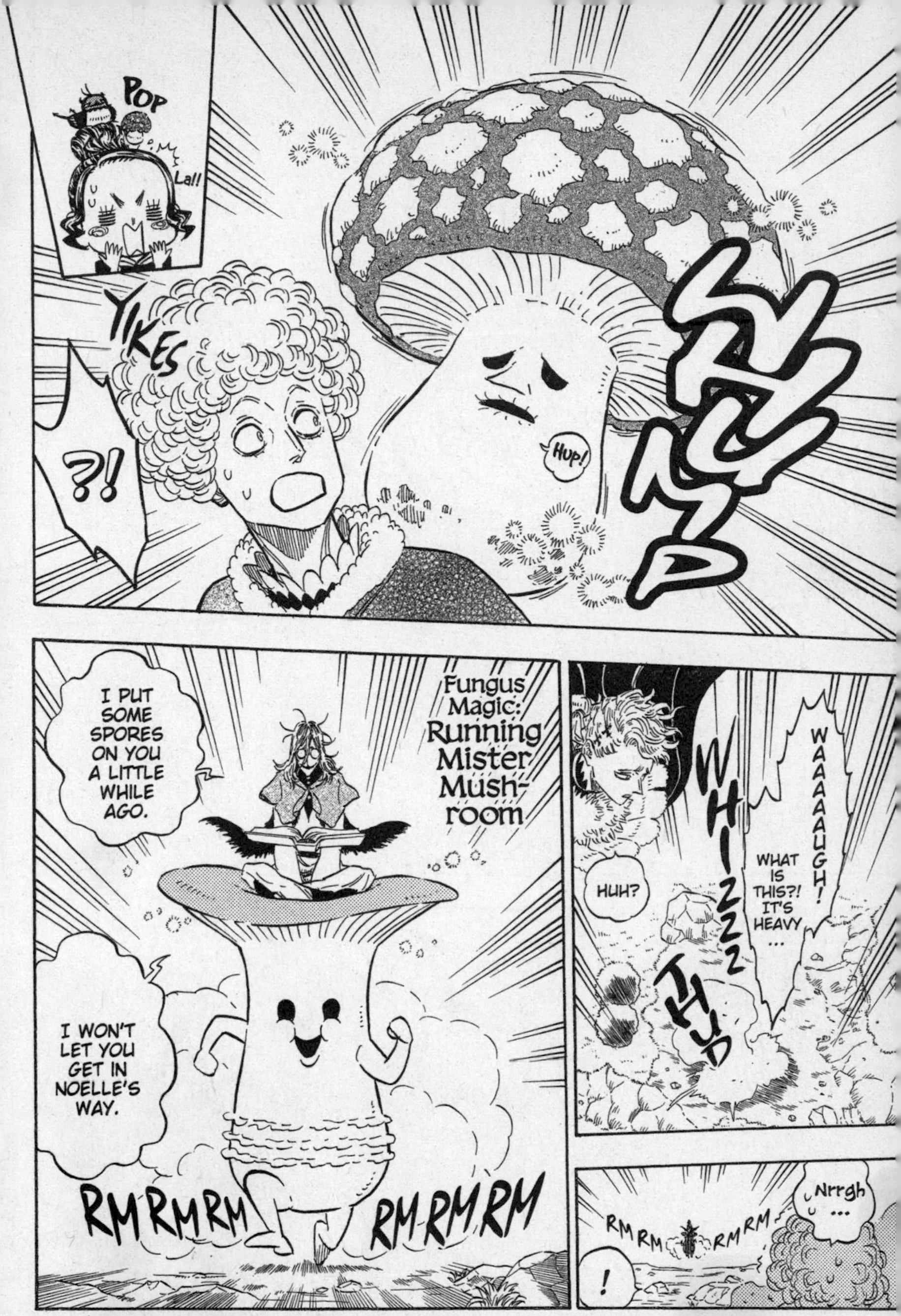
SLUMP
Hup!
?!
YIKES
POP
Lal!
WAAAAAAUGH!
WHIZZZ
WHAT IS THIS?! IT'S HEAVY...
HUH?
THUD
Nrrgh...
RM RM RM RM
!
Fungus Magic: Running Mister Mushroom
I PUT SOME SPORES ON YOU A LITTLE WHILE AGO.
I WON'T LET YOU GET IN NOELLE'S WAY.
RM RM RM
RM RM RM

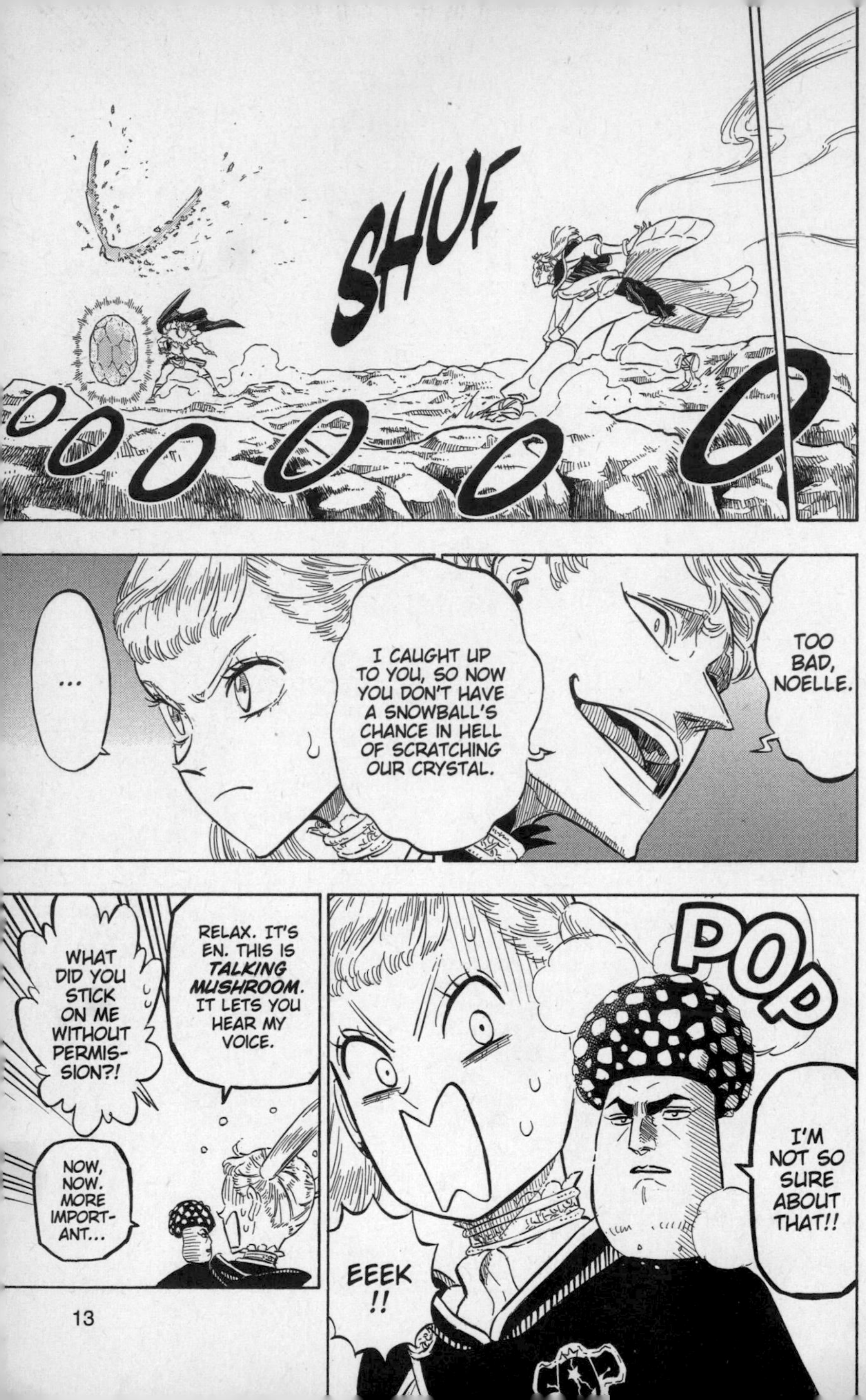
SHUF
OOOOOO
TOO BAD, NOELLE.
I CAUGHT UP TO YOU, SO NOW YOU DON'T HAVE A SNOWBALL'S CHANCE IN HELL OF SCRATCHING OUR CRYSTAL.
...
POP
I'M NOT SO SURE ABOUT THAT!!
EEEK!!
RELAX. IT'S EN. THIS IS *TALKING MUSHROOM*. IT LETS YOU HEAR MY VOICE.
WHAT DID YOU STICK ON ME WITHOUT PERMISSION?!
NOW, NOW. MORE IMPORTANT...

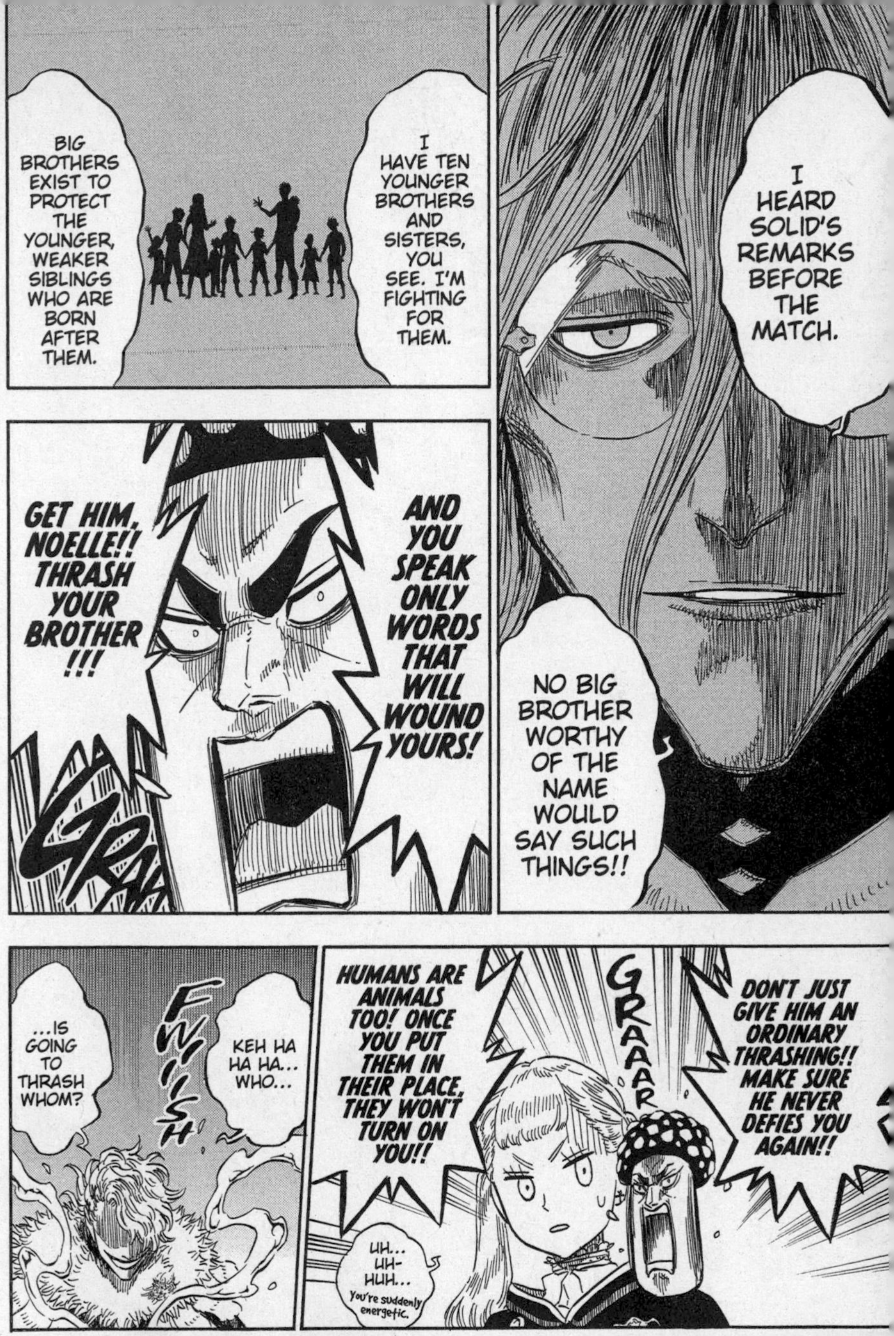
I HEARD SOLID'S REMARKS BEFORE THE MATCH.
NO BIG BROTHER WORTHY OF THE NAME WOULD SAY SUCH THINGS!!
I HAVE TEN YOUNGER BROTHERS AND SISTERS, YOU SEE. I'M FIGHTING FOR THEM.
BIG BROTHERS EXIST TO PROTECT THE YOUNGER, WEAKER SIBLINGS WHO ARE BORN AFTER THEM.
AND YOU SPEAK ONLY WORDS THAT WILL WOUND YOURS!
GET HIM, NOELLE!! THRASH YOUR BROTHER!!!
DON'T JUST GIVE HIM AN ORDINARY THRASHING!! MAKE SURE HE NEVER DEFIES YOU AGAIN!!
GRAAAR
HUMANS ARE ANIMALS TOO! ONCE YOU PUT THEM IN THEIR PLACE, THEY WON'T TURN ON YOU!!
UH... UH-HUH...
You're suddenly energetic.
KEH HA HA HA... WHO...
FWIISH
...IS GOING TO THRASH WHOM?

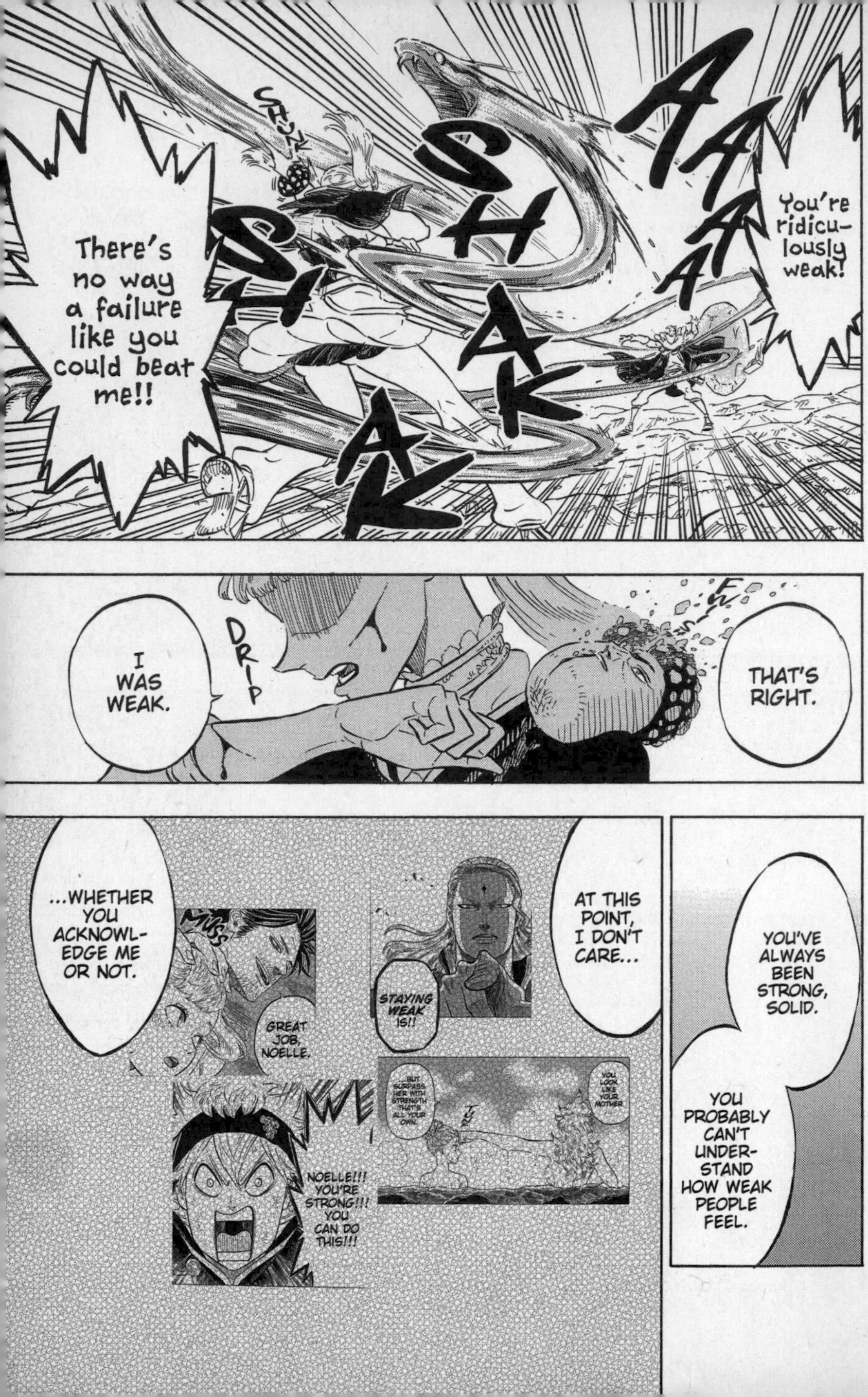
AAAA
You're ridiculously weak!
SHAK
SHAK
SHUNK
There's no way a failure like you could beat me!!
THAT'S RIGHT.
FWSH
DRIP
I WAS WEAK.
YOU'VE ALWAYS BEEN STRONG, SOLID.
YOU PROBABLY CAN'T UNDERSTAND HOW WEAK PEOPLE FEEL.
AT THIS POINT, I DON'T CARE...
STAYING WEAK IS!!
...WHETHER YOU ACKNOWLEDGE ME OR NOT.
MUSS
GREAT JOB, NOELLE.
YOU LOOK LIKE YOUR MOTHER...
...BUT SURPASS HER WITH STRENGTH THAT'S ALL YOUR OWN.
NOELLE!!! YOU'RE STRONG!!! YOU CAN DO THIS!!!

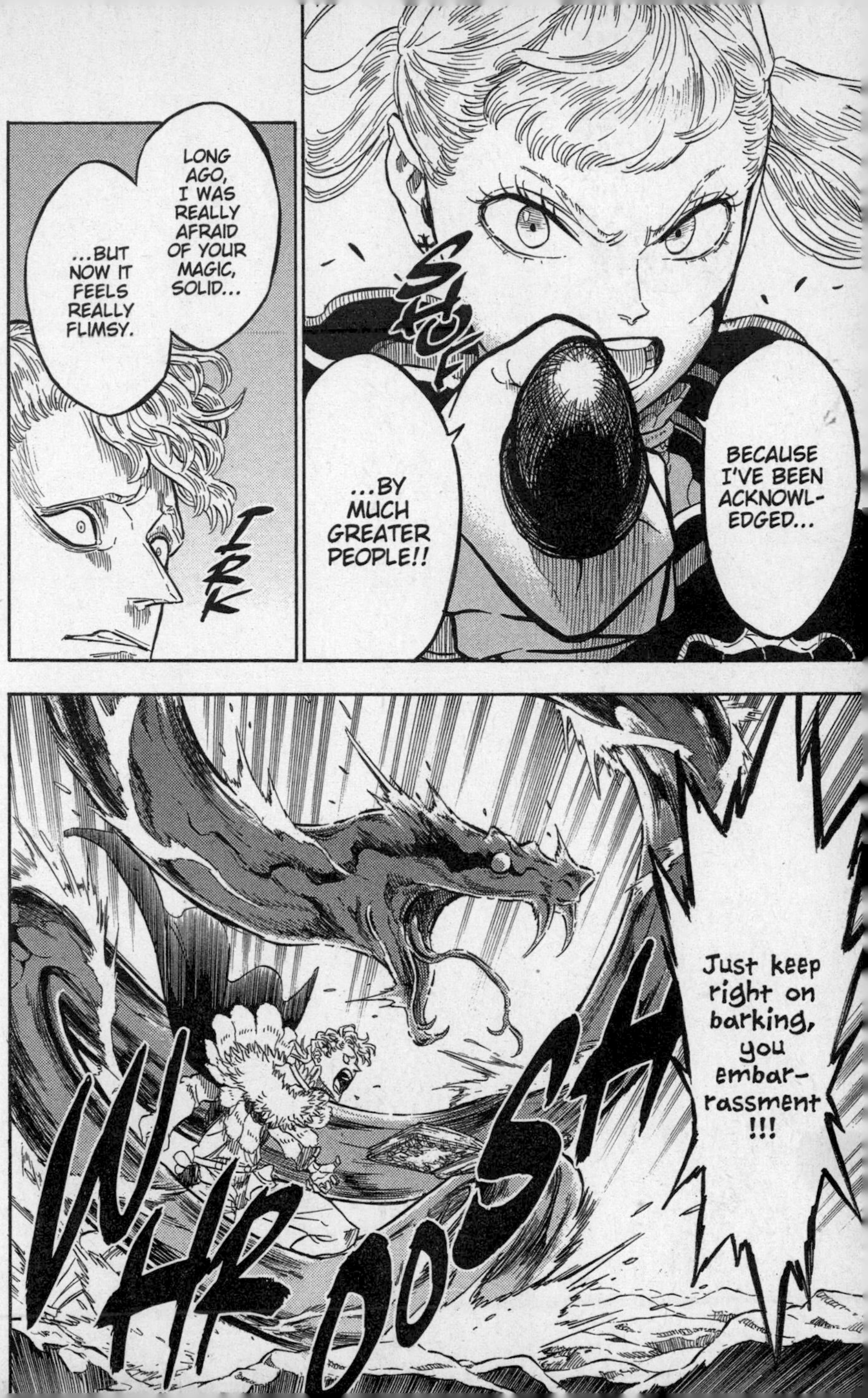
BECAUSE I'VE BEEN ACKNOWL-EDGED...
...BY MUCH GREATER PEOPLE!!
LONG AGO, I WAS REALLY AFRAID OF YOUR MAGIC, SOLID...
...BUT NOW IT FEELS REALLY FLIMSY.
IRK
Just keep right on barking, you embar-rassment!!!
WHROOSH

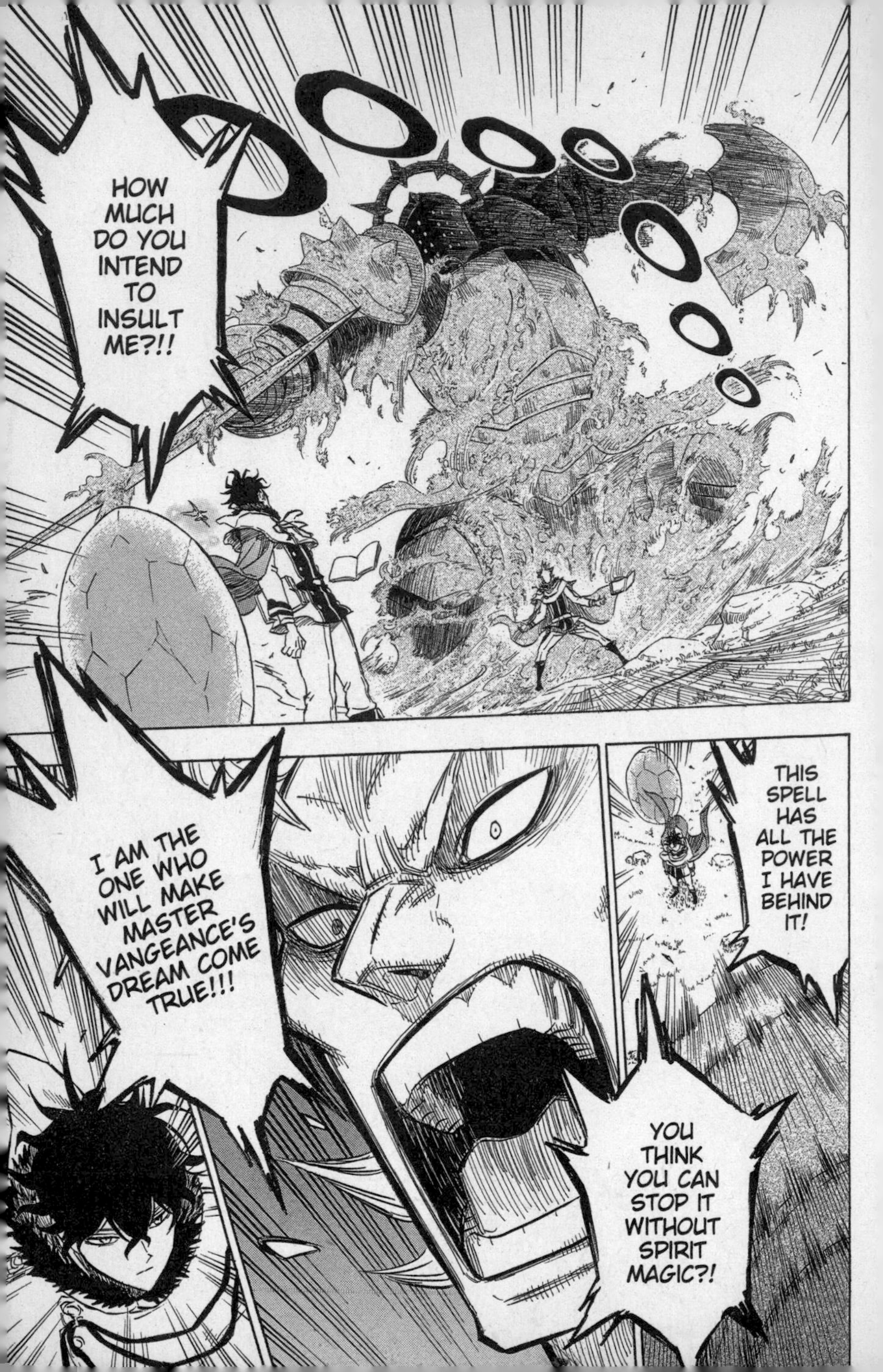
HOW MUCH DO YOU INTEND TO INSULT ME?!!
DOOOOOOO
THIS SPELL HAS ALL THE POWER I HAVE BEHIND IT!
YOU THINK YOU CAN STOP IT WITHOUT SPIRIT MAGIC?!
I AM THE ONE WHO WILL MAKE MASTER VANGEANCE'S DREAM COME TRUE!!!

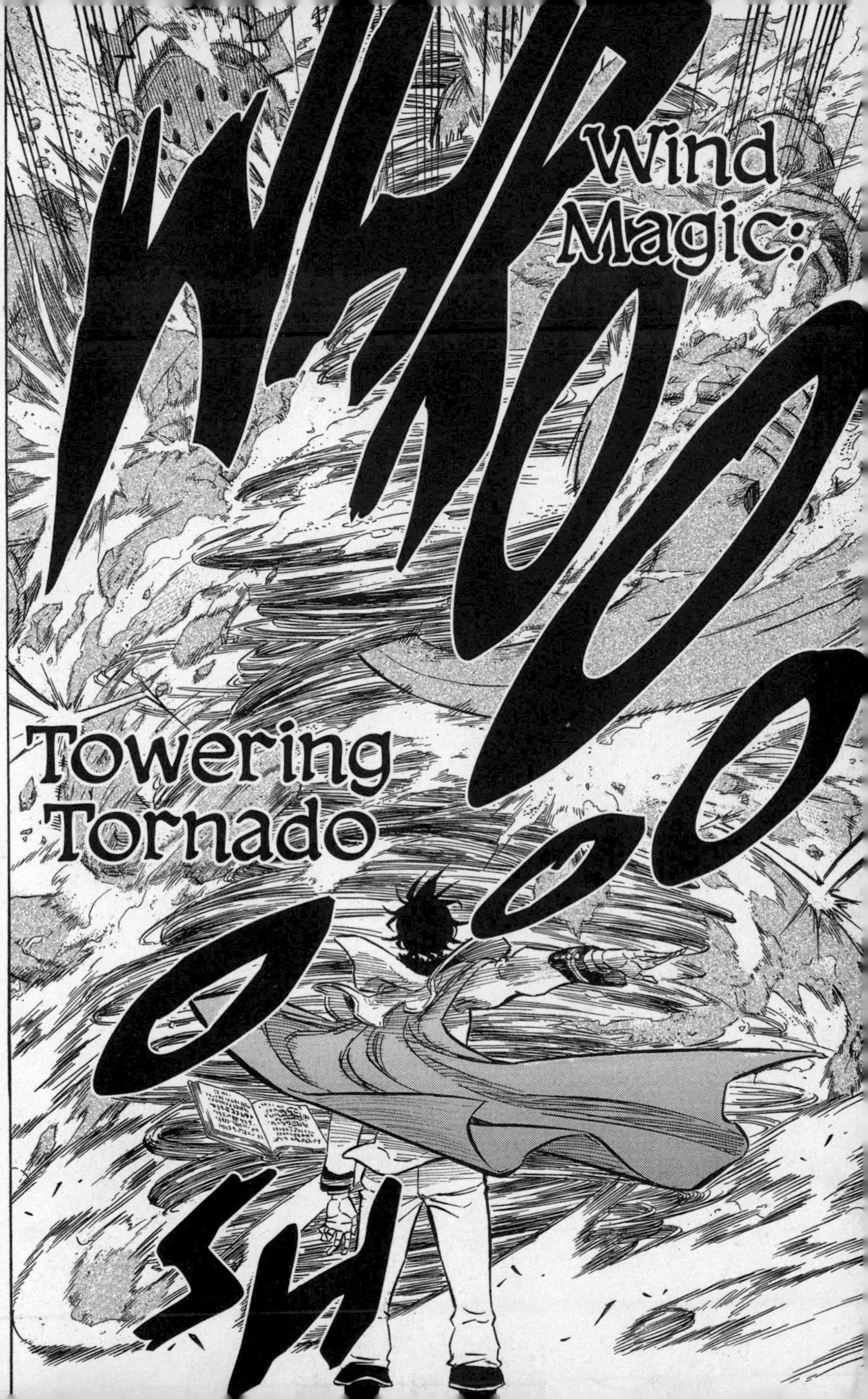
Wind Magic:
Towering Tornado

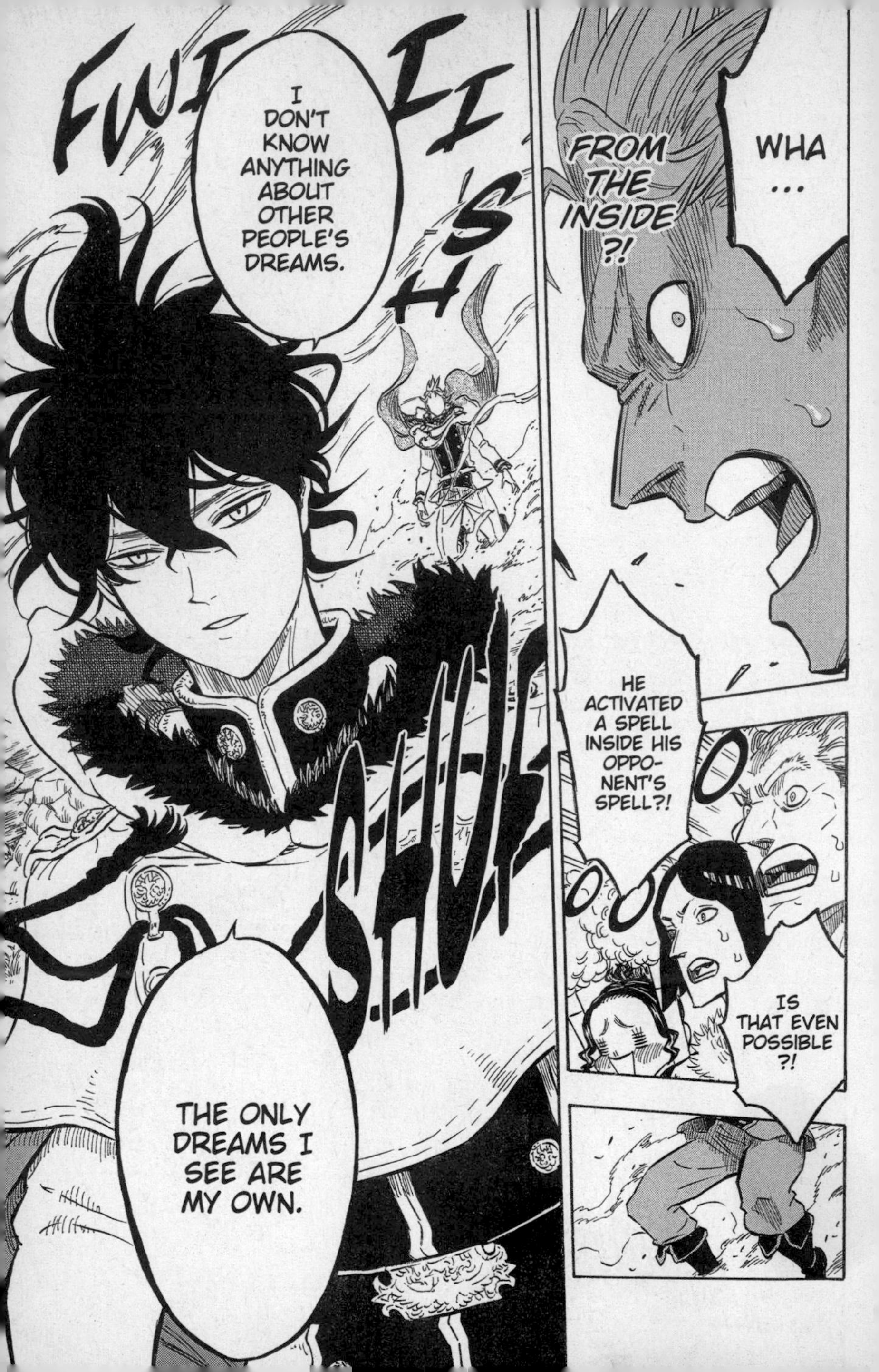
WHA...
FROM THE INSIDE?!
HE ACTIVATED A SPELL INSIDE HIS OPPONENT'S SPELL?!
IS THAT EVEN POSSIBLE?!
FWIIISH
I DON'T KNOW ANYTHING ABOUT OTHER PEOPLE'S DREAMS.
SHUF
THE ONLY DREAMS I SEE ARE MY OWN.

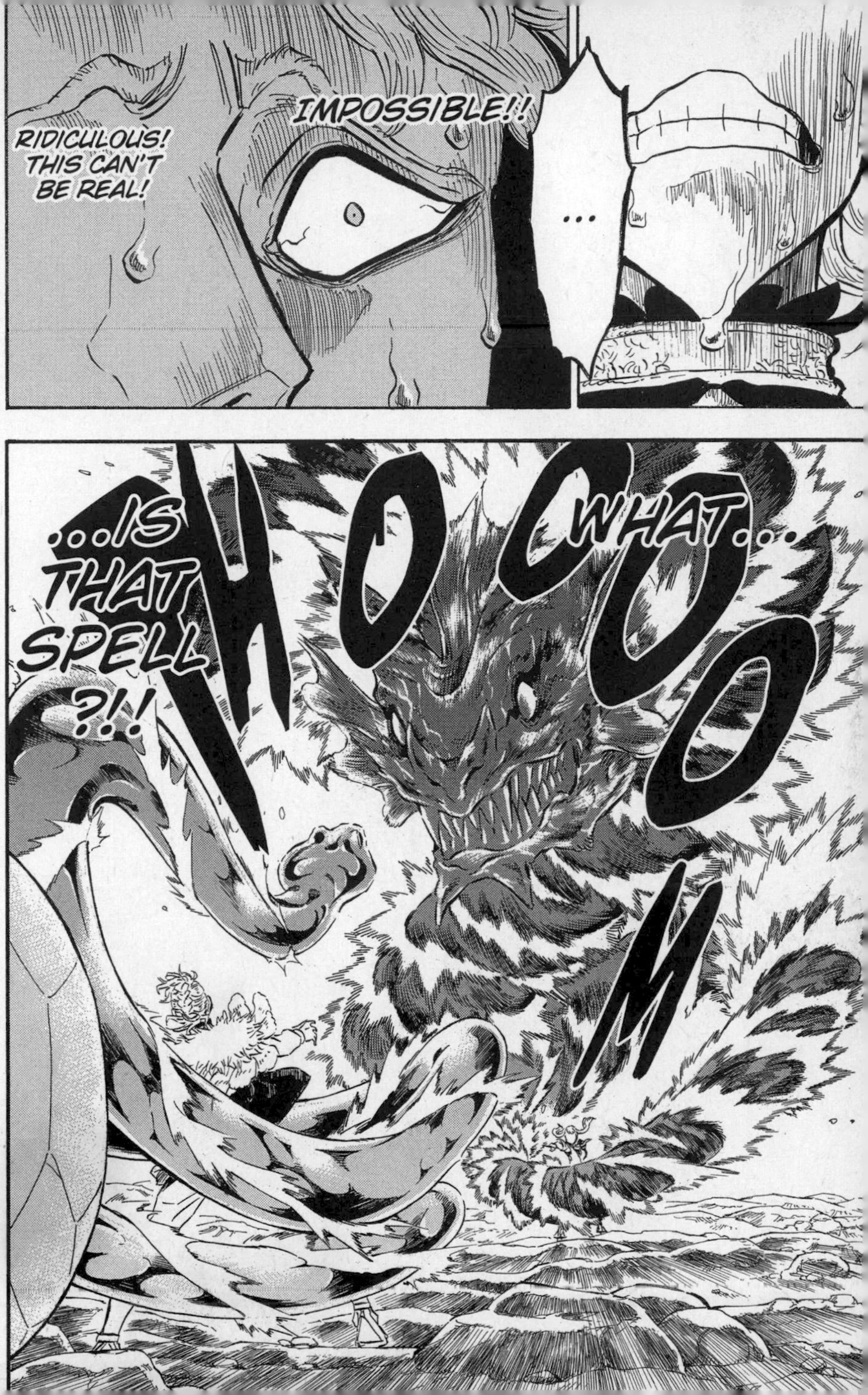
...
IMPOSSIBLE!!
RIDICULOUS! THIS CAN'T BE REAL!
WHAT...
HOOOOM
...IS THAT SPELL ?!!

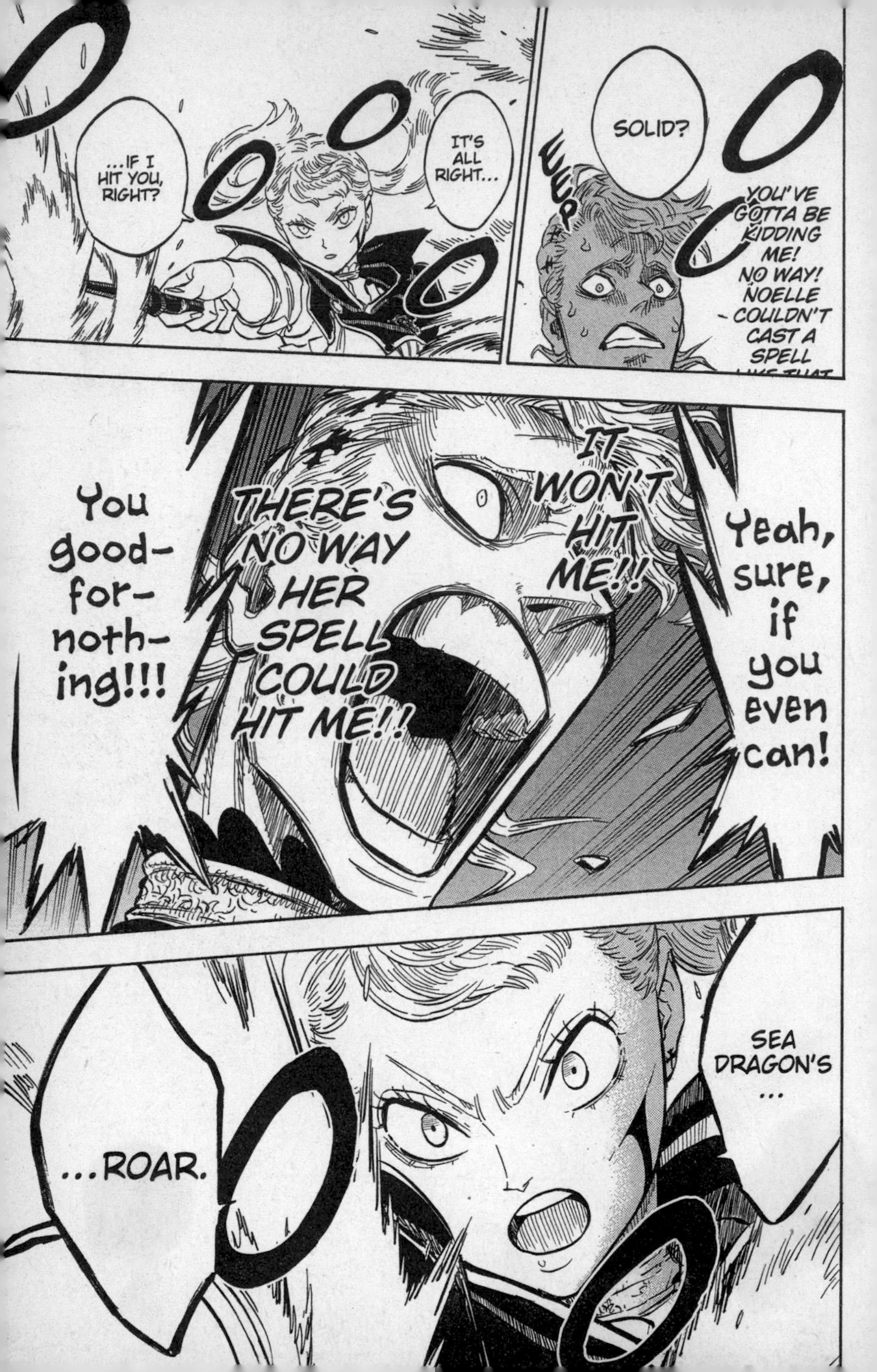
SOLID?
EEP
YOU'VE GOTTA BE KIDDING ME! NO WAY! NOELLE COULDN'T CAST A SPELL
IT'S ALL RIGHT...
...IF I HIT YOU, RIGHT?
Yeah, sure, if you even can!
IT WON'T HIT ME!!
THERE'S NO WAY HER SPELL COULD HIT ME!!
You good-for-nothing!!!
SEA DRAGON'S...
...ROAR.

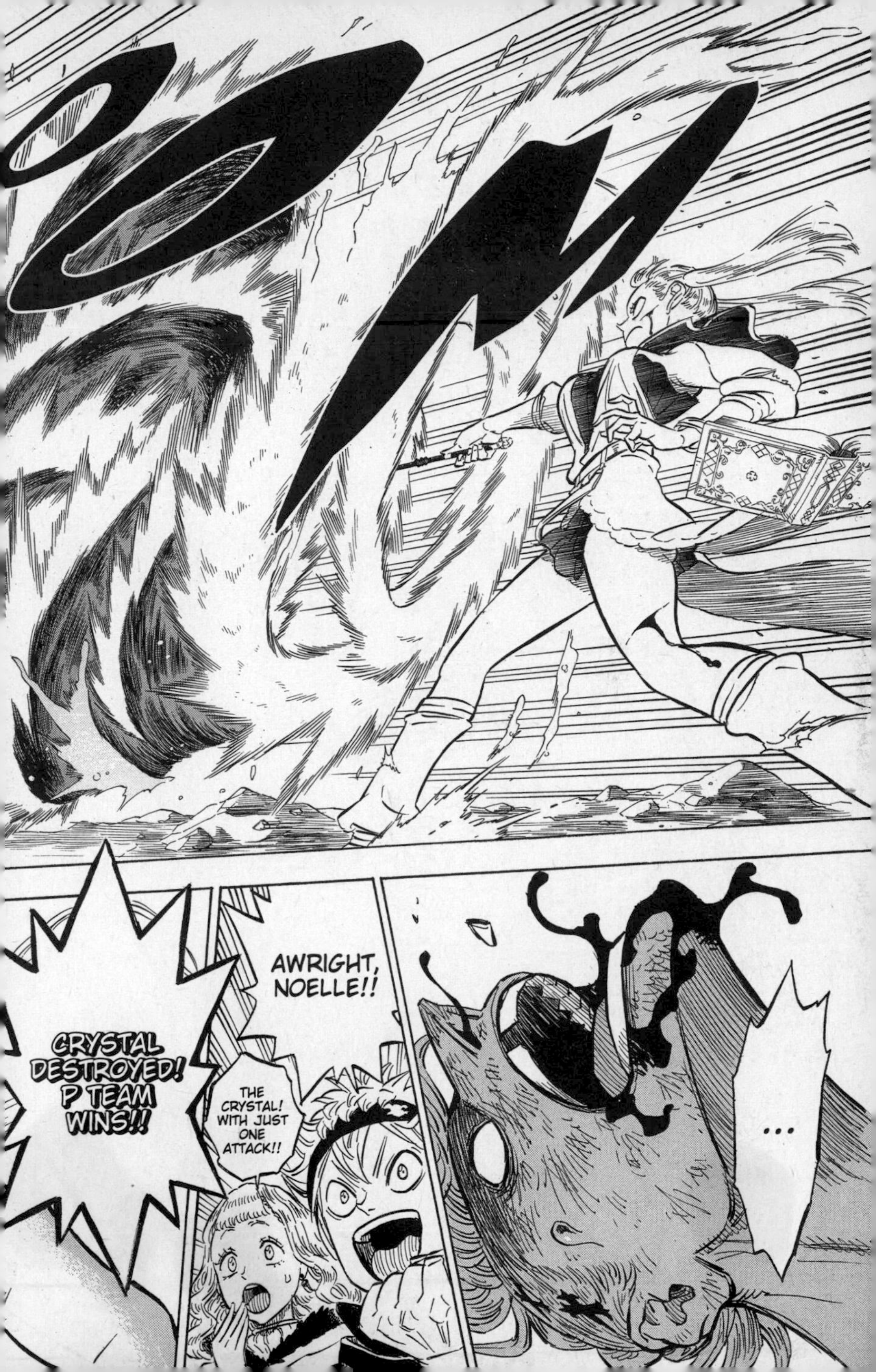
...
AWRIGHT, NOELLE!!
CRYSTAL DESTROYED! P TEAM WINS!!
THE CRYSTAL! WITH JUST ONE ATTACK!!

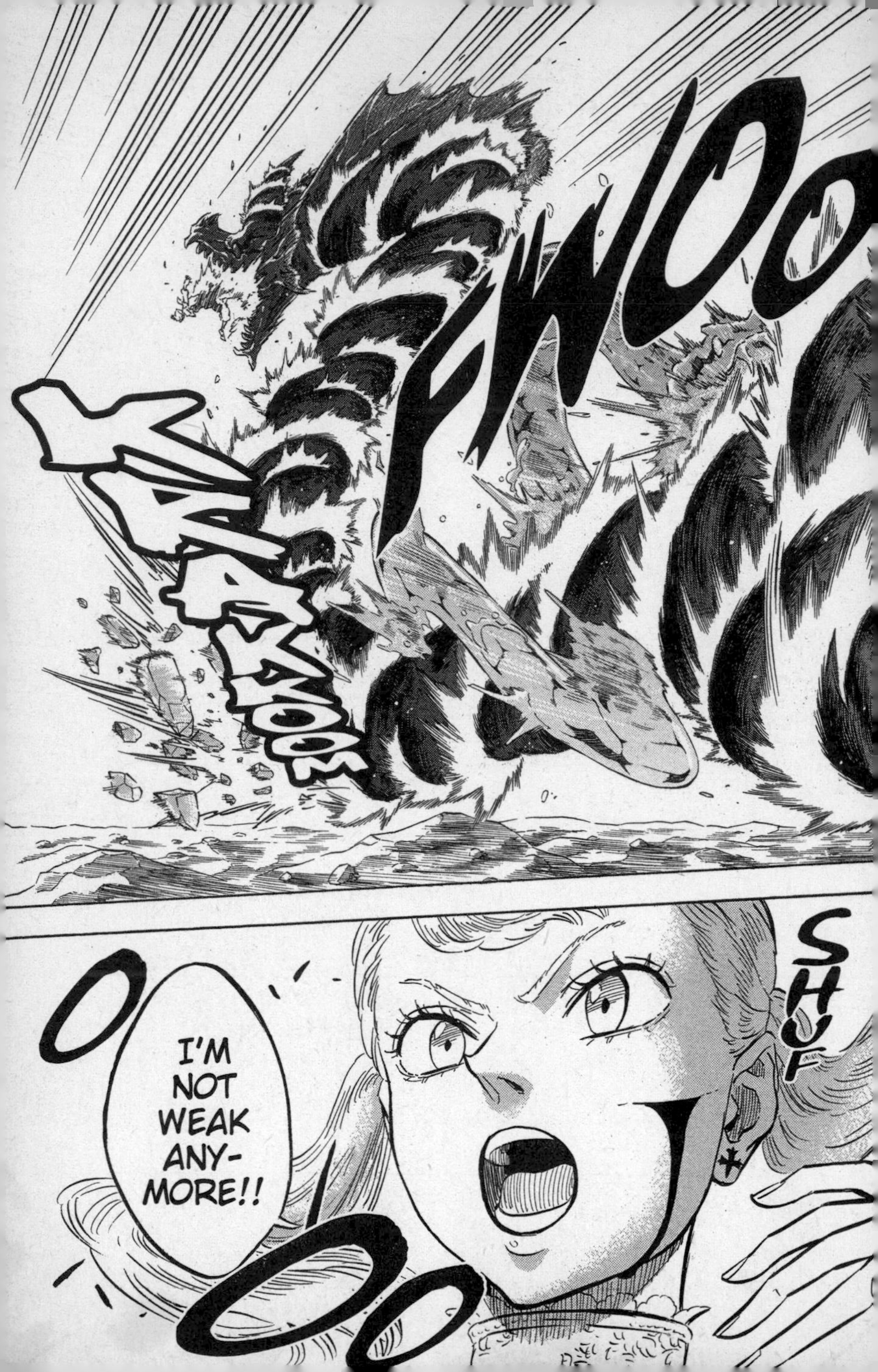
FWOO
KABOOM
SHUF
I'M NOT WEAK ANY-MORE!!

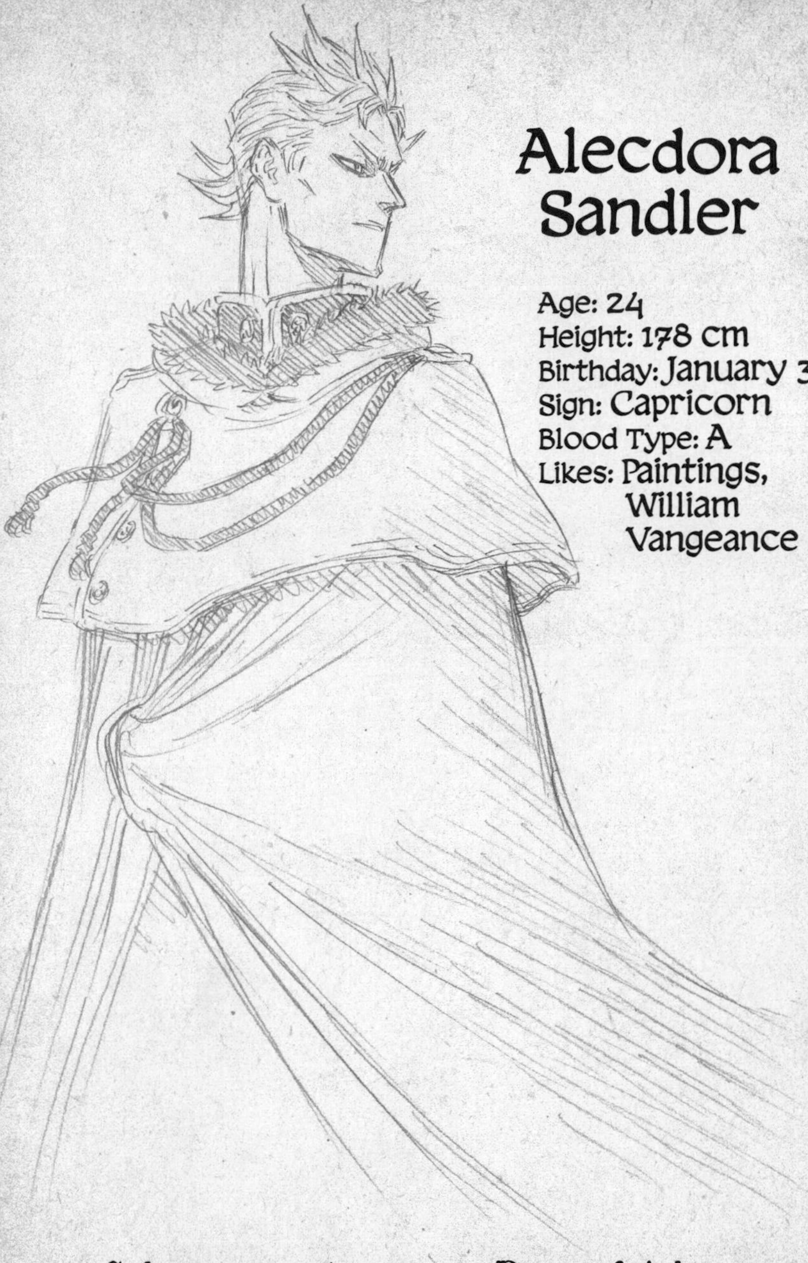

Alecdora Sandler

Age: 24
Height: 178 cm
Birthday: January 3
Sign: Capricorn
Blood Type: A
Likes: Paintings, William Vangeance

Character Profile

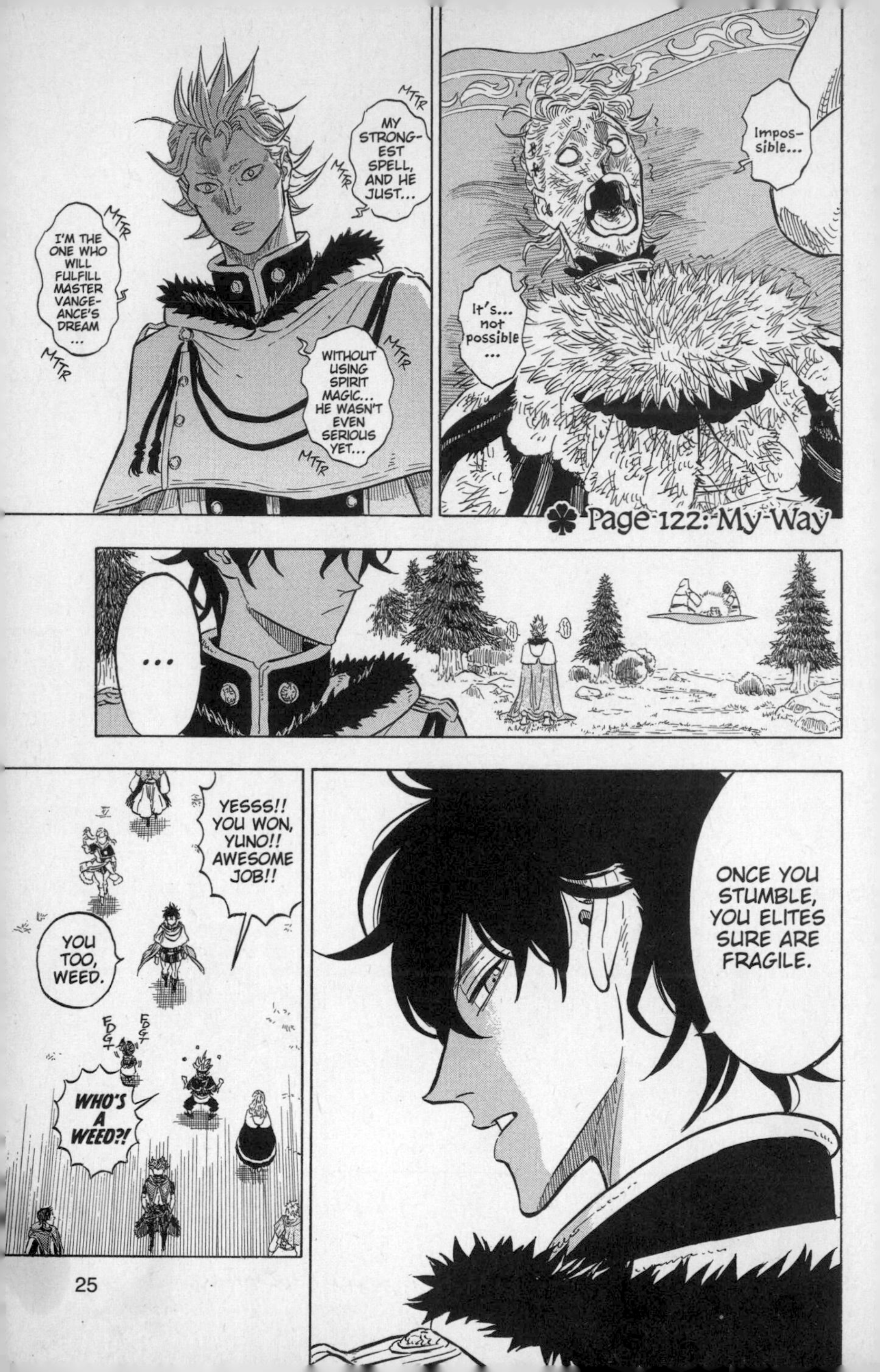
Impos-sible...
It's... not possible...
MTTR
MY STRONG-EST SPELL, AND HE JUST...
I'M THE ONE WHO WILL FULFILL MASTER VANGE-ANCE'S DREAM...
WITHOUT USING SPIRIT MAGIC... HE WASN'T EVEN SERIOUS YET...
Page 122: My Way
...
ONCE YOU STUMBLE, YOU ELITES SURE ARE FRAGILE.
YESSS!! YOU WON, YUNO!! AWESOME JOB!!
YOU TOO, WEED.
FDGT
WHO'S A WEED?!

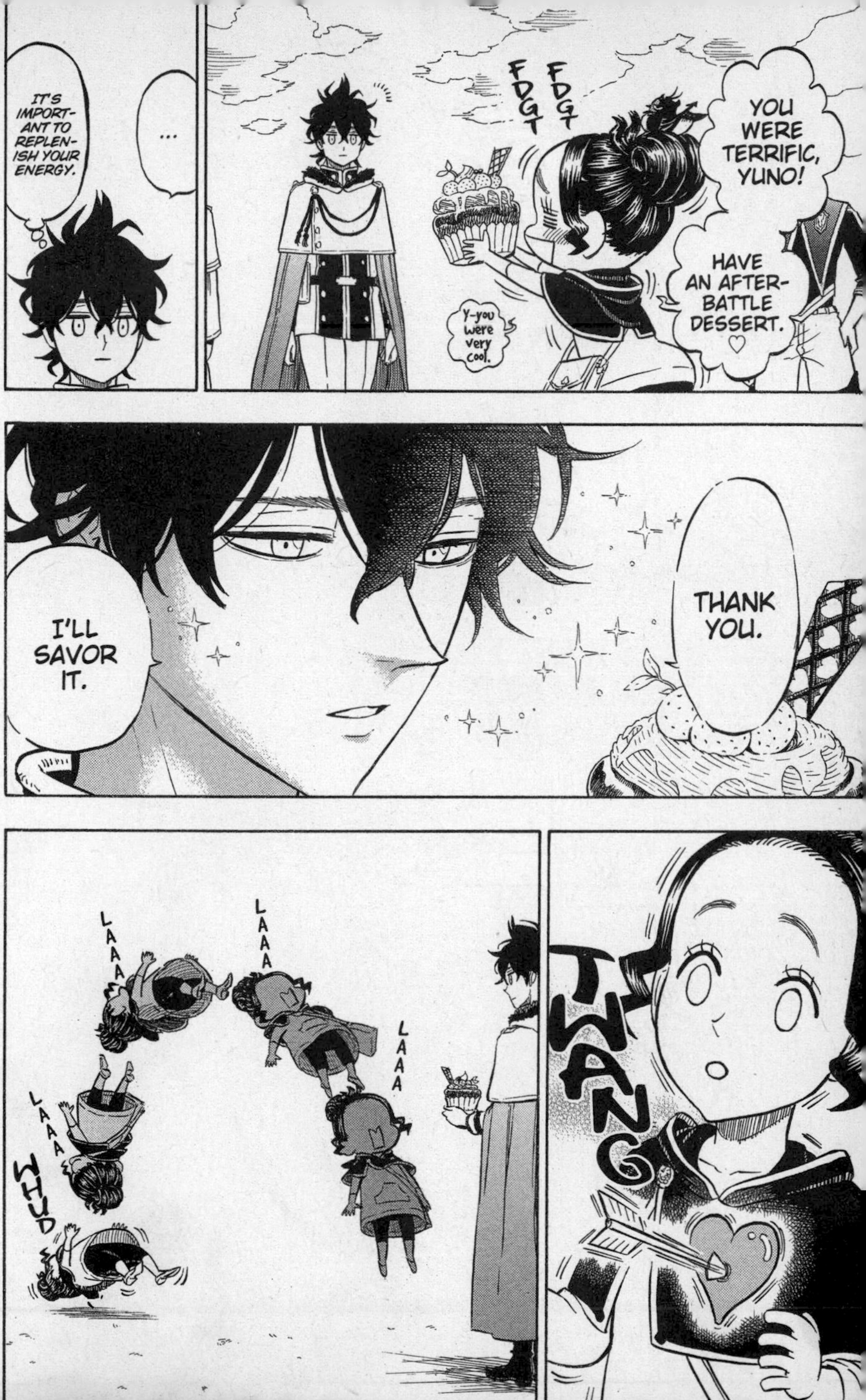

YOU WERE TERRIFIC, YUNO!
FDGT
FDGT
HAVE AN AFTER-BATTLE DESSERT. ♡
Y-you were very cool.
...
IT'S IMPORTANT TO REPLENISH YOUR ENERGY.
THANK YOU.
I'LL SAVOR IT.
THWANG
LAAA
LAAA
LAAA
LAAA
WHUD

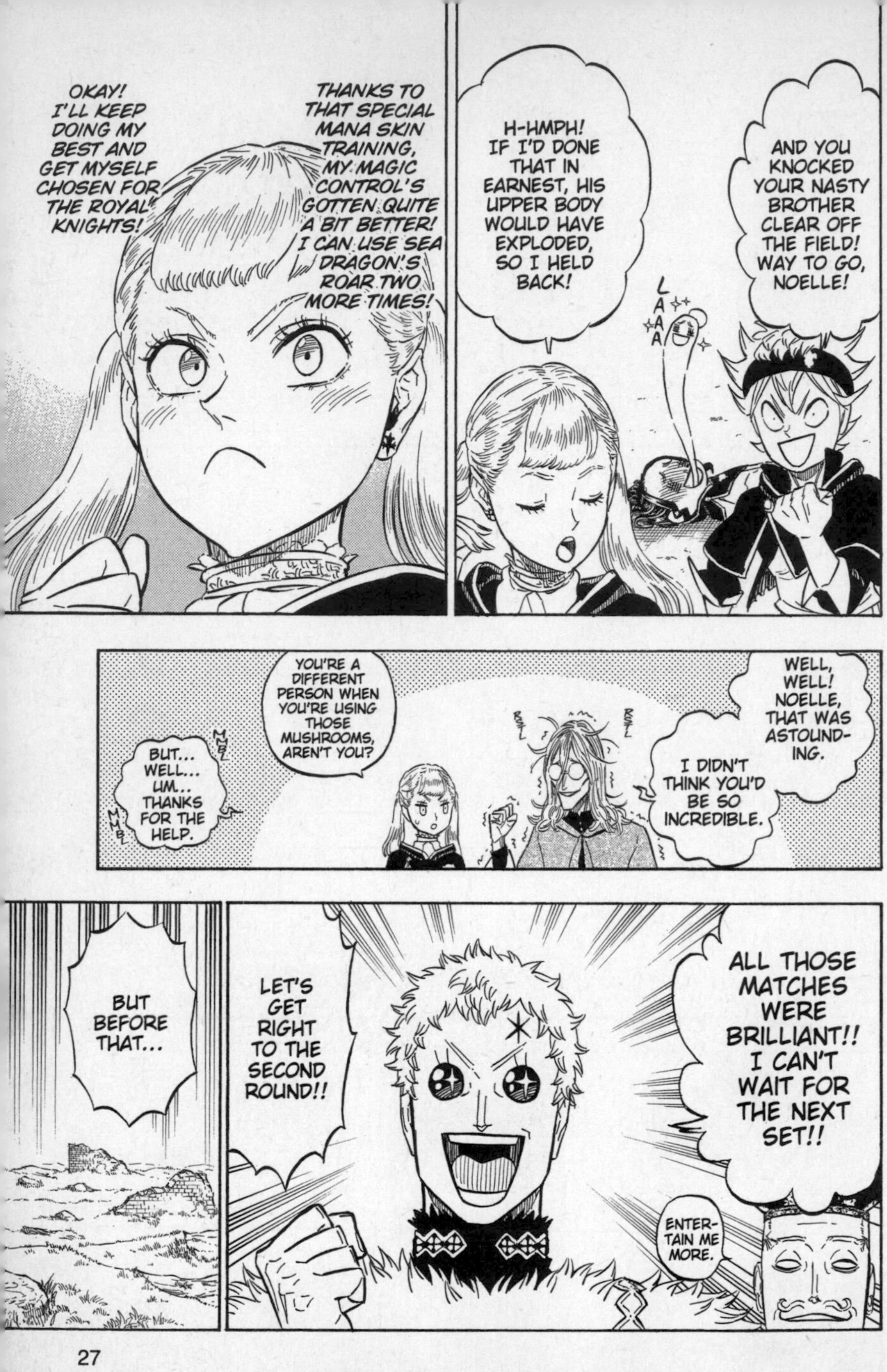
AND YOU KNOCKED YOUR NASTY BROTHER CLEAR OFF THE FIELD! WAY TO GO, NOELLE!
H-HMPH! IF I'D DONE THAT IN EARNEST, HIS UPPER BODY WOULD HAVE EXPLODED, SO I HELD BACK!
LAAAA
THANKS TO THAT SPECIAL MANA SKIN TRAINING, MY MAGIC CONTROL'S GOTTEN QUITE A BIT BETTER! I CAN USE SEA DRAGON'S ROAR TWO MORE TIMES!
OKAY! I'LL KEEP DOING MY BEST AND GET MYSELF CHOSEN FOR THE ROYAL KNIGHTS!
WELL, WELL! NOELLE, THAT WAS ASTOUNDING.
I DIDN'T THINK YOU'D BE SO INCREDIBLE.
RSL
RSL
YOU'RE A DIFFERENT PERSON WHEN YOU'RE USING THOSE MUSHROOMS, AREN'T YOU?
MMBL
BUT... WELL... UM... THANKS FOR THE HELP.
MMBL
ALL THOSE MATCHES WERE BRILLIANT!! I CAN'T WAIT FOR THE NEXT SET!!
ENTERTAIN ME MORE.
LET'S GET RIGHT TO THE SECOND ROUND!!
BUT BEFORE THAT...

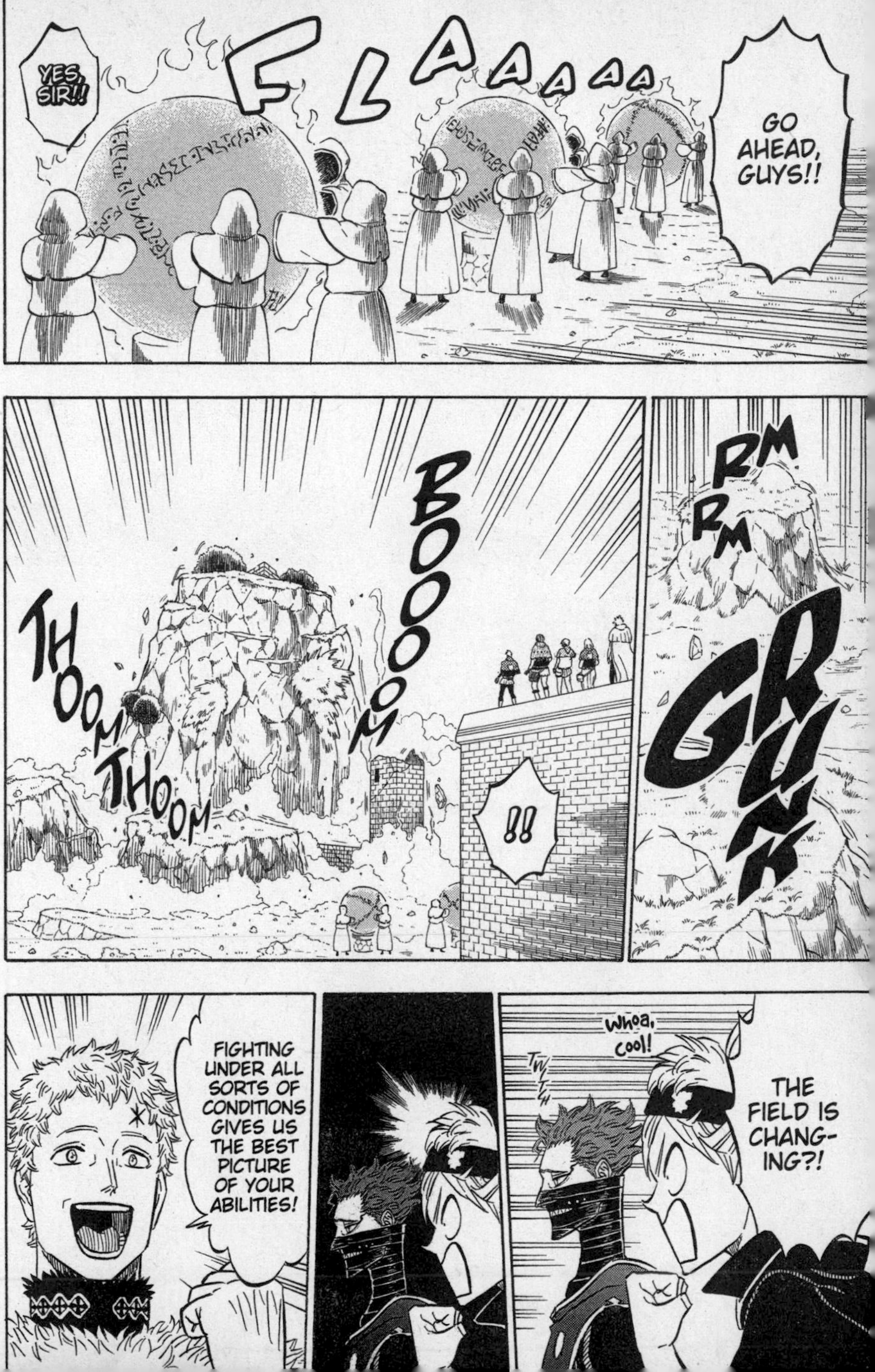
GO AHEAD, GUYS!!
FLAAAAA
YES, SIR!!
RM RM
GRUNK
BOOOOOM
THOOM THOOM
!!
THE FIELD IS CHANG-ING?!
Whoa, cool!
TWITCH
FIGHTING UNDER ALL SORTS OF CONDITIONS GIVES US THE BEST PICTURE OF YOUR ABILITIES!

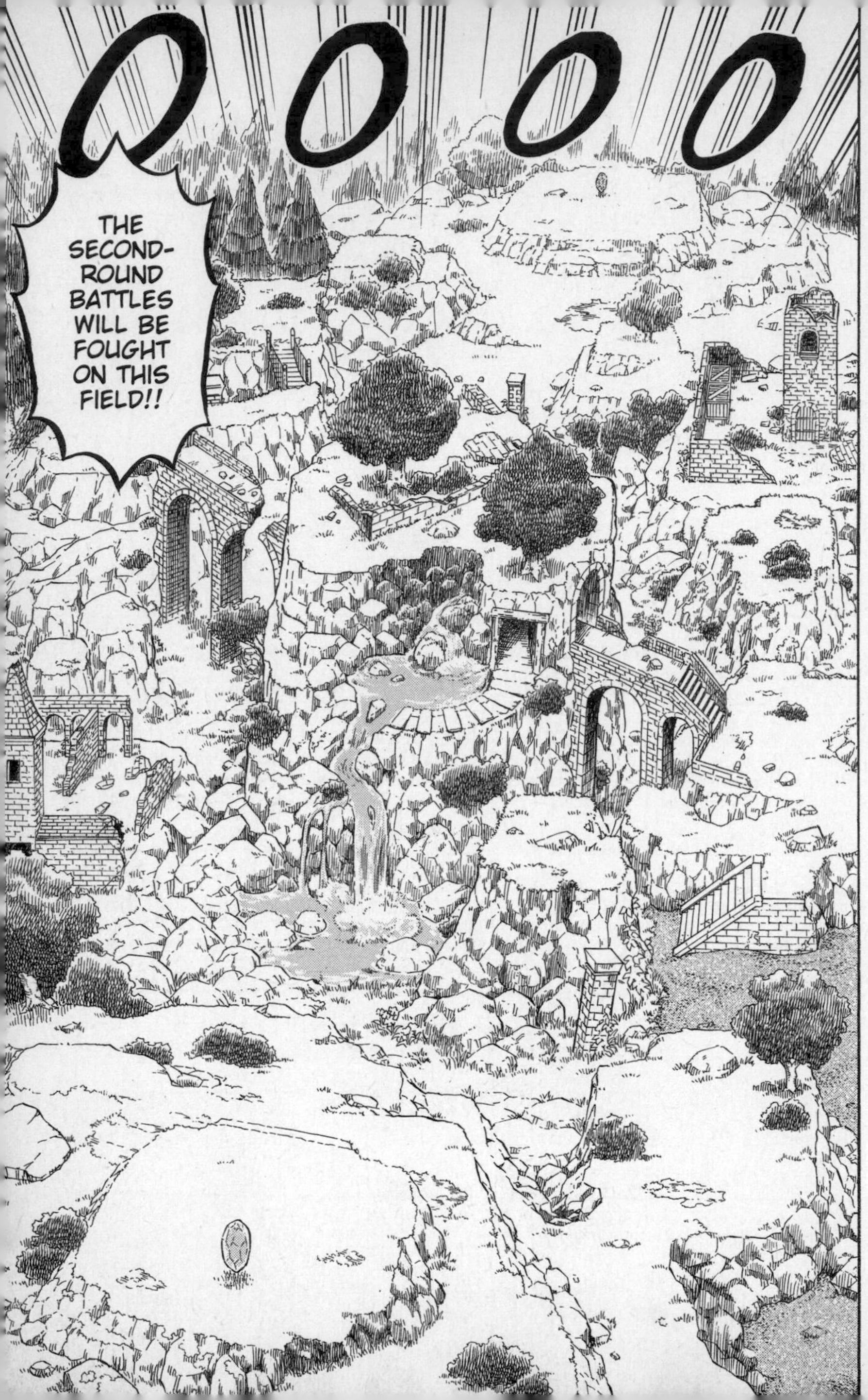
OOOO
THE SECOND-ROUND BATTLES WILL BE FOUGHT ON THIS FIELD!!

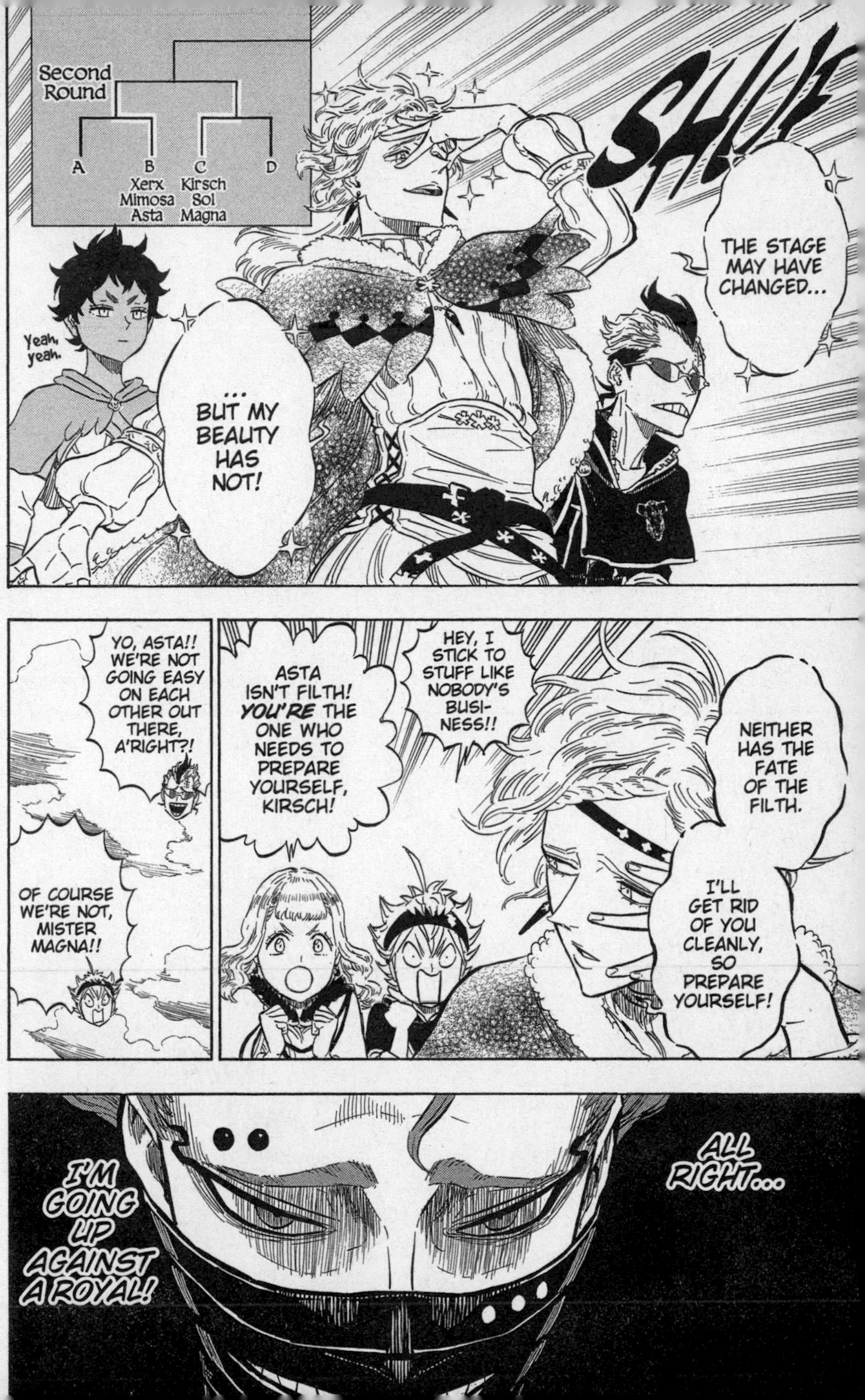
Second Round
A
B
C
D
Xerx Mimosa Asta
Kirsch Sol Magna
THE STAGE MAY HAVE CHANGED...
... BUT MY BEAUTY HAS NOT!
Yeah, yeah.
NEITHER HAS THE FATE OF THE FILTH.
I'LL GET RID OF YOU CLEANLY, SO PREPARE YOURSELF!
HEY, I STICK TO STUFF LIKE NOBODY'S BUSI-NESS!!
ASTA ISN'T FILTH! *YOU'RE* THE ONE WHO NEEDS TO PREPARE YOURSELF, KIRSCH!
YO, ASTA!! WE'RE NOT GOING EASY ON EACH OTHER OUT THERE, A'RIGHT?!
OF COURSE WE'RE NOT, MISTER MAGNA!!
ALL RIGHT...
I'M GOING UP AGAINST A ROYAL!

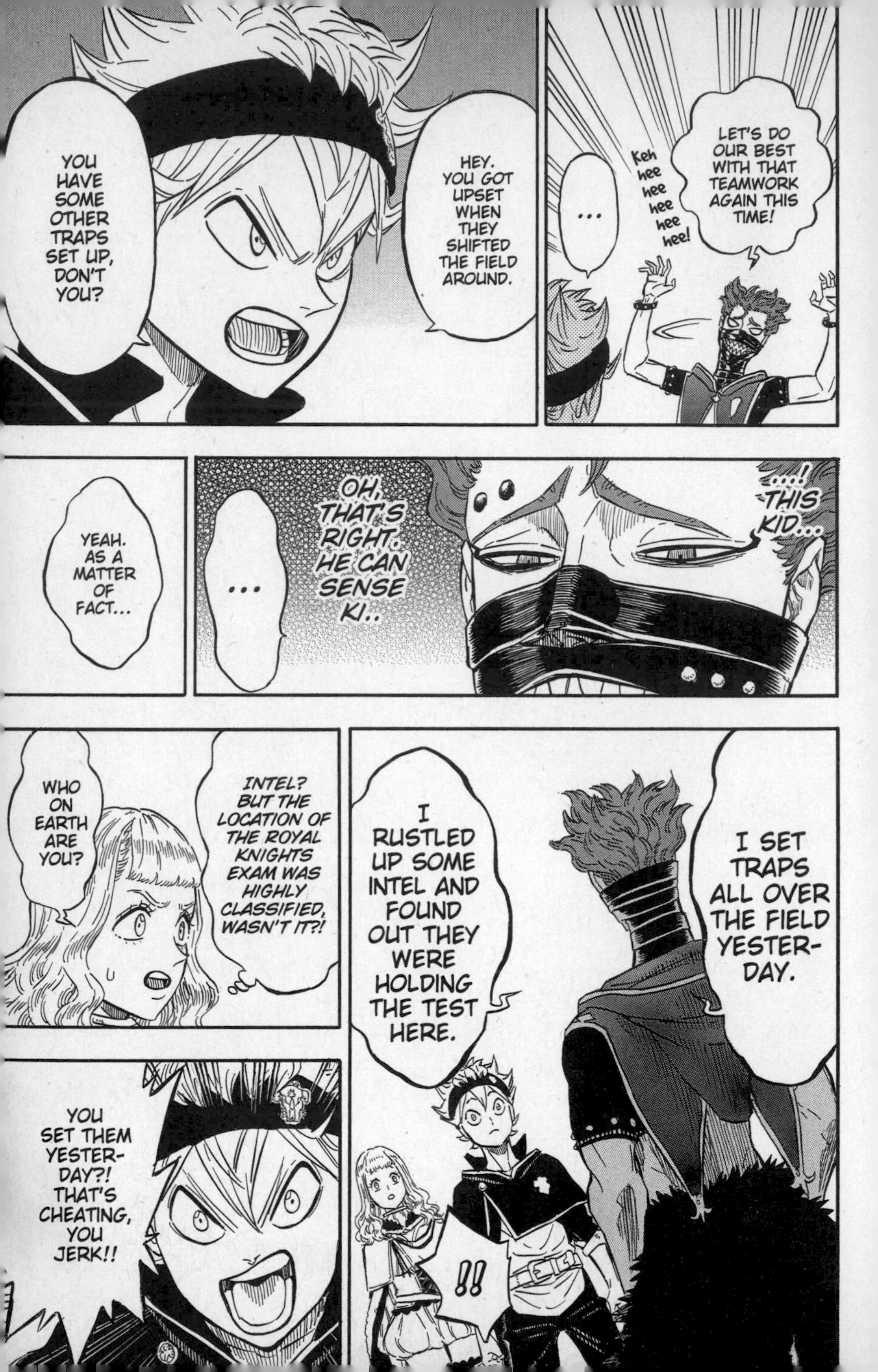
LET'S DO OUR BEST WITH THAT TEAMWORK AGAIN THIS TIME!
Keh hee hee hee hee hee!
...
HEY. YOU GOT UPSET WHEN THEY SHIFTED THE FIELD AROUND.
YOU HAVE SOME OTHER TRAPS SET UP, DON'T YOU?
...! THIS KID...
OH, THAT'S RIGHT. HE CAN SENSE KI..
...
YEAH. AS A MATTER OF FACT...
I SET TRAPS ALL OVER THE FIELD YESTER-DAY.
I RUSTLED UP SOME INTEL AND FOUND OUT THEY WERE HOLDING THE TEST HERE.
!!
INTEL? BUT THE LOCATION OF THE ROYAL KNIGHTS EXAM WAS HIGHLY CLASSIFIED, WASN'T IT?!
WHO ON EARTH ARE YOU?
YOU SET THEM YESTER-DAY?! THAT'S CHEATING, YOU JERK!!

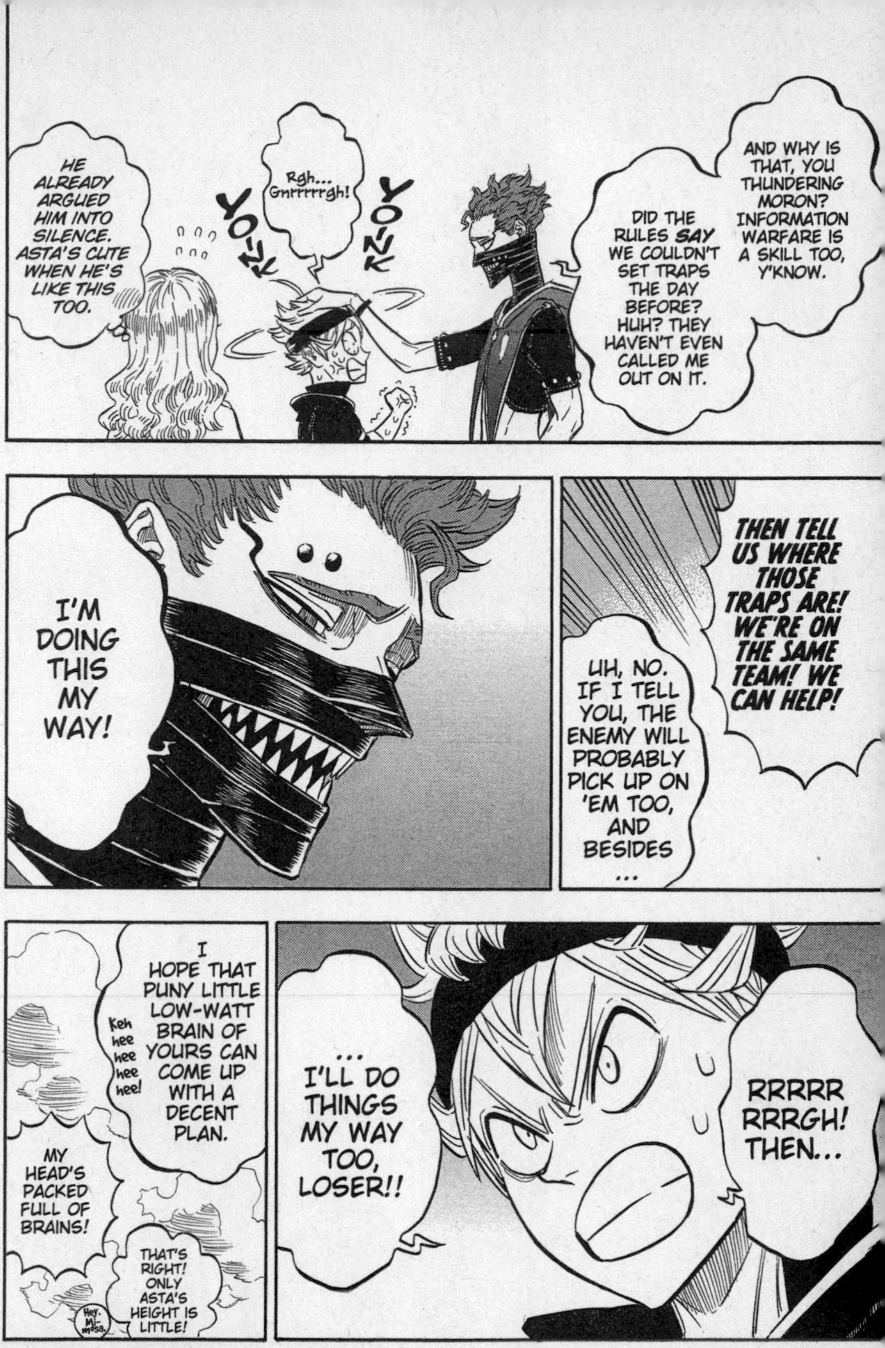
AND WHY IS THAT, YOU THUNDERING MORON? INFORMATION WARFARE IS A SKILL TOO, Y'KNOW.
DID THE RULES SAY WE COULDN'T SET TRAPS THE DAY BEFORE? HUH? THEY HAVEN'T EVEN CALLED ME OUT ON IT.
YOINK
Rgh... Gnrrrrrgh!
YOINK
HE ALREADY ARGUED HIM INTO SILENCE. ASTA'S CUTE WHEN HE'S LIKE THIS TOO.
THEN TELL US WHERE THOSE TRAPS ARE! WE'RE ON THE SAME TEAM! WE CAN HELP!
UH, NO. IF I TELL YOU, THE ENEMY WILL PROBABLY PICK UP ON 'EM TOO, AND BESIDES...
I'M DOING THIS MY WAY!
RRRRR RRRGH! THEN...
... I'LL DO THINGS MY WAY TOO, LOSER!!
I HOPE THAT PUNY LITTLE LOW-WATT BRAIN OF YOURS CAN COME UP WITH A DECENT PLAN.
Keh hee hee hee hee!
MY HEAD'S PACKED FULL OF BRAINS!
THAT'S RIGHT! ONLY ASTA'S HEIGHT IS LITTLE!
Hey. Mimosa.

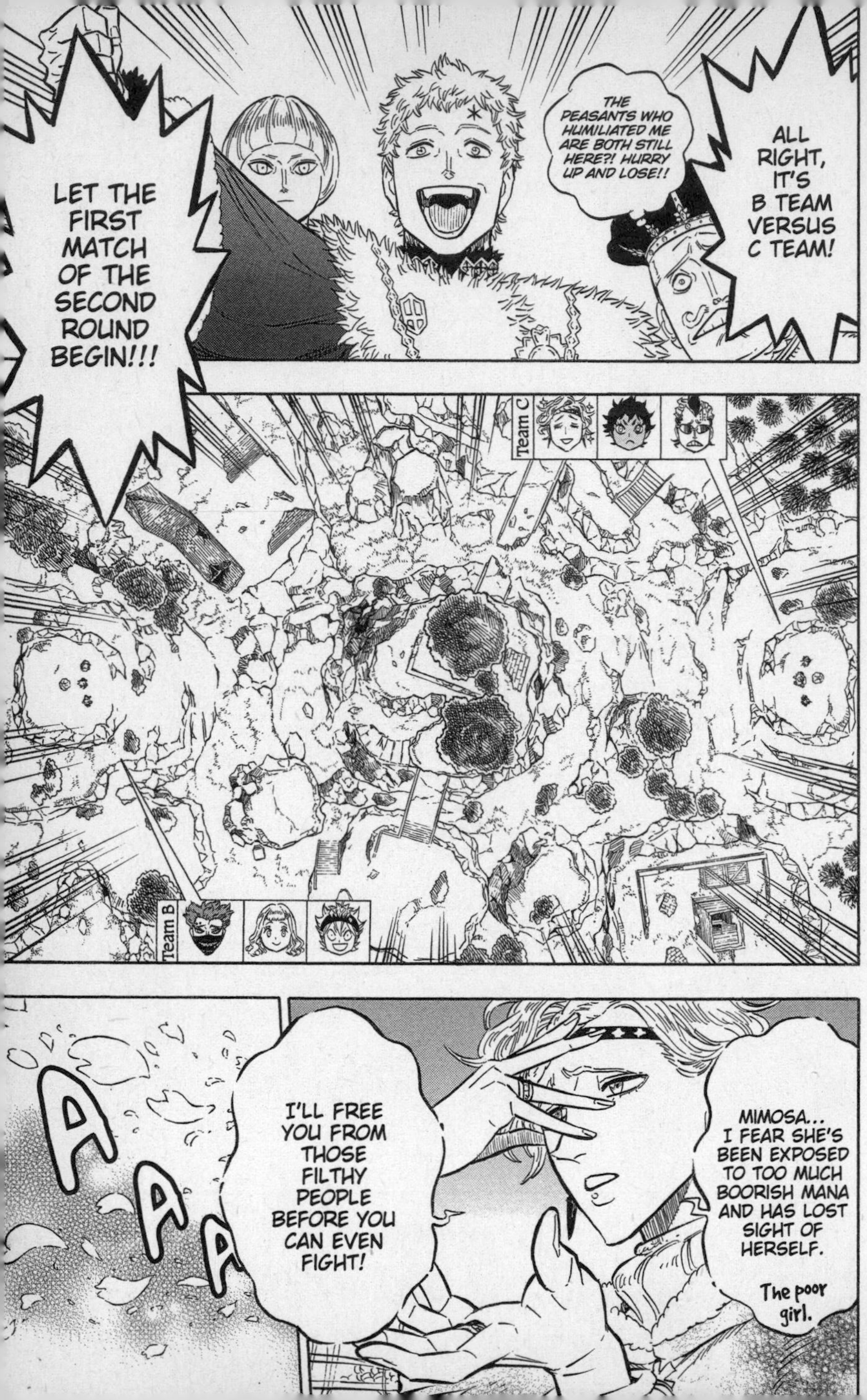
ALL RIGHT, IT'S B TEAM VERSUS C TEAM!
THE PEASANTS WHO HUMILIATED ME ARE BOTH STILL HERE?! HURRY UP AND LOSE!!
LET THE FIRST MATCH OF THE SECOND ROUND BEGIN!!!
Team C
Team B
MIMOSA... I FEAR SHE'S BEEN EXPOSED TO TOO MUCH BOORISH MANA AND HAS LOST SIGHT OF HERSELF.
The poor girl.
I'LL FREE YOU FROM THOSE FILTHY PEOPLE BEFORE YOU CAN EVEN FIGHT!
AAA

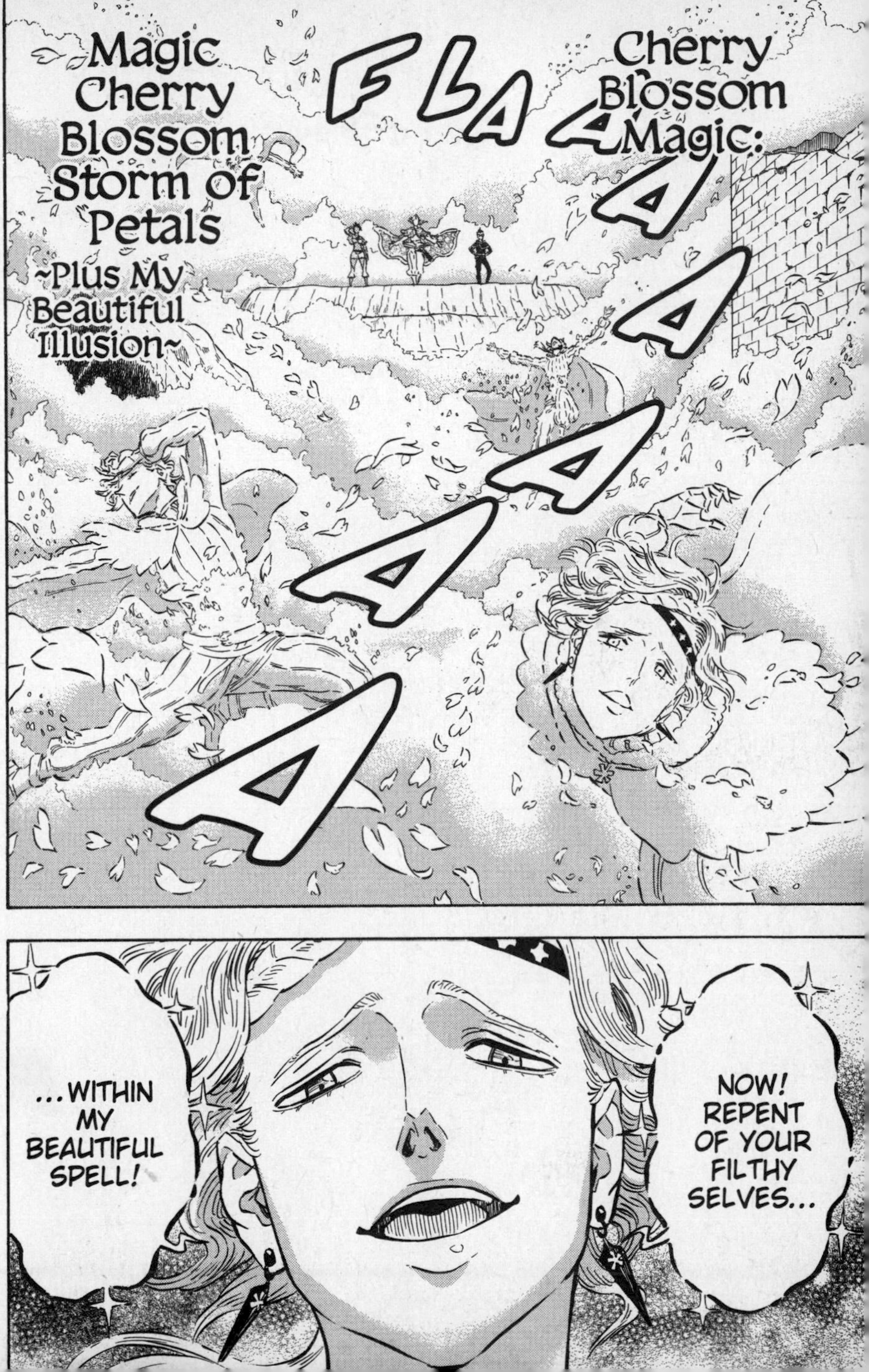
Cherry Blossom Magic:
Magic Cherry Blossom Storm of Petals ~Plus My Beautiful Illusion~
FLAAAAAAA
NOW! REPENT OF YOUR FILTHY SELVES...
...WITHIN MY BEAUTIFUL SPELL!

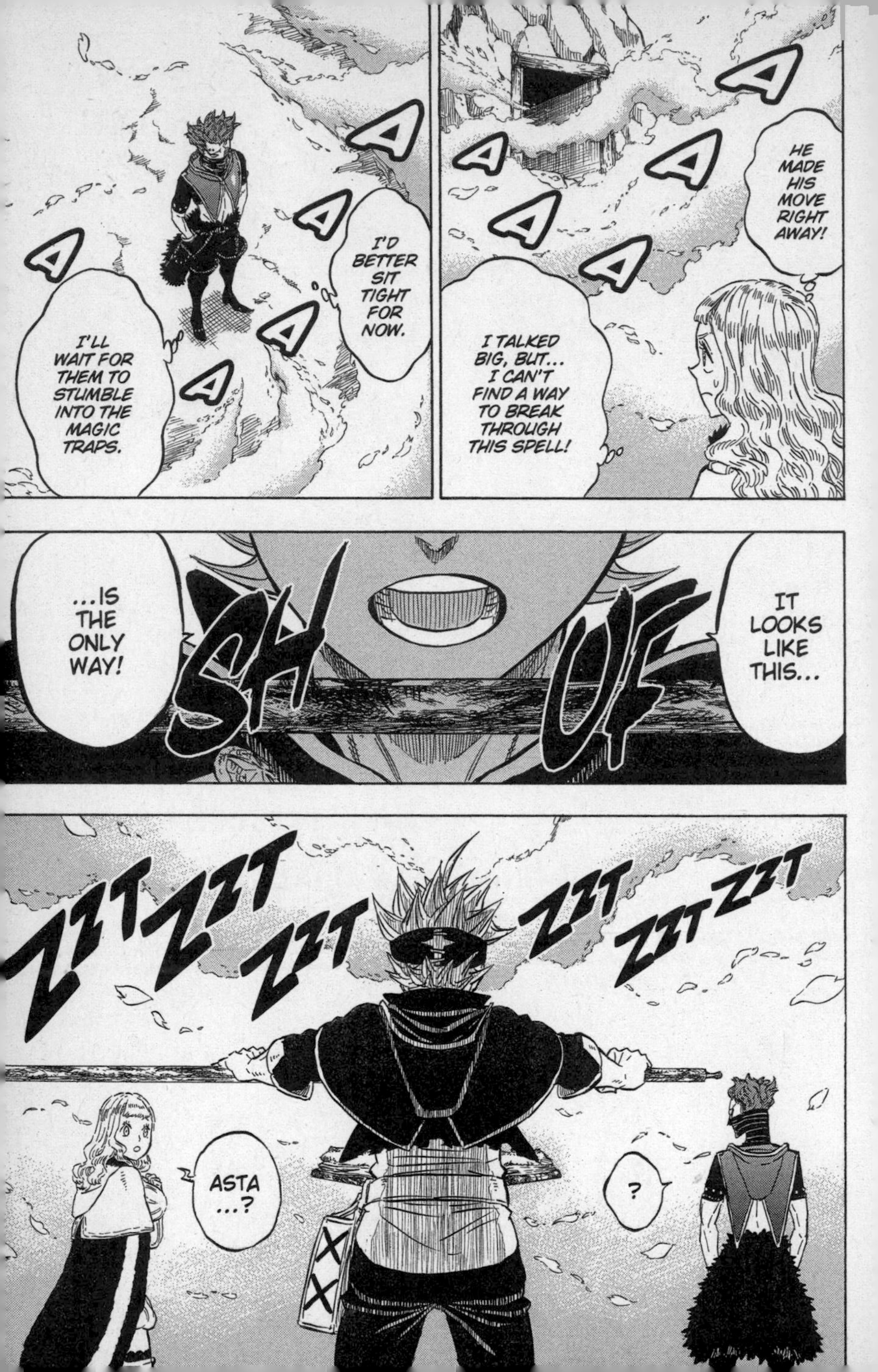

HE MADE HIS MOVE RIGHT AWAY!
A A A A A A
I TALKED BIG, BUT... I CAN'T FIND A WAY TO BREAK THROUGH THIS SPELL!
I'D BETTER SIT TIGHT FOR NOW.
A A A A A
I'LL WAIT FOR THEM TO STUMBLE INTO THE MAGIC TRAPS.
IT LOOKS LIKE THIS...
SH UF
...IS THE ONLY WAY!
ZZT ZZT ZZT ZZT ZZT ZZT
?
ASTA ...?

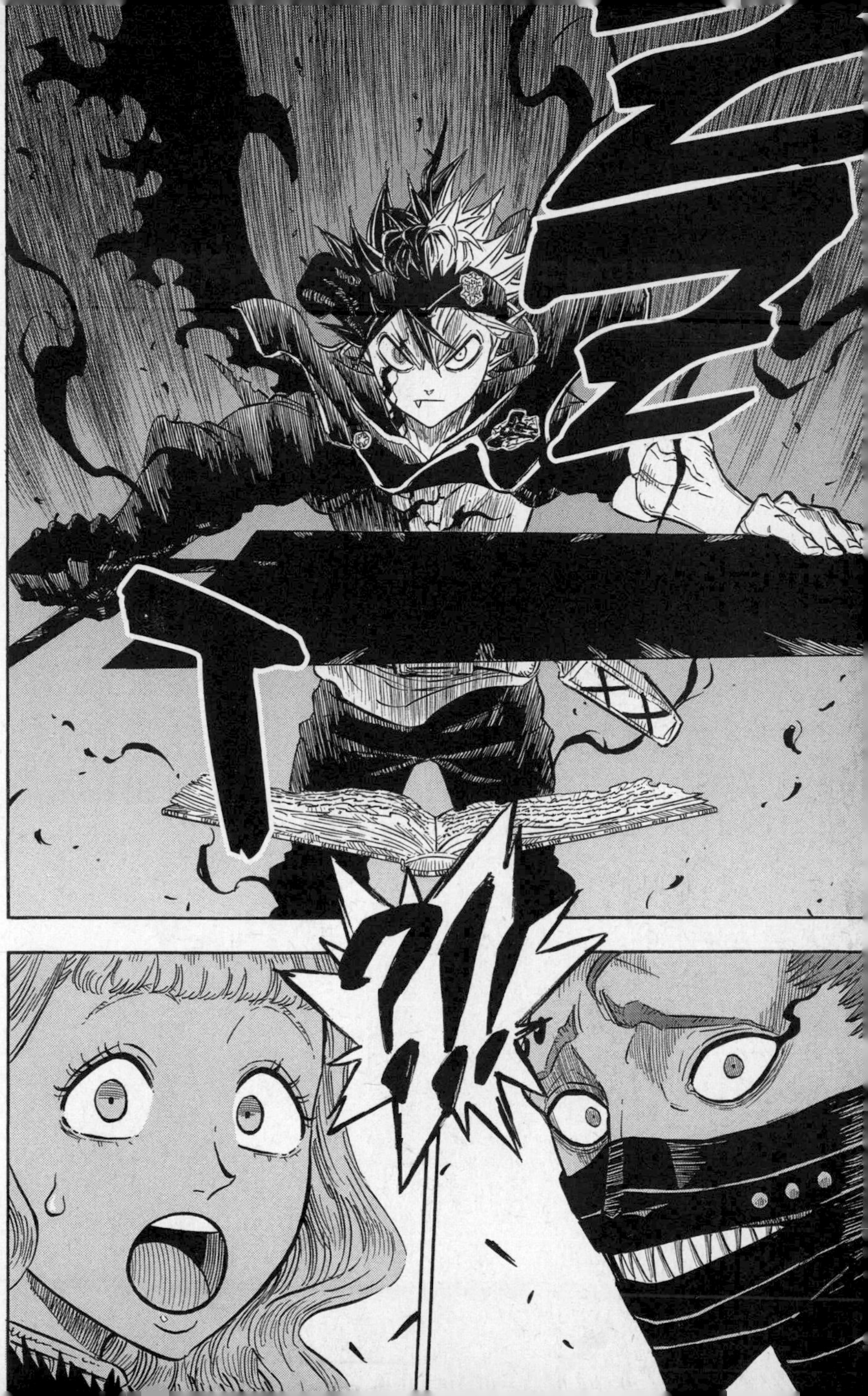
?!!

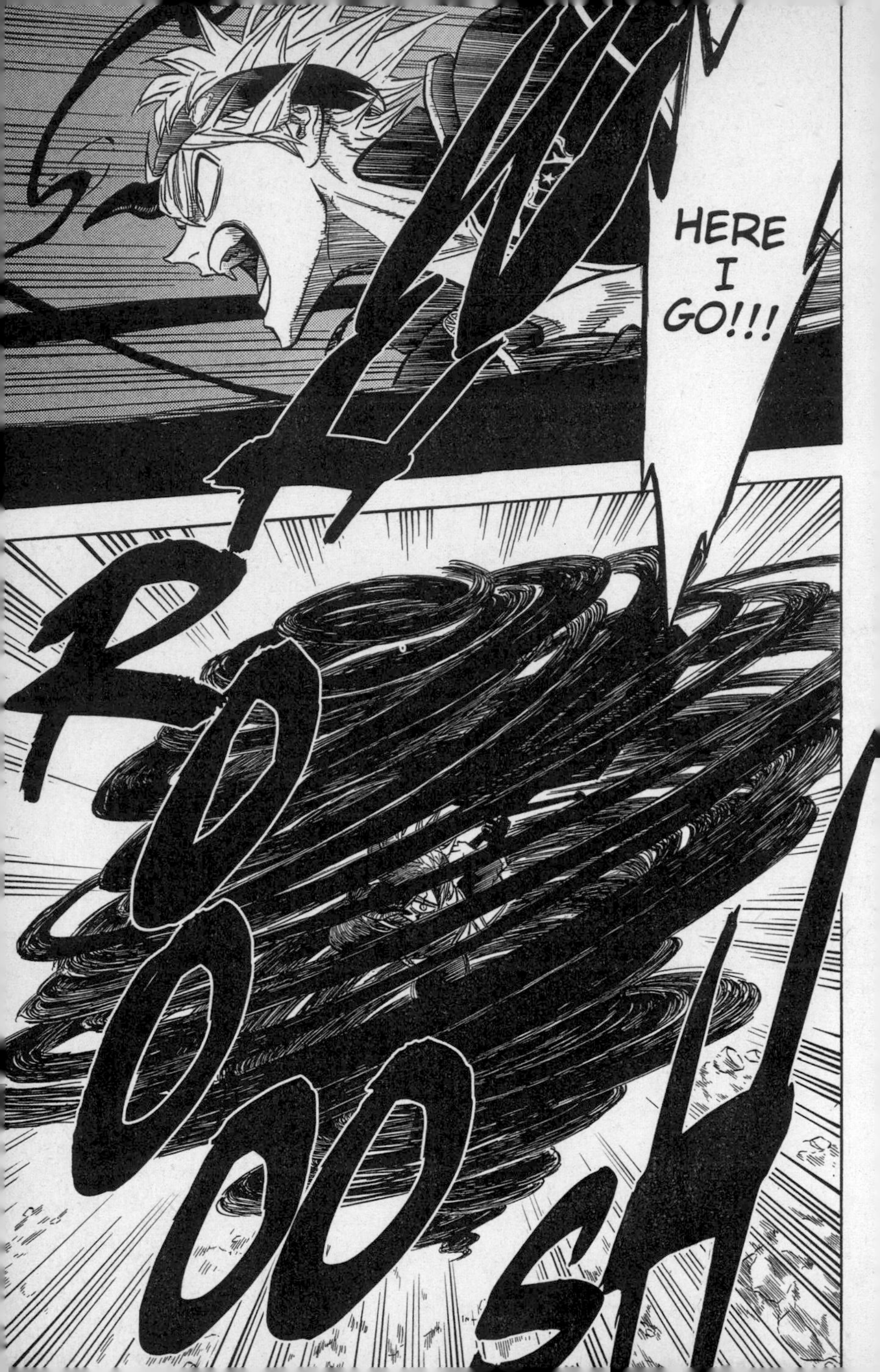
HERE I GO!!!

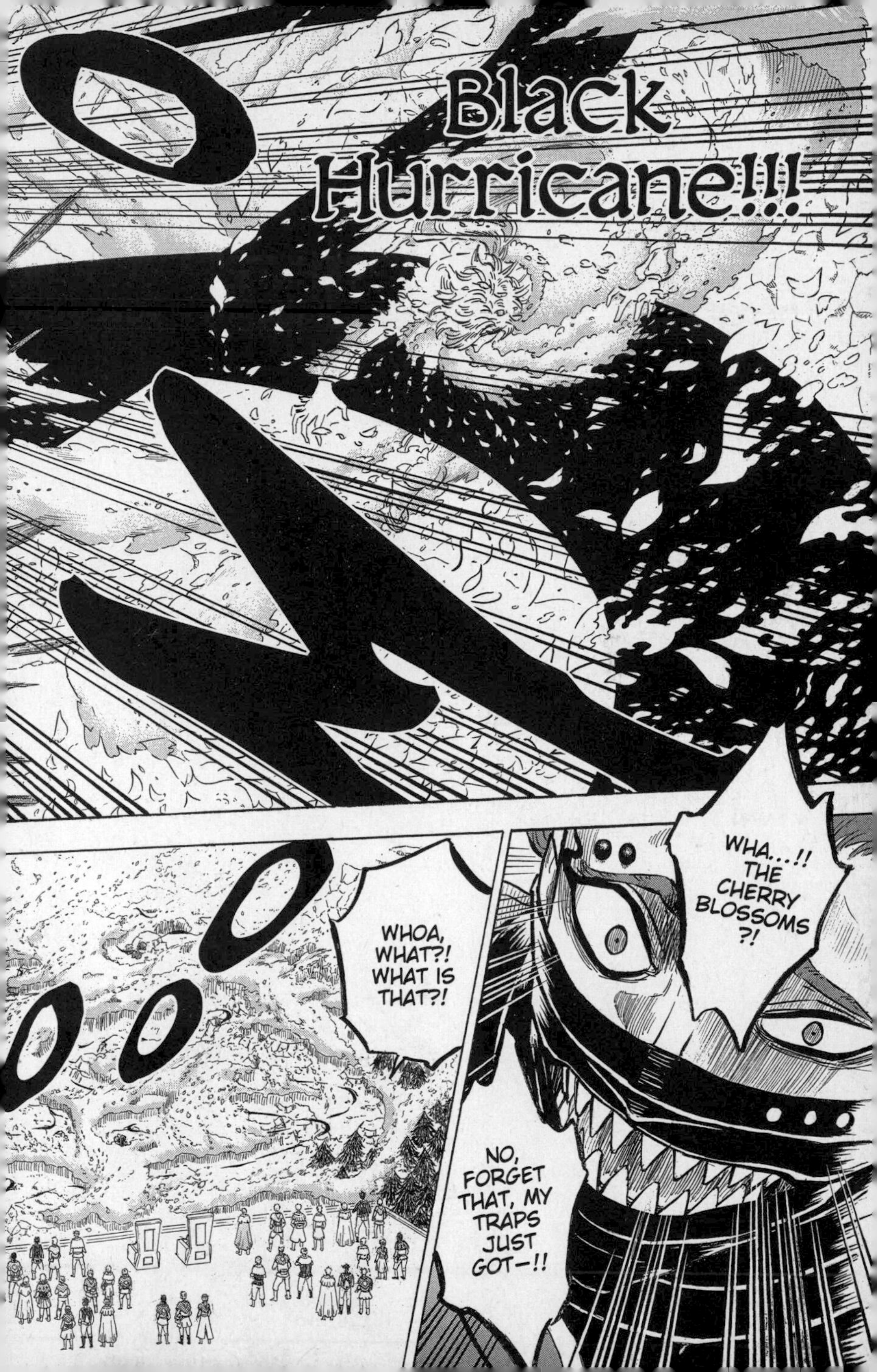
Black Hurricane!!!
WHA...!! THE CHERRY BLOSSOMS?!
NO, FORGET THAT, MY TRAPS JUST GOT-!!
WHOA, WHAT?! WHAT IS THAT?!

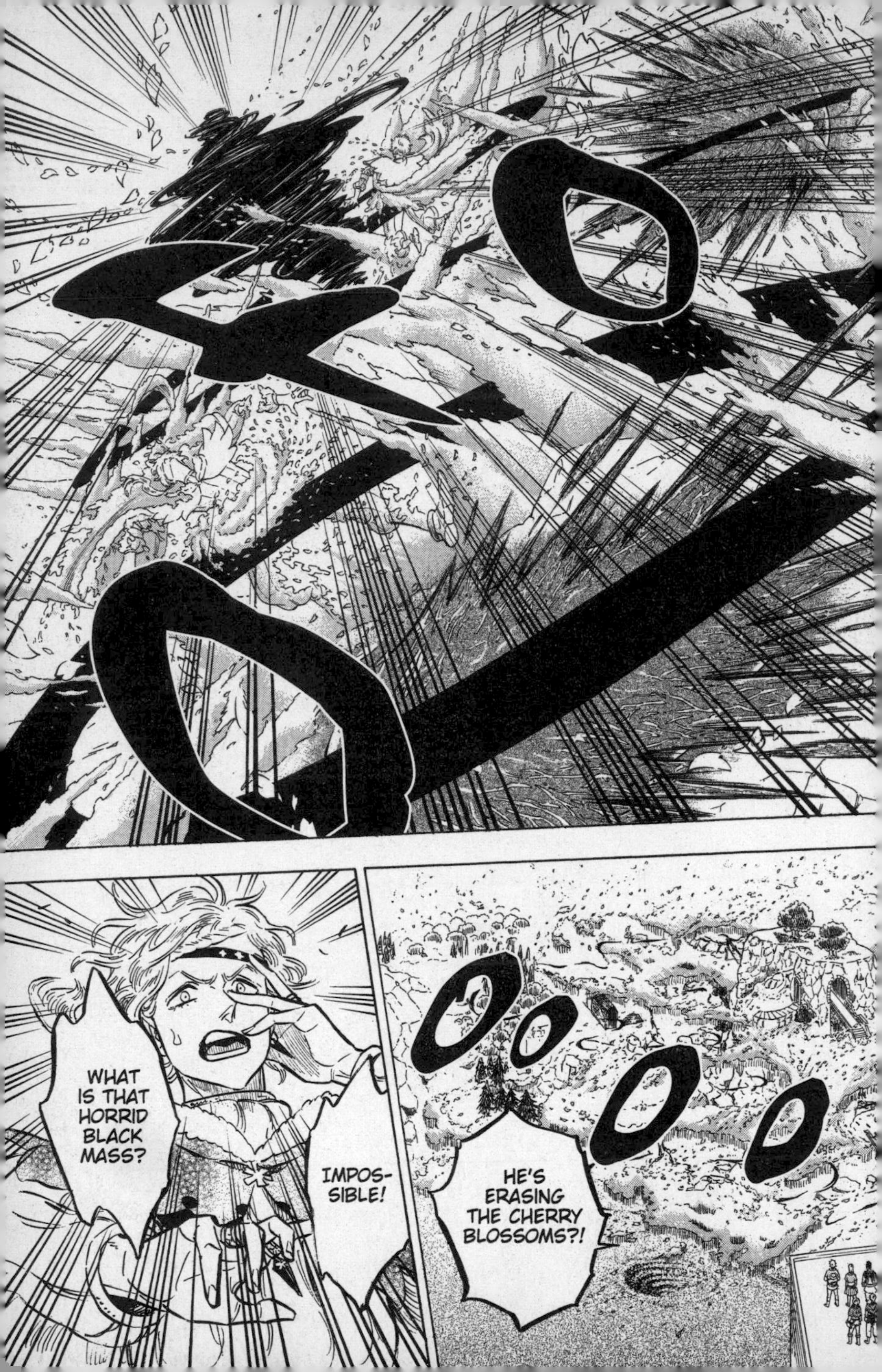
HE'S ERASING THE CHERRY BLOSSOMS?!
IMPOS-SIBLE!
WHAT IS THAT HORRID BLACK MASS?

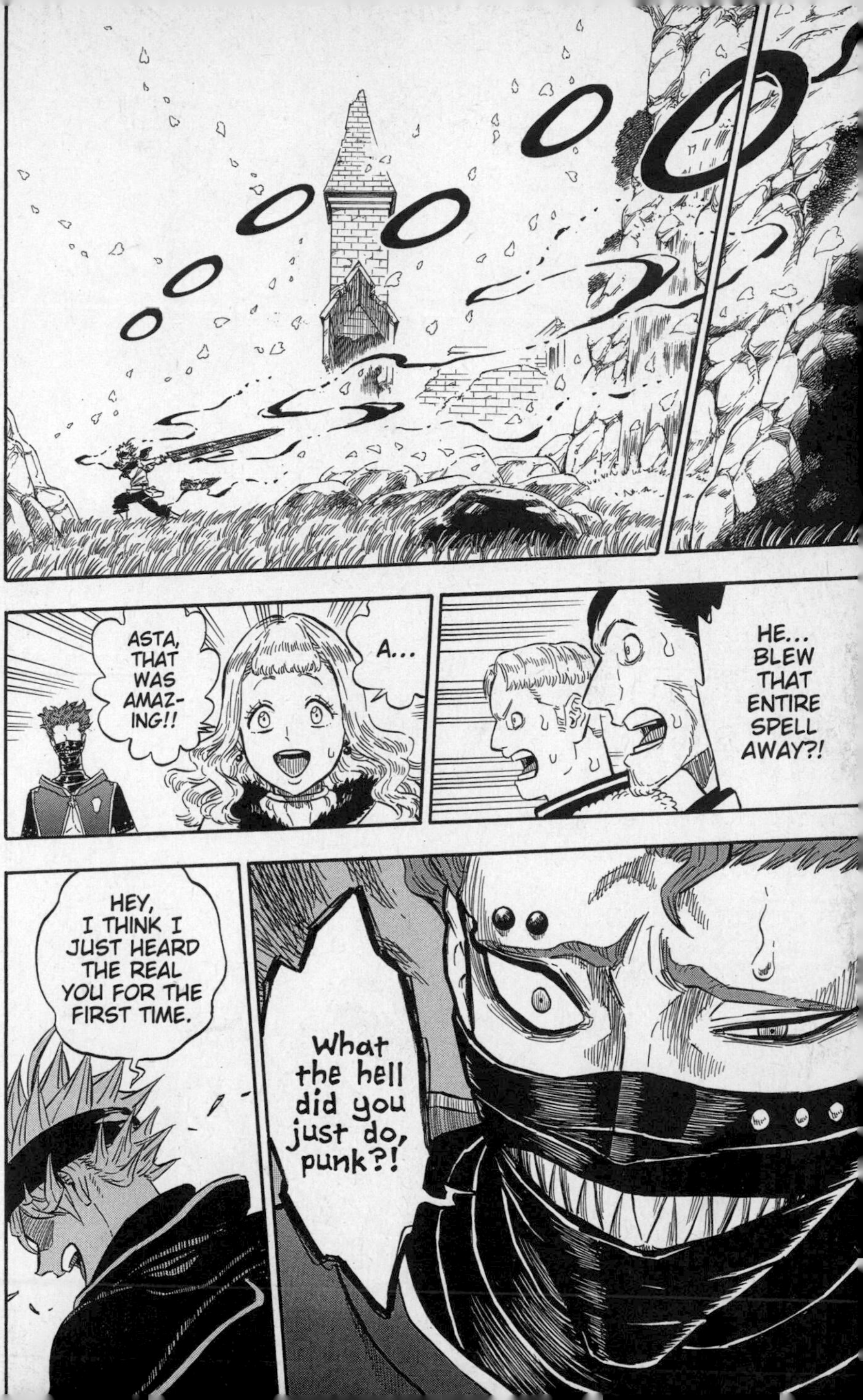
HE... BLEW THAT ENTIRE SPELL AWAY?!
A...
ASTA, THAT WAS AMAZ-ING!!
What the hell did you just do, punk?!
HEY, I THINK I JUST HEARD THE REAL YOU FOR THE FIRST TIME.

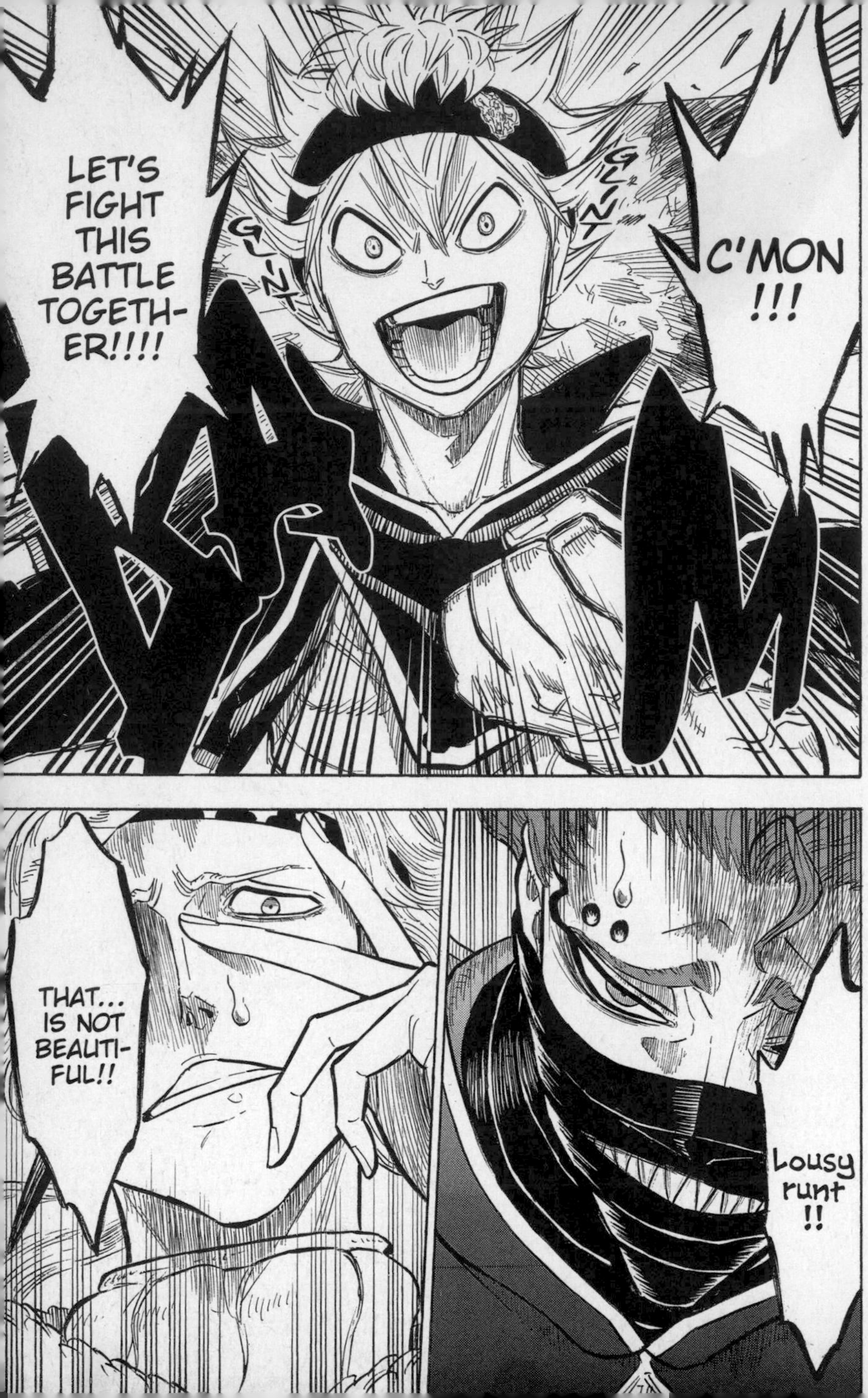
C'MON!!!
GLINT
GLINT
LET'S FIGHT THIS BATTLE TOGETHER!!!!
Lousy runt!!
THAT... IS NOT BEAUTIFUL!!

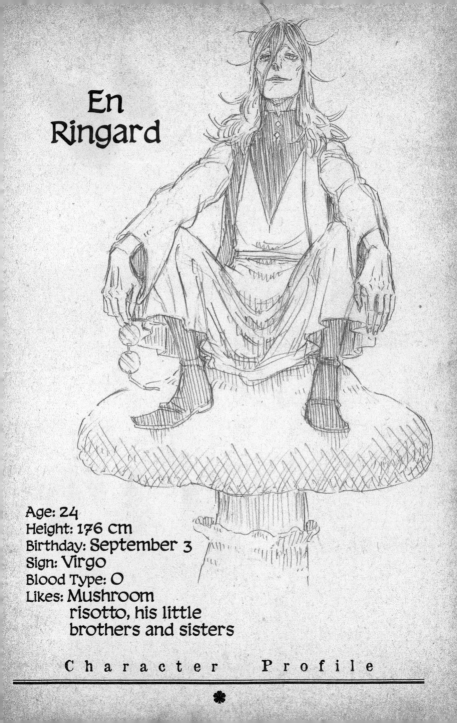

En Ringard

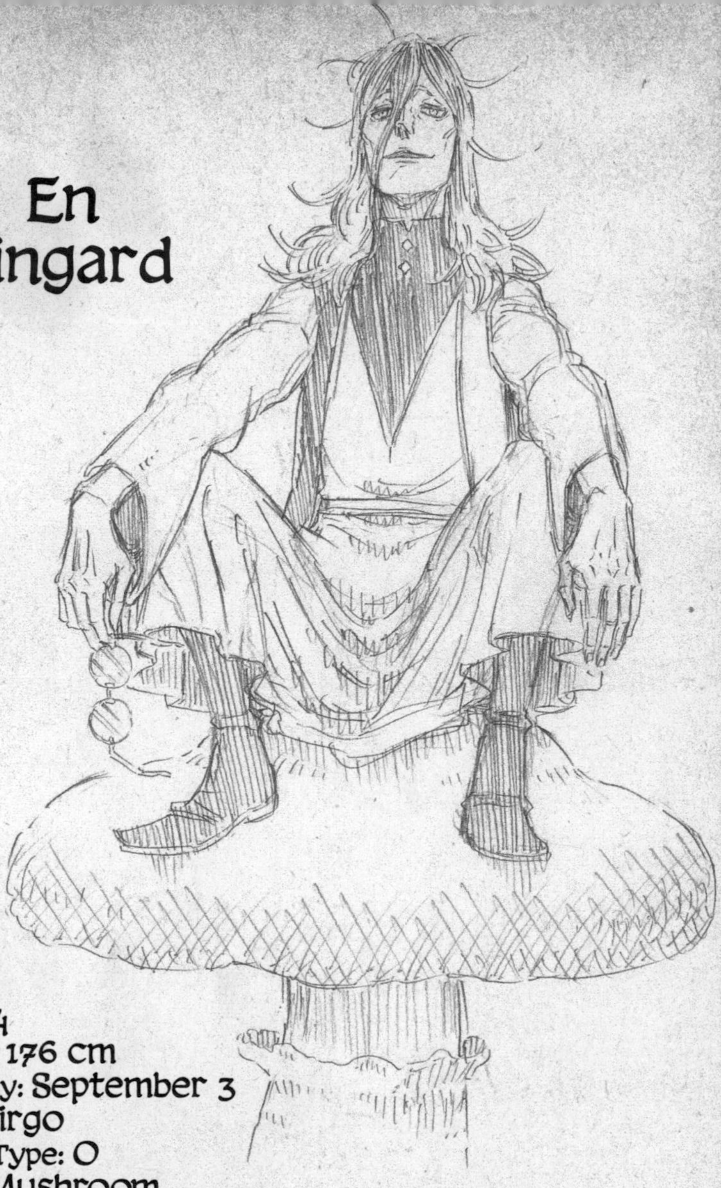

Age: 24
Height: 176 cm
Birthday: September 3
Sign: Virgo
Blood Type: O
Likes: Mushroom risotto, his little brothers and sisters

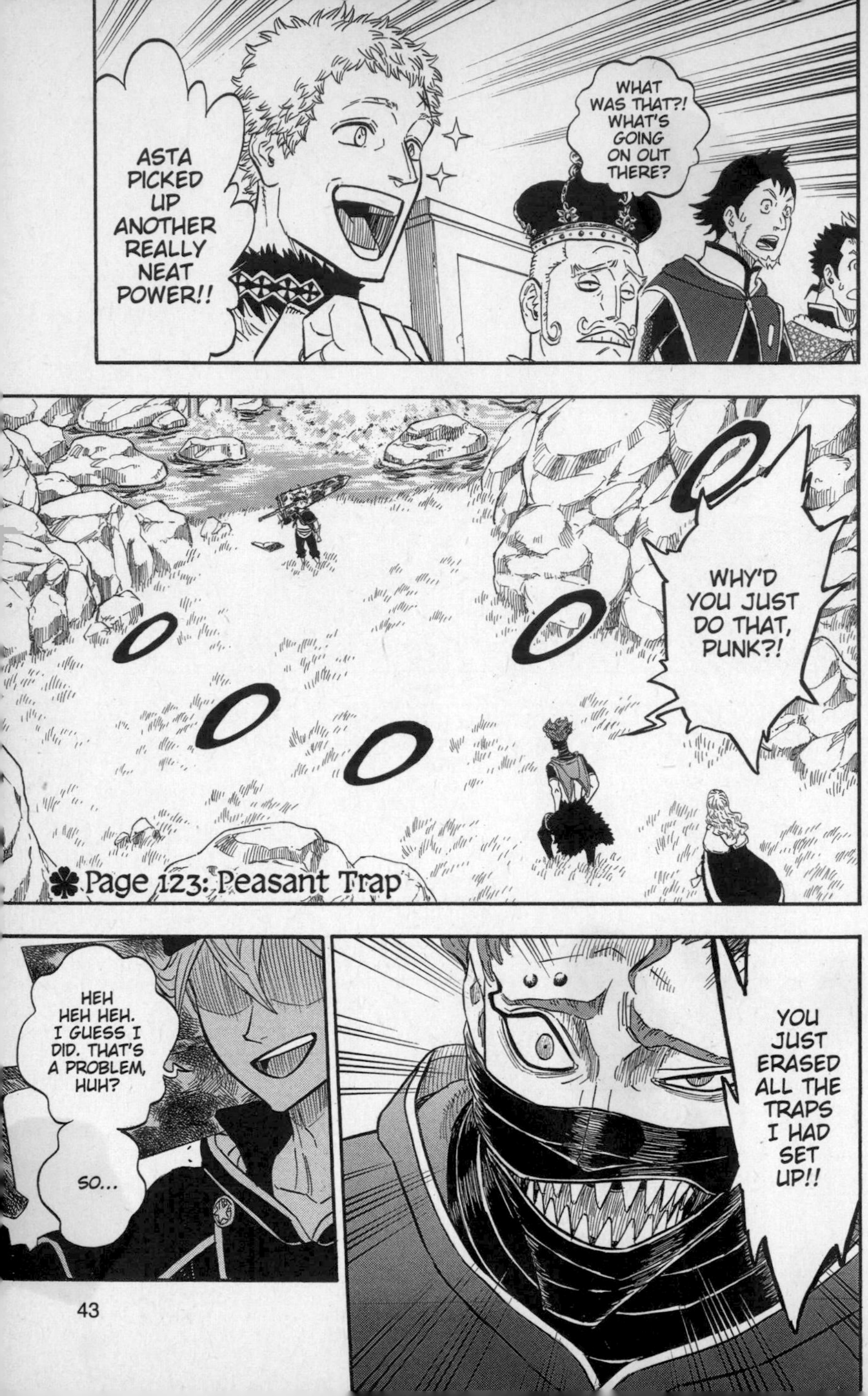
WHAT WAS THAT?! WHAT'S GOING ON OUT THERE?
ASTA PICKED UP ANOTHER REALLY NEAT POWER!!
WHY'D YOU JUST DO THAT, PUNK?!
Page 123: Peasant Trap
YOU JUST ERASED ALL THE TRAPS I HAD SET UP!!
HEH HEH HEH. I GUESS I DID. THAT'S A PROBLEM, HUH?
SO...

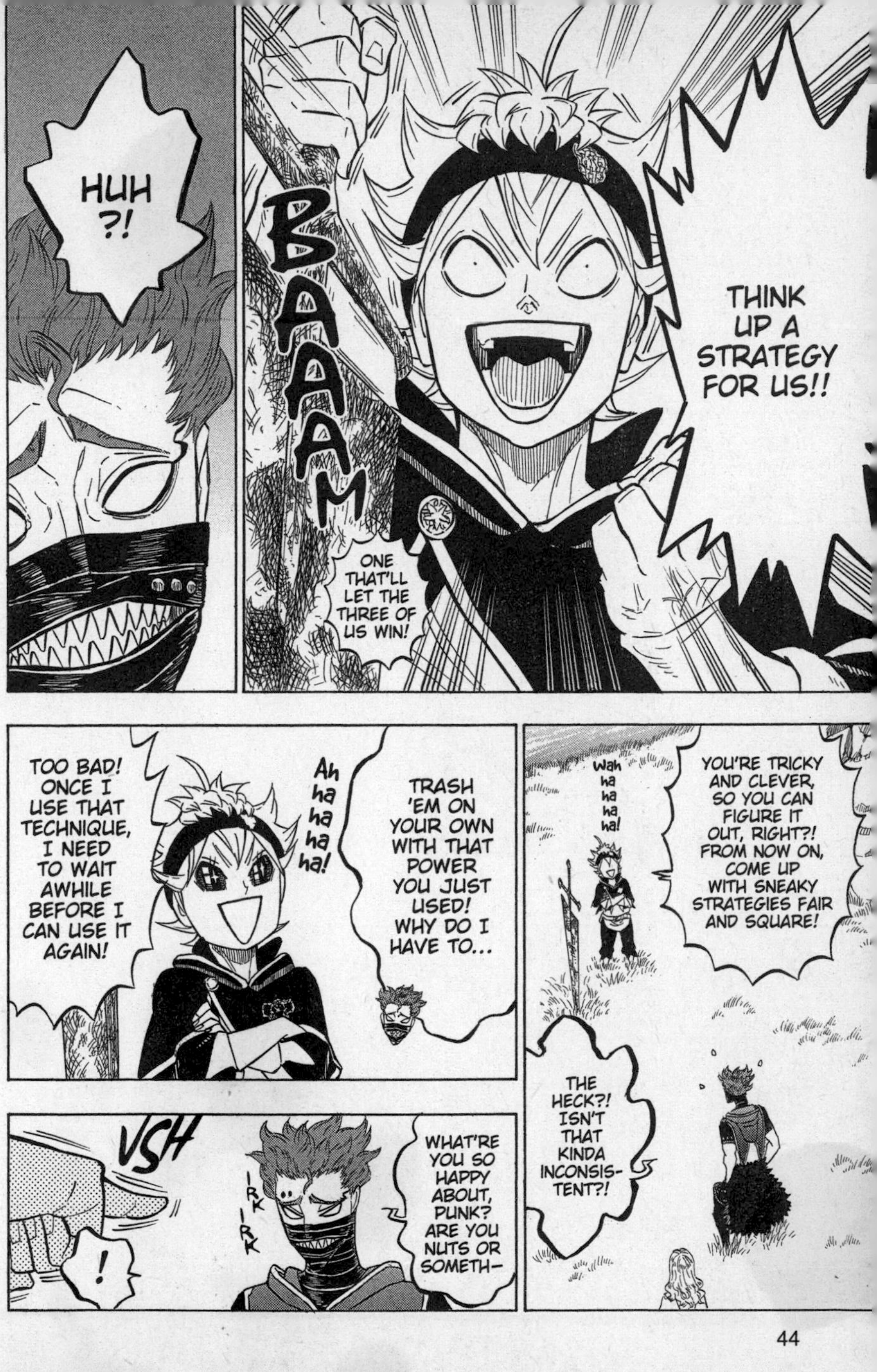
BAAAAM
THINK UP A STRATEGY FOR US!!
ONE THAT'LL LET THE THREE OF US WIN!
HUH ?!
Wah ha ha ha ha!
YOU'RE TRICKY AND CLEVER, SO YOU CAN FIGURE IT OUT, RIGHT?! FROM NOW ON, COME UP WITH SNEAKY STRATEGIES FAIR AND SQUARE!
THE HECK?! ISN'T THAT KINDA INCONSIS- TENT?!
TRASH 'EM ON YOUR OWN WITH THAT POWER YOU JUST USED! WHY DO I HAVE TO...
Ah ha ha ha ha!
TOO BAD! ONCE I USE THAT TECHNIQUE, I NEED TO WAIT AWHILE BEFORE I CAN USE IT AGAIN!
WHAT'RE YOU SO HAPPY ABOUT, PUNK? ARE YOU NUTS OR SOMETH—
IRK IRK
VSH
!

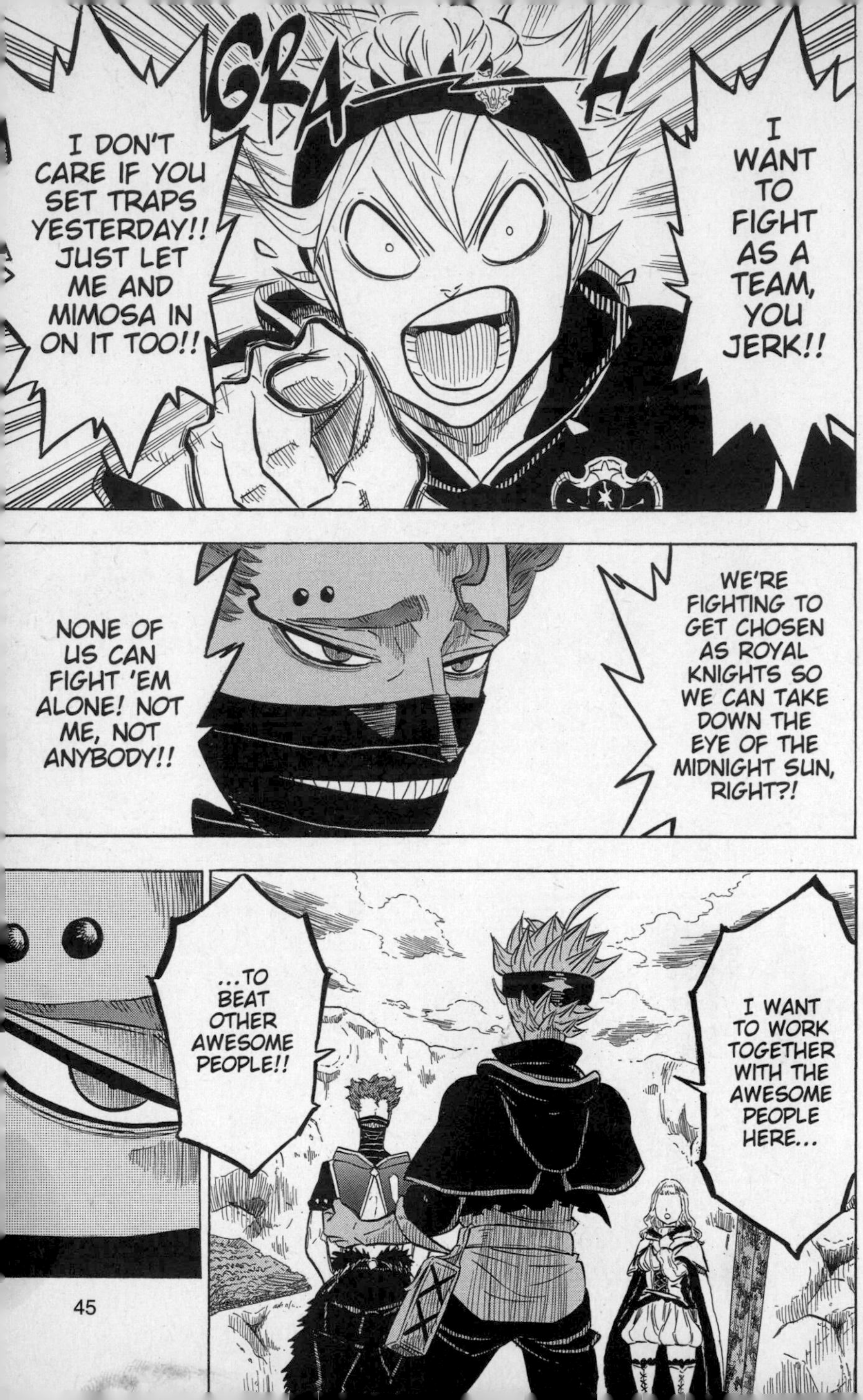
GRA H
I WANT TO FIGHT AS A TEAM, YOU JERK!!
I DON'T CARE IF YOU SET TRAPS YESTERDAY!! JUST LET ME AND MIMOSA IN ON IT TOO!!
WE'RE FIGHTING TO GET CHOSEN AS ROYAL KNIGHTS SO WE CAN TAKE DOWN THE EYE OF THE MIDNIGHT SUN, RIGHT?!
NONE OF US CAN FIGHT 'EM ALONE! NOT ME, NOT ANYBODY!!
I WANT TO WORK TOGETHER WITH THE AWESOME PEOPLE HERE...
...TO BEAT OTHER AWESOME PEOPLE!!

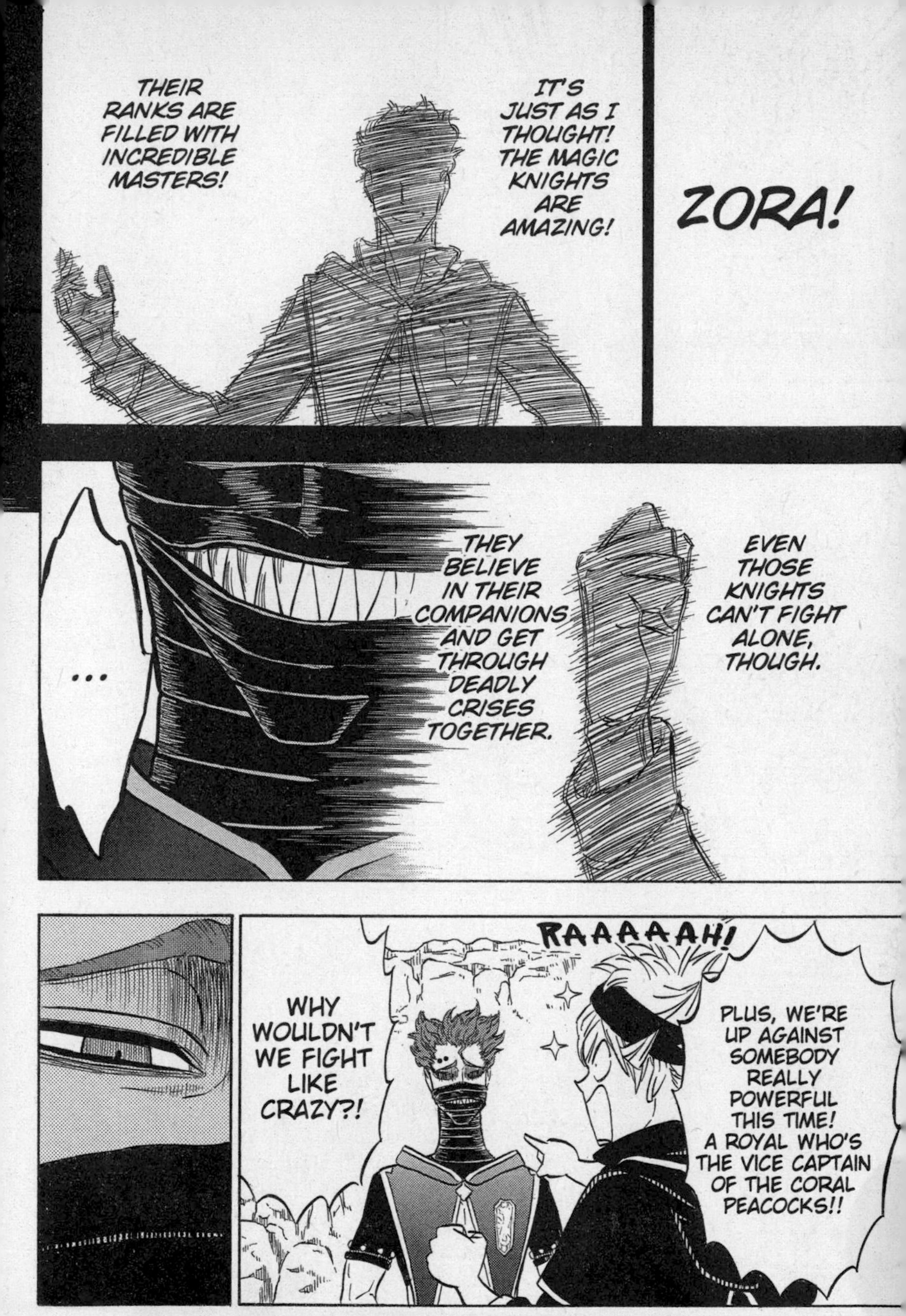
ZORA!
IT'S JUST AS I THOUGHT! THE MAGIC KNIGHTS ARE AMAZING!
THEIR RANKS ARE FILLED WITH INCREDIBLE MASTERS!
EVEN THOSE KNIGHTS CAN'T FIGHT ALONE, THOUGH.
THEY BELIEVE IN THEIR COMPANIONS AND GET THROUGH DEADLY CRISES TOGETHER.
...
RAAAAAH!
PLUS, WE'RE UP AGAINST SOMEBODY REALLY POWERFUL THIS TIME! A ROYAL WHO'S THE VICE CAPTAIN OF THE CORAL PEACOCKS!!
WHY WOULDN'T WE FIGHT LIKE CRAZY?!

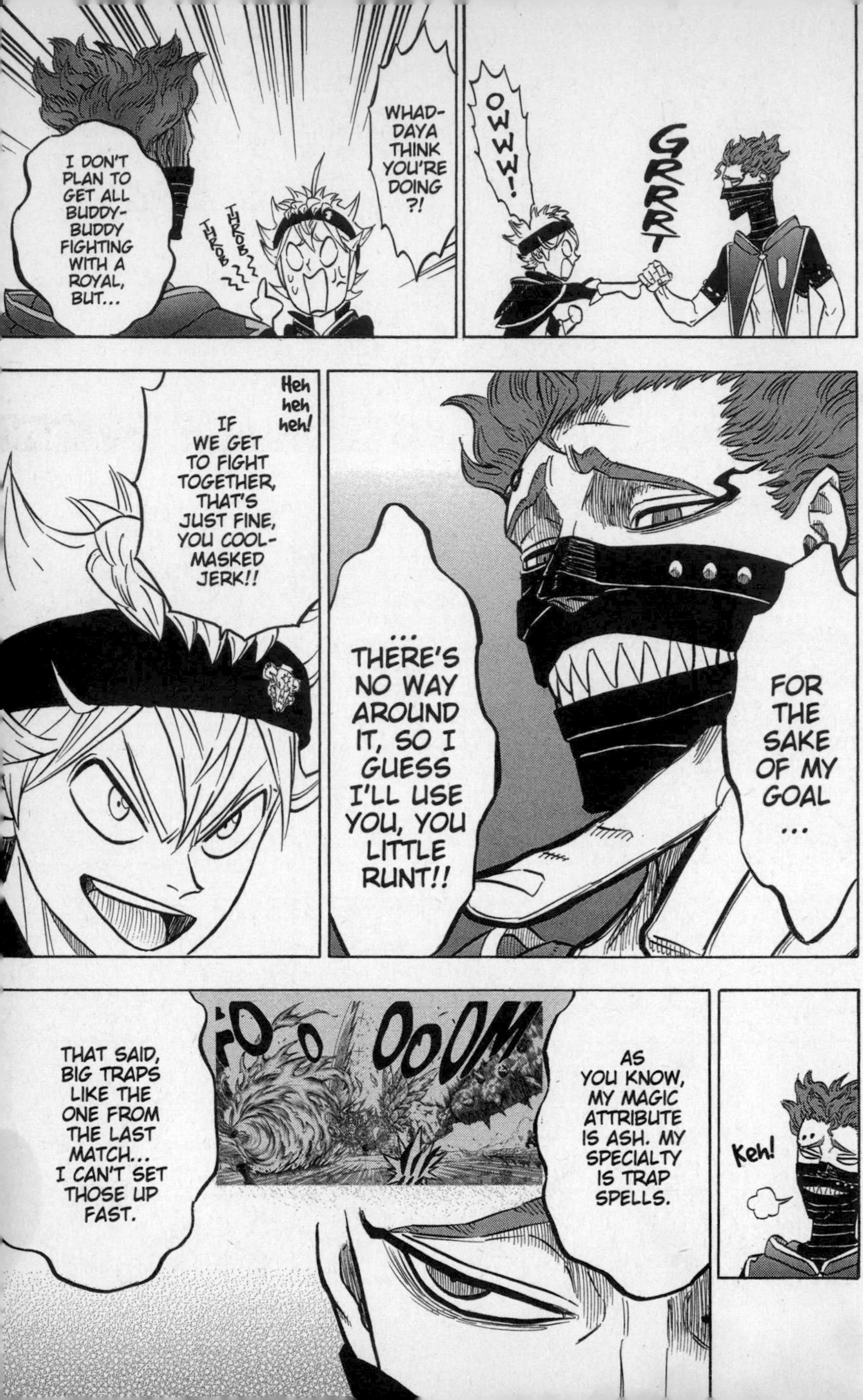
GRRRT
OWWW!
WHAD-DAYA THINK YOU'RE DOING?!
THROB THROB
I DON'T PLAN TO GET ALL BUDDY-BUDDY FIGHTING WITH A ROYAL, BUT...
FOR THE SAKE OF MY GOAL...
...THERE'S NO WAY AROUND IT, SO I GUESS I'LL USE YOU, YOU LITTLE RUNT!!
Heh heh heh!
IF WE GET TO FIGHT TOGETHER, THAT'S JUST FINE, YOU COOL-MASKED JERK!!
Keh!
AS YOU KNOW, MY MAGIC ATTRIBUTE IS ASH. MY SPECIALTY IS TRAP SPELLS.
FOOOOOM
THAT SAID, BIG TRAPS LIKE THE ONE FROM THE LAST MATCH... I CAN'T SET THOSE UP FAST.

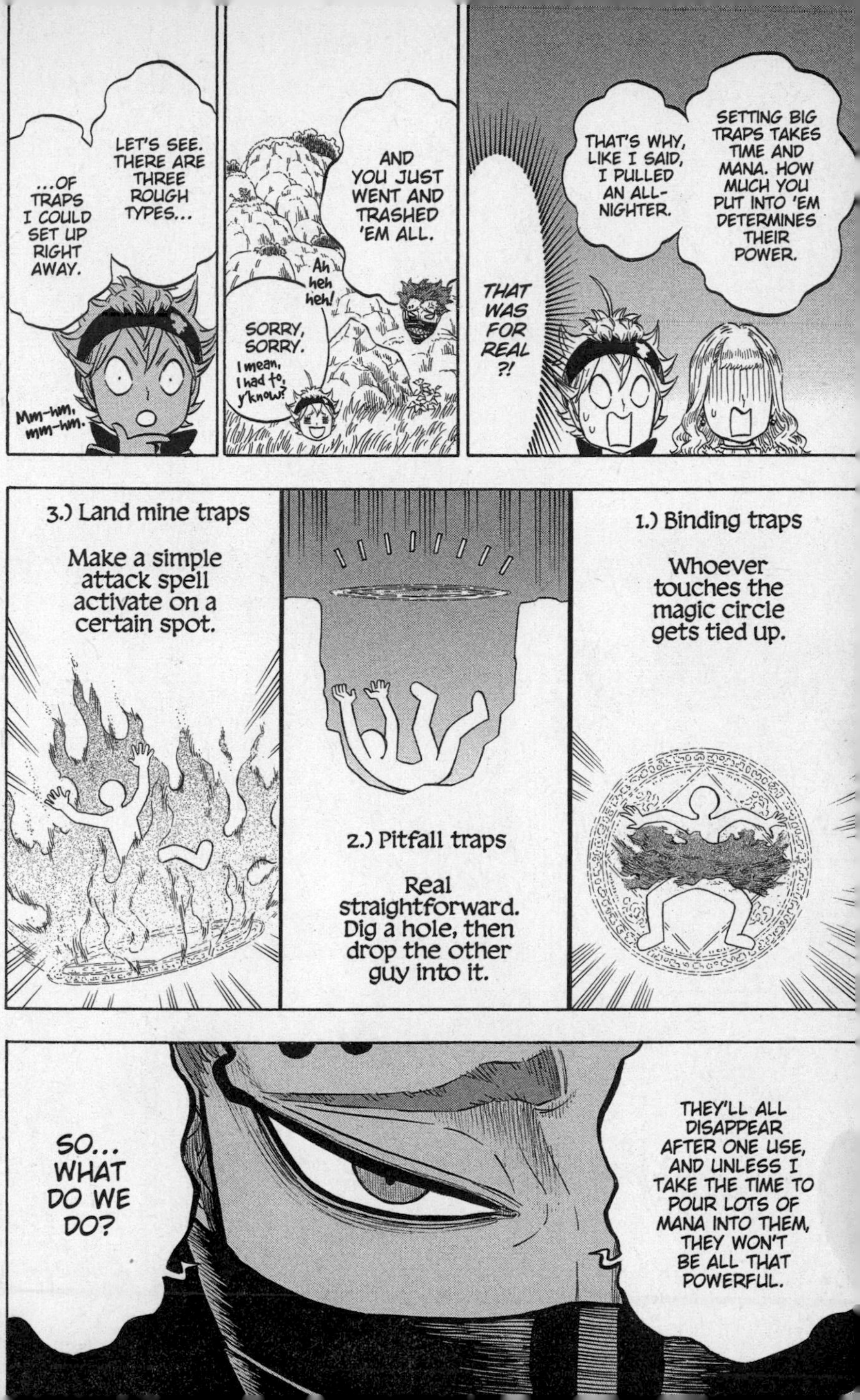

SETTING BIG TRAPS TAKES TIME AND MANA. HOW MUCH YOU PUT INTO 'EM DETERMINES THEIR POWER.
THAT'S WHY, LIKE I SAID, I PULLED AN ALL-NIGHTER.
THAT WAS FOR REAL ?!
AND YOU JUST WENT AND TRASHED 'EM ALL.
Ah heh heh!
SORRY, SORRY.
I mean, I had to, y'know?
LET'S SEE. THERE ARE THREE ROUGH TYPES...
...OF TRAPS I COULD SET UP RIGHT AWAY.
Mm-hm, mm-hm.
1.) Binding traps
Whoever touches the magic circle gets tied up.
2.) Pitfall traps
Real straightforward. Dig a hole, then drop the other guy into it.
3.) Land mine traps
Make a simple attack spell activate on a certain spot.
THEY'LL ALL DISAPPEAR AFTER ONE USE, AND UNLESS I TAKE THE TIME TO POUR LOTS OF MANA INTO THEM, THEY WON'T BE ALL THAT POWERFUL.
SO... WHAT DO WE DO?

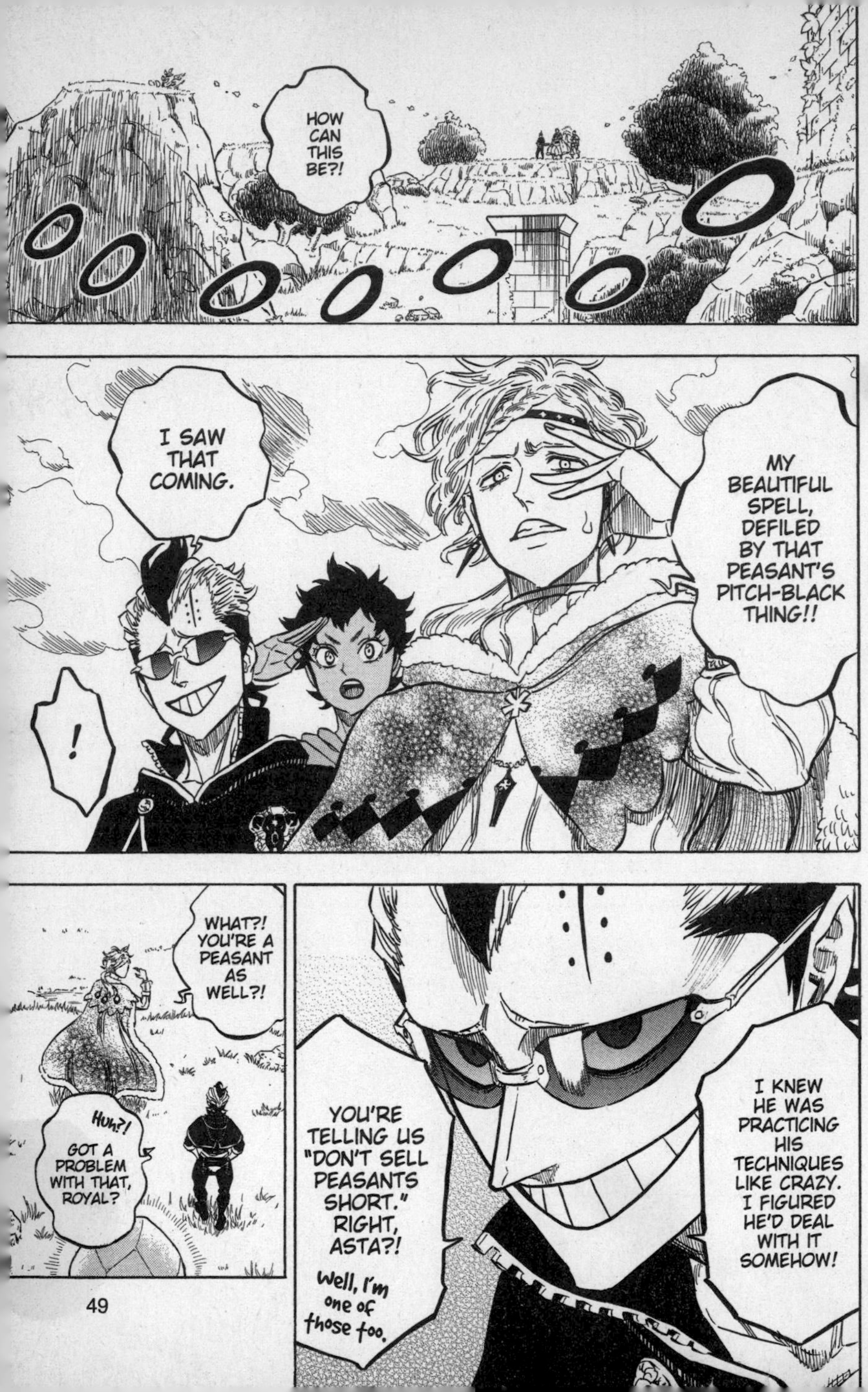
HOW CAN THIS BE?!
MY BEAUTIFUL SPELL, DEFILED BY THAT PEASANT'S PITCH-BLACK THING!!
I SAW THAT COMING.
!
I KNEW HE WAS PRACTICING HIS TECHNIQUES LIKE CRAZY. I FIGURED HE'D DEAL WITH IT SOMEHOW!
YOU'RE TELLING US "DON'T SELL PEASANTS SHORT." RIGHT, ASTA?!
Well, I'm one of those too.
WHAT?! YOU'RE A PEASANT AS WELL?!
Huh?!
GOT A PROBLEM WITH THAT, ROYAL?

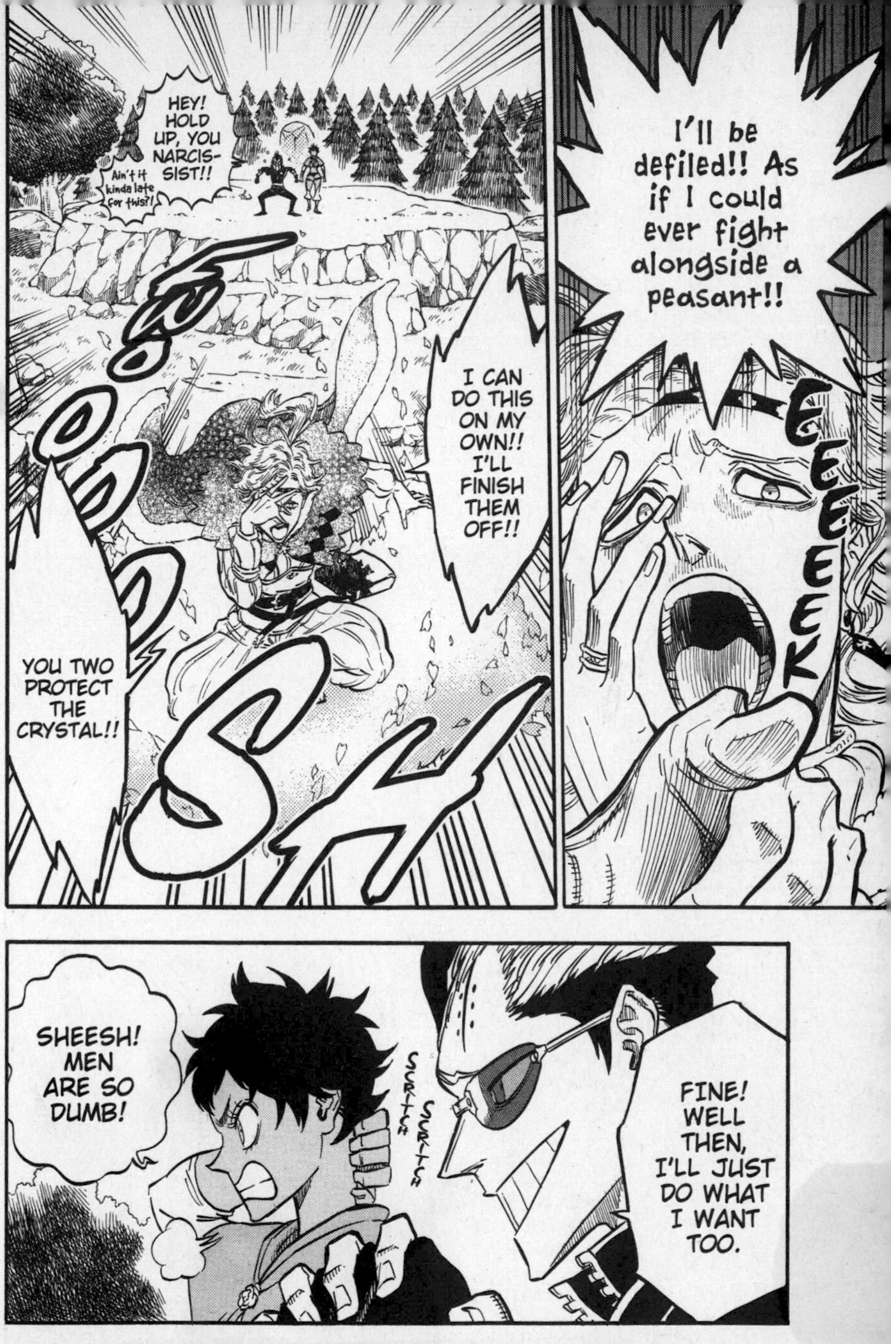
I'll be defiled!! As if I could ever fight alongside a peasant!!
EEEEEEK
HEY! HOLD UP, YOU NARCIS-SIST!!
Ain't it kinda late for this?!
I CAN DO THIS ON MY OWN!! I'LL FINISH THEM OFF!!
YOU TWO PROTECT THE CRYSTAL!!
SH
FINE! WELL THEN, I'LL JUST DO WHAT I WANT TOO.
SCRITCH SCRITCH
SHEESH! MEN ARE SO DUMB!

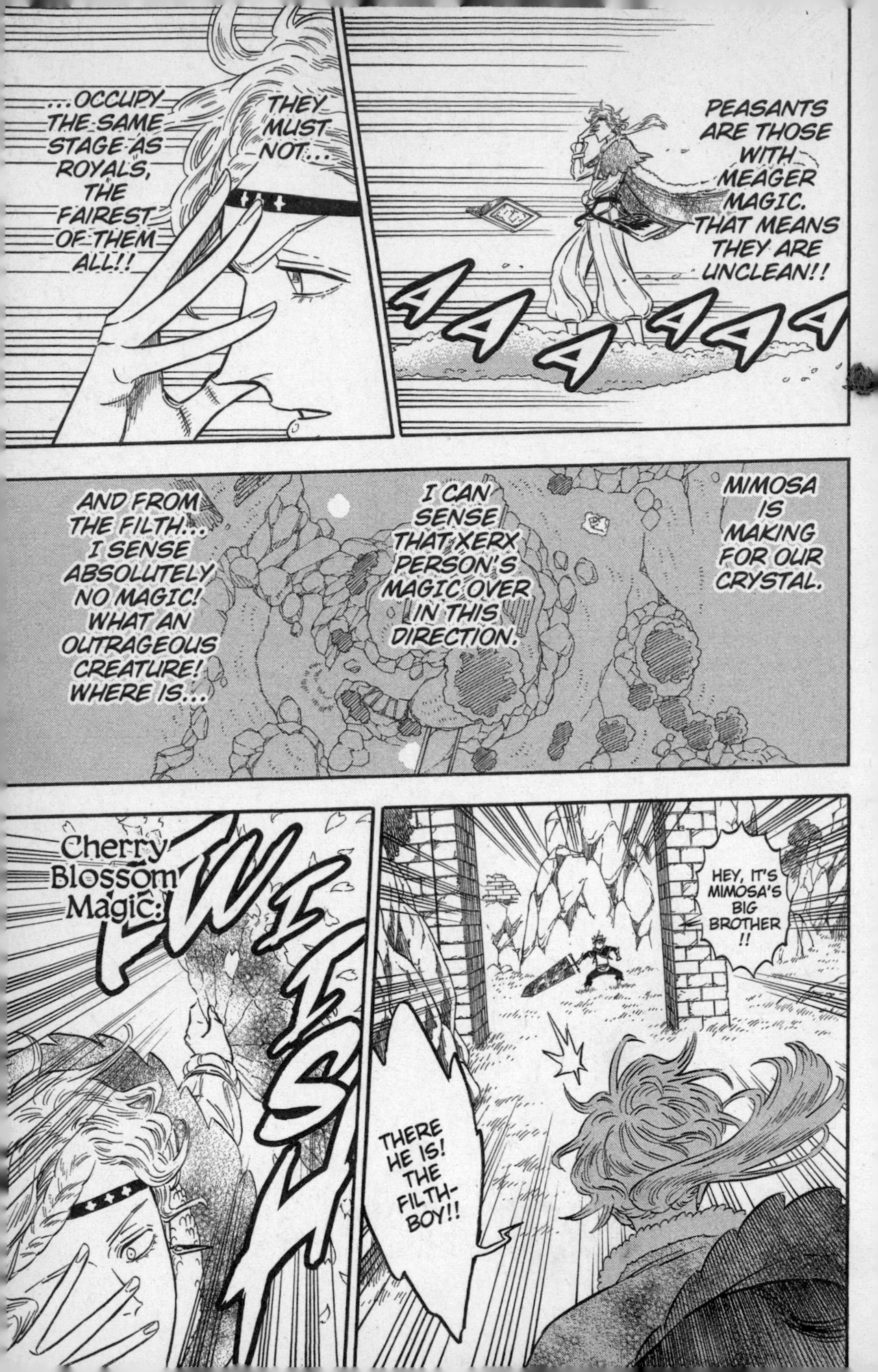
PEASANTS ARE THOSE WITH MEAGER MAGIC. THAT MEANS THEY ARE UNCLEAN!!
THEY MUST NOT...
...OCCUPY THE SAME STAGE AS ROYALS, THE FAIREST OF THEM ALL!!
MIMOSA IS MAKING FOR OUR CRYSTAL.
I CAN SENSE THAT XERX PERSON'S MAGIC OVER IN THIS DIRECTION.
AND FROM THE FILTH... I SENSE ABSOLUTELY NO MAGIC! WHAT AN OUTRAGEOUS CREATURE! WHERE IS...
HEY, IT'S MIMOSA'S BIG BROTHER!!
THERE HE IS! THE FILTH-BOY!!
Cherry Blossom Magic:
WHISH

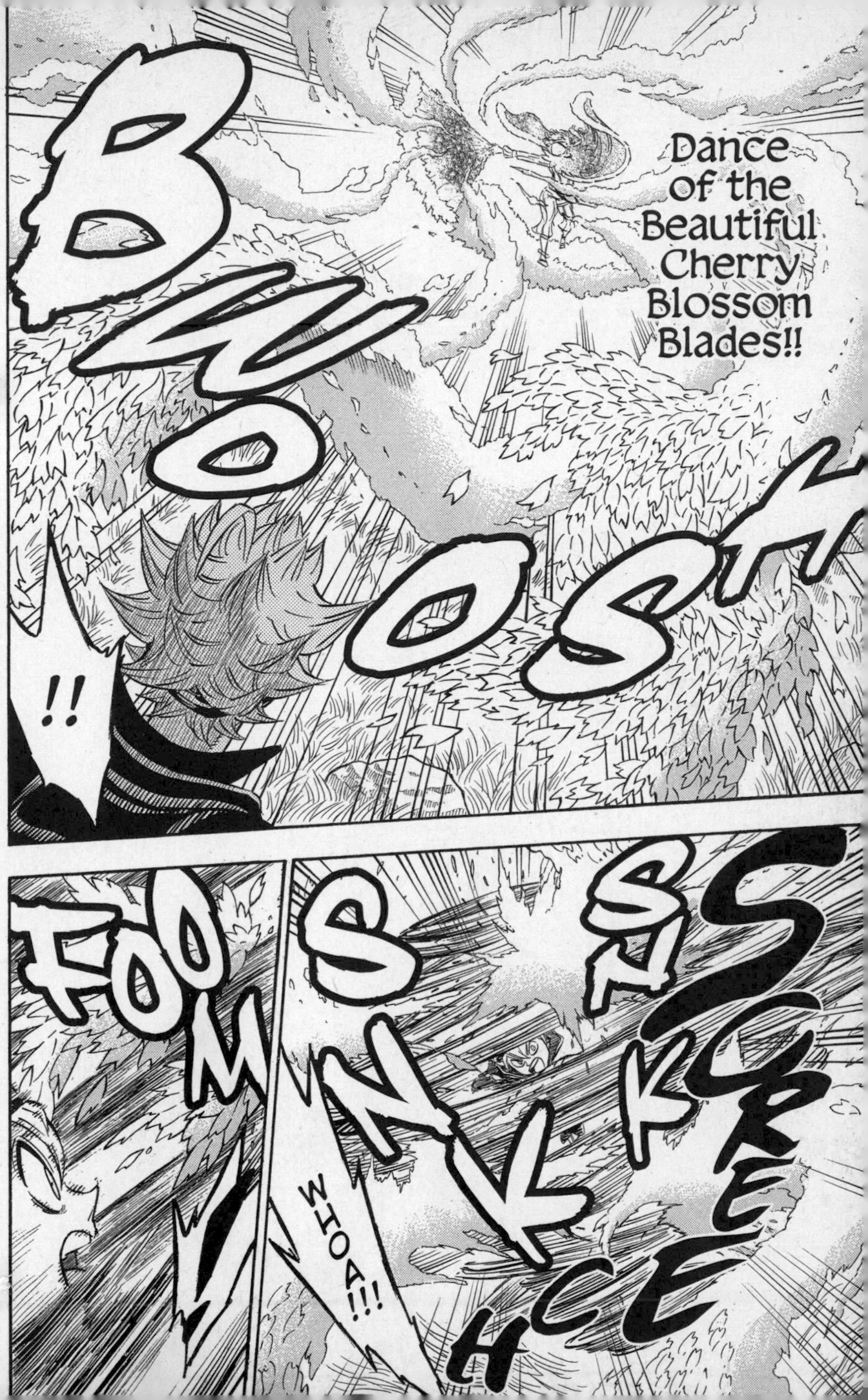
Dance of the Beautiful Cherry Blossom Blades!!
BWOOSH
!!
WHOA!!!
FOOM

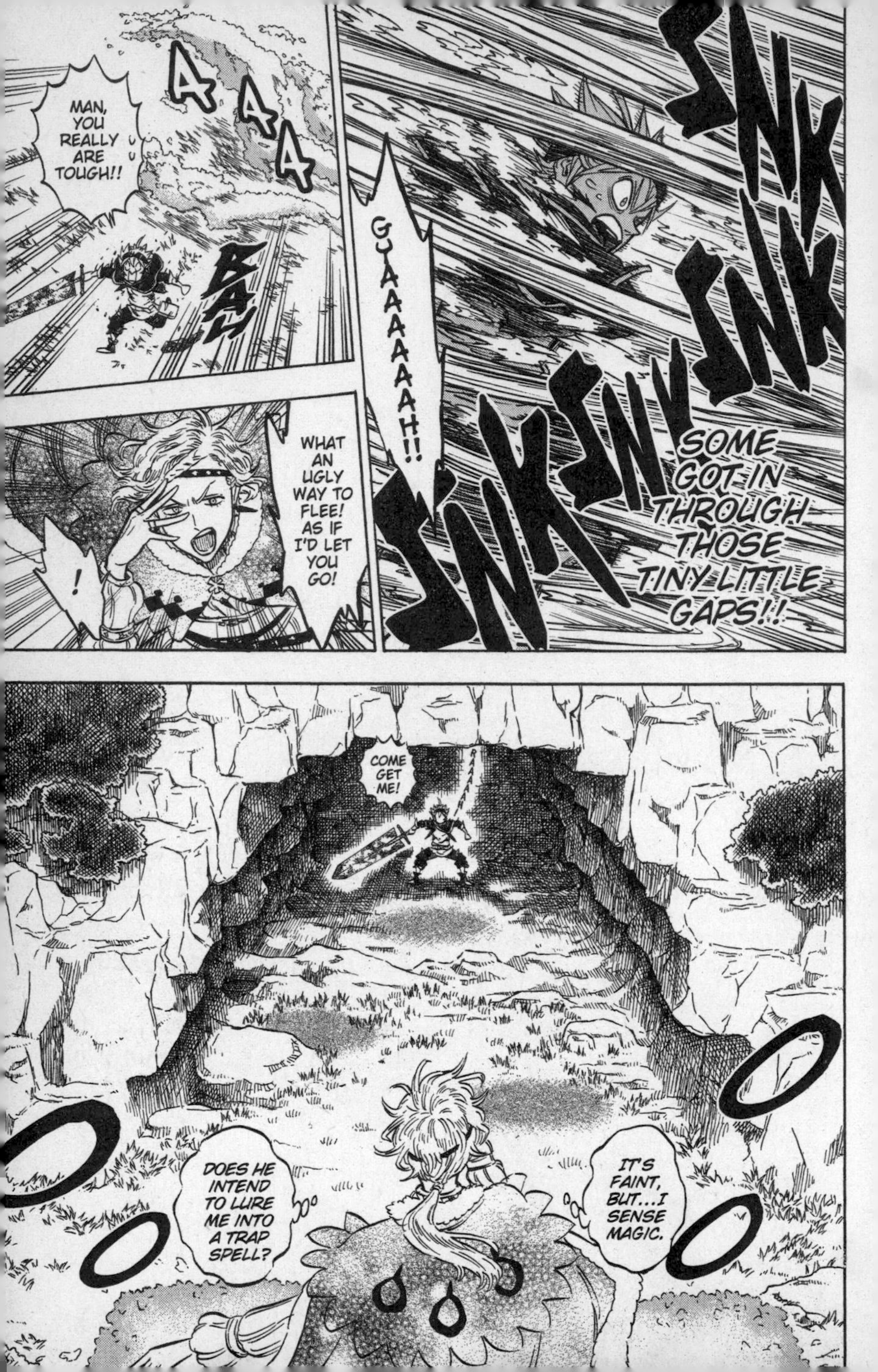
SNK SNK SNK SNK
GUAAAAAAAH!!
SOME GOT IN THROUGH THOSE TINY LITTLE GAPS!!
MAN, YOU REALLY ARE TOUGH!!
BAM
!
WHAT AN UGLY WAY TO FLEE! AS IF I'D LET YOU GO!
COME GET ME!
IT'S FAINT, BUT...I SENSE MAGIC.
DOES HE INTEND TO LURE ME INTO A TRAP SPELL?

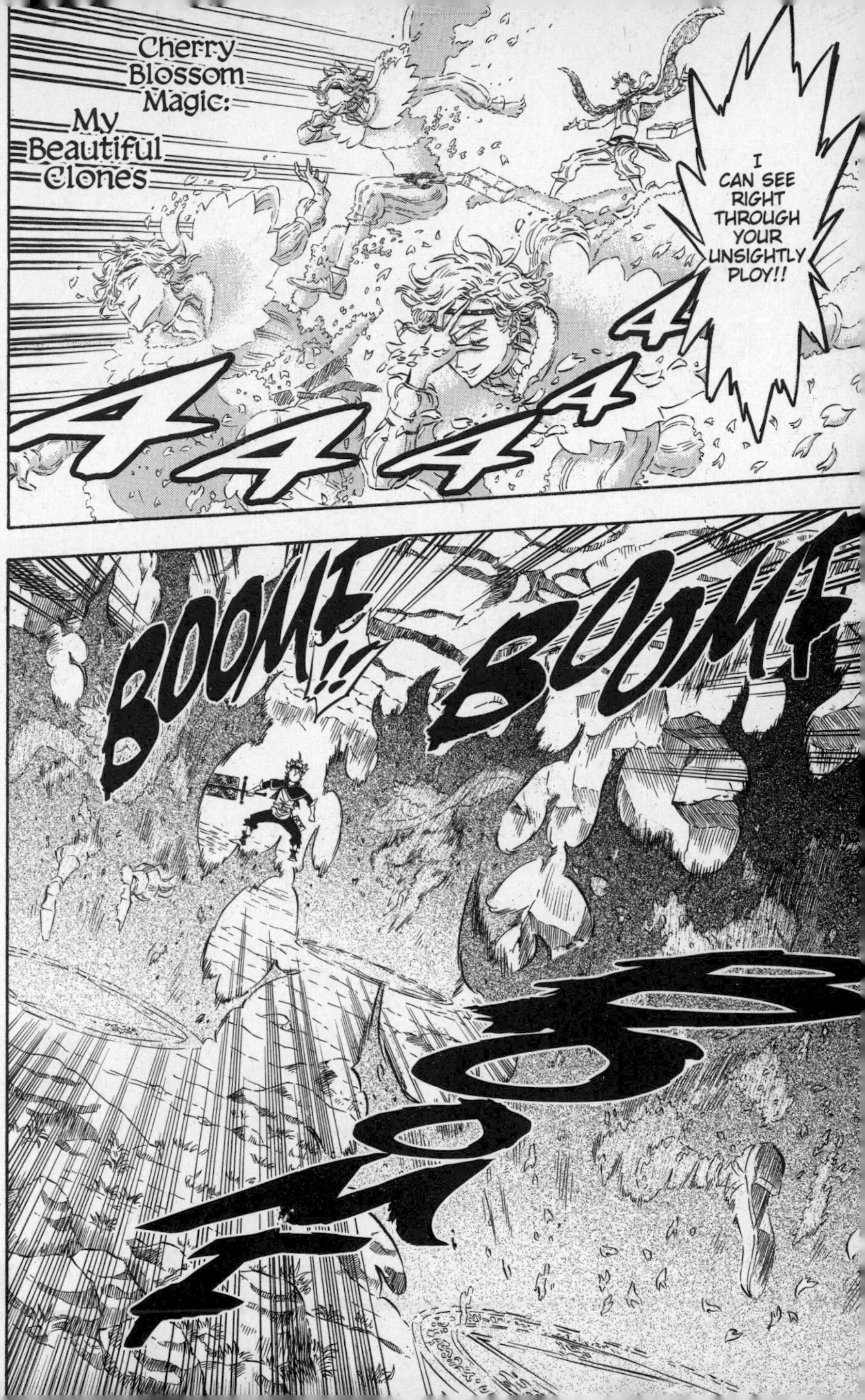
I CAN SEE RIGHT THROUGH YOUR UNSIGHTLY PLOY!!
Cherry Blossom Magic: My Beautiful Clones
BOOM
BOOM!!

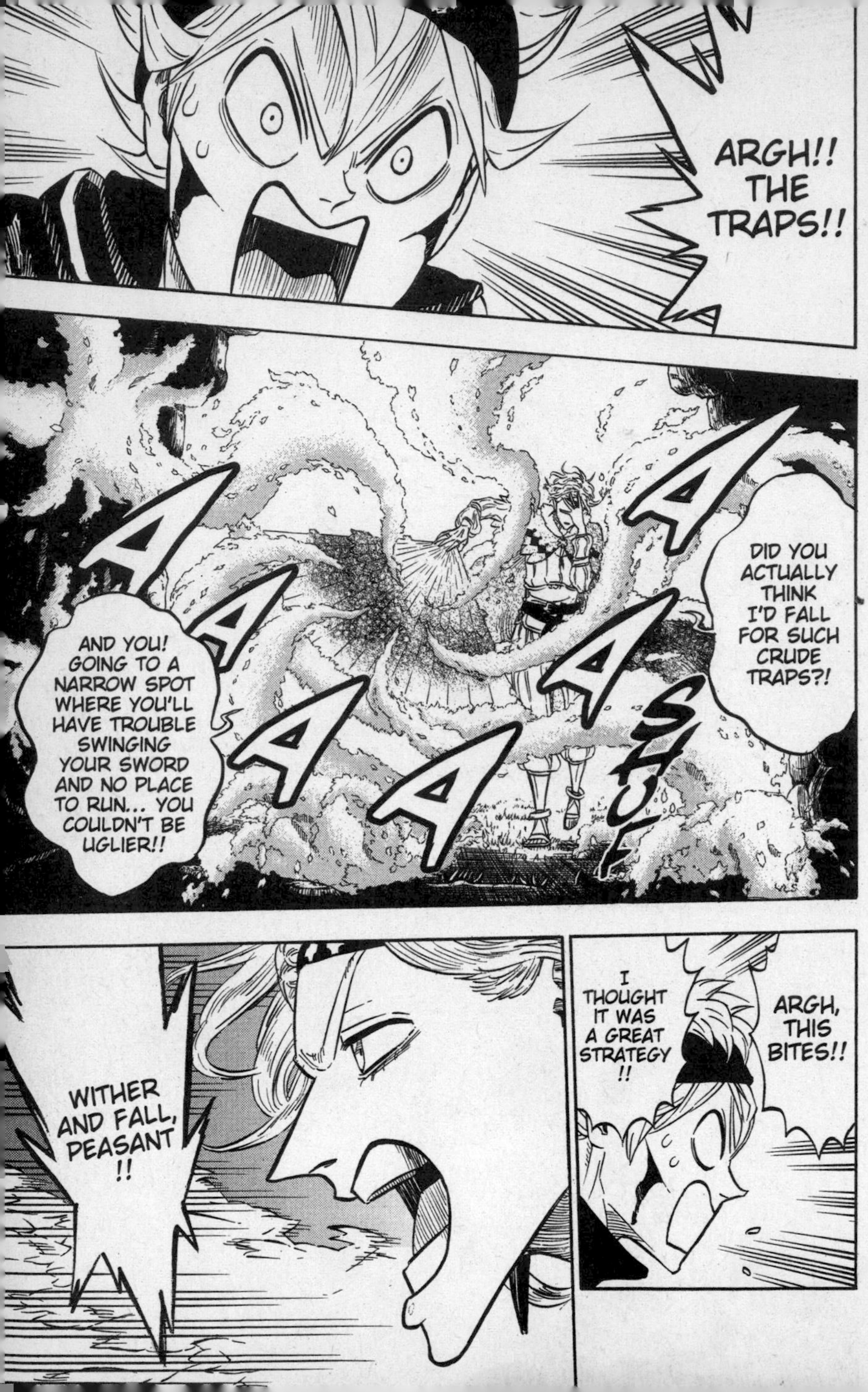
ARGH!! THE TRAPS!!
DID YOU ACTUALLY THINK I'D FALL FOR SUCH CRUDE TRAPS?!
AND YOU! GOING TO A NARROW SPOT WHERE YOU'LL HAVE TROUBLE SWINGING YOUR SWORD AND NO PLACE TO RUN... YOU COULDN'T BE UGLIER!!
AAAAAA
SHUF
ARGH, THIS BITES!!
I THOUGHT IT WAS A GREAT STRATEGY!!
WITHER AND FALL, PEASANT!!

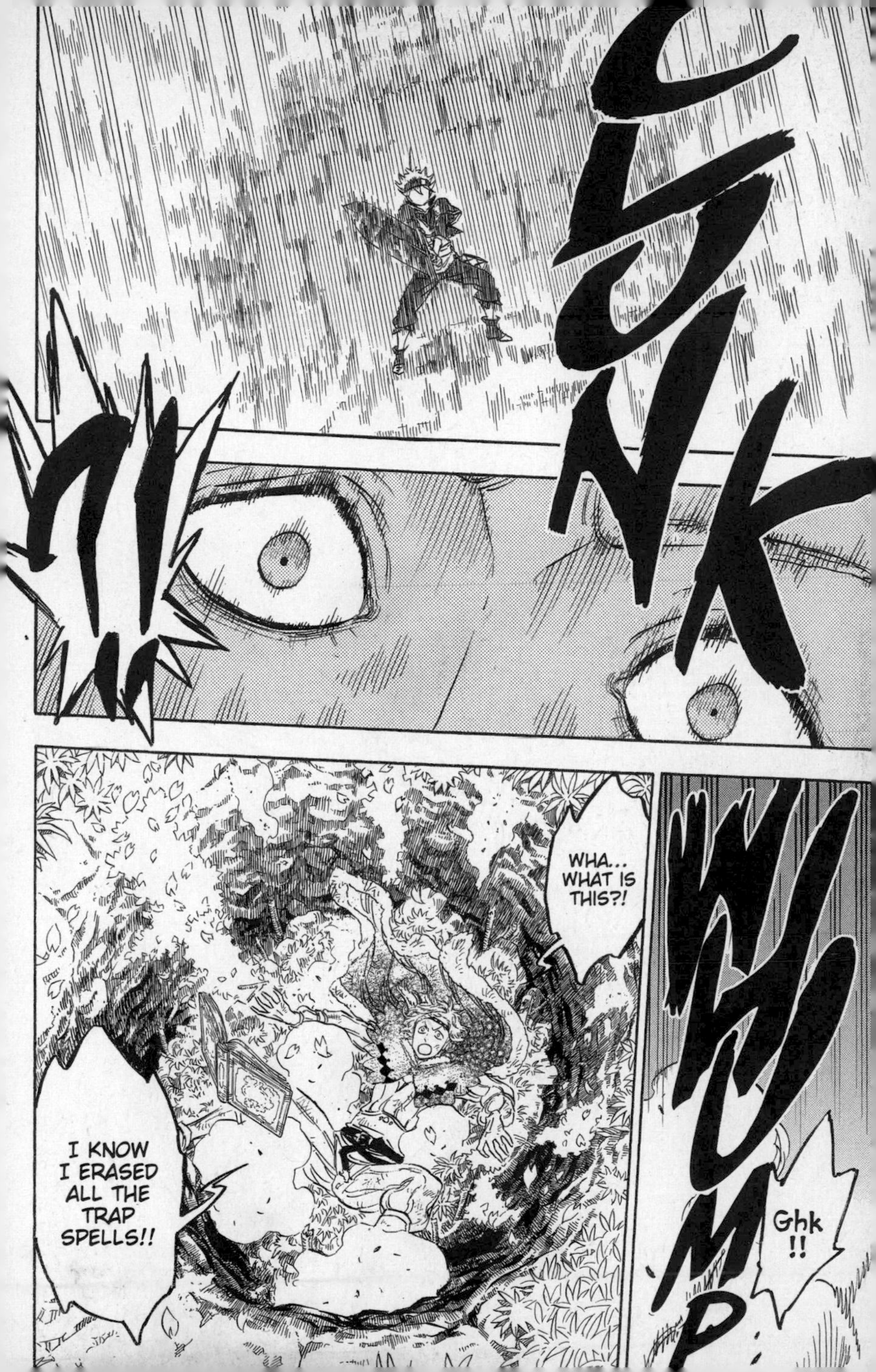
CLUNK
WHUMP
Ghk !!
WHA... WHAT IS THIS?!
I KNOW I ERASED ALL THE TRAP SPELLS!!

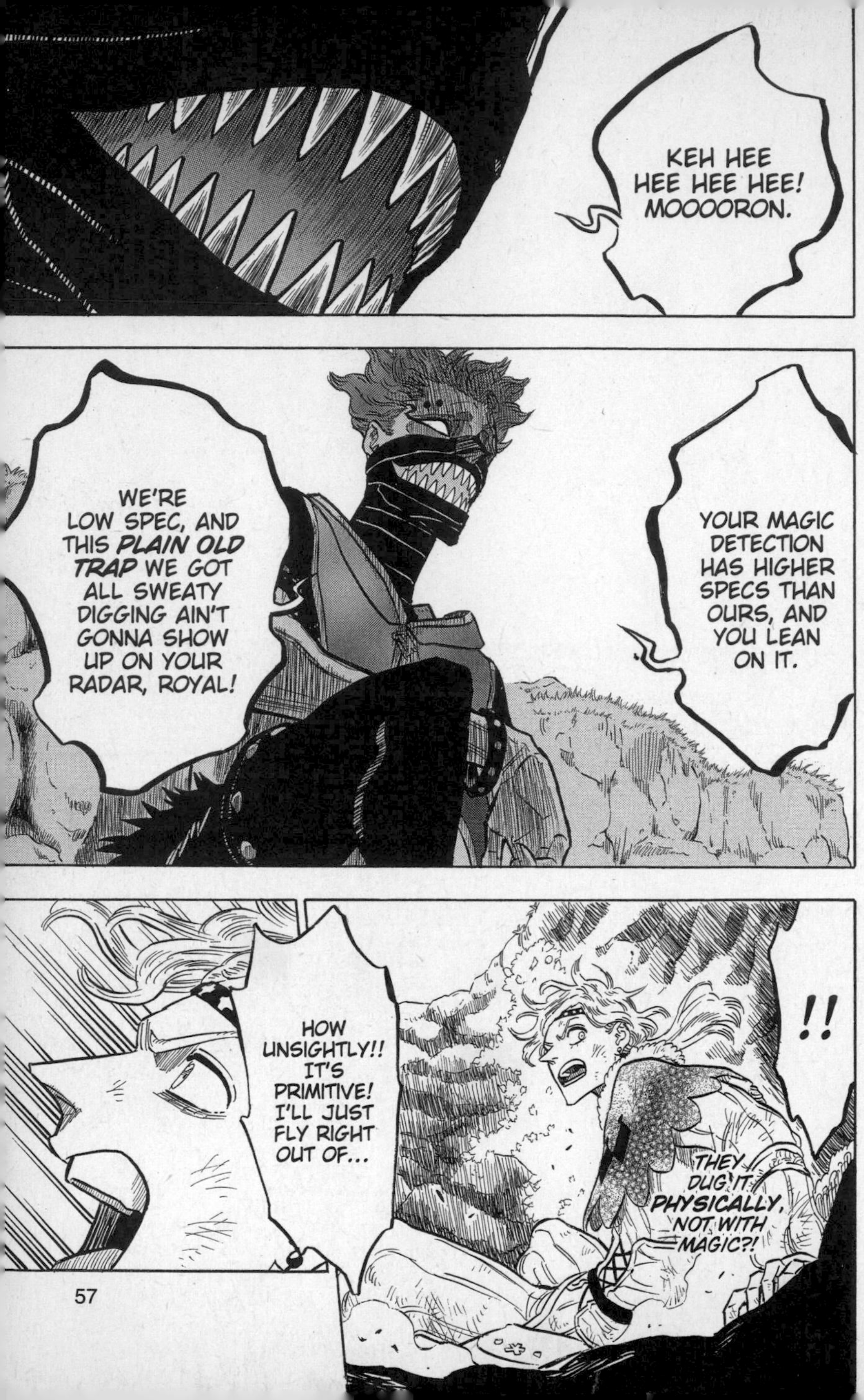
KEH HEE HEE HEE HEE! MOOOORON.
YOUR MAGIC DETECTION HAS HIGHER SPECS THAN OURS, AND YOU LEAN ON IT.
WE'RE LOW SPEC, AND THIS *PLAIN OLD TRAP* WE GOT ALL SWEATY DIGGING AIN'T GONNA SHOW UP ON YOUR RADAR, ROYAL!
!!
THEY DUG IT *PHYSICALLY*, NOT WITH MAGIC?!
HOW UNSIGHTLY!! IT'S PRIMITIVE! I'LL JUST FLY RIGHT OUT OF...

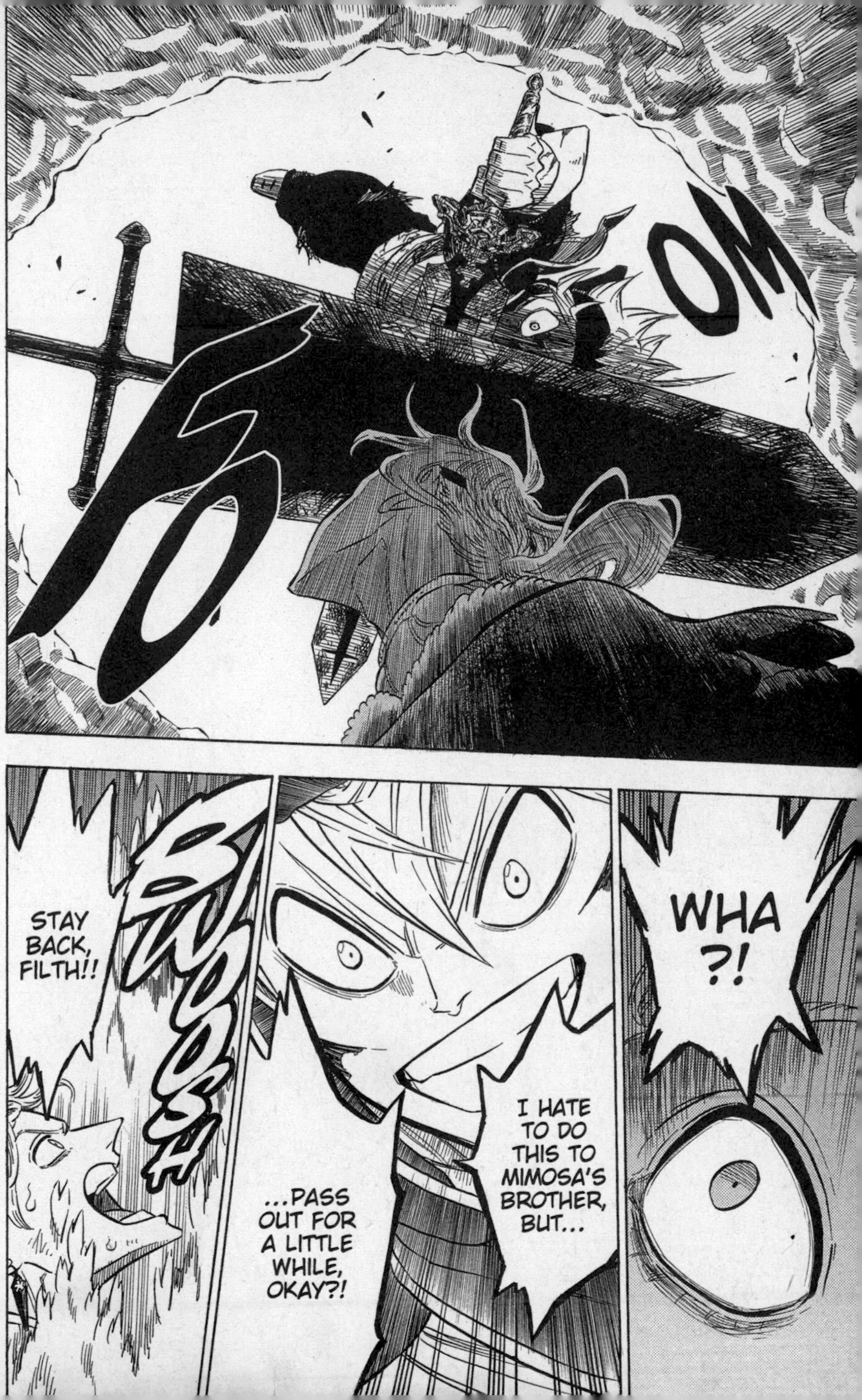
WHA ?!
I HATE TO DO THIS TO MIMOSA'S BROTHER, BUT...
...PASS OUT FOR A LITTLE WHILE, OKAY?!
STAY BACK, FILTH!!

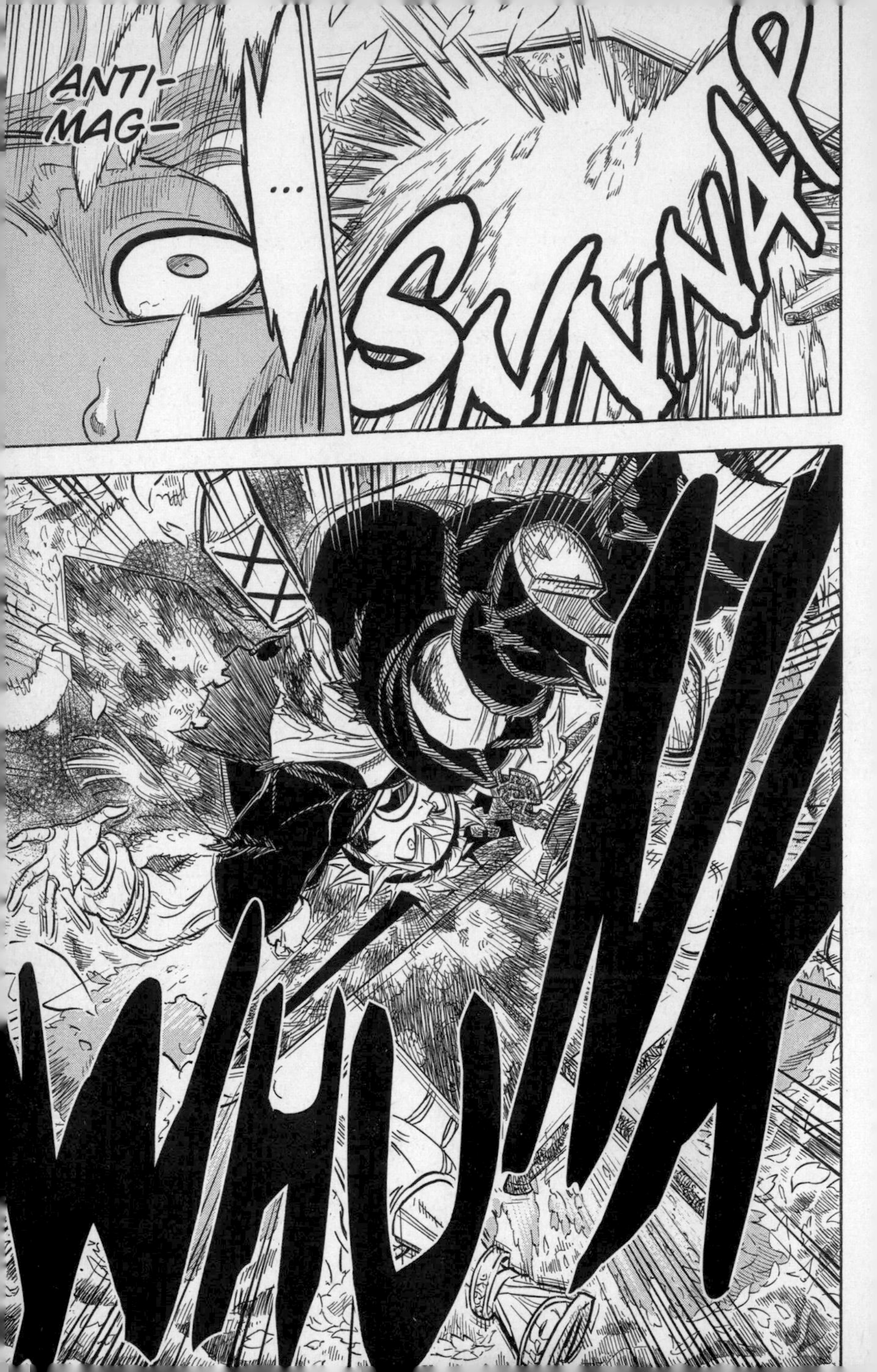
SNAP
ANTI-
MAG–
...

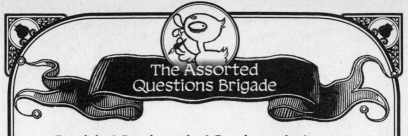

The Assorted Questions Brigade

Good day! Good evening! Good morning!

It's time for the letters corner. This time, we've got a ranking that will make you want to hear them sing (?) in spite of yourself.

Q: Give us a list of who's best at singing! (Tapioca)

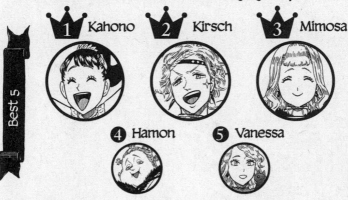

Best 5

1 Kahono

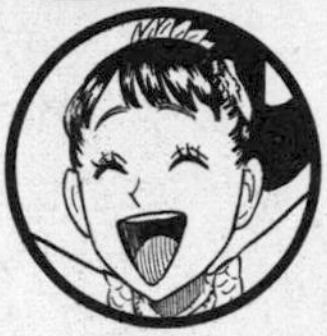

2 Kirsch

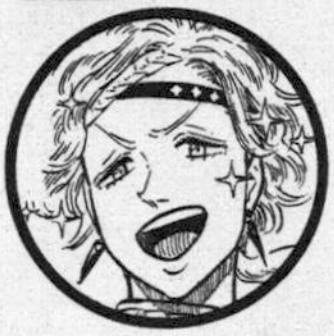

3 Mimosa

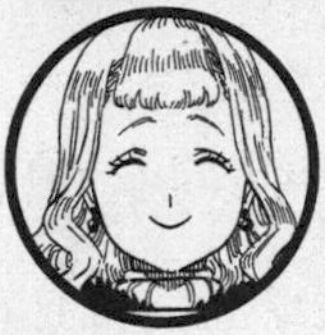

4 Hamon

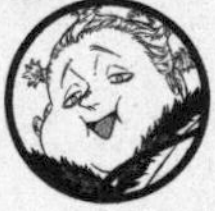

5 Vanessa

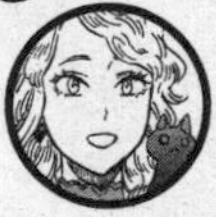

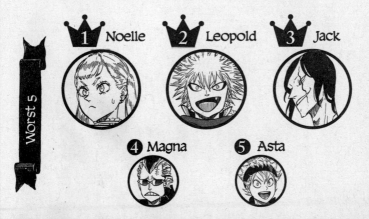

Worst 5

1 Noelle

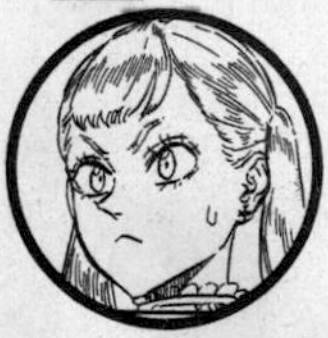

2 Leopold

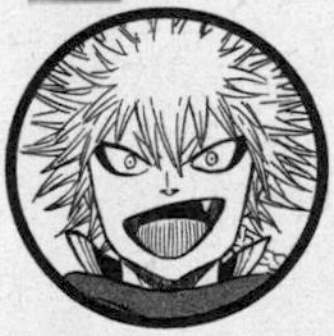

3 Jack

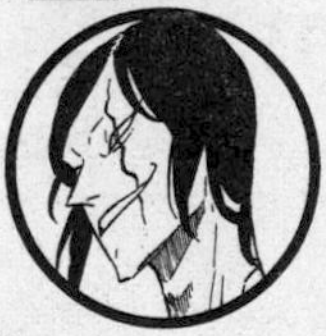

4 Magna

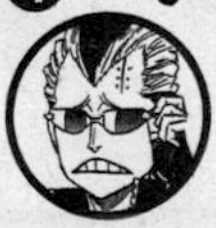

5 Asta

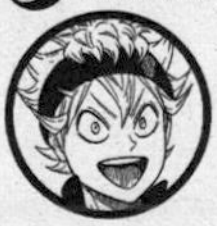

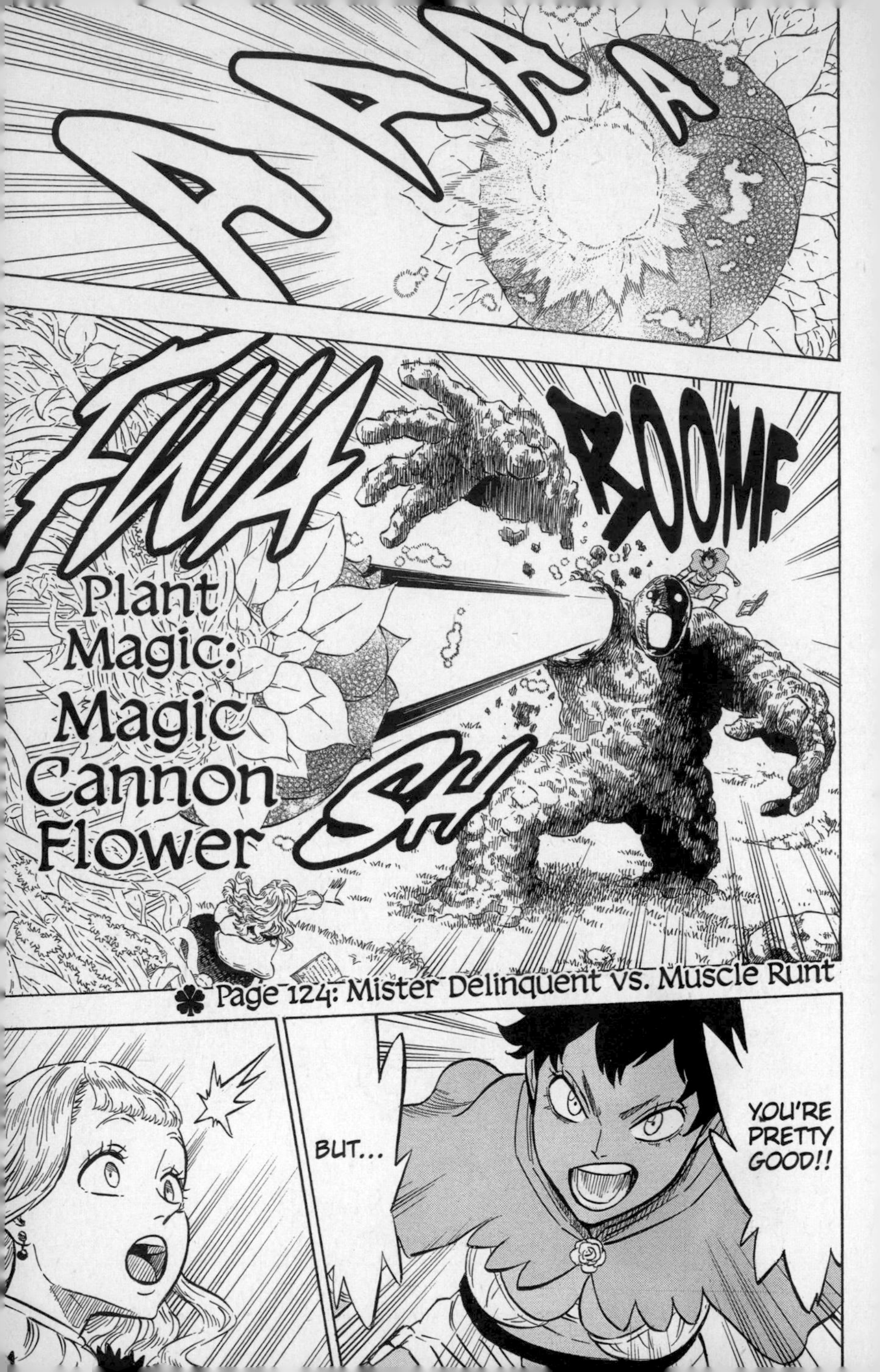
BOOMF
Plant Magic: Magic Cannon Flower
Page 124: Mister Delinquent vs. Muscle Runt
YOU'RE PRETTY GOOD!!
BUT...

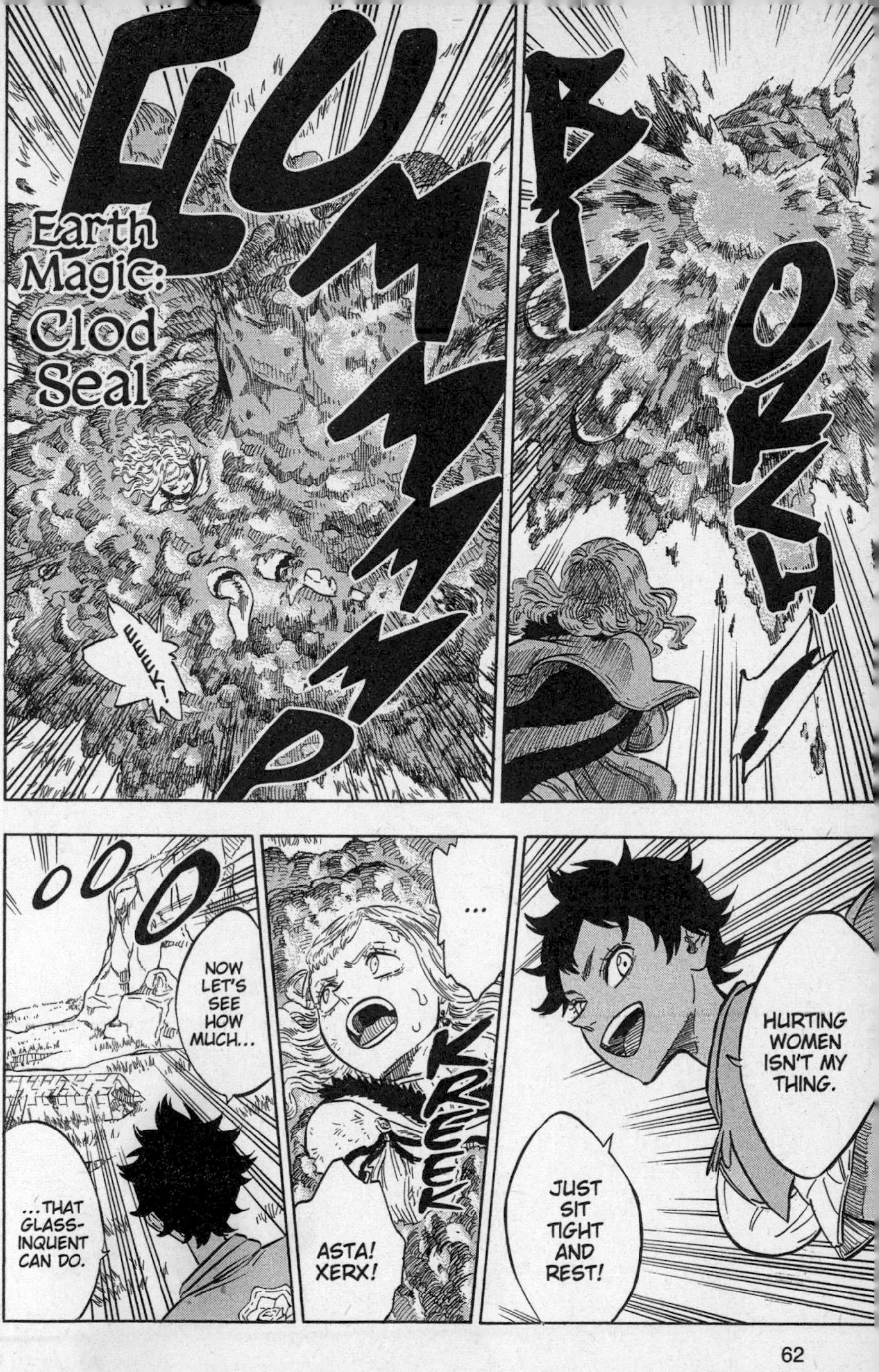
BLOOSH!
Earth Magic: Clod Seal
FLUMMMMP
EEEK!
HURTING WOMEN ISN'T MY THING.
JUST SIT TIGHT AND REST!
...
ASTA! XERX!
KREEEN
oOO
NOW LET'S SEE HOW MUCH...
...THAT GLASS-INQUENT CAN DO.

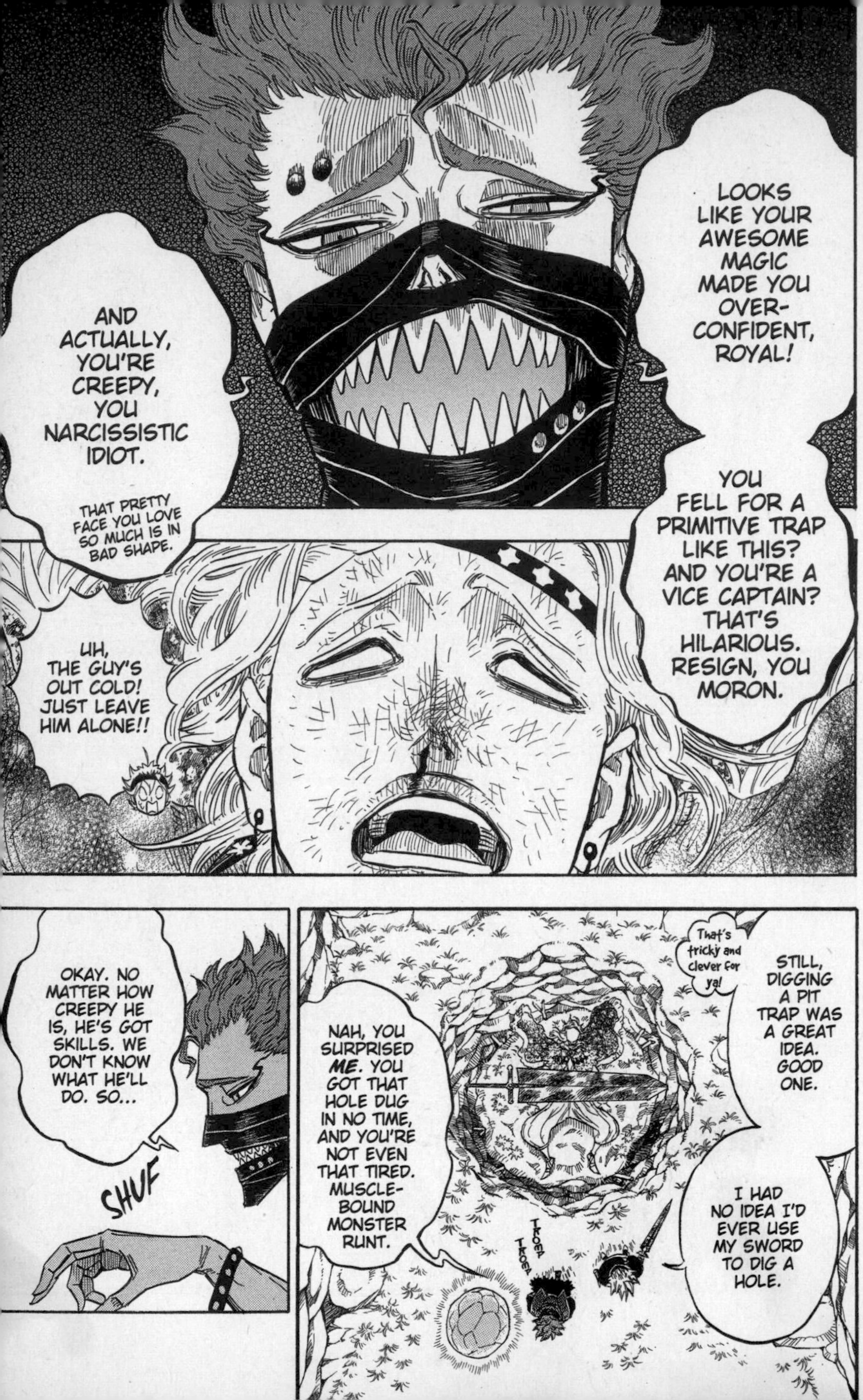
LOOKS LIKE YOUR AWESOME MAGIC MADE YOU OVER-CONFIDENT, ROYAL!
AND ACTUALLY, YOU'RE CREEPY, YOU NARCISSISTIC IDIOT.
YOU FELL FOR A PRIMITIVE TRAP LIKE THIS? AND YOU'RE A VICE CAPTAIN? THAT'S HILARIOUS. RESIGN, YOU MORON.
THAT PRETTY FACE YOU LOVE SO MUCH IS IN BAD SHAPE.
UH, THE GUY'S OUT COLD! JUST LEAVE HIM ALONE!!
STILL, DIGGING A PIT TRAP WAS A GREAT IDEA. GOOD ONE.
That's tricky and clever for ya!
I HAD NO IDEA I'D EVER USE MY SWORD TO DIG A HOLE.
NAH, YOU SURPRISED *ME*. YOU GOT THAT HOLE DUG IN NO TIME, AND YOU'RE NOT EVEN THAT TIRED. MUSCLE-BOUND MONSTER RUNT.
TROMP TROMP
OKAY. NO MATTER HOW CREEPY HE IS, HE'S GOT SKILLS. WE DON'T KNOW WHAT HE'LL DO. SO...
SHUF

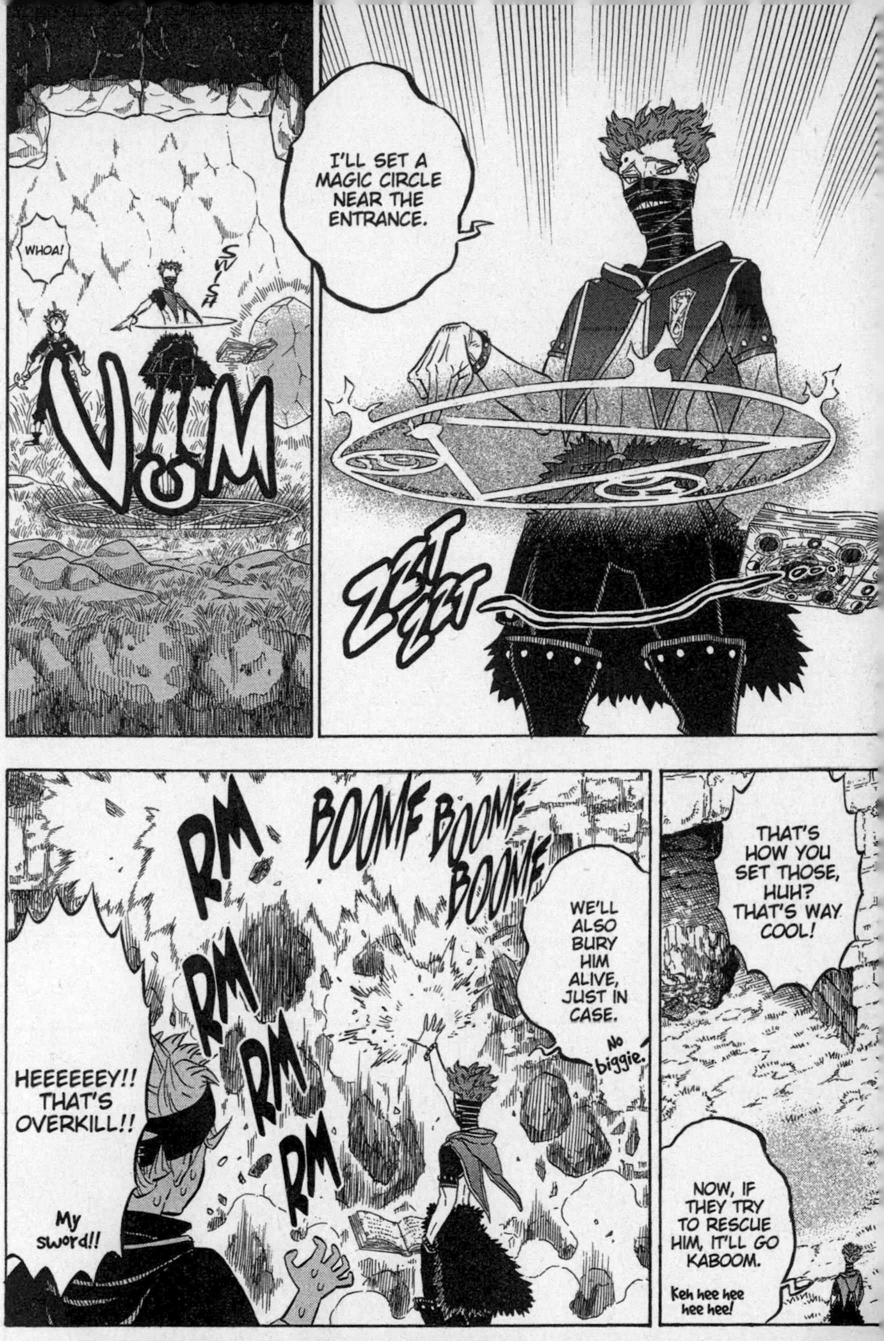
I'LL SET A MAGIC CIRCLE NEAR THE ENTRANCE.
WHOA!
SWISH
THAT'S HOW YOU SET THOSE, HUH? THAT'S WAY COOL!
NOW, IF THEY TRY TO RESCUE HIM, IT'LL GO KABOOM.
Keh hee hee hee hee!
BOOMF BOOMF BOOMF
WE'LL ALSO BURY HIM ALIVE, JUST IN CASE.
No biggie.
RM RM RM RM RM
HEEEEEEY!! THAT'S OVERKILL!!
My sword!!

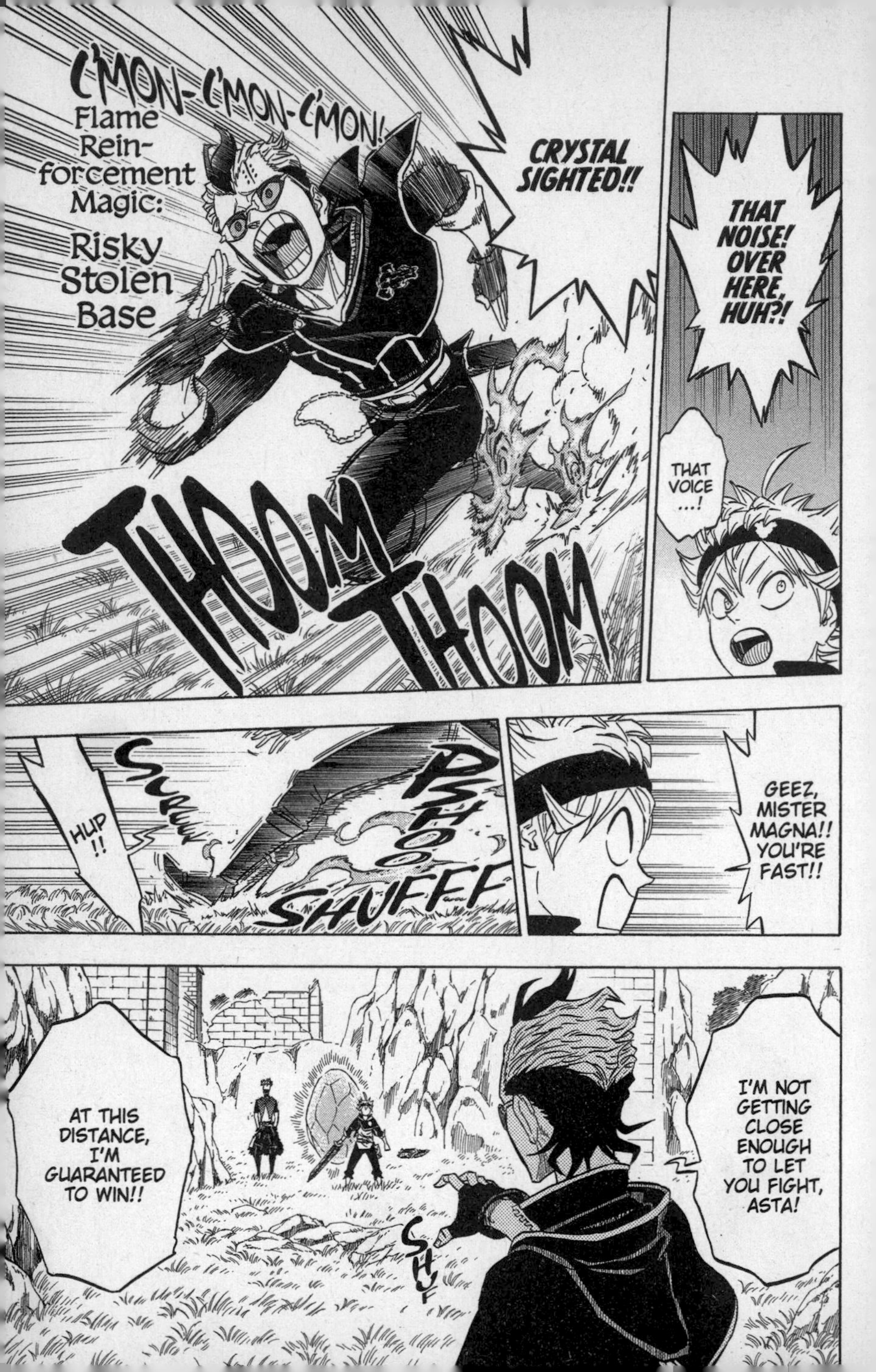
THAT NOISE! OVER HERE, HUH?!
THAT VOICE ...!
CRYSTAL SIGHTED!!
C'MON-C'MON-C'MON!
Flame Reinforcement Magic: Risky Stolen Base
THOOM THOOM
GEEZ, MISTER MAGNA!! YOU'RE FAST!!
HUP!!
SHUFFF
I'M NOT GETTING CLOSE ENOUGH TO LET YOU FIGHT, ASTA!
SHU
AT THIS DISTANCE, I'M GUARANTEED TO WIN!!

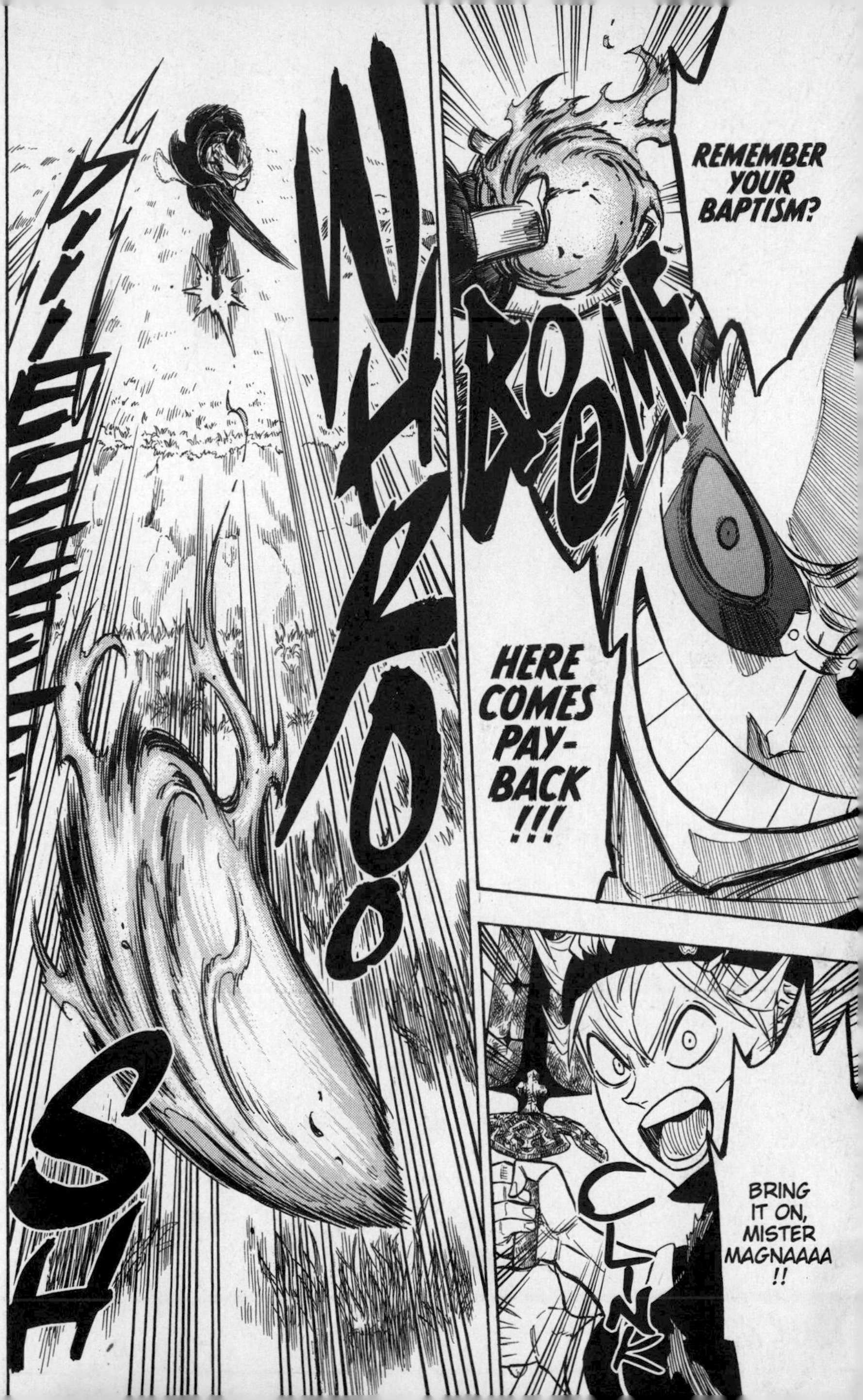
REMEMBER YOUR BAPTISM?
HERE COMES PAY-BACK !!!
BRING IT ON, MISTER MAGNAAAA !!
CLINK

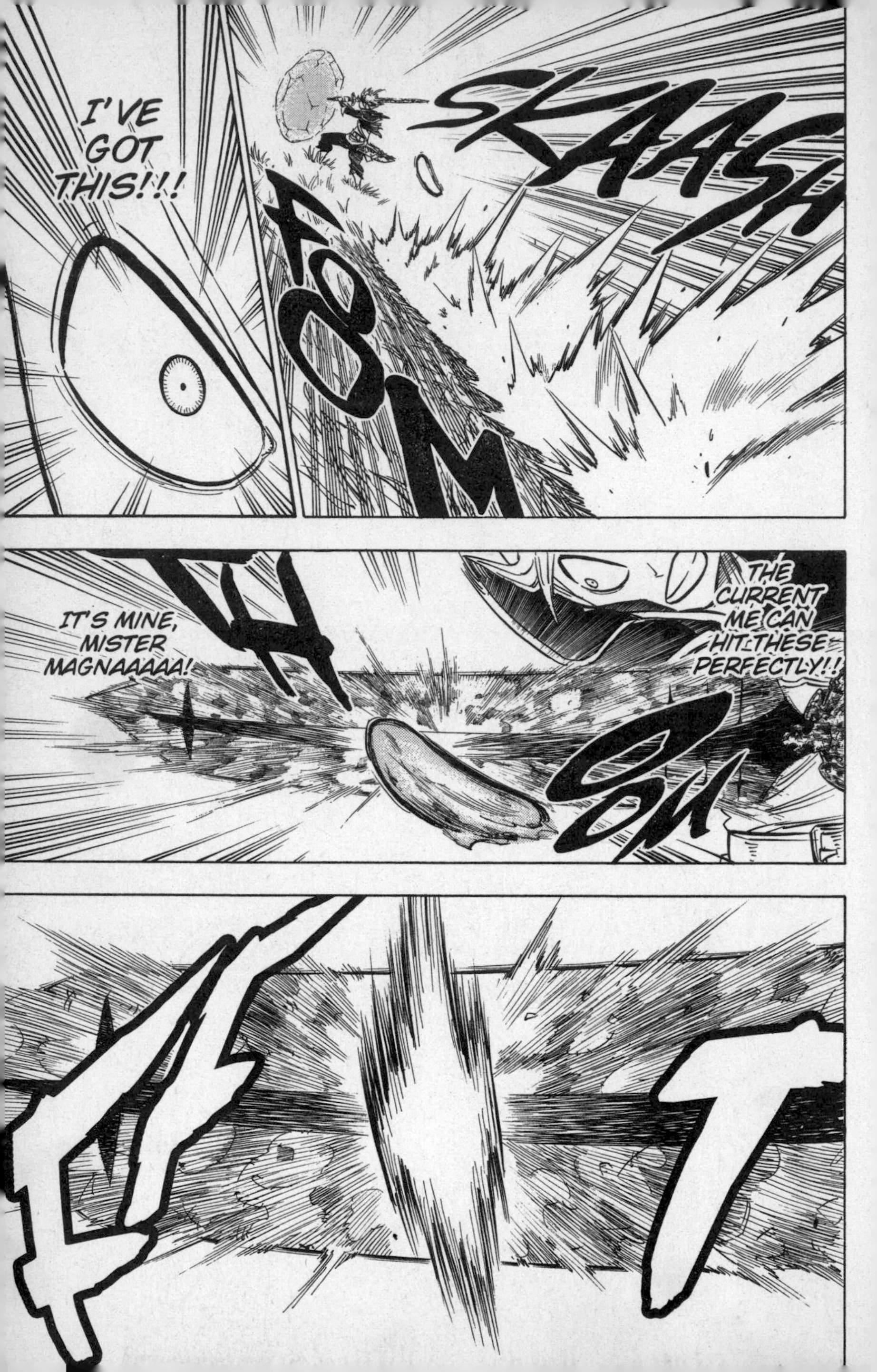
SKAASH
FOOM
I'VE GOT THIS!!!
THE CURRENT ME CAN HIT THESE PERFECTLY!!
IT'S MINE, MISTER MAGNAAAAA!

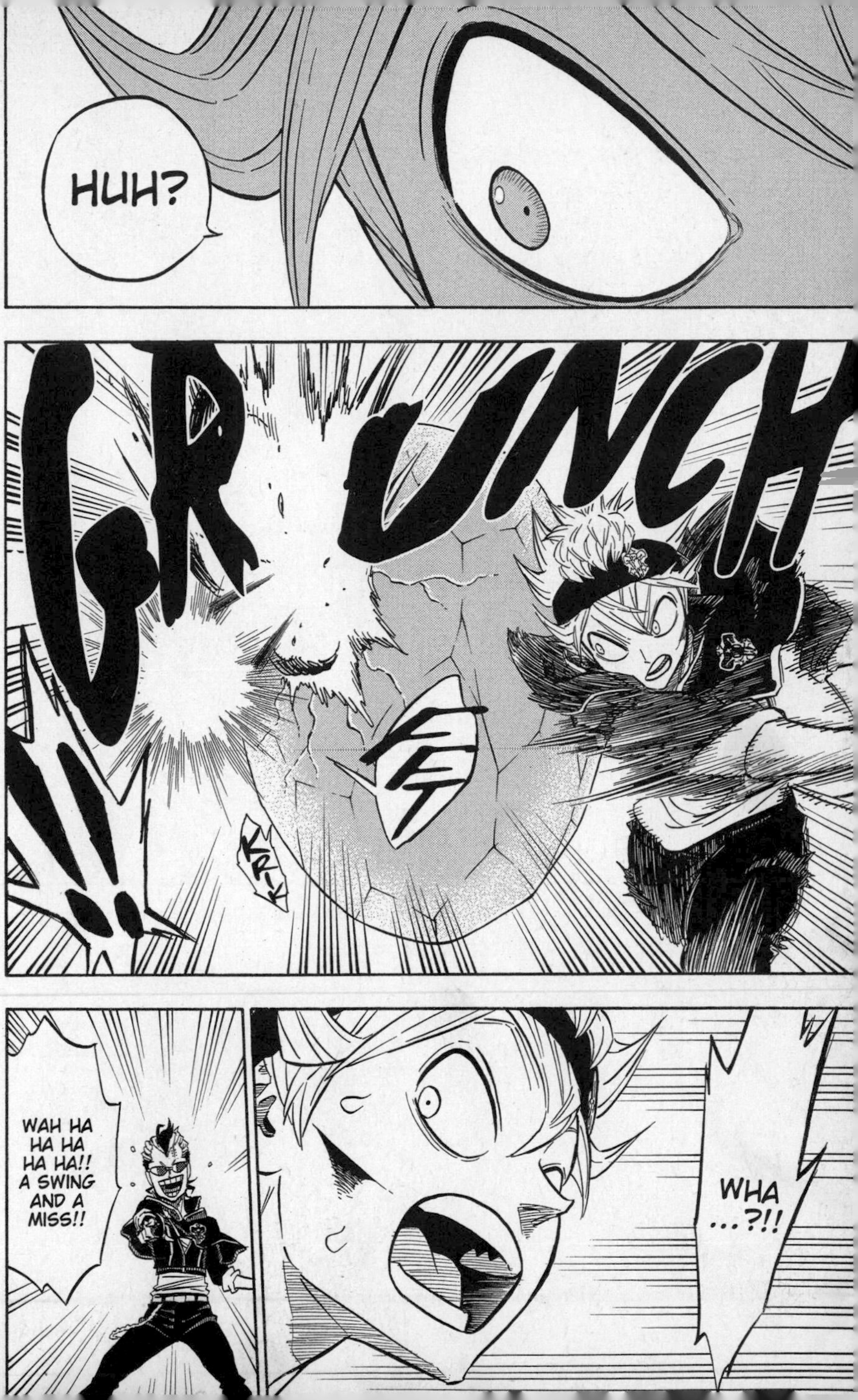
HUH?
CRUNCH!!
KRIK
WHA ...?!!
WAH HA HA HA HA HA!! A SWING AND A MISS!!

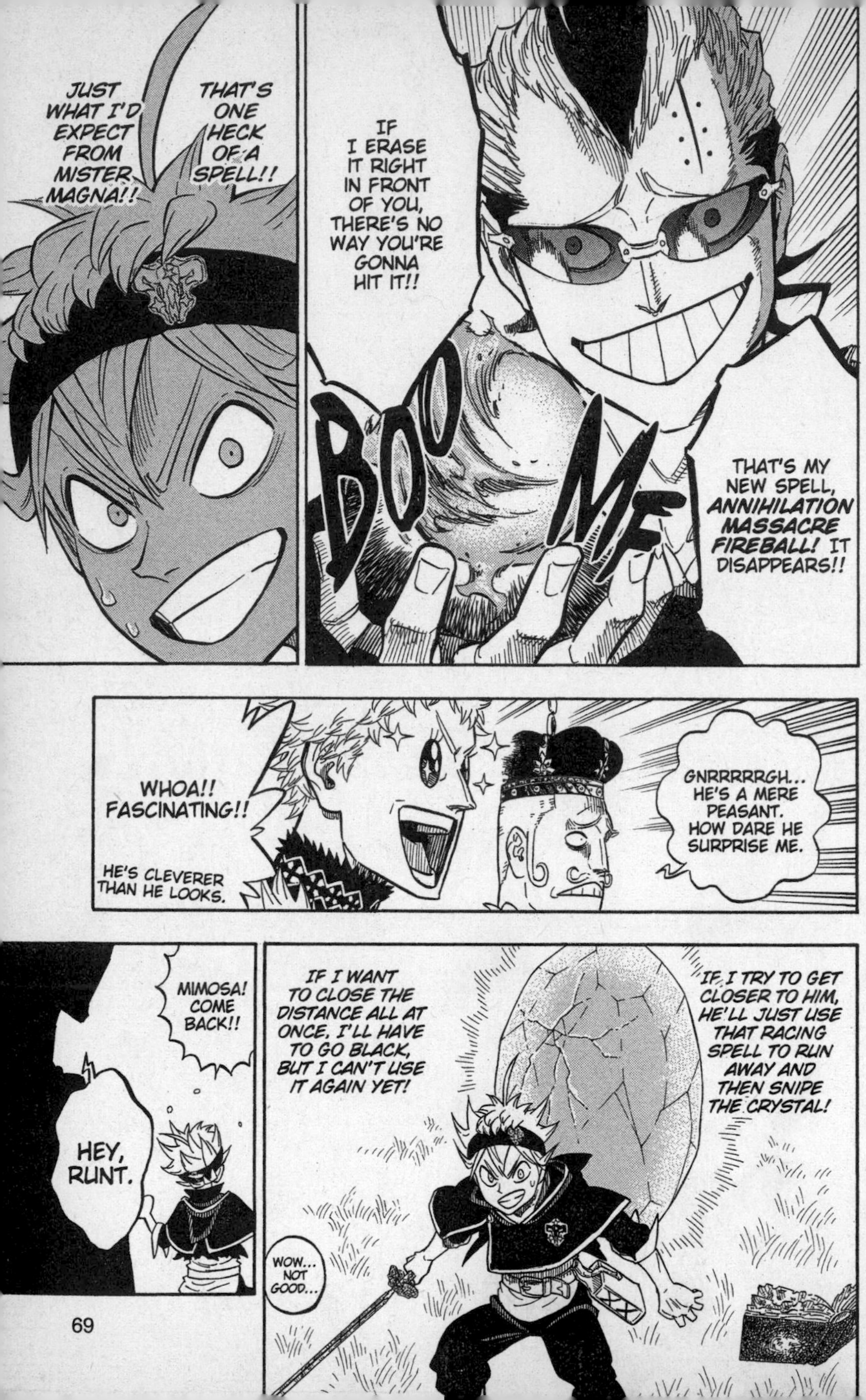
THAT'S MY NEW SPELL, ANNIHILATION MASSACRE FIREBALL! IT DISAPPEARS!!
IF I ERASE IT RIGHT IN FRONT OF YOU, THERE'S NO WAY YOU'RE GONNA HIT IT!!
BOOM
THAT'S ONE HECK OF A SPELL!!
JUST WHAT I'D EXPECT FROM MISTER MAGNA!!
GNRRRRRGH... HE'S A MERE PEASANT. HOW DARE HE SURPRISE ME.
WHOA!! FASCINATING!!
HE'S CLEVERER THAN HE LOOKS.
IF I TRY TO GET CLOSER TO HIM, HE'LL JUST USE THAT RACING SPELL TO RUN AWAY AND THEN SNIPE THE CRYSTAL!
IF I WANT TO CLOSE THE DISTANCE ALL AT ONCE, I'LL HAVE TO GO BLACK, BUT I CAN'T USE IT AGAIN YET!
WOW... NOT GOOD...
MIMOSA! COME BACK!!
HEY, RUNT.

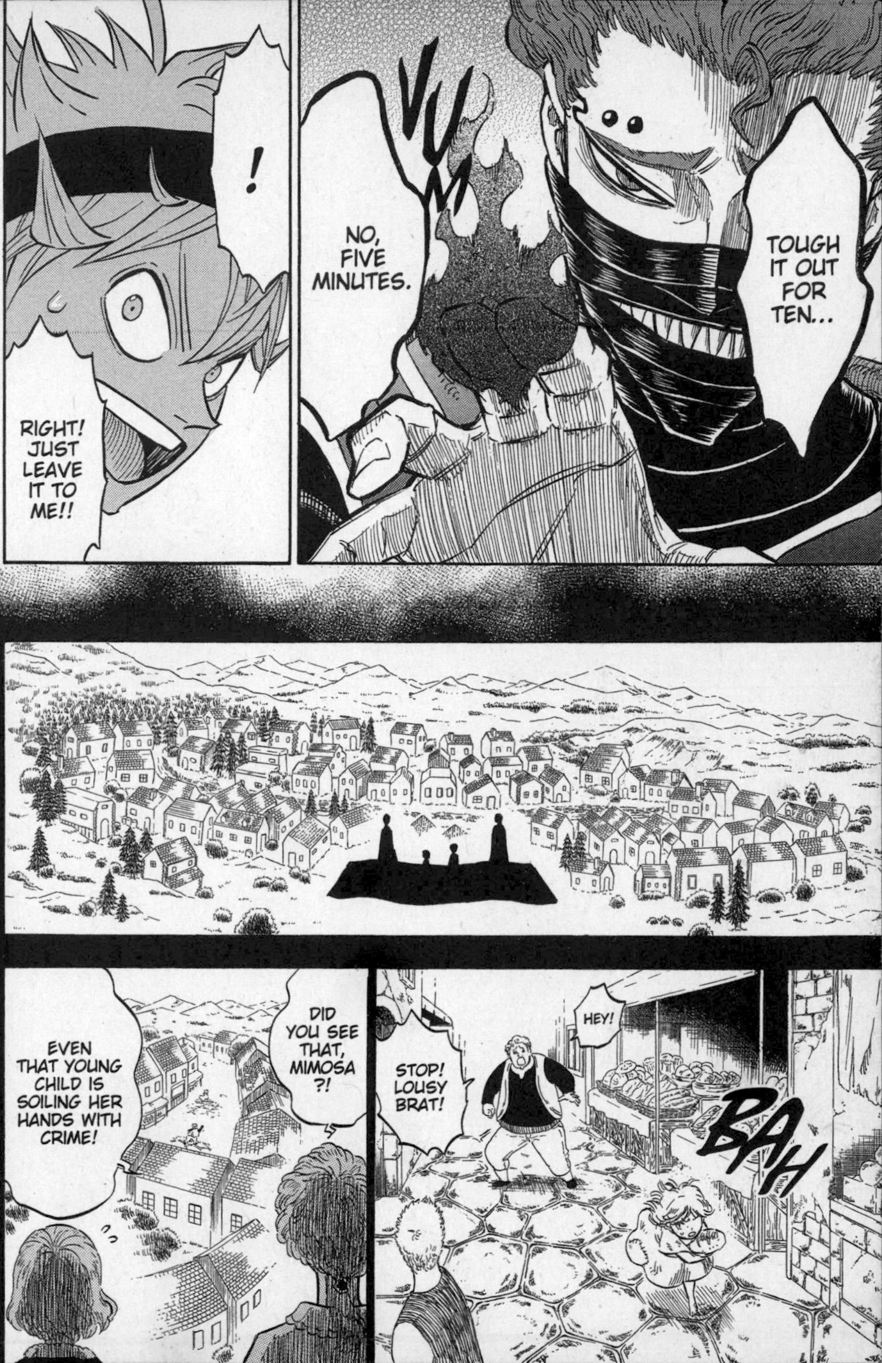
TOUGH IT OUT FOR TEN...
NO, FIVE MINUTES.
!
RIGHT! JUST LEAVE IT TO ME!!
HEY!
STOP! LOUSY BRAT!
BAH
DID YOU SEE THAT, MIMOSA?!
EVEN THAT YOUNG CHILD IS SOILING HER HANDS WITH CRIME!

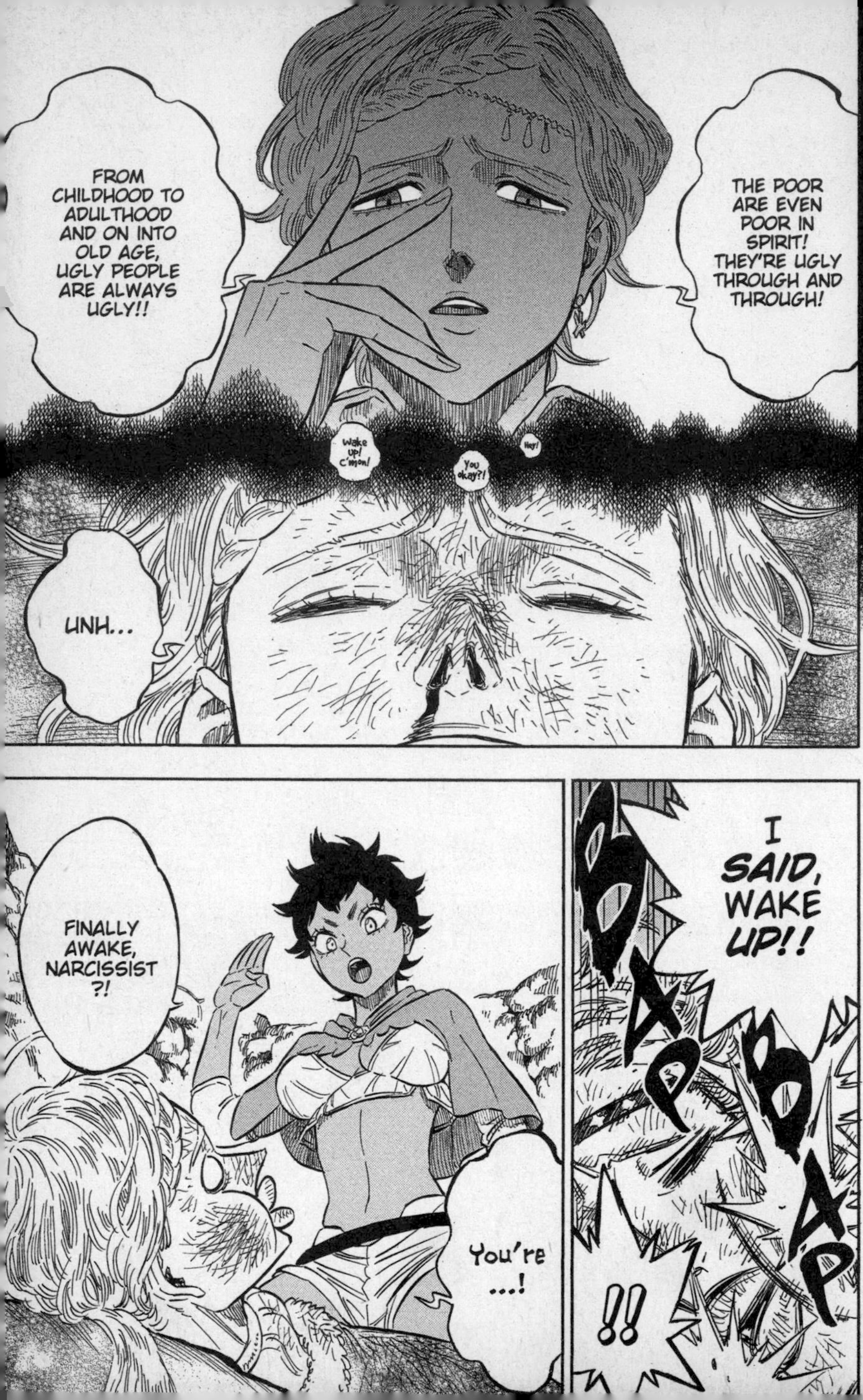
THE POOR ARE EVEN POOR IN SPIRIT! THEY'RE UGLY THROUGH AND THROUGH!
FROM CHILDHOOD TO ADULTHOOD AND ON INTO OLD AGE, UGLY PEOPLE ARE ALWAYS UGLY!!
Hey!
You okay?!
Wake up! C'mon!
UNH...
I SAID, WAKE UP!!
BAP
BAP
!!
FINALLY AWAKE, NARCISSIST?!
You're ...!

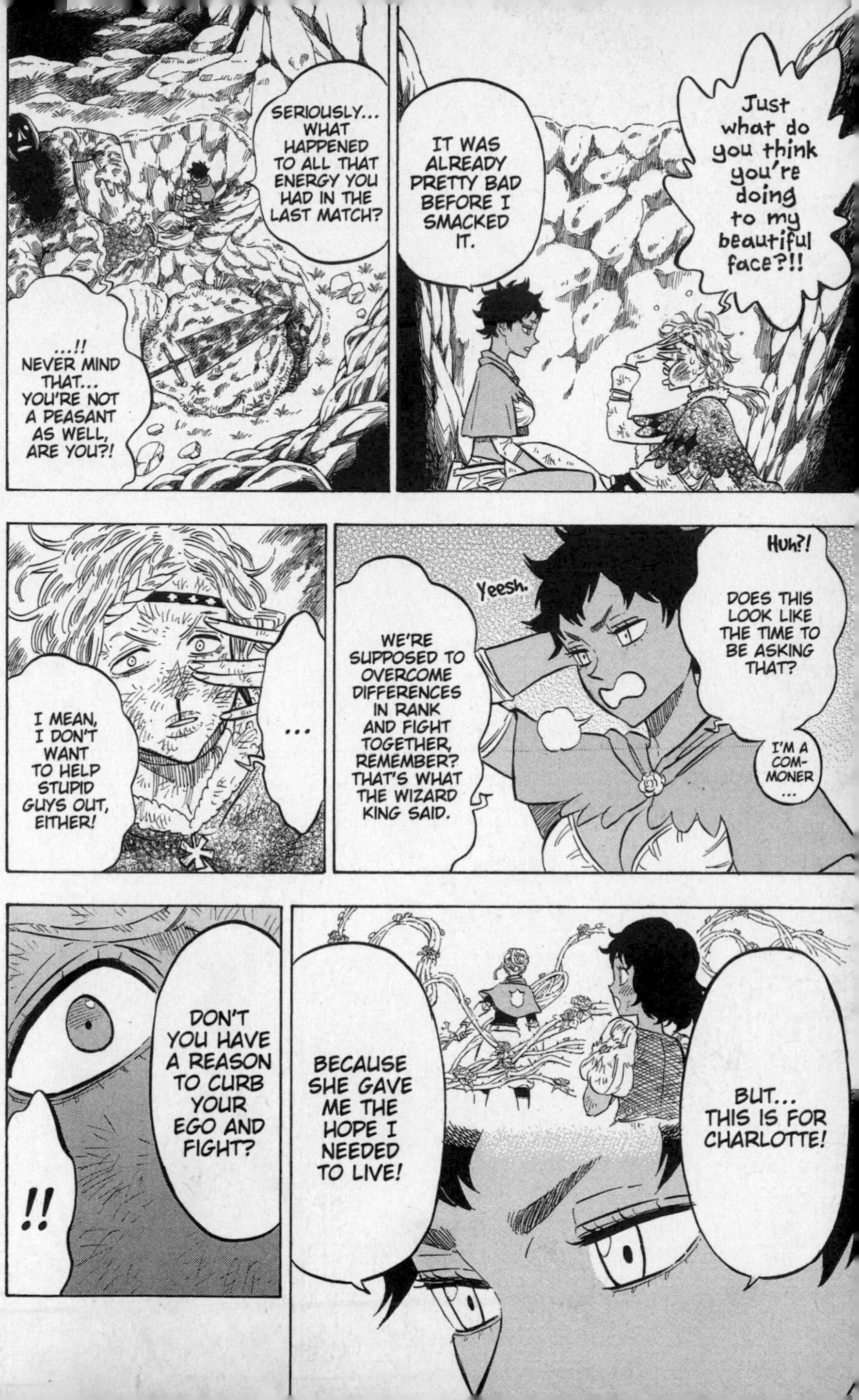
Just what do you think you're doing to my beautiful face?!!
IT WAS ALREADY PRETTY BAD BEFORE I SMACKED IT.
SERIOUSLY... WHAT HAPPENED TO ALL THAT ENERGY YOU HAD IN THE LAST MATCH?
...!! NEVER MIND THAT... YOU'RE NOT A PEASANT AS WELL, ARE YOU?!
Huh?!
DOES THIS LOOK LIKE THE TIME TO BE ASKING THAT?
I'M A COMMONER...
Yeesh.
WE'RE SUPPOSED TO OVERCOME DIFFERENCES IN RANK AND FIGHT TOGETHER, REMEMBER? THAT'S WHAT THE WIZARD KING SAID.
...
I MEAN, I DON'T WANT TO HELP STUPID GUYS OUT, EITHER!
BUT... THIS IS FOR CHARLOTTE!
BECAUSE SHE GAVE ME THE HOPE I NEEDED TO LIVE!
DON'T YOU HAVE A REASON TO CURB YOUR EGO AND FIGHT?
!!

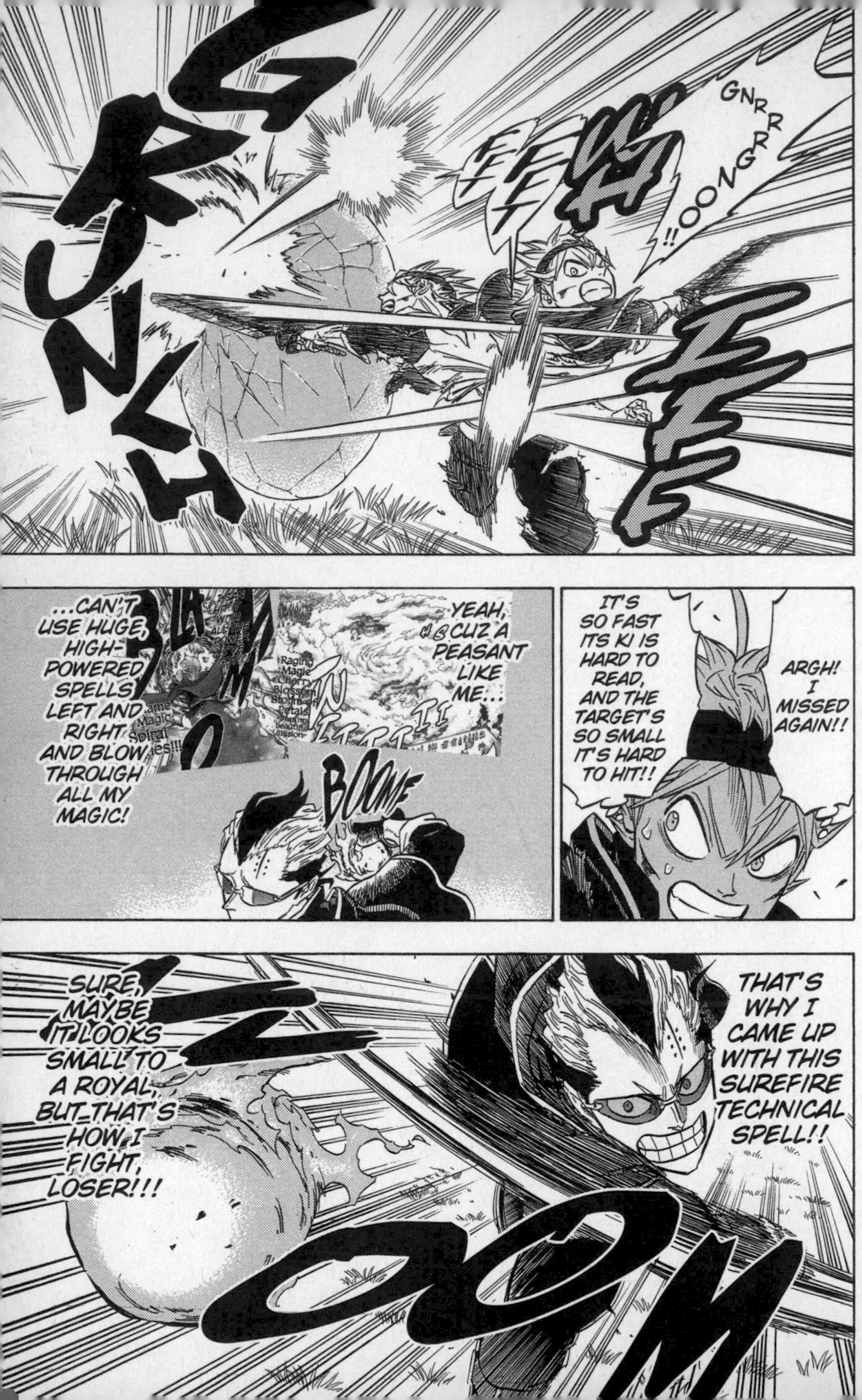
GNRRR
OONGRR!!
ARGH! I MISSED AGAIN!!
IT'S SO FAST ITS KI IS HARD TO READ, AND THE TARGET'S SO SMALL IT'S HARD TO HIT!!
YEAH, CUZ A PEASANT LIKE ME...
...CAN'T USE HUGE, HIGH-POWERED SPELLS LEFT AND RIGHT AND BLOW THROUGH ALL MY MAGIC!
BOOM
THAT'S WHY I CAME UP WITH THIS SUREFIRE TECHNICAL SPELL!!
SURE, MAYBE IT LOOKS SMALL TO A ROYAL, BUT THAT'S HOW I FIGHT, LOSER!!!

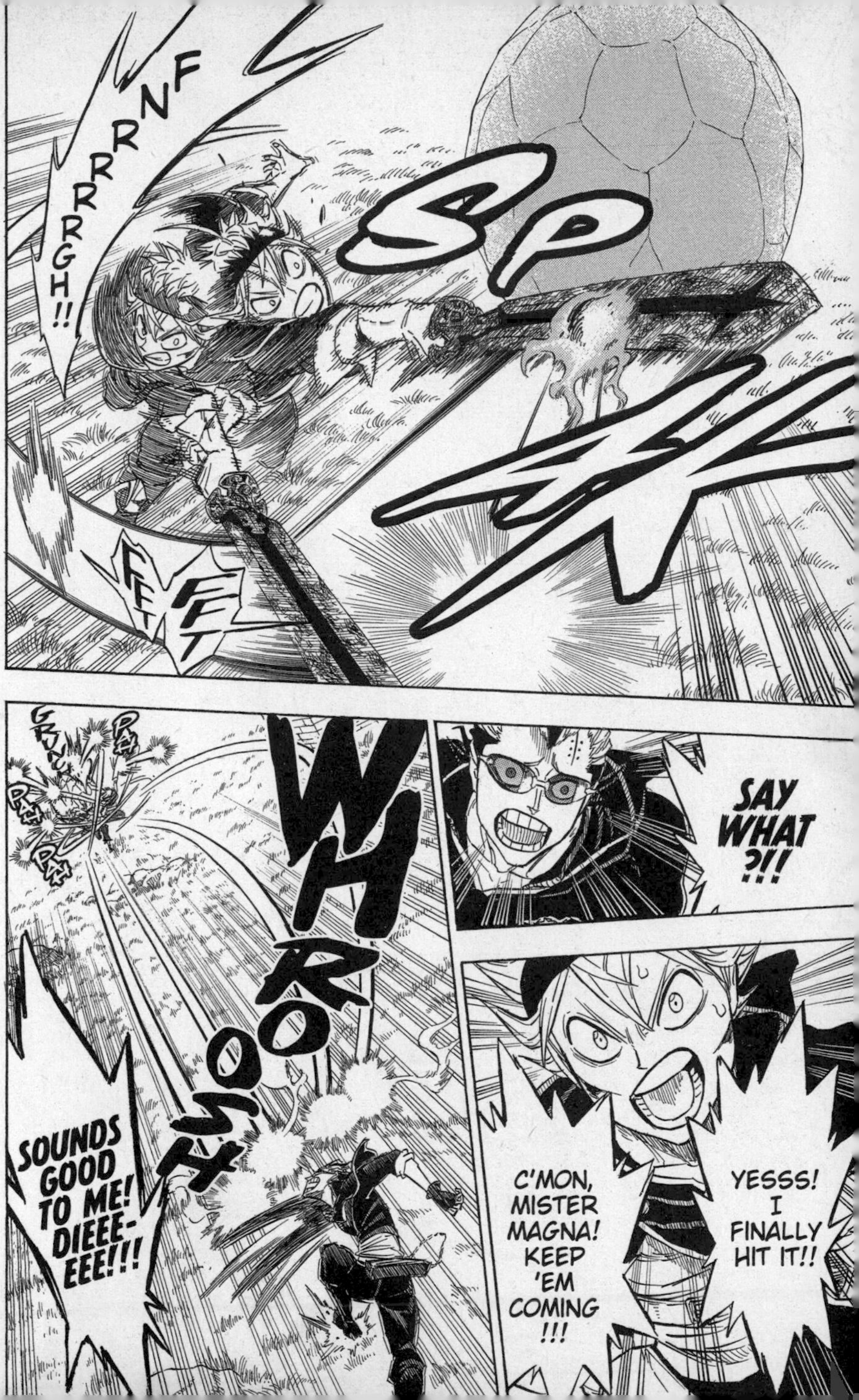
FFT
FFT
SAY WHAT?!!
YESSS! I FINALLY HIT IT!!
C'MON, MISTER MAGNA! KEEP 'EM COMING!!!
WHROOSH
SOUNDS GOOD TO ME! DIEEE-EEE!!!

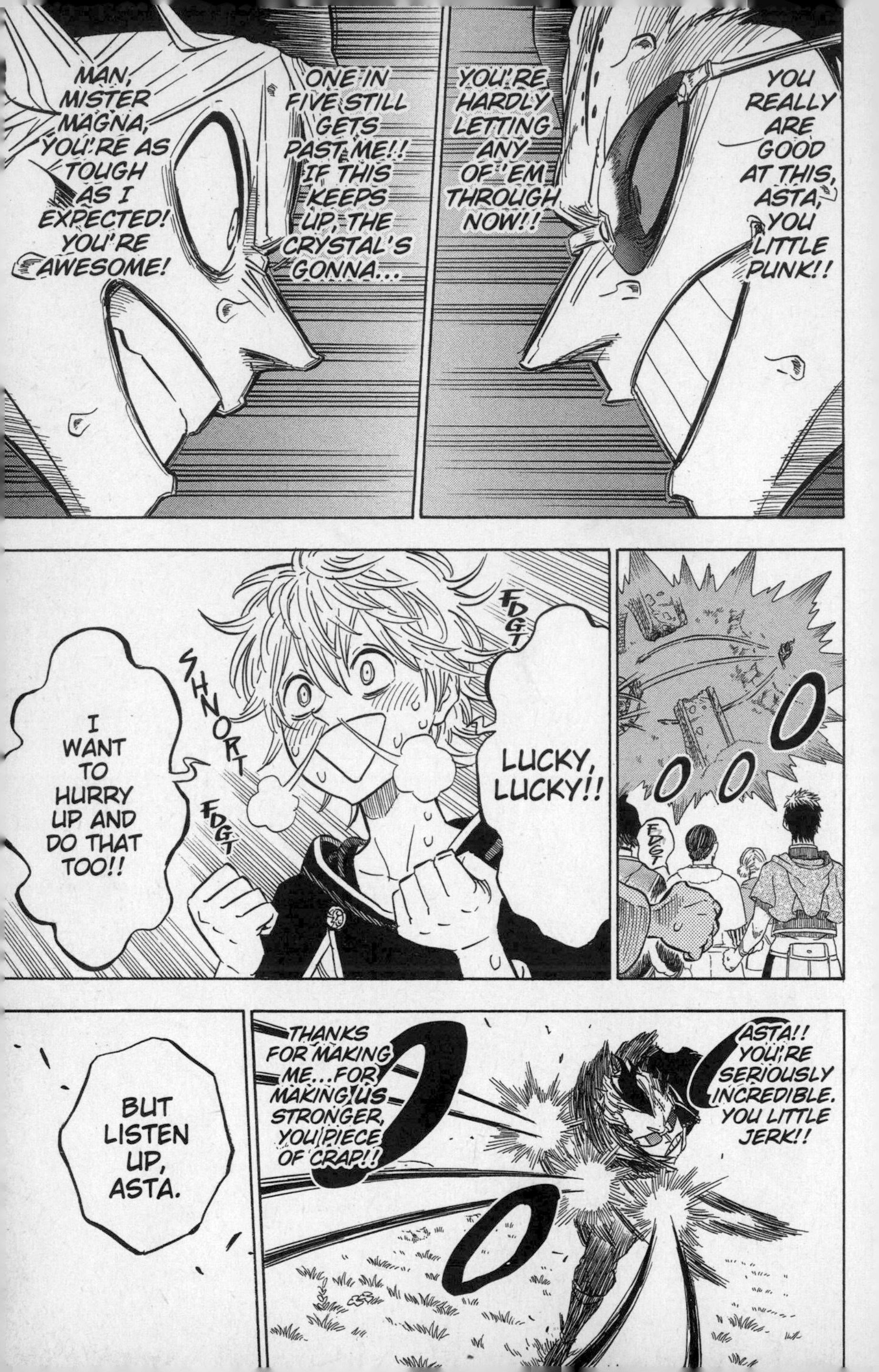
YOU REALLY ARE GOOD AT THIS, ASTA, YOU LITTLE PUNK!!
YOU'RE HARDLY LETTING ANY OF 'EM THROUGH NOW!!
ONE IN FIVE STILL GETS PAST ME!! IF THIS KEEPS UP, THE CRYSTAL'S GONNA...
MAN, MISTER MAGNA, YOU'RE AS TOUGH AS I EXPECTED! YOU'RE AWESOME!
FDGT
FDGT
LUCKY, LUCKY!!
SHNORT
FDGT
I WANT TO HURRY UP AND DO THAT TOO!!
ASTA!! YOU'RE SERIOUSLY INCREDIBLE. YOU LITTLE JERK!!
THANKS FOR MAKING ME...FOR MAKING US STRONGER, YOU PIECE OF CRAP!!
BUT LISTEN UP, ASTA.

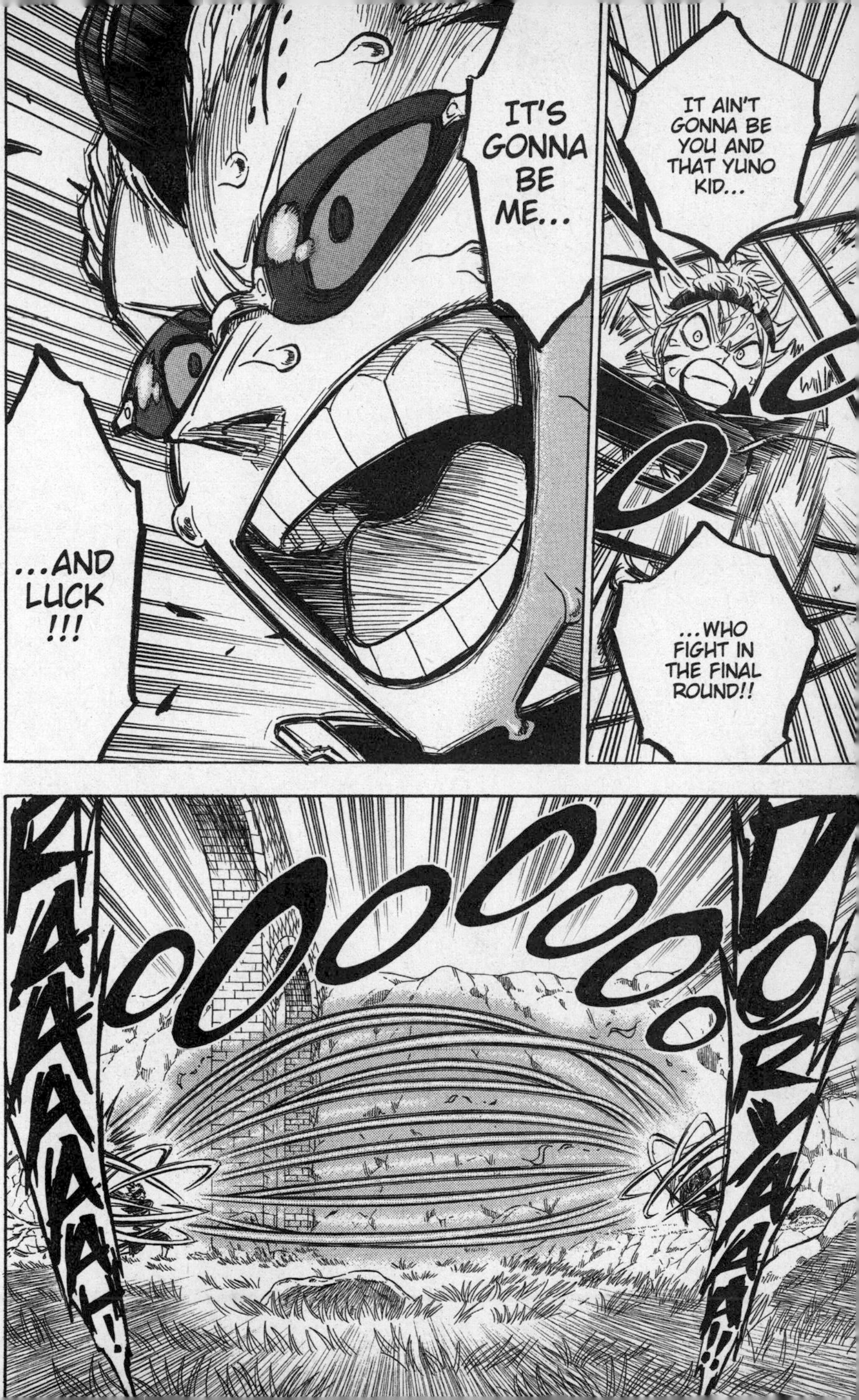
IT AIN'T GONNA BE YOU AND THAT YUNO KID...
...WHO FIGHT IN THE FINAL ROUND!!
IT'S GONNA BE ME...
...AND LUCK!!!

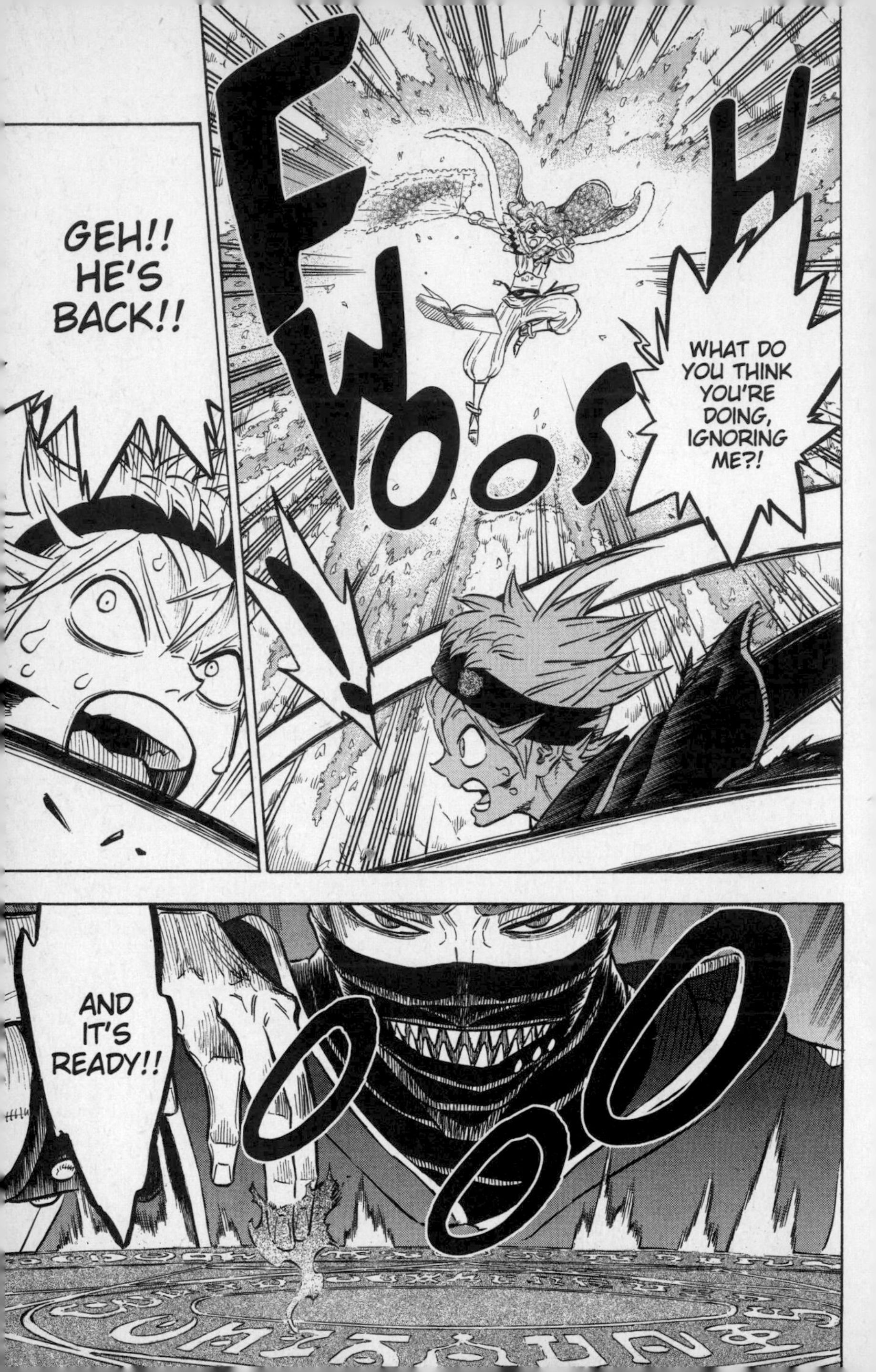
FWOOSH
WHAT DO YOU THINK YOU'RE DOING, IGNORING ME?!
GEH!! HE'S BACK!!
AND IT'S READY!!

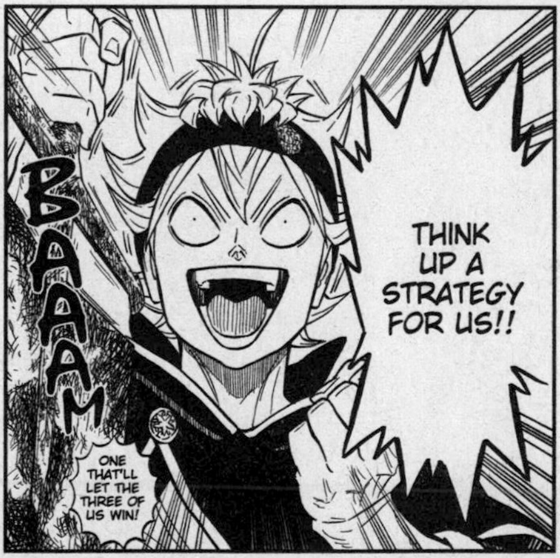
THINK UP A STRATEGY FOR US!!
BAAAM
ONE THAT'LL LET THE THREE OF US WIN!

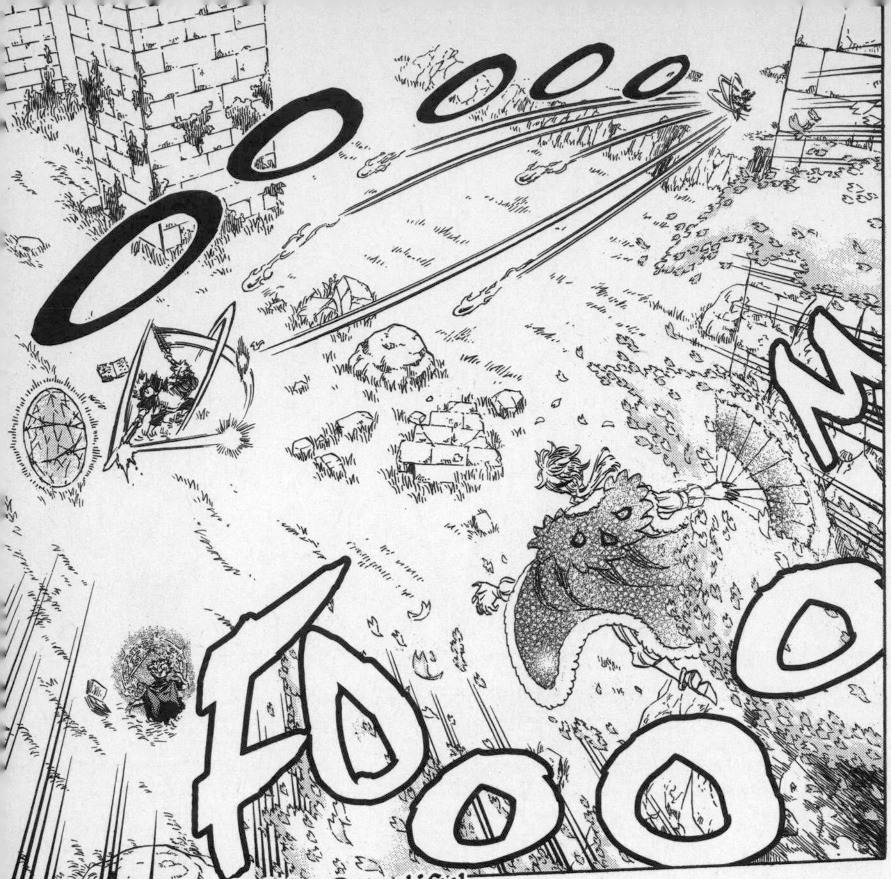

Page 125: It Was Beautiful

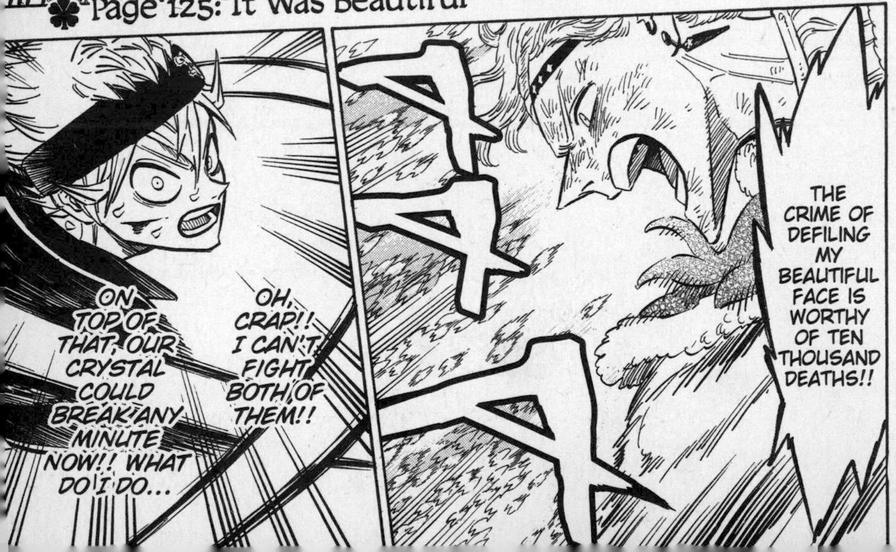

THE CRIME OF DEFILING MY BEAUTIFUL FACE IS WORTHY OF TEN THOUSAND DEATHS!!
OH, CRAP!! I CAN'T FIGHT BOTH OF THEM!!
ON TOP OF THAT, OUR CRYSTAL COULD BREAK ANY MINUTE NOW!! WHAT DO I DO...

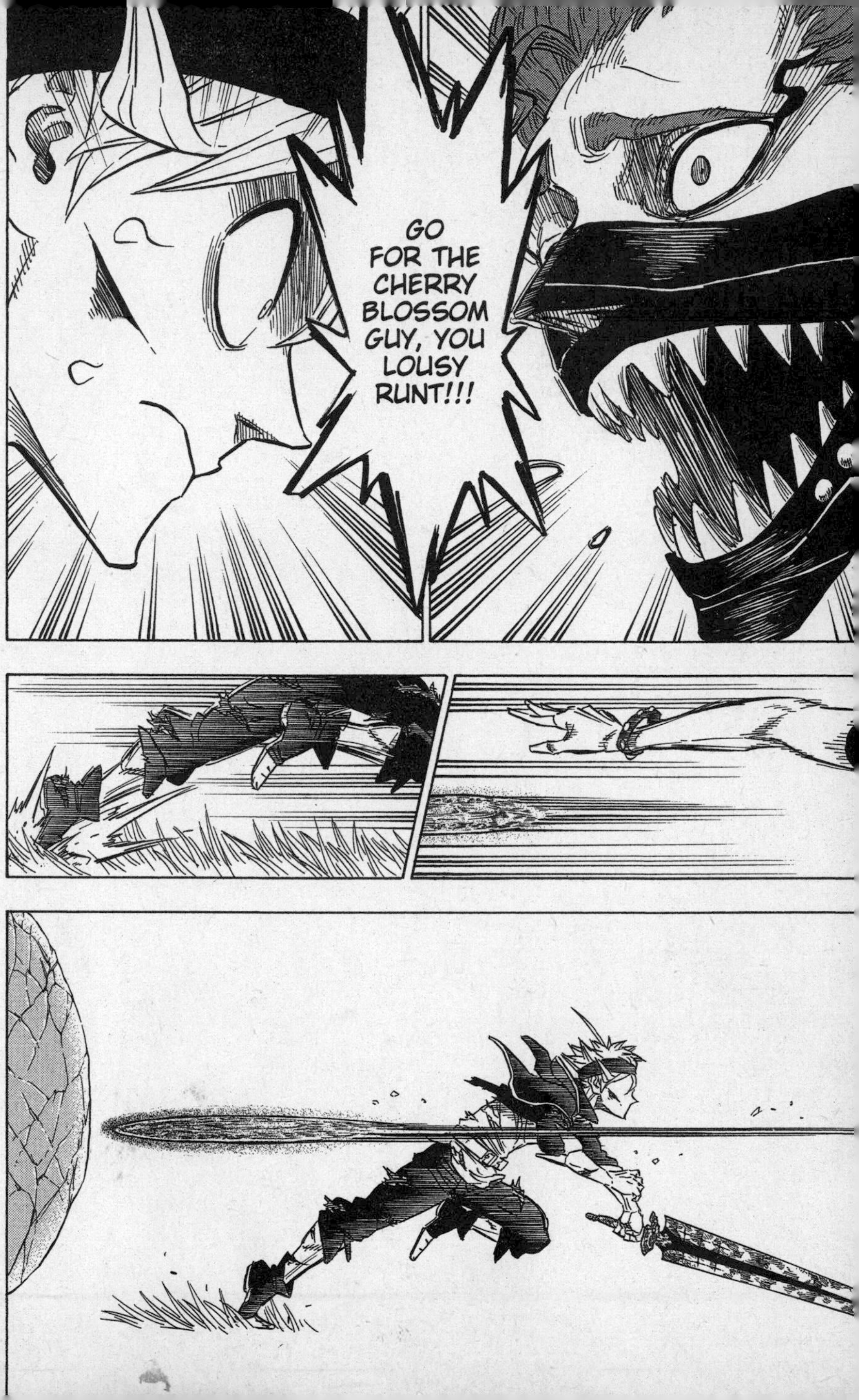
GO FOR THE CHERRY BLOSSOM GUY, YOU LOUSY RUNT!!!

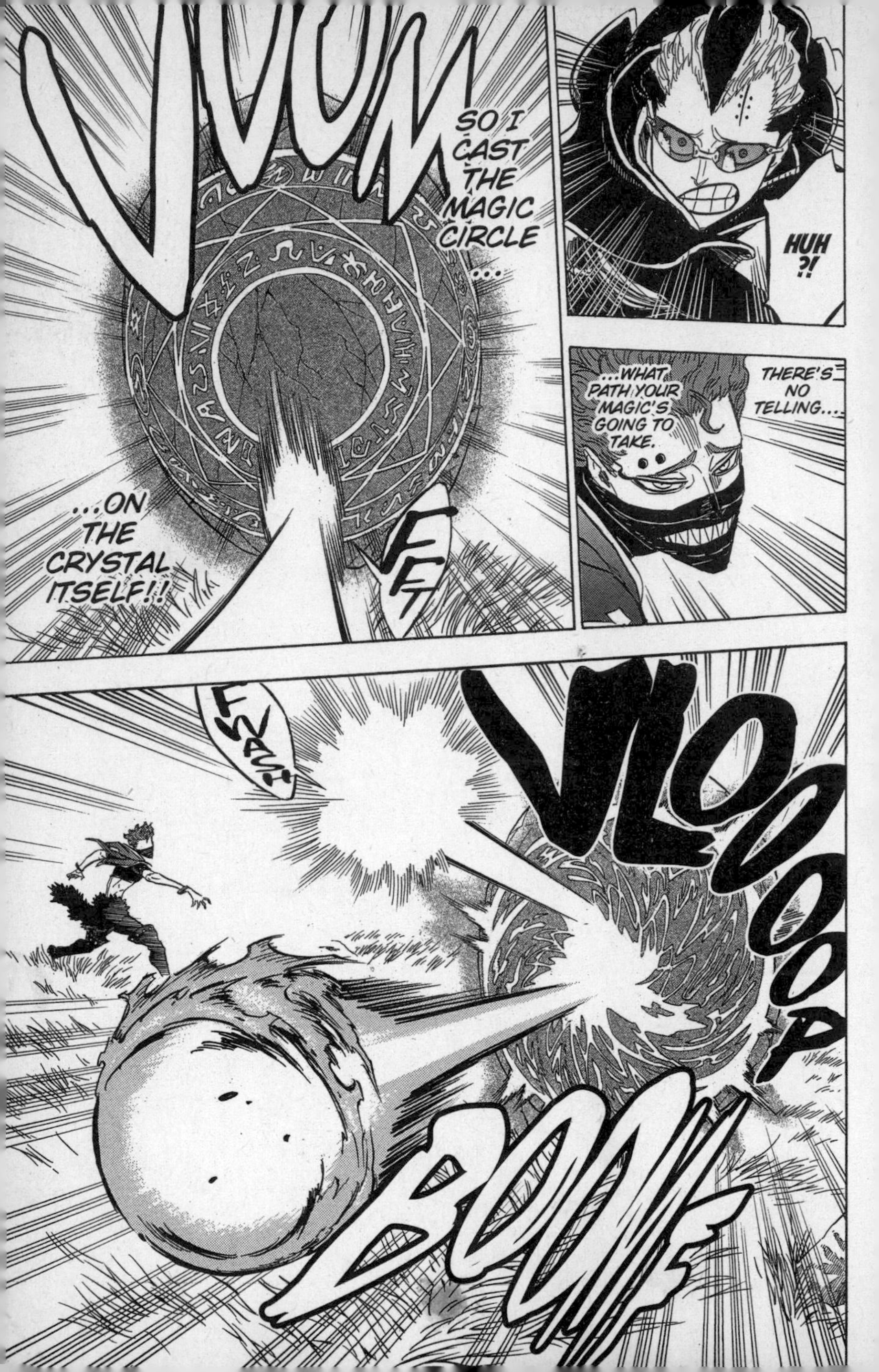
HUH ?!
THERE'S NO TELLING...
...WHAT PATH YOUR MAGIC'S GOING TO TAKE.
VVUM
SO I CAST THE MAGIC CIRCLE...
...ON THE CRYSTAL ITSELF!!
FFT
FWASH
VLOOOOOP
BOOM

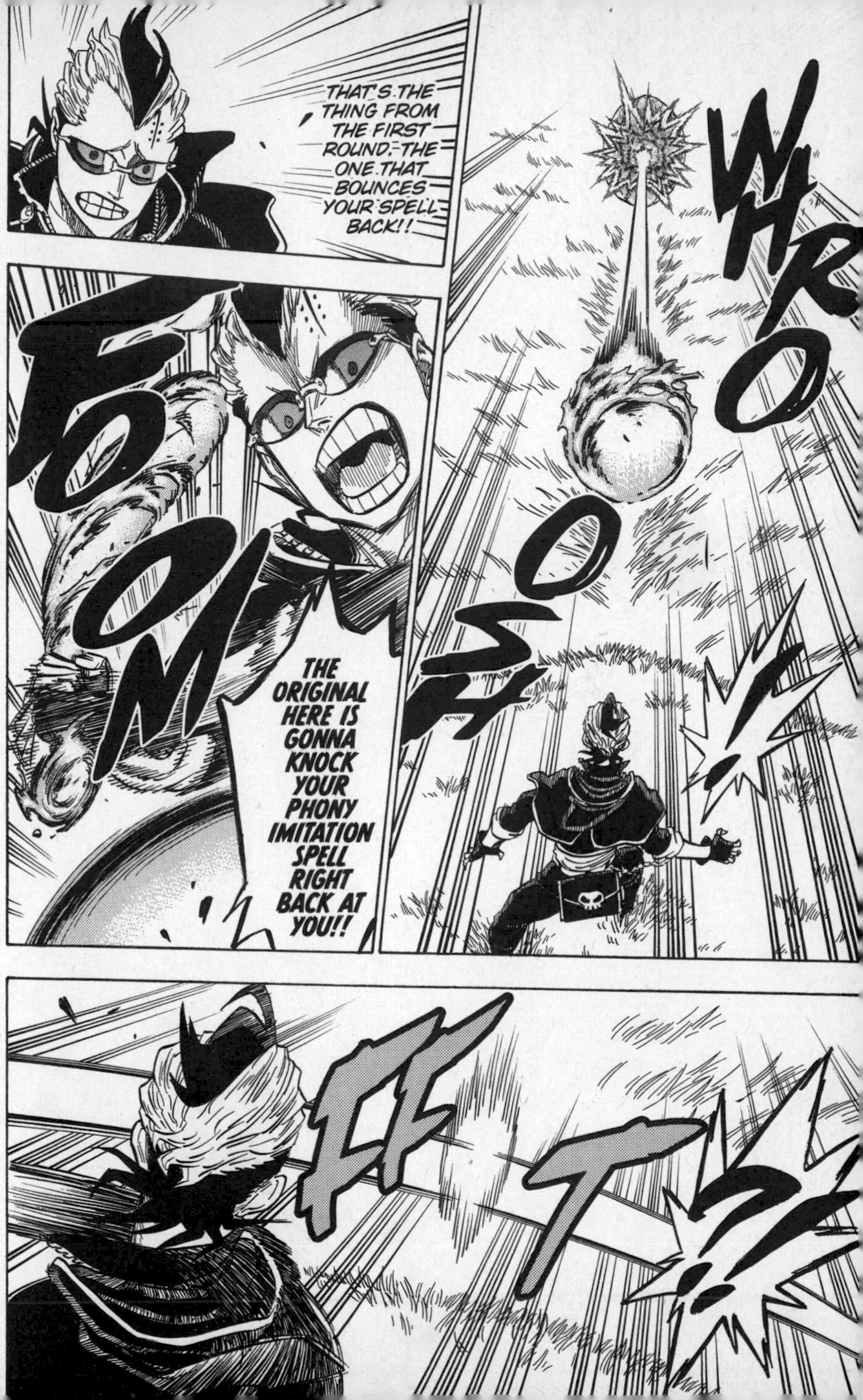
WHROOOSH
THAT'S THE THING FROM THE FIRST ROUND. THE ONE THAT BOUNCES YOUR SPELL BACK!!
BOOM
THE ORIGINAL HERE IS GONNA KNOCK YOUR PHONY IMITATION SPELL RIGHT BACK AT YOU!!
FFT

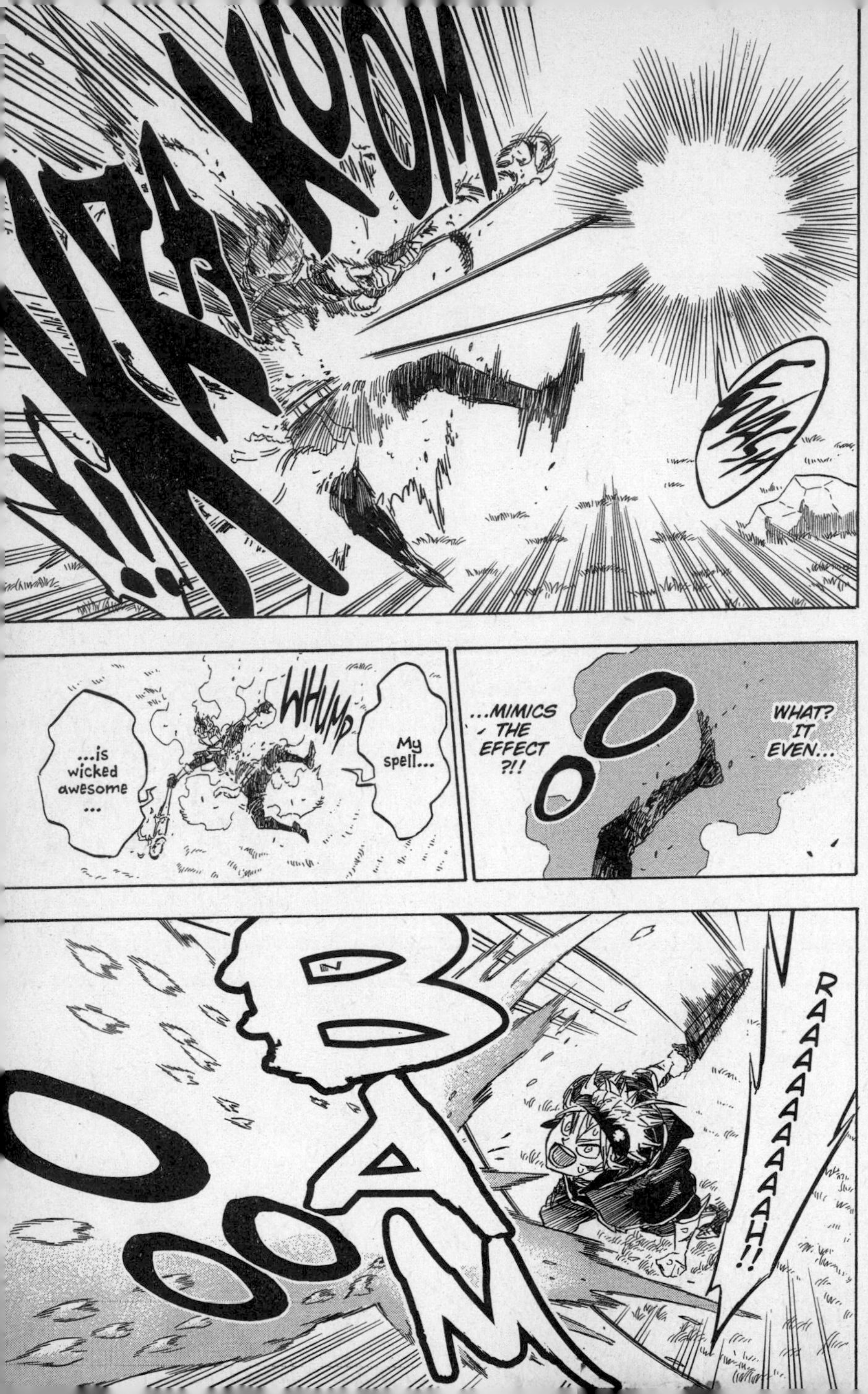
WHAT? IT EVEN...
...MIMICS THE EFFECT?!!
WHUMP
My spell...
...is wicked awesome...

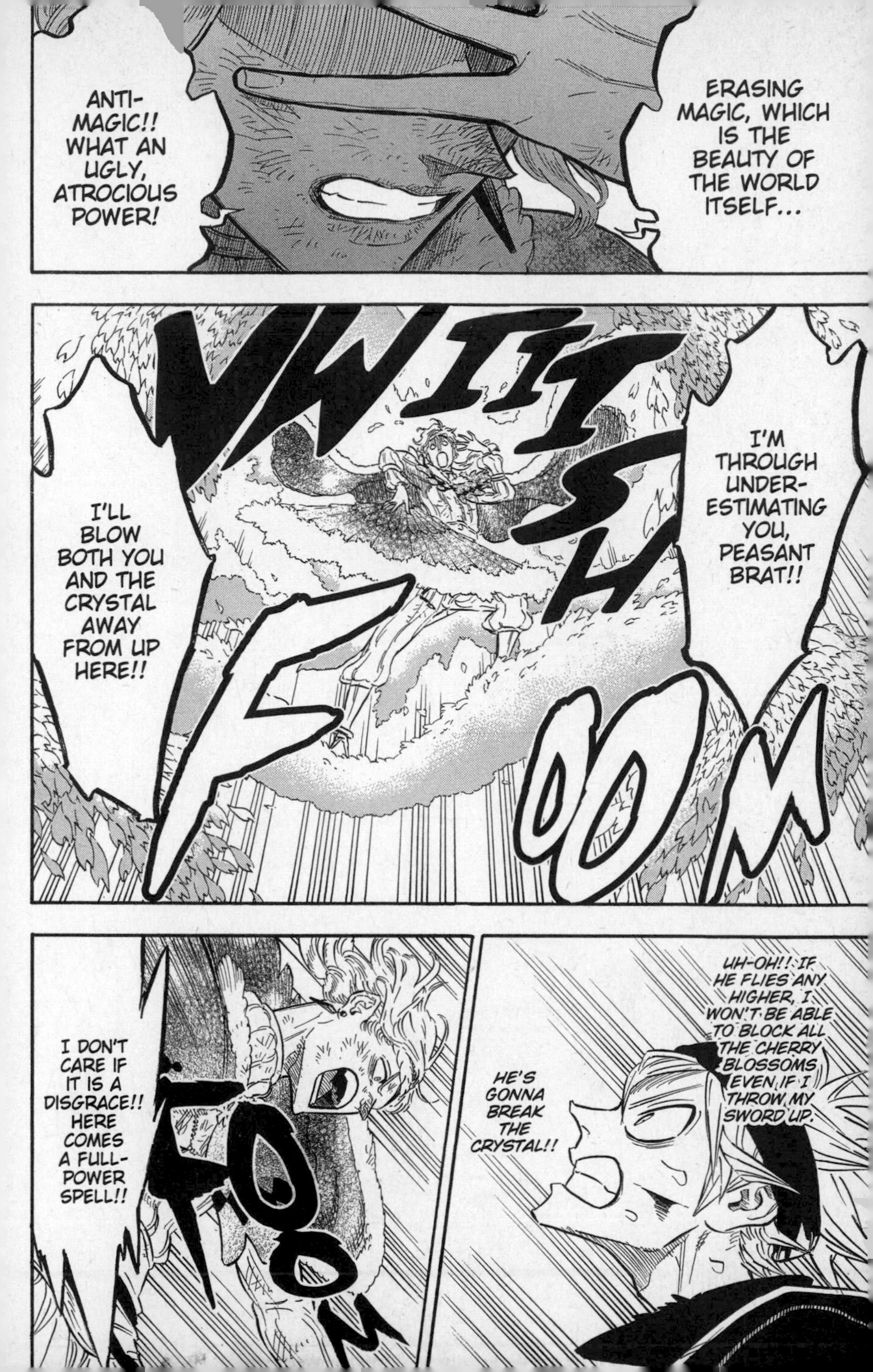
ERASING MAGIC, WHICH IS THE BEAUTY OF THE WORLD ITSELF...
ANTI-MAGIC!! WHAT AN UGLY, ATROCIOUS POWER!
VWIISH
I'M THROUGH UNDER-ESTIMATING YOU, PEASANT BRAT!!
I'LL BLOW BOTH YOU AND THE CRYSTAL AWAY FROM UP HERE!!
UH-OH!! IF HE FLIES ANY HIGHER, I WON'T BE ABLE TO BLOCK ALL THE CHERRY BLOSSOMS EVEN IF I THROW MY SWORD UP.
HE'S GONNA BREAK THE CRYSTAL!!
I DON'T CARE IF IT IS A DISGRACE!! HERE COMES A FULL-POWER SPELL!!
FOOM

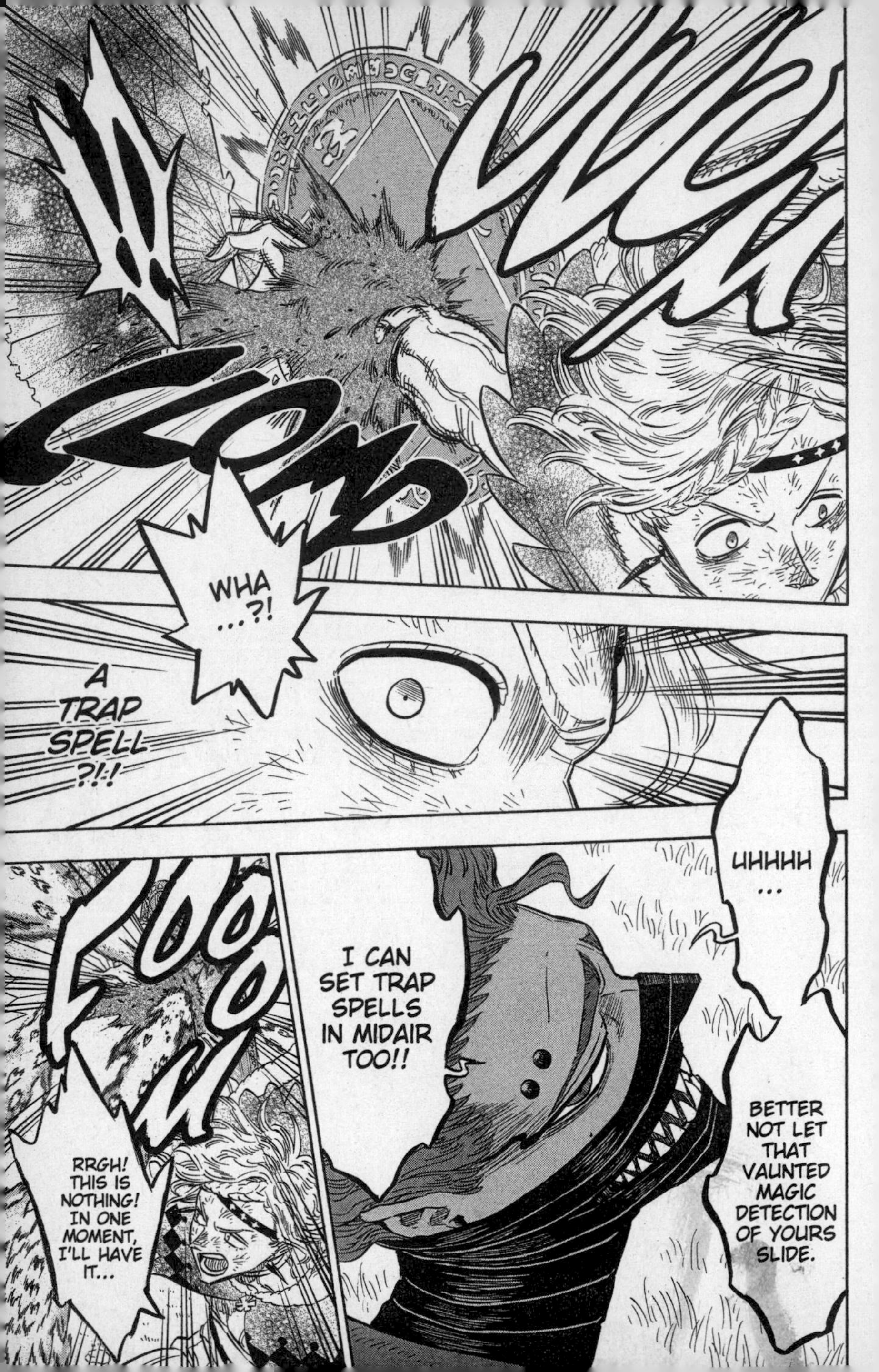
WHA ...?!
A TRAP SPELL ?!?!
UHHHH ...
I CAN SET TRAP SPELLS IN MIDAIR TOO!!
BETTER NOT LET THAT VAUNTED MAGIC DETECTION OF YOURS SLIDE.
RRGH! THIS IS NOTHING! IN ONE MOMENT, I'LL HAVE IT...

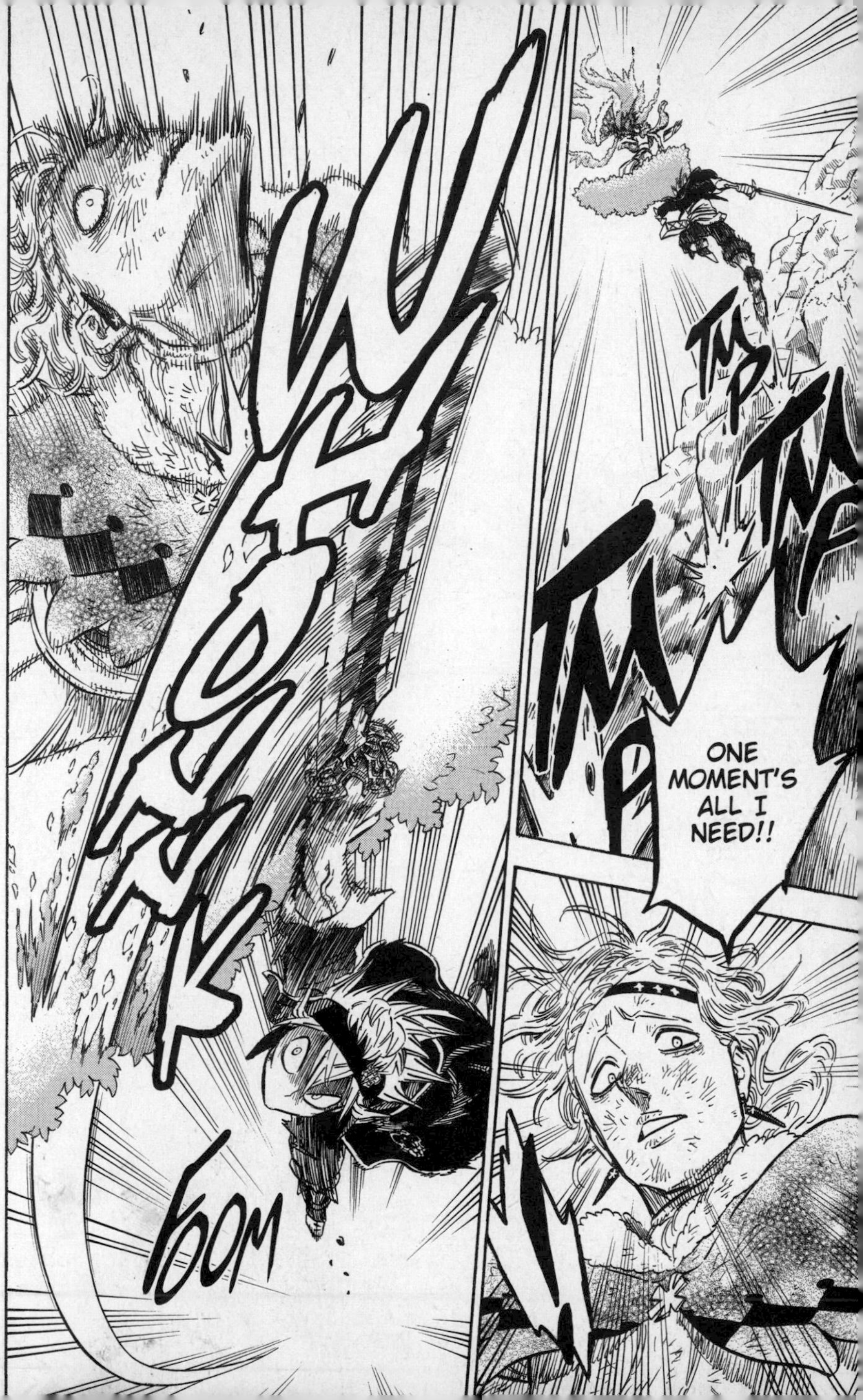
TMP
TMP
TMP
ONE MOMENT'S ALL I NEED!!
!

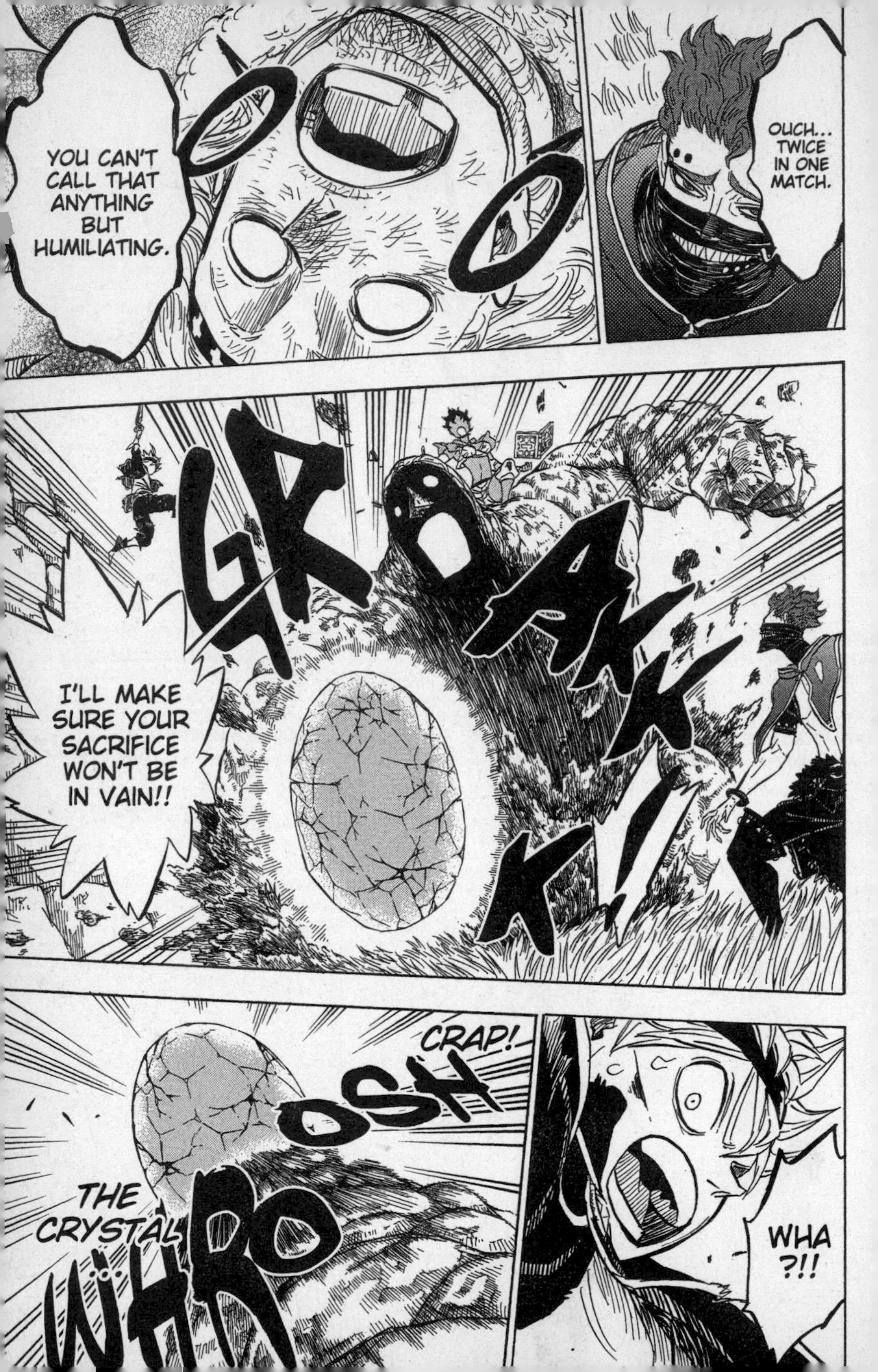
OUCH... TWICE IN ONE MATCH.
YOU CAN'T CALL THAT ANYTHING BUT HUMILIATING.
GRAKKK!
I'LL MAKE SURE YOUR SACRIFICE WON'T BE IN VAIN!!
WHA ?!!
CRAP!
THE CRYSTAL...

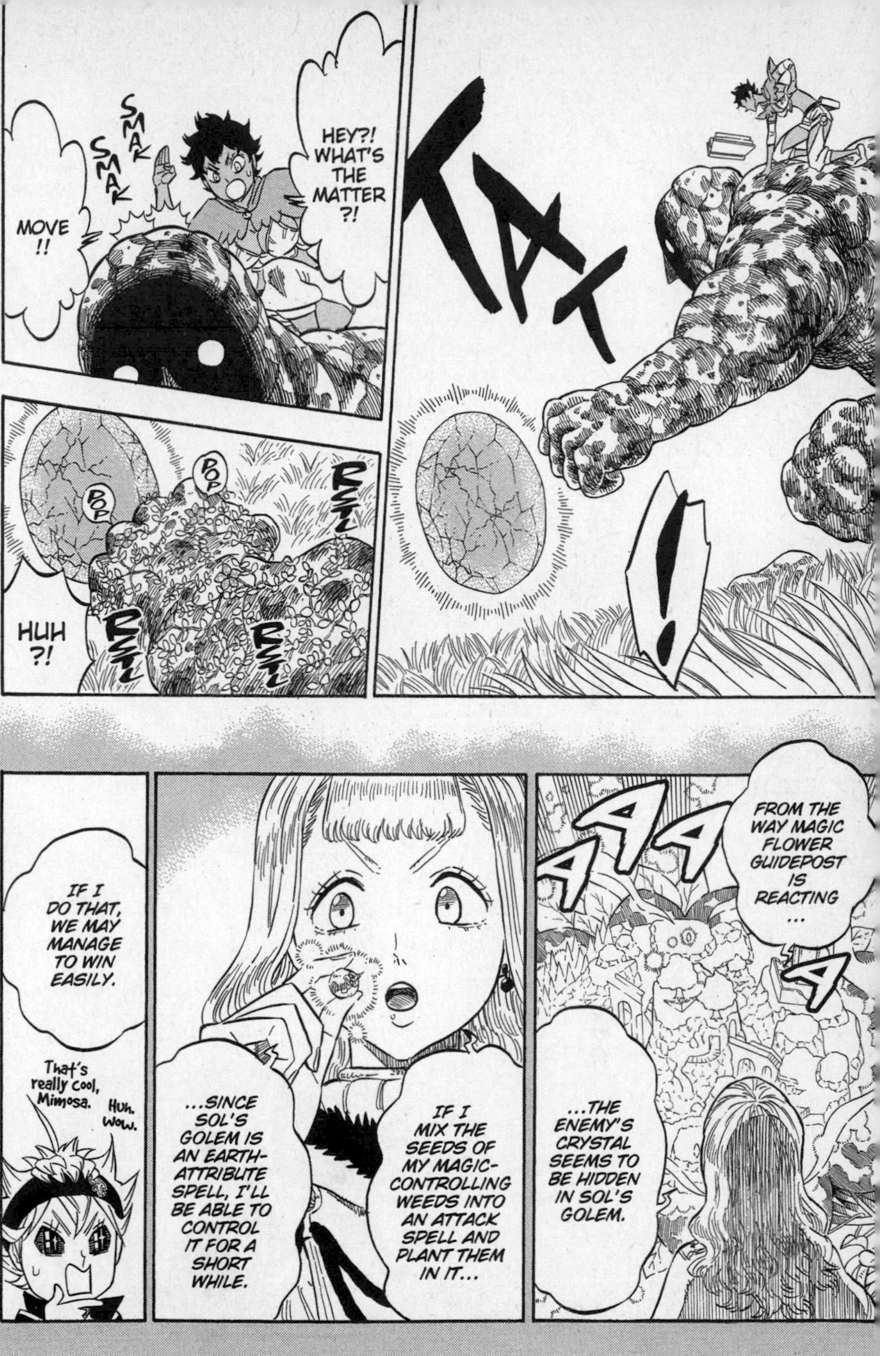
TAT
!
HEY?! WHAT'S THE MATTER ?!
SMAK SMAK
MOVE !!
POP
POP
RSTL
RSTL
RSTL
HUH ?!
FROM THE WAY MAGIC FLOWER GUIDEPOST IS REACTING ...
AAAA
A
...THE ENEMY'S CRYSTAL SEEMS TO BE HIDDEN IN SOL'S GOLEM.
IF I MIX THE SEEDS OF MY MAGIC-CONTROLLING WEEDS INTO AN ATTACK SPELL AND PLANT THEM IN IT...
...SINCE SOL'S GOLEM IS AN EARTH-ATTRIBUTE SPELL, I'LL BE ABLE TO CONTROL IT FOR A SHORT WHILE.
IF I DO THAT, WE MAY MANAGE TO WIN EASILY.
Huh. Wow.
That's really cool, Mimosa.

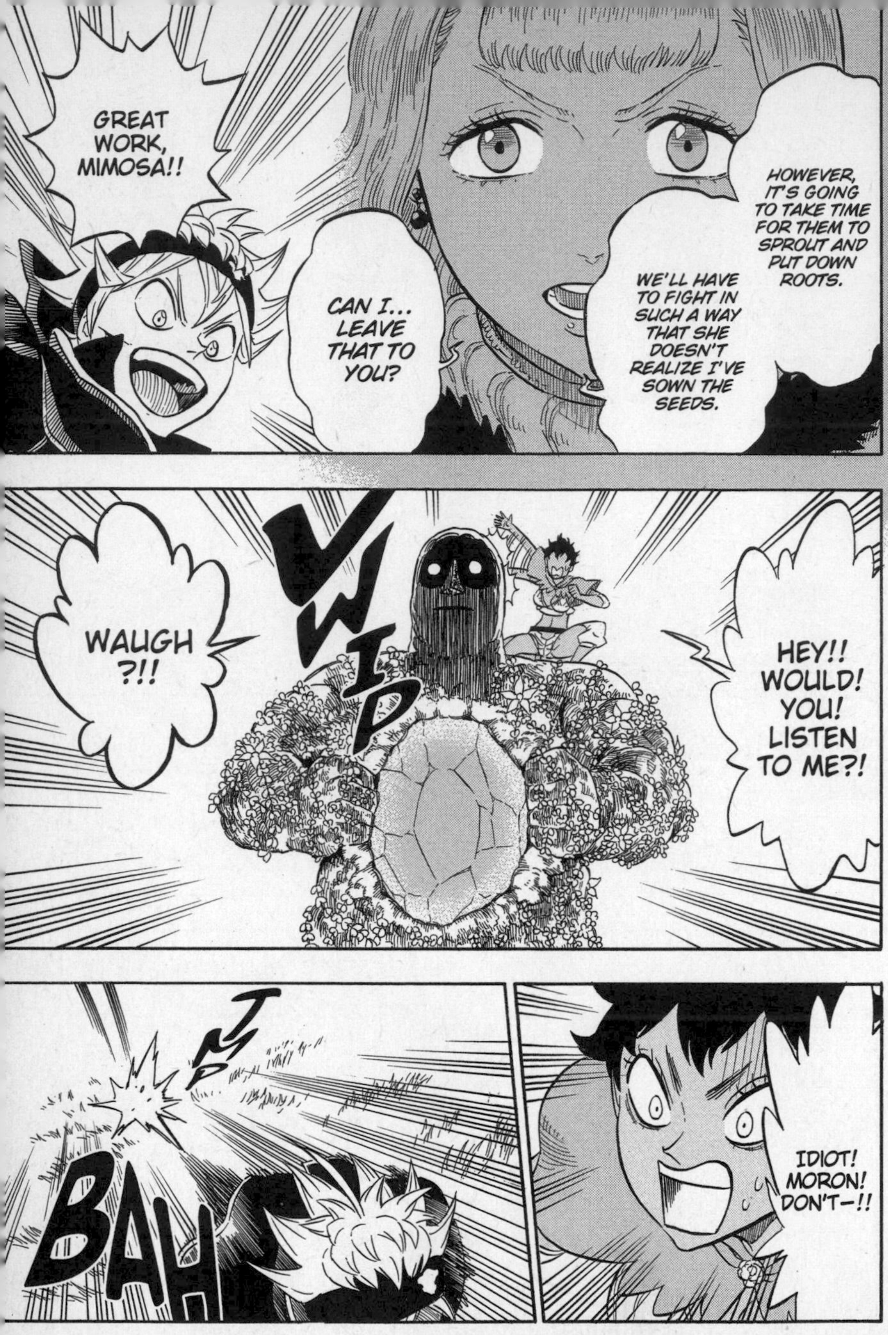
HOWEVER, IT'S GOING TO TAKE TIME FOR THEM TO SPROUT AND PUT DOWN ROOTS.
WE'LL HAVE TO FIGHT IN SUCH A WAY THAT SHE DOESN'T REALIZE I'VE SOWN THE SEEDS.
CAN I... LEAVE THAT TO YOU?
GREAT WORK, MIMOSA!!
HEY!! WOULD! YOU! LISTEN TO ME?!
VWIP
WAUGH ?!!
IDIOT! MORON! DON'T—!!
BAH

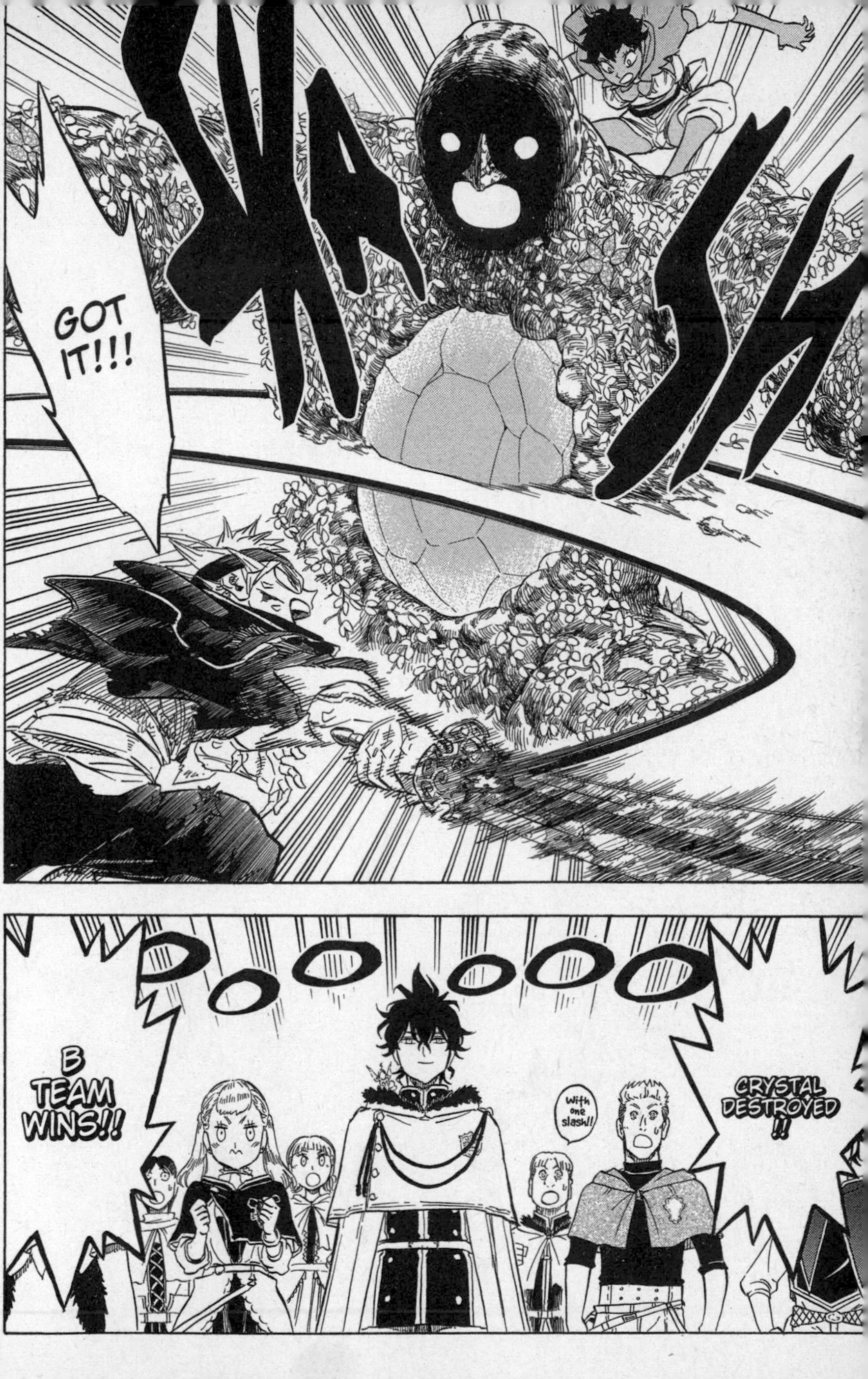
GOT IT!!!
CRYSTAL DESTROYED!!
With one slash!!
B TEAM WINS!!

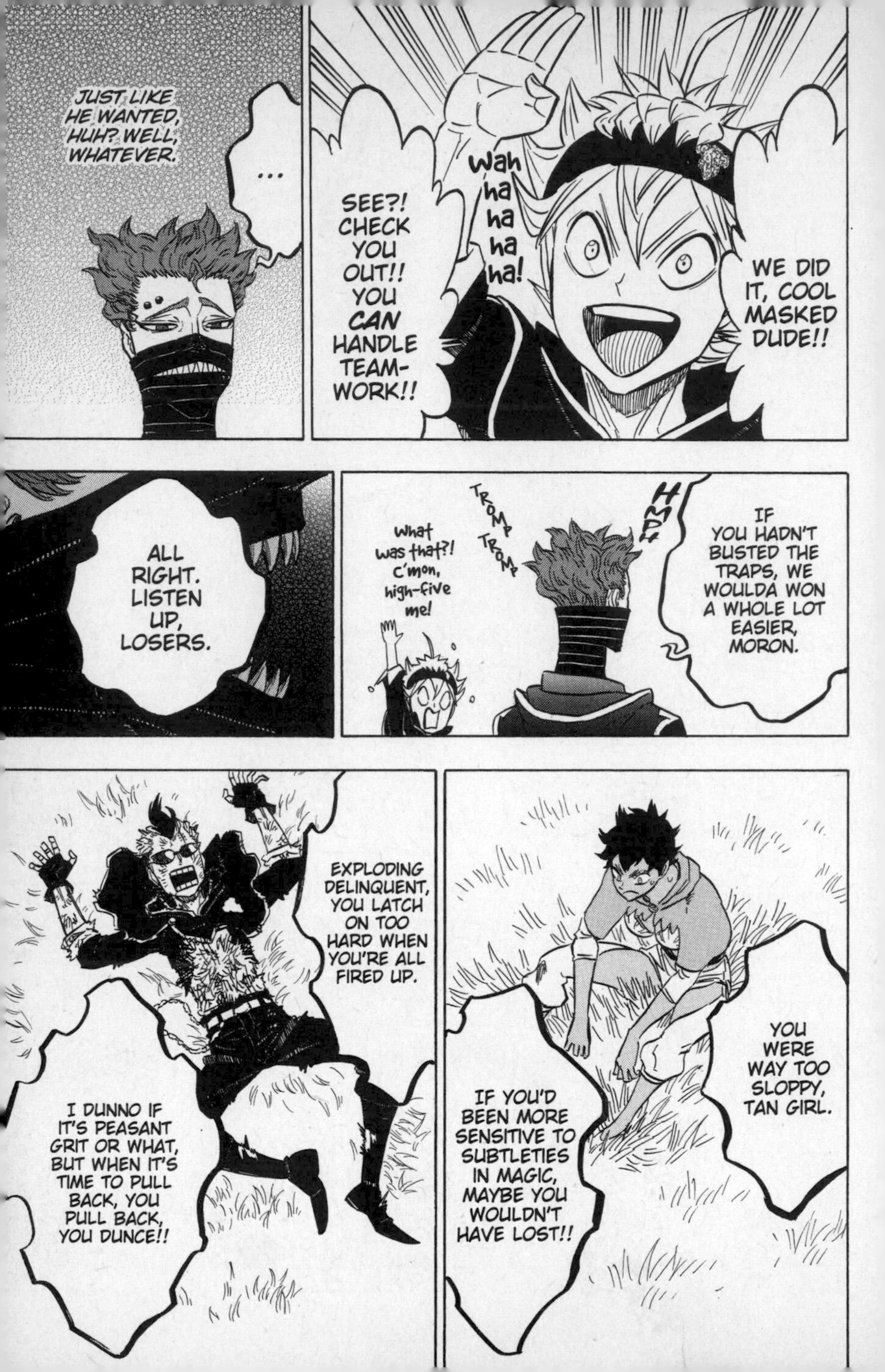
WE DID IT, COOL MASKED DUDE!!
Wah ha ha ha ha!
SEE?! CHECK YOU OUT!! YOU CAN HANDLE TEAM-WORK!!
...
JUST LIKE HE WANTED, HUH? WELL, WHATEVER.
IF YOU HADN'T BUSTED THE TRAPS, WE WOULDA WON A WHOLE LOT EASIER, MORON.
HMPH
TROMP TROMP
What was that?! C'mon, high-five me!
ALL RIGHT. LISTEN UP, LOSERS.
YOU WERE WAY TOO SLOPPY, TAN GIRL.
IF YOU'D BEEN MORE SENSITIVE TO SUBTLETIES IN MAGIC, MAYBE YOU WOULDN'T HAVE LOST!!
EXPLODING DELINQUENT, YOU LATCH ON TOO HARD WHEN YOU'RE ALL FIRED UP.
I DUNNO IF IT'S PEASANT GRIT OR WHAT, BUT WHEN IT'S TIME TO PULL BACK, YOU PULL BACK, YOU DUNCE!!

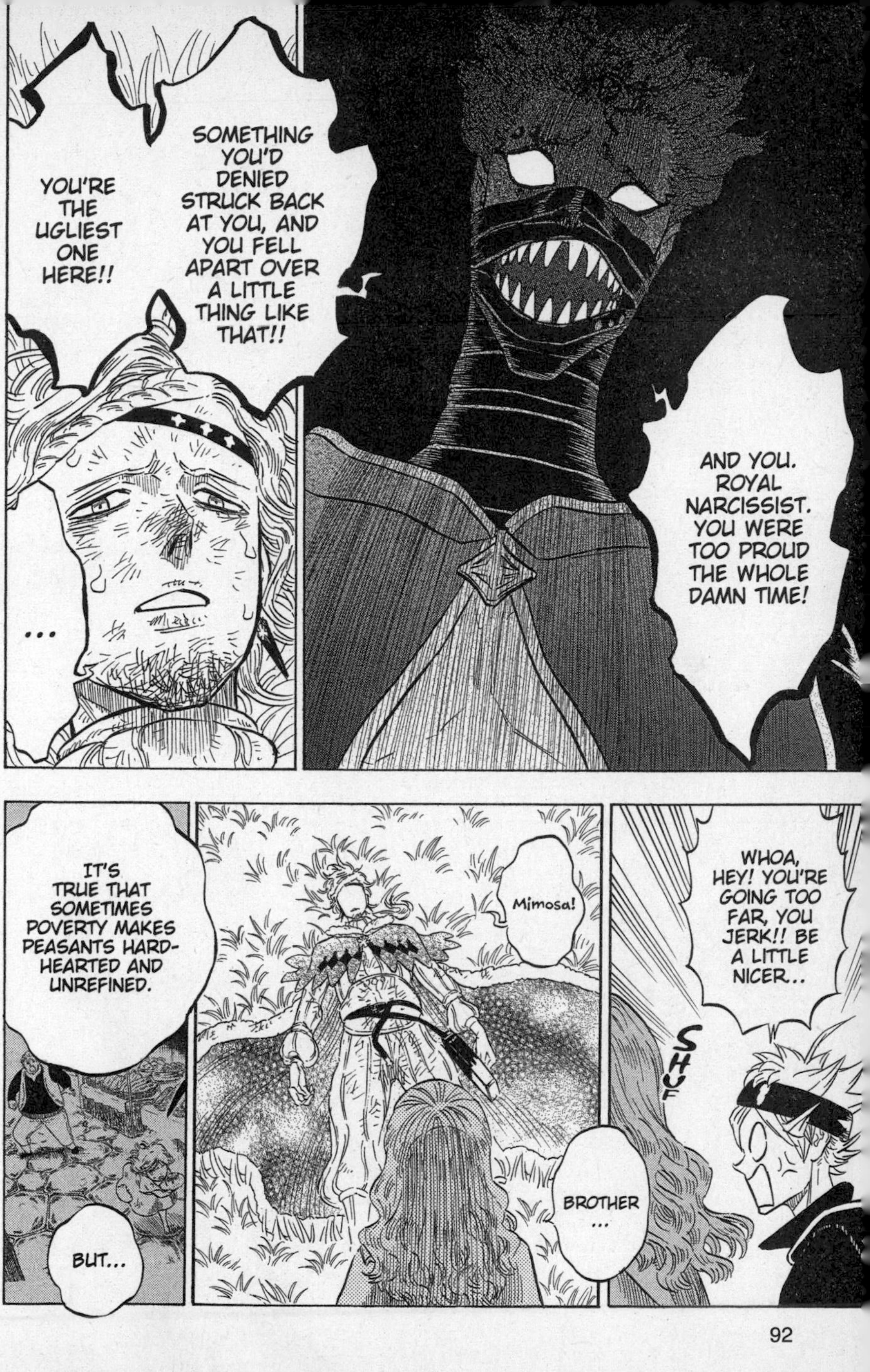
AND YOU. ROYAL NARCISSIST. YOU WERE TOO PROUD THE WHOLE DAMN TIME!
SOMETHING YOU'D DENIED STRUCK BACK AT YOU, AND YOU FELL APART OVER A LITTLE THING LIKE THAT!!
YOU'RE THE UGLIEST ONE HERE!!
...
WHOA, HEY! YOU'RE GOING TOO FAR, YOU JERK!! BE A LITTLE NICER...
SHUF
Mimosa!
BROTHER ...
IT'S TRUE THAT SOMETIMES POVERTY MAKES PEASANTS HARD-HEARTED AND UNREFINED.
BUT...

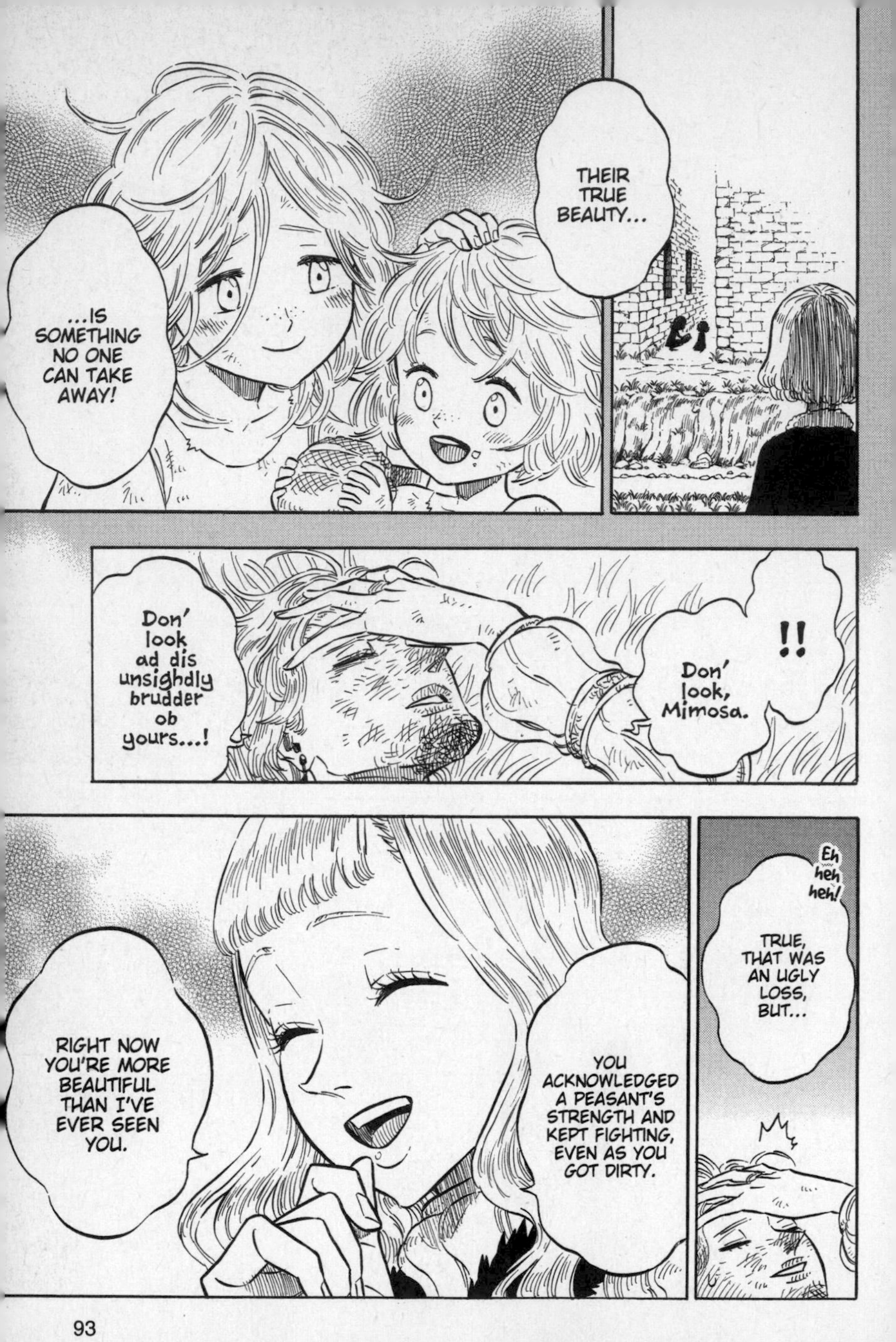
THEIR TRUE BEAUTY...
...IS SOMETHING NO ONE CAN TAKE AWAY!
!!
Don' look, Mimosa.
Don' look ad dis unsightly brudder ob yours...!
Eh heh heh!
TRUE, THAT WAS AN UGLY LOSS, BUT...
YOU ACKNOWLEDGED A PEASANT'S STRENGTH AND KEPT FIGHTING, EVEN AS YOU GOT DIRTY.
RIGHT NOW YOU'RE MORE BEAUTIFUL THAN I'VE EVER SEEN YOU.

I DIDN'T WANT TO ADMIT IT, BUT...

OOOOOOOOOO

THAT WAS... ...BEAUTIFUL.

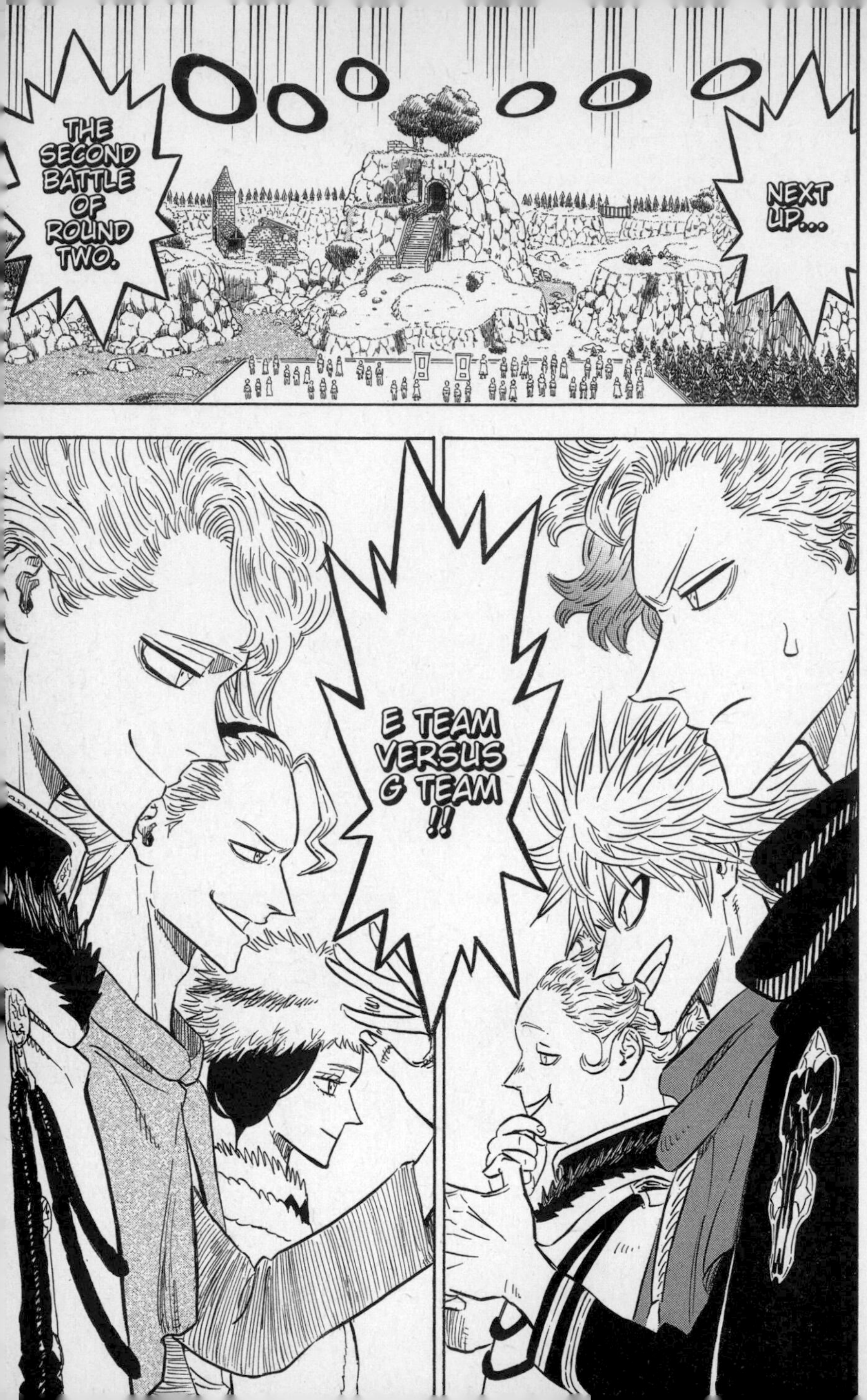
NEXT UP...
OOOOOO
THE SECOND BATTLE OF ROUND TWO.
E TEAM VERSUS G TEAM!!

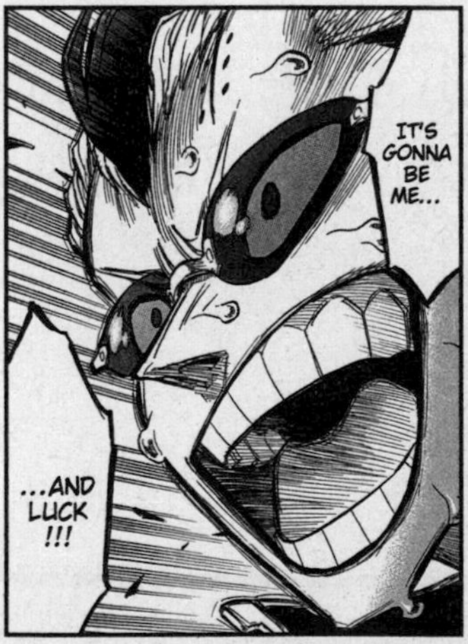
IT'S GONNA BE ME...
...AND LUCK !!!

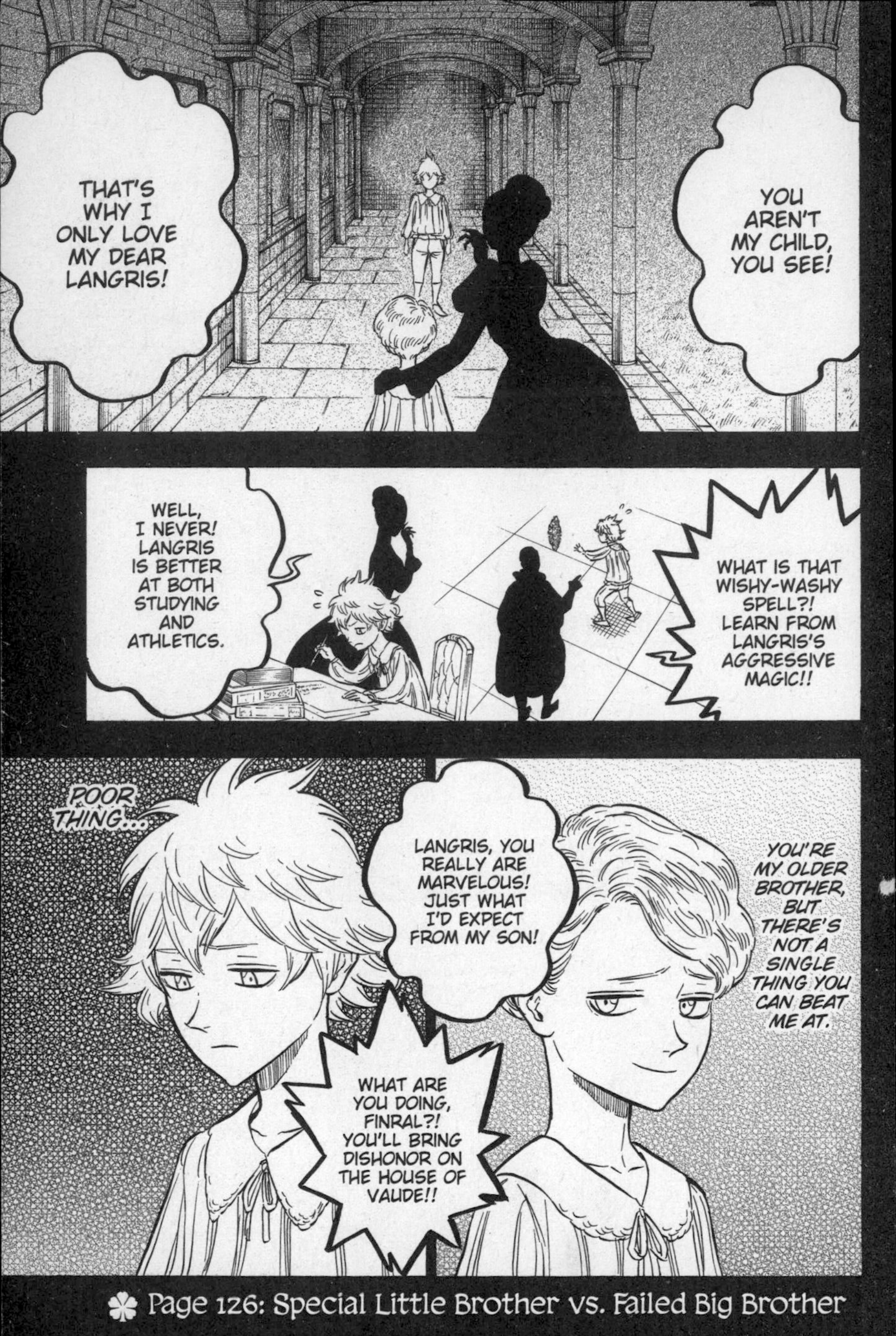
YOU AREN'T MY CHILD, YOU SEE!
THAT'S WHY I ONLY LOVE MY DEAR LANGRIS!
WHAT IS THAT WISHY-WASHY SPELL?! LEARN FROM LANGRIS'S AGGRESSIVE MAGIC!!
WELL, I NEVER! LANGRIS IS BETTER AT BOTH STUDYING AND ATHLETICS.
YOU'RE MY OLDER BROTHER, BUT THERE'S NOT A SINGLE THING YOU CAN BEAT ME AT.
LANGRIS, YOU REALLY ARE MARVELOUS! JUST WHAT I'D EXPECT FROM MY SON!
WHAT ARE YOU DOING, FINRAL?! YOU'LL BRING DISHONOR ON THE HOUSE OF VAUDE!!
POOR THING...

Page 126: Special Little Brother vs. Failed Big Brother

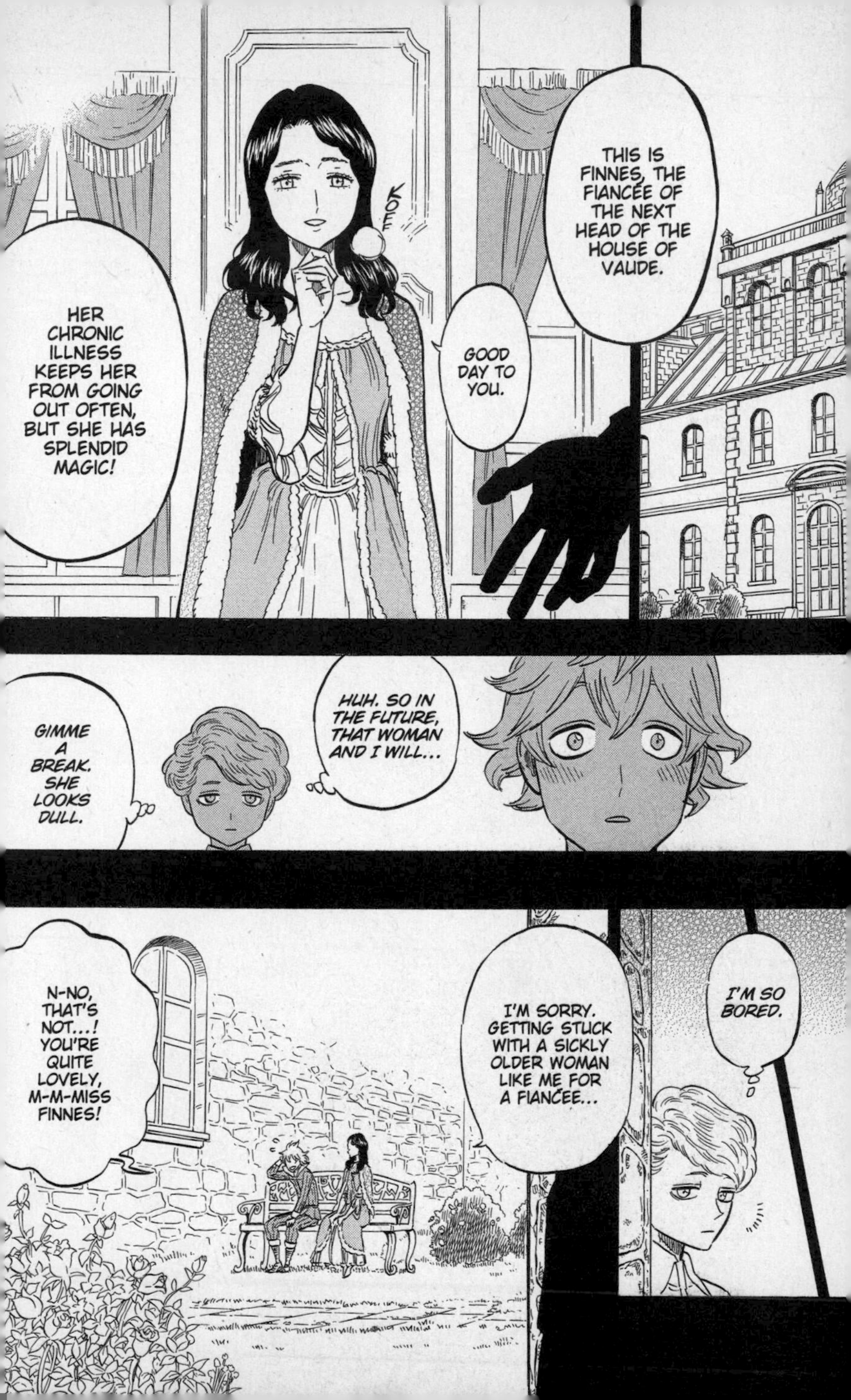
THIS IS FINNES, THE FIANCÉE OF THE NEXT HEAD OF THE HOUSE OF VAUDE.
KOFF
GOOD DAY TO YOU.
HER CHRONIC ILLNESS KEEPS HER FROM GOING OUT OFTEN, BUT SHE HAS SPLENDID MAGIC!
HUH. SO IN THE FUTURE, THAT WOMAN AND I WILL...
GIMME A BREAK. SHE LOOKS DULL.
I'M SO BORED.
I'M SORRY. GETTING STUCK WITH A SICKLY OLDER WOMAN LIKE ME FOR A FIANCÉE...
N-NO, THAT'S NOT...! YOU'RE QUITE LOVELY, M-M-MISS FINNES!

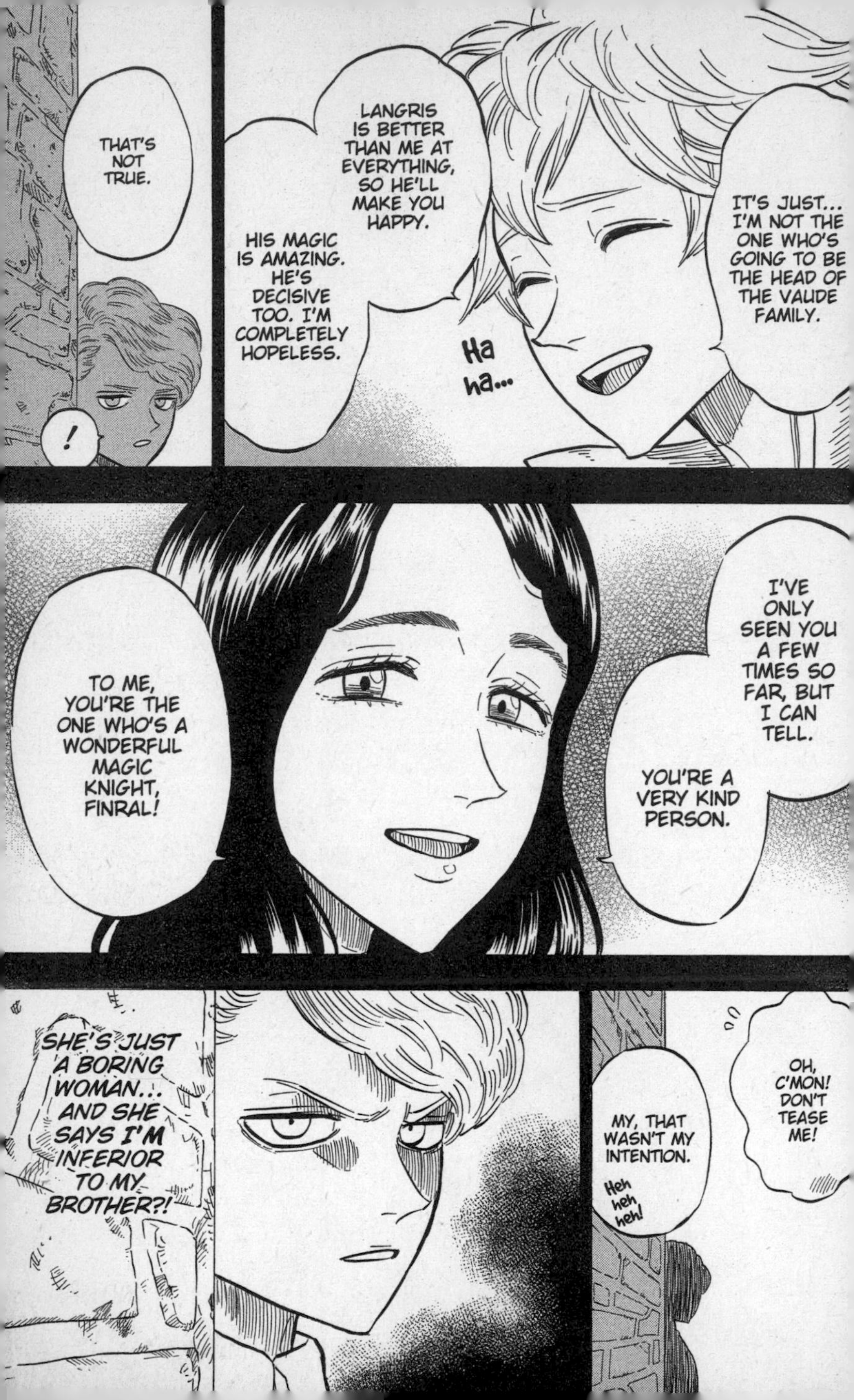
IT'S JUST... I'M NOT THE ONE WHO'S GOING TO BE THE HEAD OF THE VAUDE FAMILY.
Ha ha...
LANGRIS IS BETTER THAN ME AT EVERYTHING, SO HE'LL MAKE YOU HAPPY.
HIS MAGIC IS AMAZING. HE'S DECISIVE TOO. I'M COMPLETELY HOPELESS.
THAT'S NOT TRUE.
!
I'VE ONLY SEEN YOU A FEW TIMES SO FAR, BUT I CAN TELL.
YOU'RE A VERY KIND PERSON.
TO ME, YOU'RE THE ONE WHO'S A WONDERFUL MAGIC KNIGHT, FINRAL!
OH, C'MON! DON'T TEASE ME!
MY, THAT WASN'T MY INTENTION.
Heh heh heh!
SHE'S JUST A BORING WOMAN... AND SHE SAYS I'M INFERIOR TO MY BROTHER?!

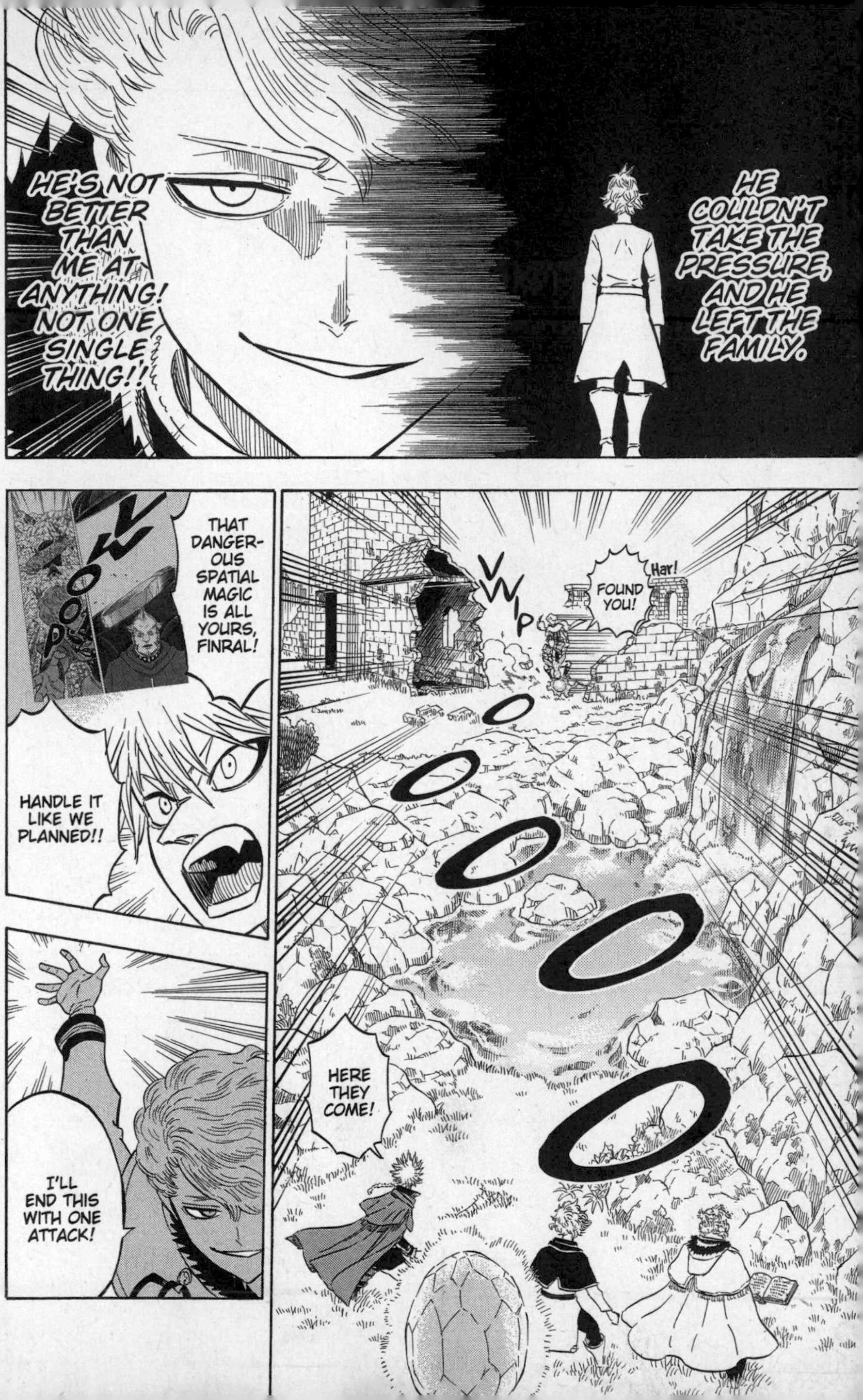
HE COULDN'T TAKE THE PRESSURE, AND HE LEFT THE FAMILY.
HE'S NOT BETTER THAN ME AT ANYTHING! NOT ONE SINGLE THING!!
FOUND YOU!
Har!
VWIP
HERE THEY COME!
VWOOOP
THAT DANGER-OUS SPATIAL MAGIC IS ALL YOURS, FINRAL!
HANDLE IT LIKE WE PLANNED!!
I'LL END THIS WITH ONE ATTACK!

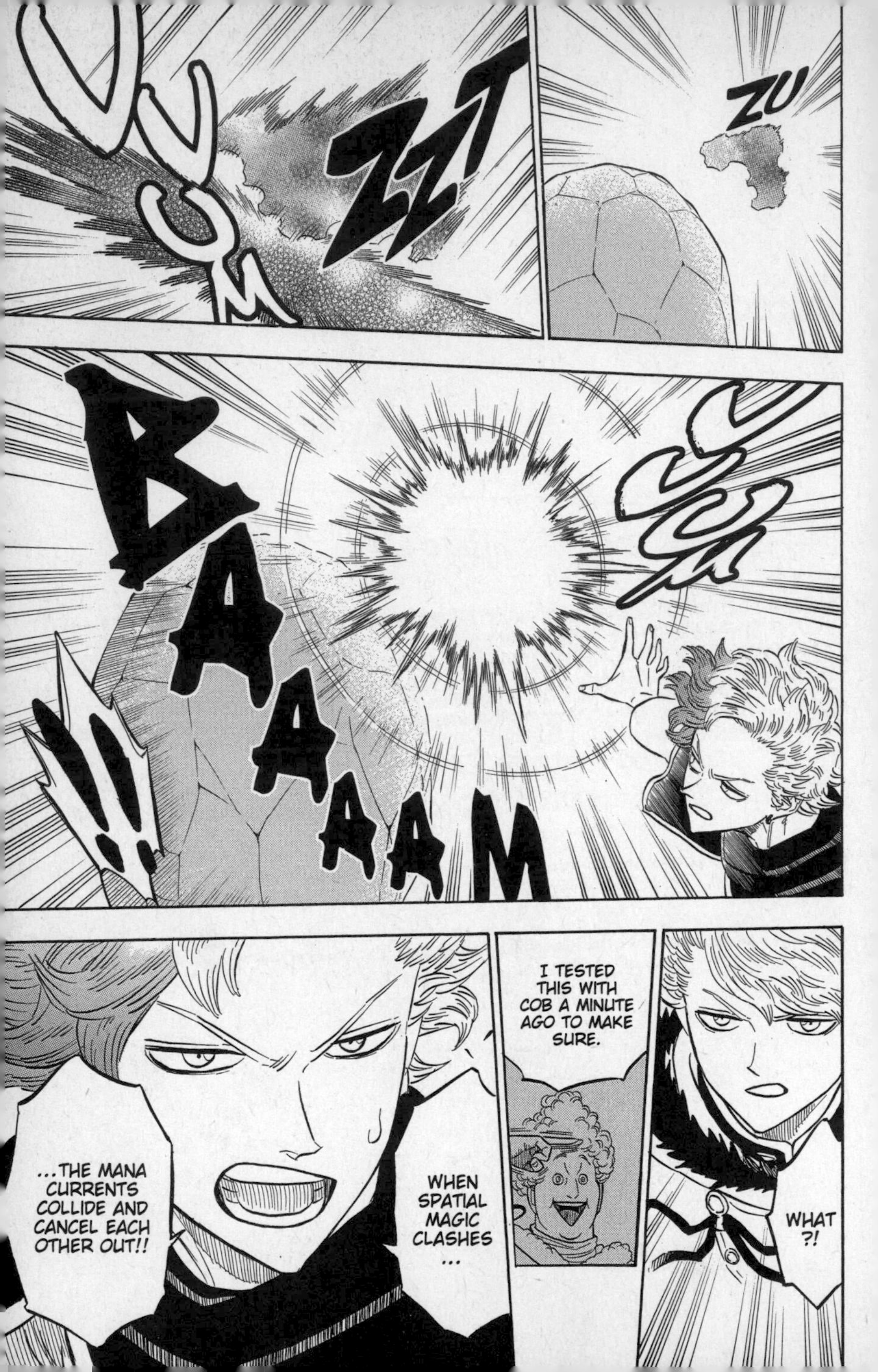
ZU
VUUM
ZZT
VUUM
BAAAAAM
!!
WHAT ?!
I TESTED THIS WITH COB A MINUTE AGO TO MAKE SURE.
WHEN SPATIAL MAGIC CLASHES ...
...THE MANA CURRENTS COLLIDE AND CANCEL EACH OTHER OUT!!

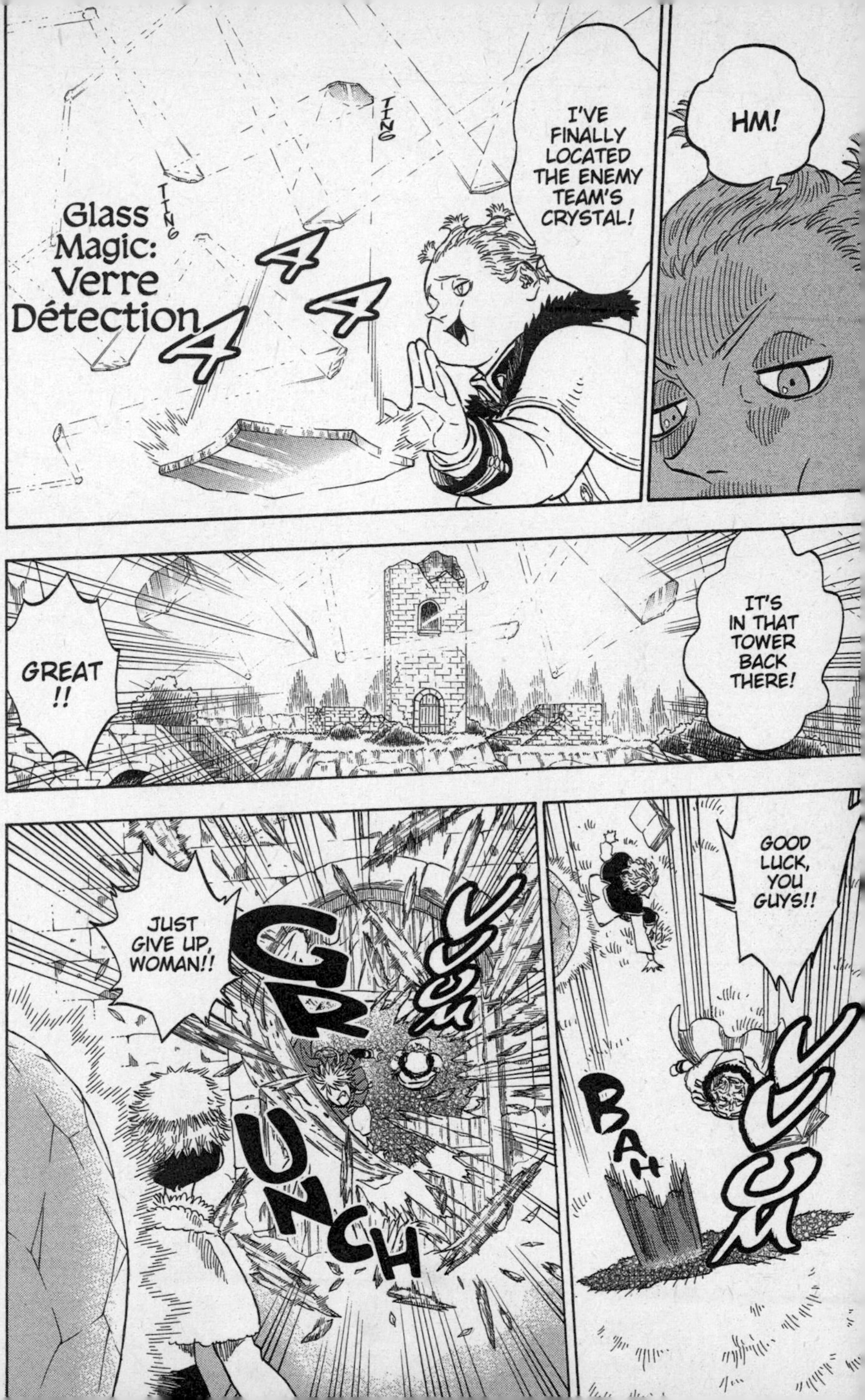
HM!
I'VE FINALLY LOCATED THE ENEMY TEAM'S CRYSTAL!
TING
TING
Glass Magic: Verre Détection
IT'S IN THAT TOWER BACK THERE!
GREAT!!
GOOD LUCK, YOU GUYS!!
VOOM
BAH
JUST GIVE UP, WOMAN!!
VOOM
GRUNCH

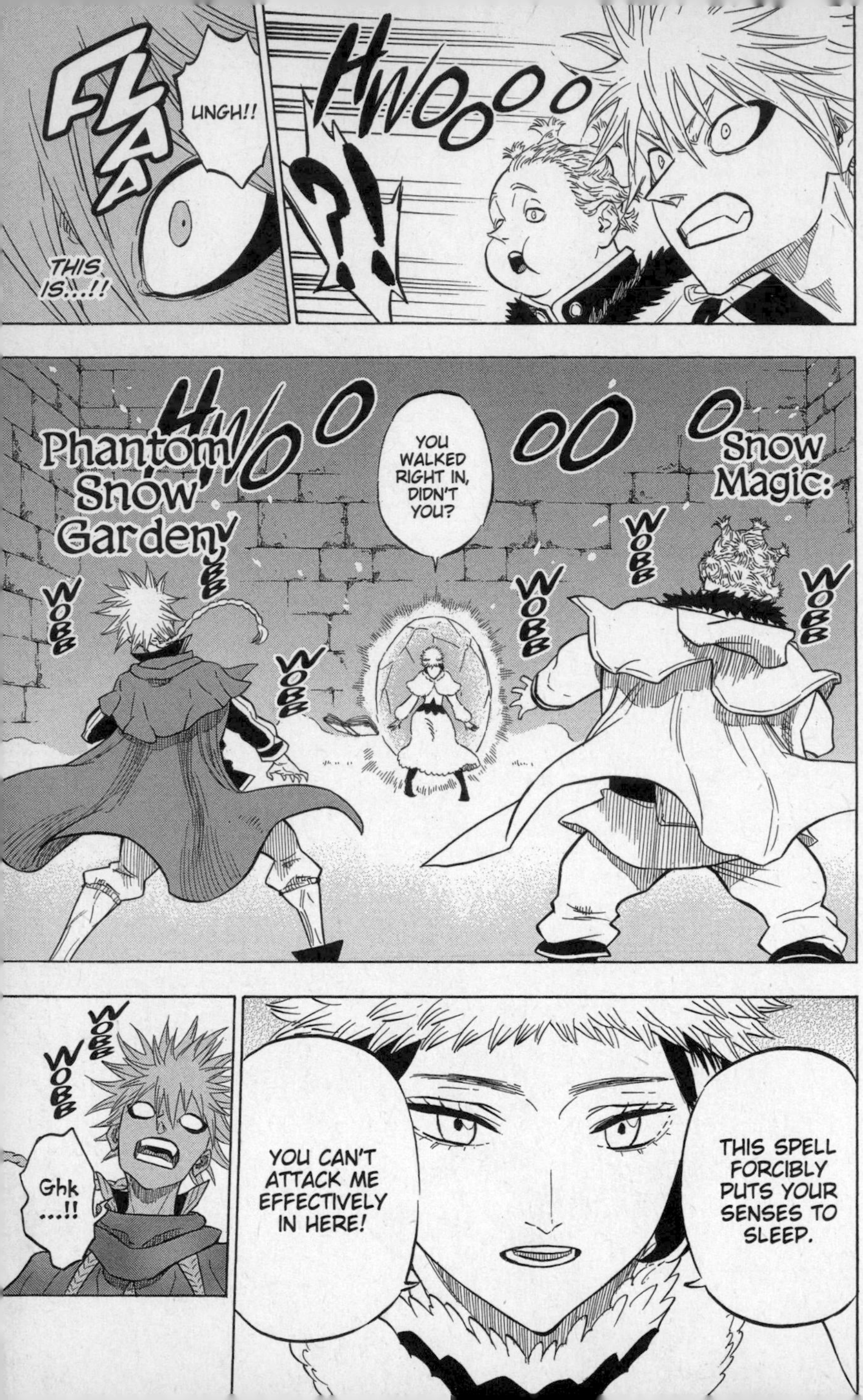
HWOOOO
?!!
FLAA
UNGH!!
THIS IS...!!
Snow Magic:
YOU WALKED RIGHT IN, DIDN'T YOU?
HWOOOOOO
Phantom Snow Garden
WOBB
WOBB
WOBB
WOBB
WOBB
WOBB
THIS SPELL FORCIBLY PUTS YOUR SENSES TO SLEEP.
YOU CAN'T ATTACK ME EFFECTIVELY IN HERE!
WOBB
WOBB
Ghk ...!!

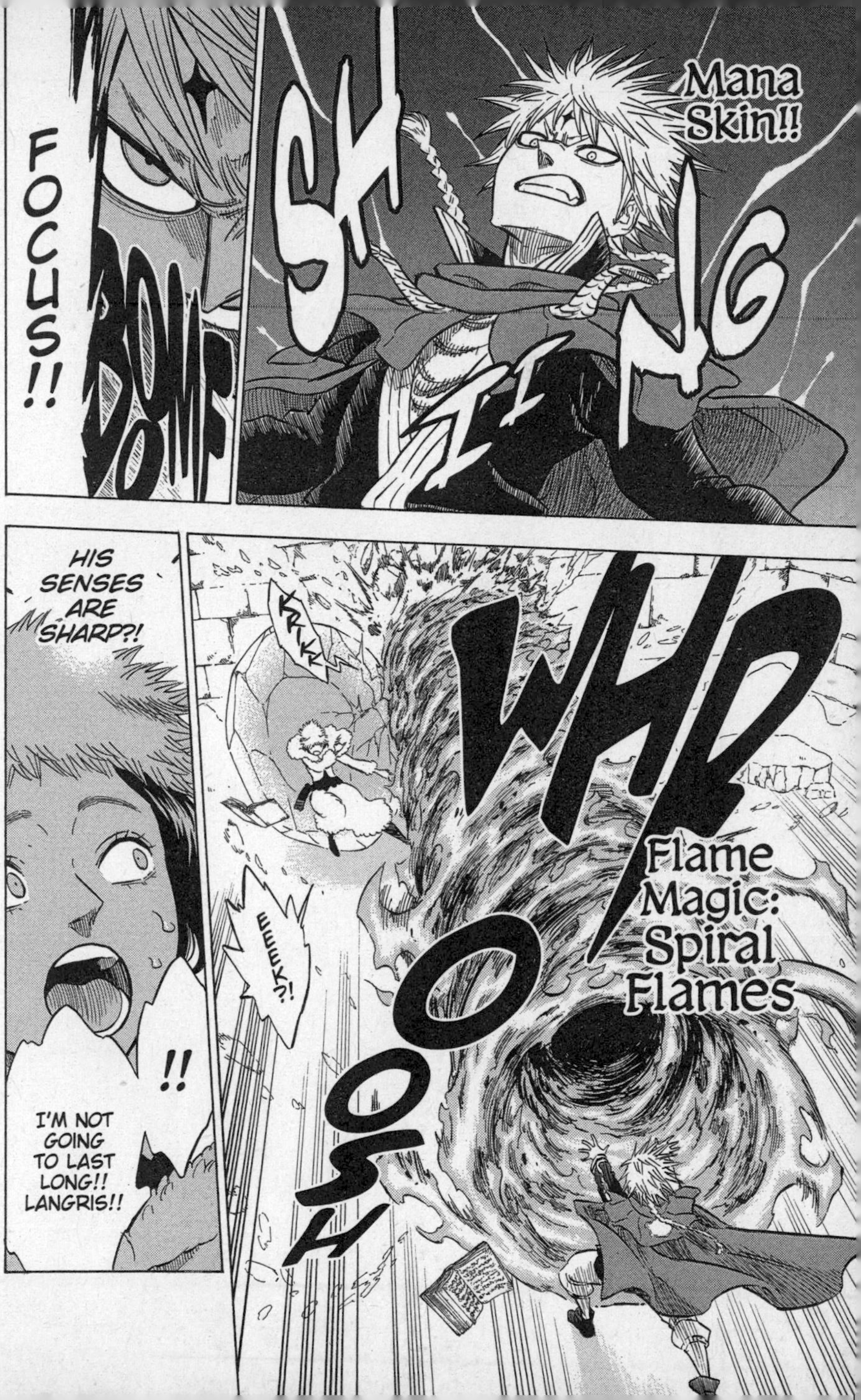
Mana Skin!!
SHIING
FOCUS!!
BOMF
WHOOSH
KRIKK
Flame Magic: Spiral Flames
EEEK?!
HIS SENSES ARE SHARP?!
!!
I'M NOT GOING TO LAST LONG!! LANGRIS!!

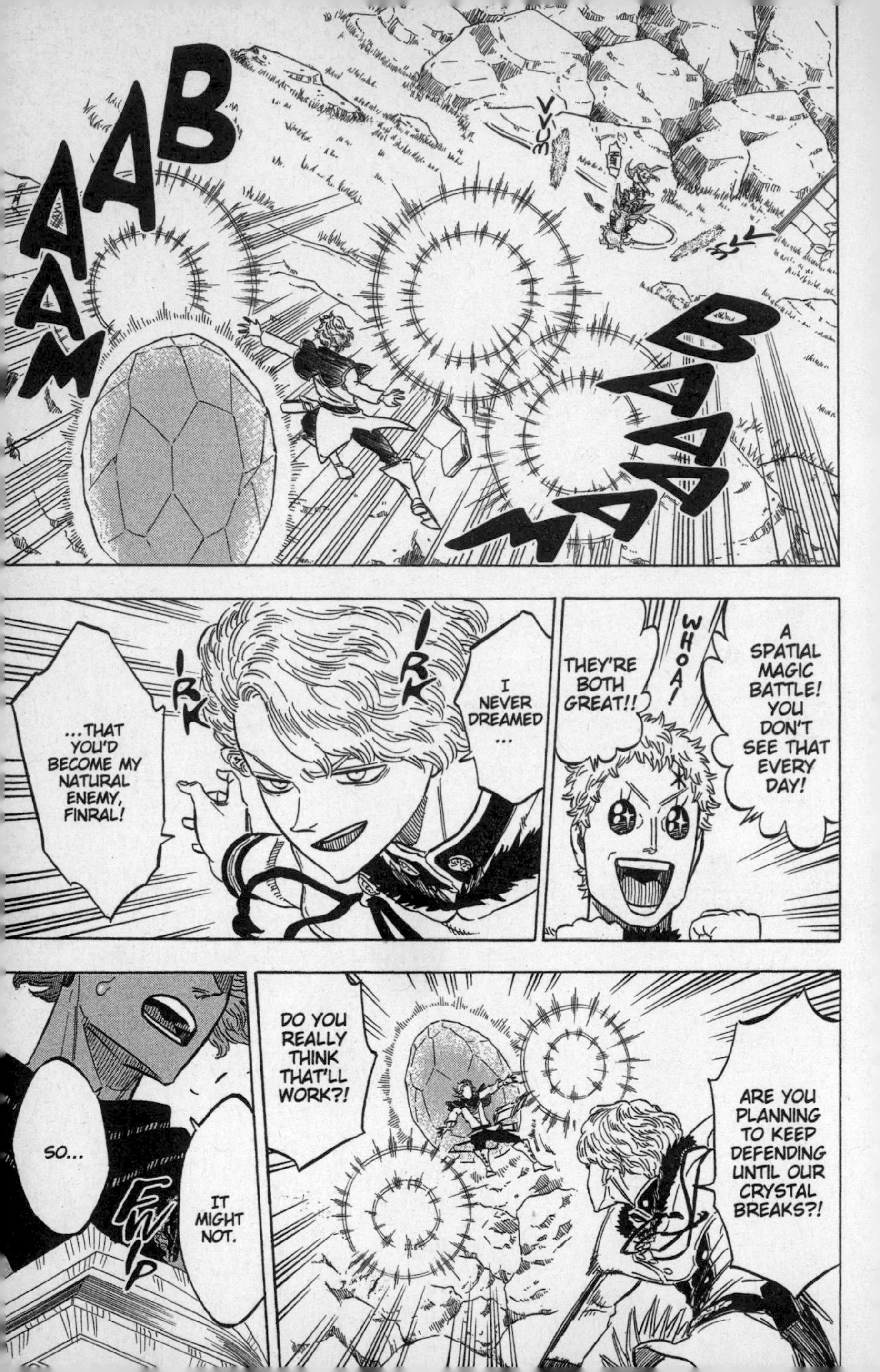
VVUM
SK
BAAAM
BAAAM
A SPATIAL MAGIC BATTLE! YOU DON'T SEE THAT EVERY DAY!
WHOA!
THEY'RE BOTH GREAT!!
IRK
I NEVER DREAMED...
IRK
...THAT YOU'D BECOME MY NATURAL ENEMY, FINRAL!
ARE YOU PLANNING TO KEEP DEFENDING UNTIL OUR CRYSTAL BREAKS?!
DO YOU REALLY THINK THAT'LL WORK?!
IT MIGHT NOT.
FWIP
SO...

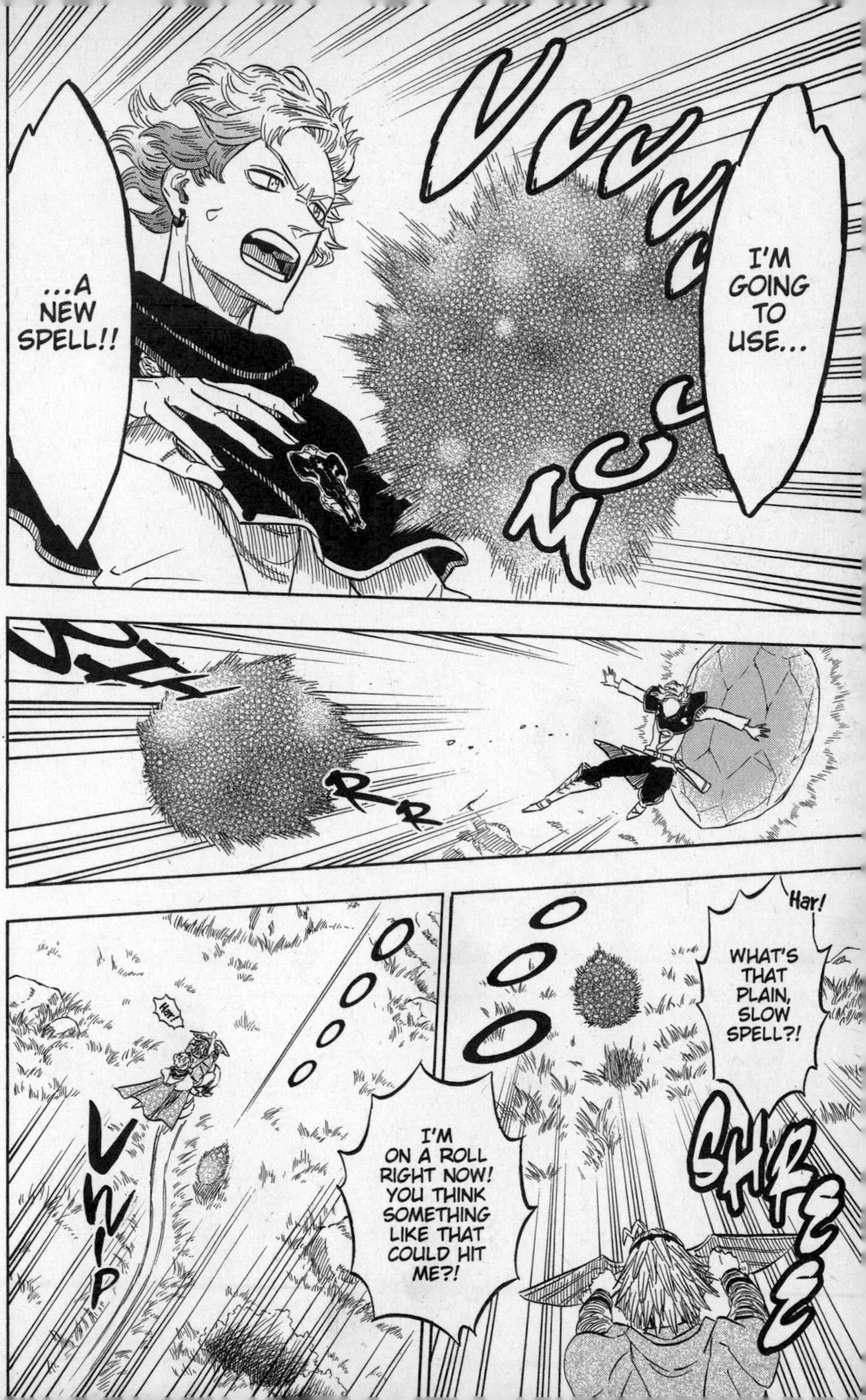
I'M GOING TO USE...
...A NEW SPELL!!
R-R
Har!
WHAT'S THAT PLAIN, SLOW SPELL?!
SHREEE
I'M ON A ROLL RIGHT NOW! YOU THINK SOMETHING LIKE THAT COULD HIT ME?!
Har!
VWIP

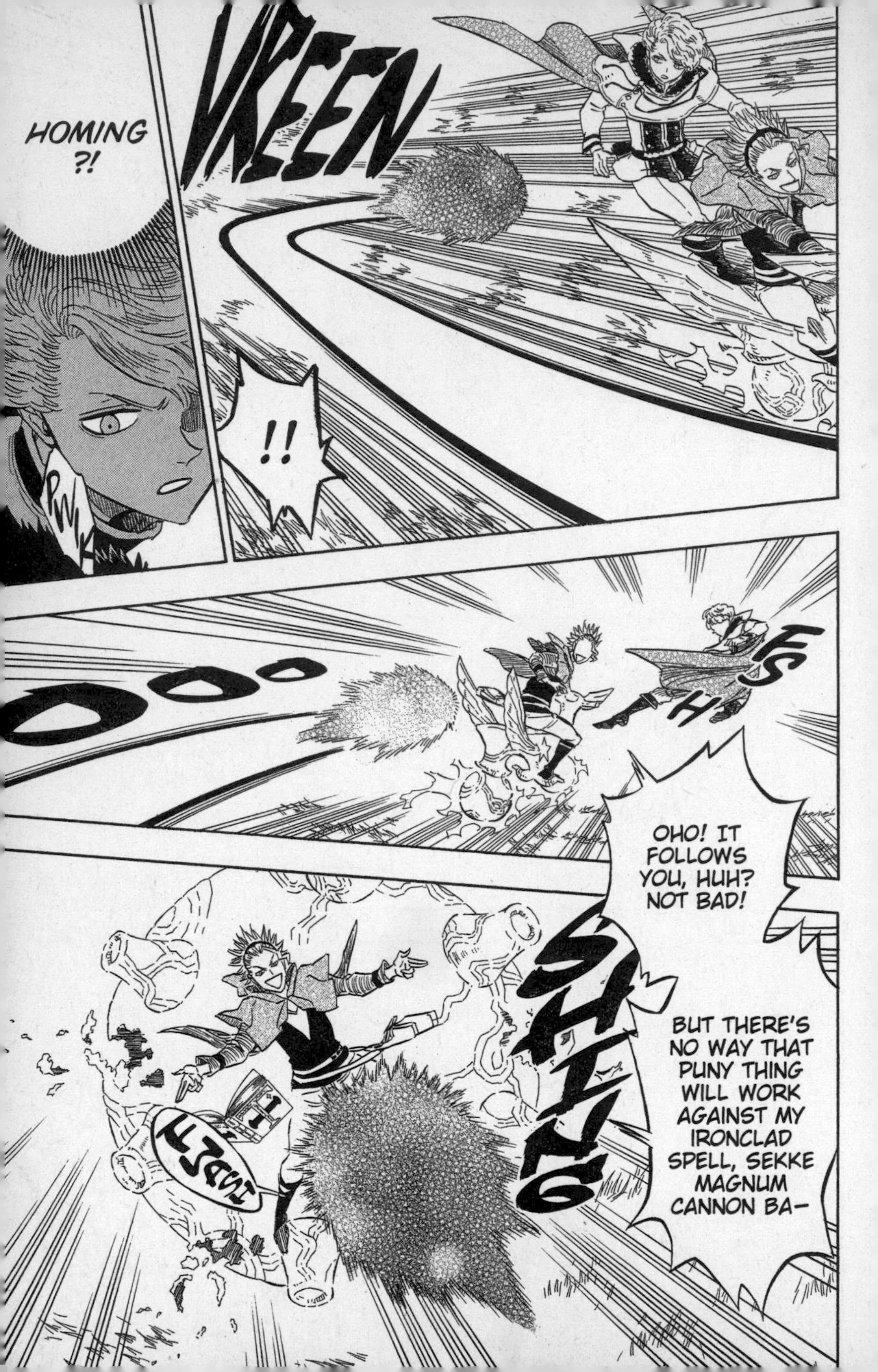
VREEN
!!
HOMING ?!
PWIK
FSH
OHO! IT FOLLOWS YOU, HUH? NOT BAD!
SHING
BUT THERE'S NO WAY THAT PUNY THING WILL WORK AGAINST MY IRONCLAD SPELL, SEKKE MAGNUM CANNON BA-

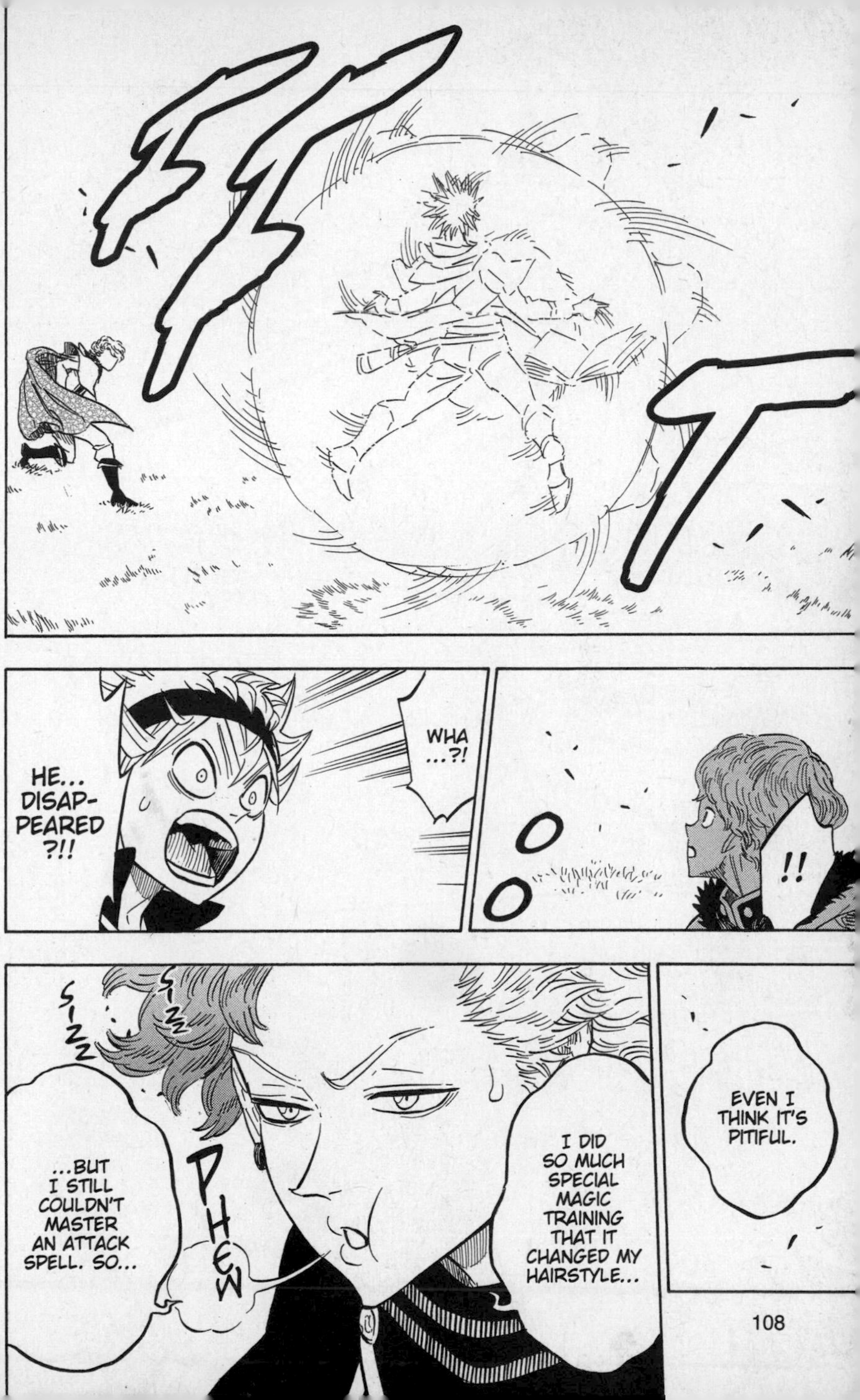
!!
WHA ...?!
HE... DISAP-PEARED ?!!
EVEN I THINK IT'S PITIFUL.
I DID SO MUCH SPECIAL MAGIC TRAINING THAT IT CHANGED MY HAIRSTYLE...
SIZZ
SIZZ
PHEW
...BUT I STILL COULDN'T MASTER AN ATTACK SPELL. SO...

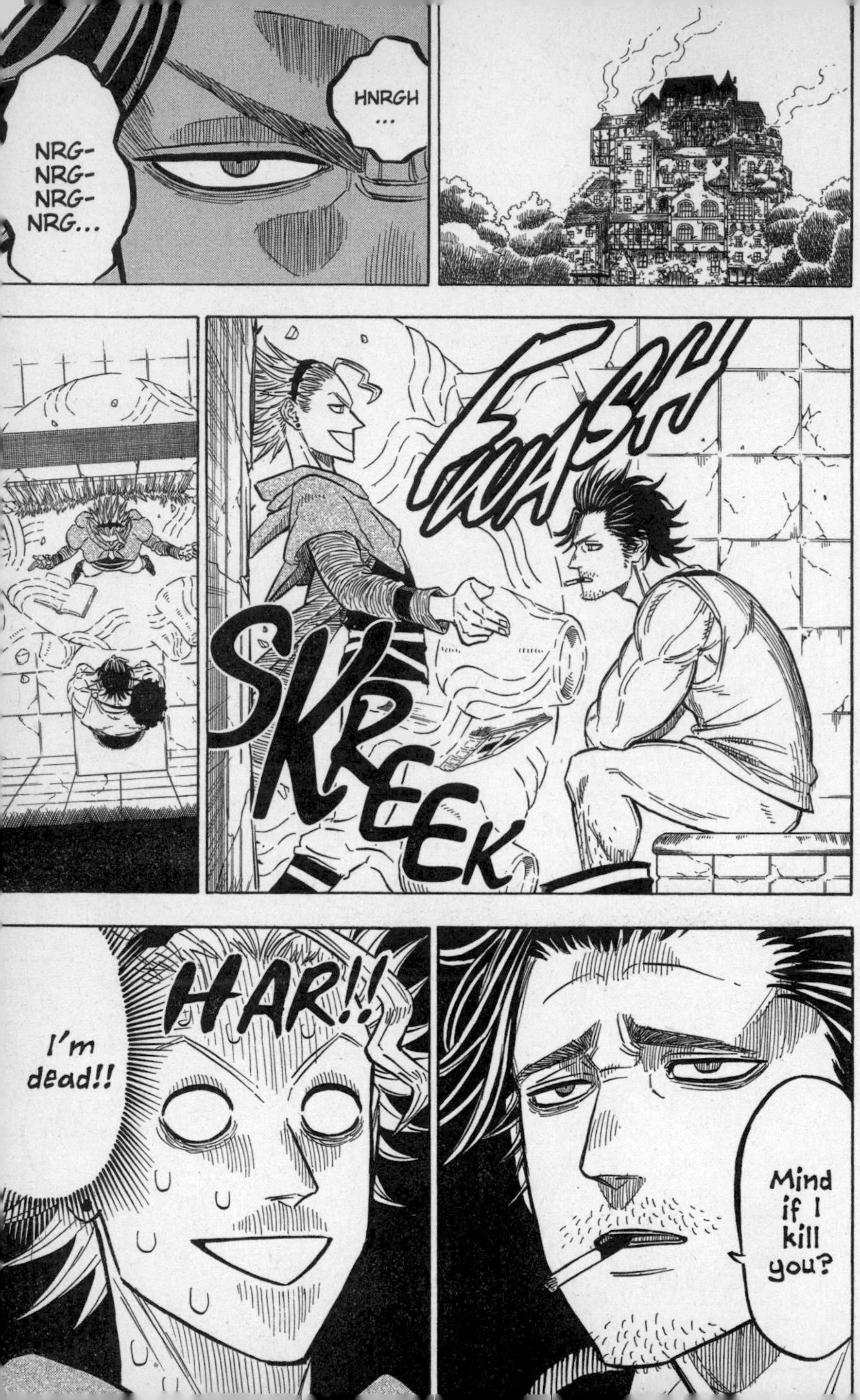
HNRGH ...
NRG- NRG- NRG- NRG...
SKREEK
Mind if I kill you?
HAR!!
I'm dead!!

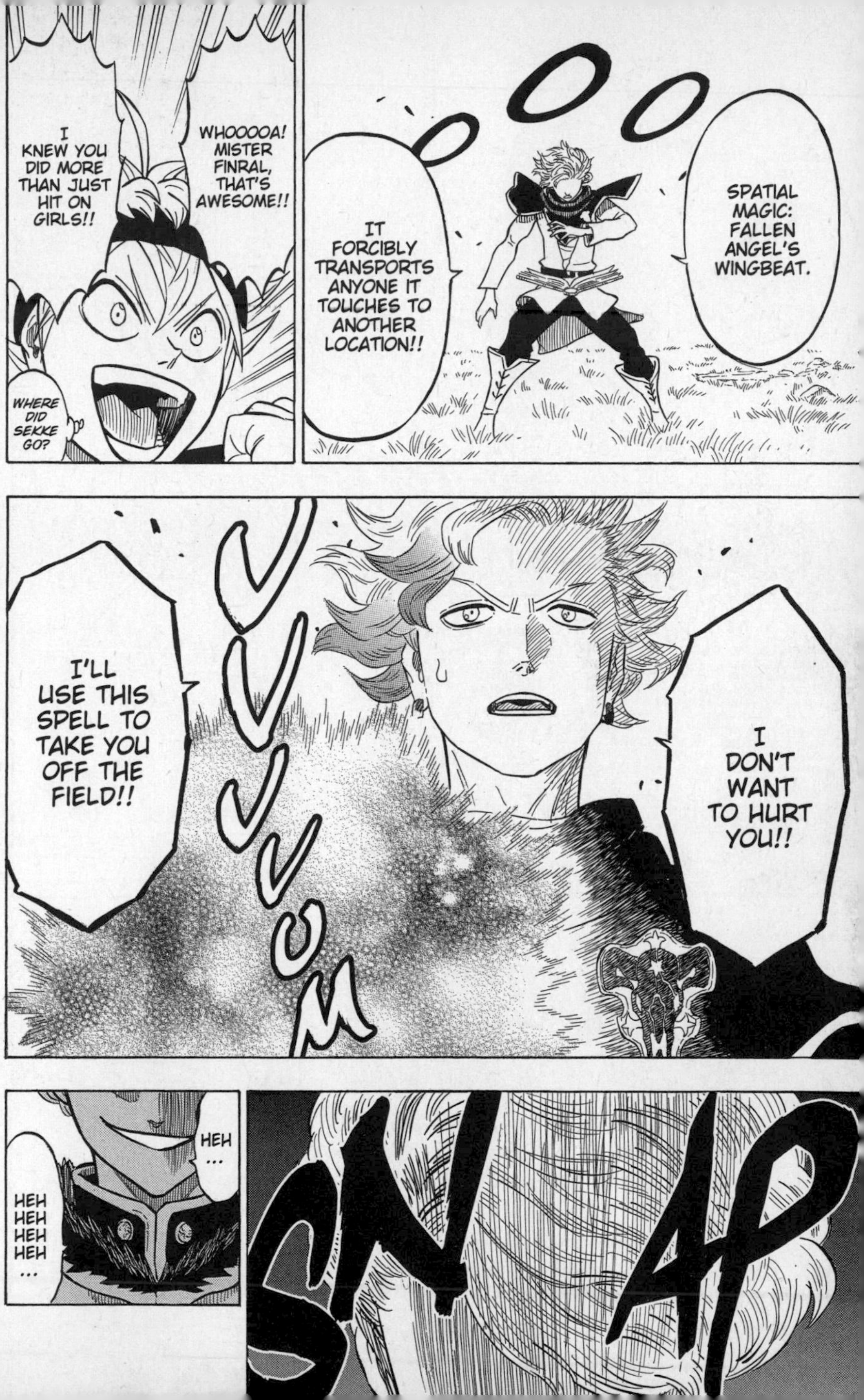
SPATIAL MAGIC: FALLEN ANGEL'S WINGBEAT.
IT FORCIBLY TRANSPORTS ANYONE IT TOUCHES TO ANOTHER LOCATION!!
WHOOOOA! MISTER FINRAL, THAT'S AWESOME!!
I KNEW YOU DID MORE THAN JUST HIT ON GIRLS!!
WHERE DID SEKKE GO?
I DON'T WANT TO HURT YOU!!
I'LL USE THIS SPELL TO TAKE YOU OFF THE FIELD!!
SNAP
HEH...
HEH HEH HEH HEH...

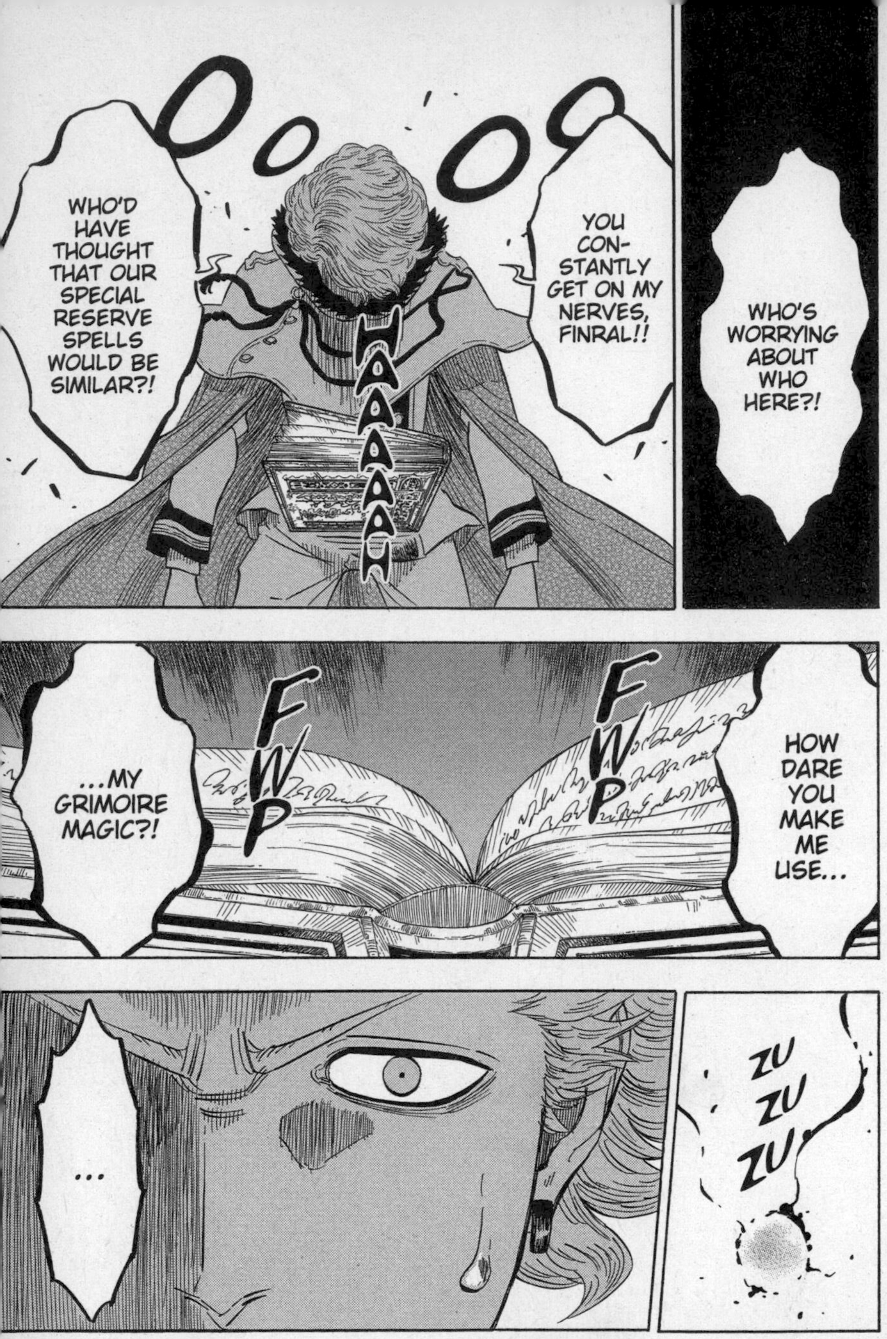

WHO'S WORRYING ABOUT WHO HERE?!
OOOO
YOU CON-STANTLY GET ON MY NERVES, FINRAL!!
WHO'D HAVE THOUGHT THAT OUR SPECIAL RESERVE SPELLS WOULD BE SIMILAR?!
HAAAAAH
HOW DARE YOU MAKE ME USE...
FWP
FWP
...MY GRIMOIRE MAGIC?!
ZU ZU ZU
...

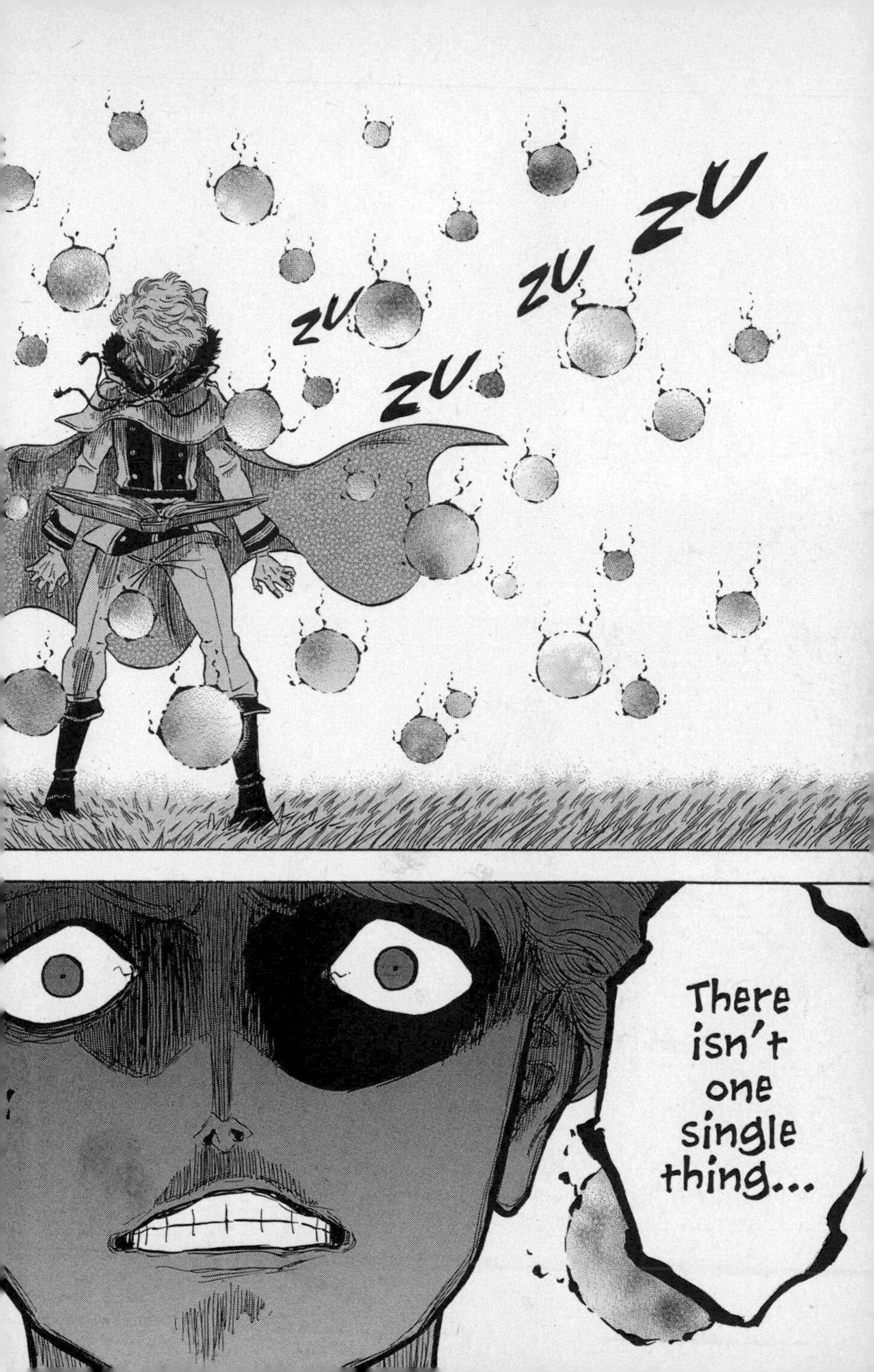
ZU ZU ZU ZU
There isn't one single thing...

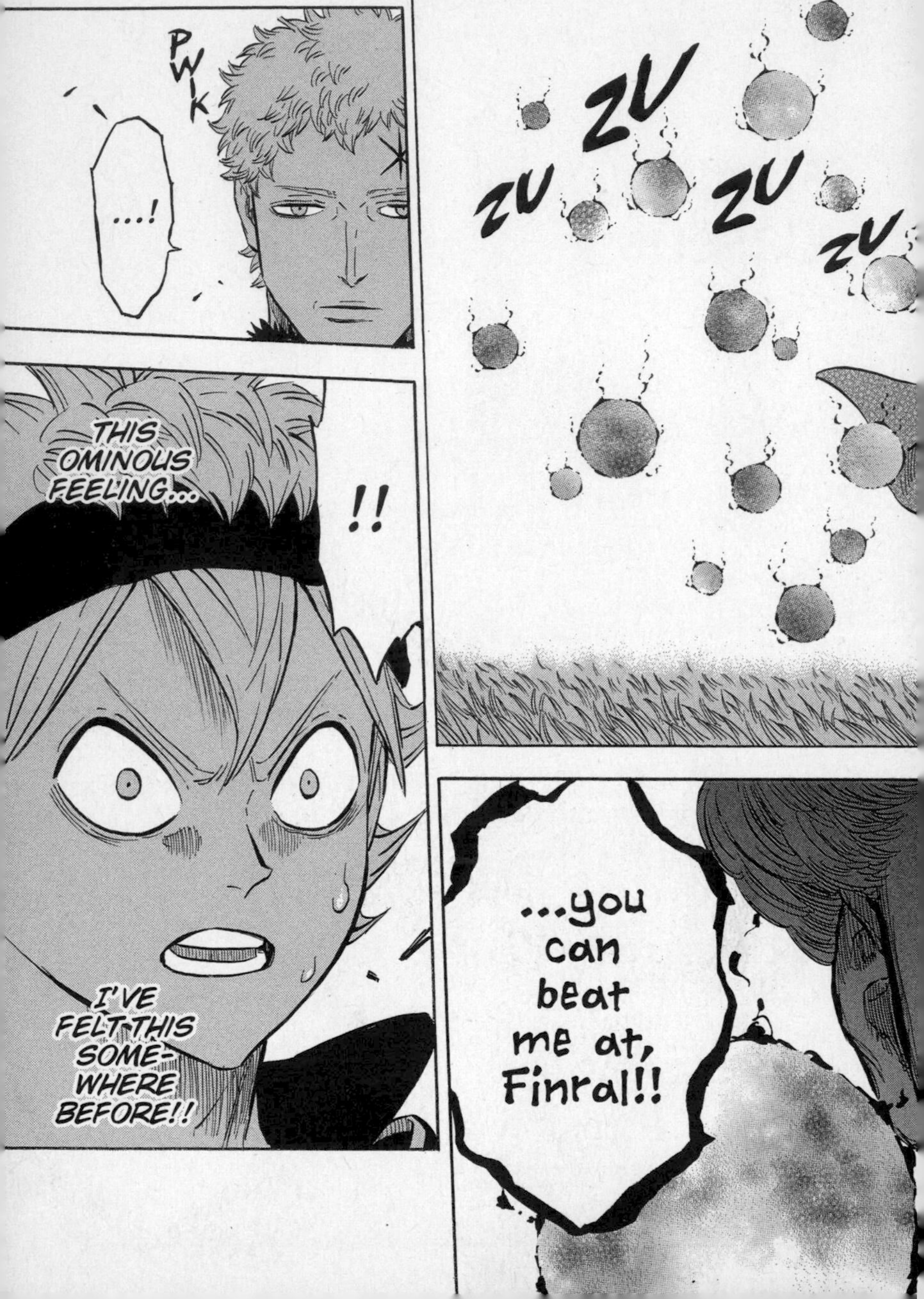
ZU
ZU
ZU
ZU
...you can beat me at, Finral!!
PWIK
...!
THIS OMINOUS FEELING...
!!
I'VE FELT THIS SOME-WHERE BEFORE!!

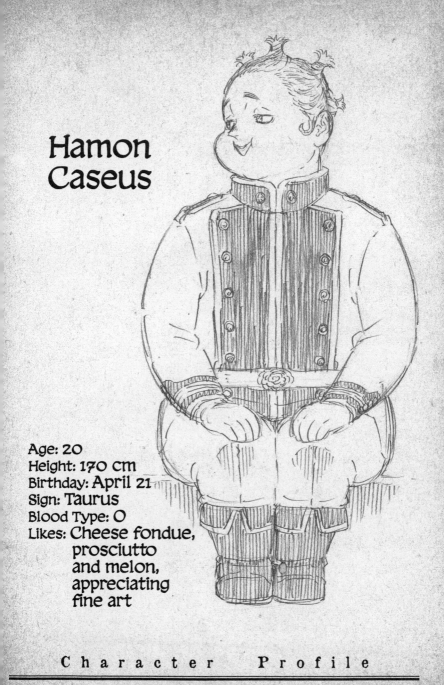

Hamon
Caseus

Age: 20
Height: 170 cm
Birthday: April 21
Sign: Taurus
Blood Type: O
Likes: Cheese fondue,
prosciutto
and melon,
appreciating
fine art

Character Profile

♣

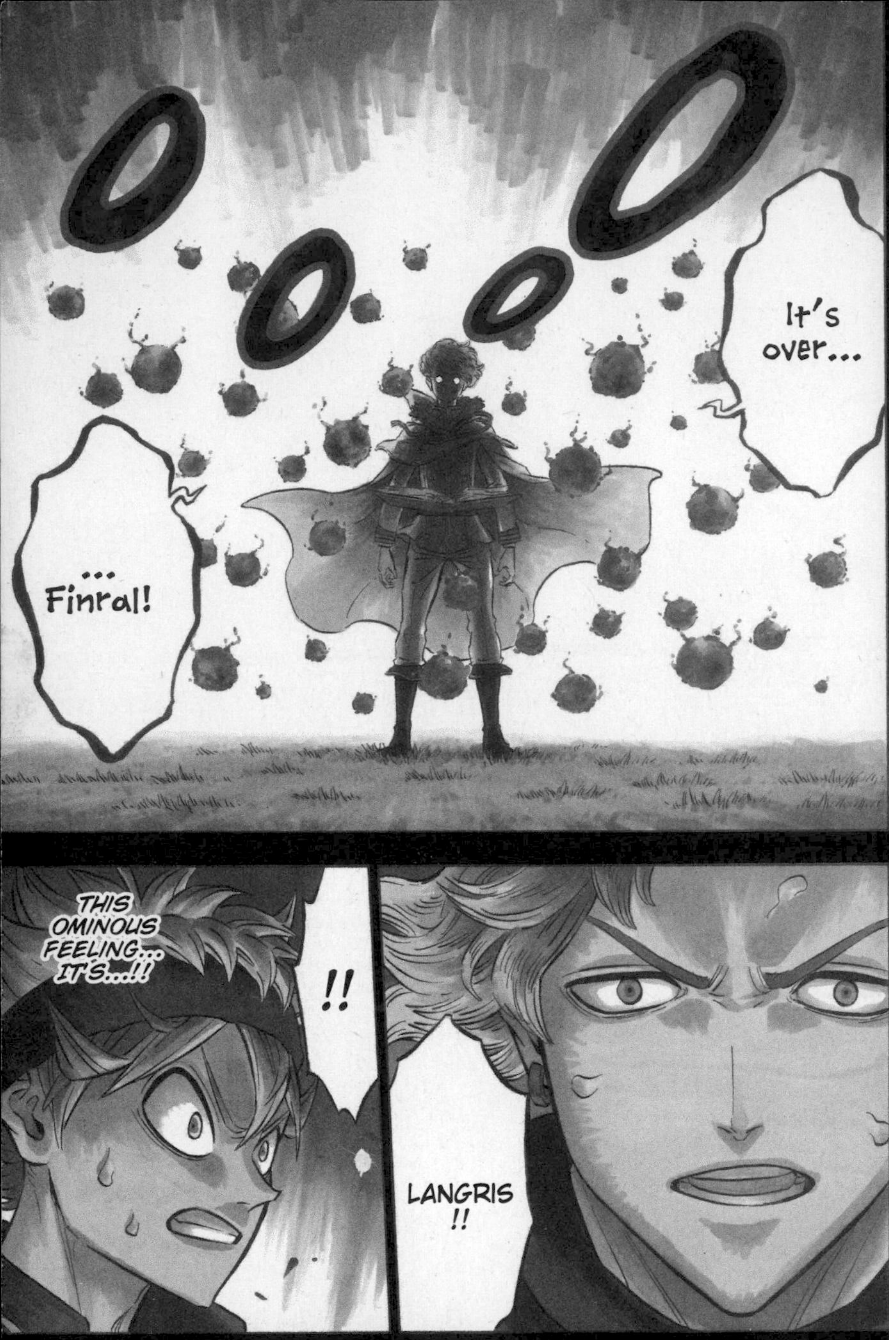
It's over...
...Finral!
LANGRIS !!
!!
THIS OMINOUS FEELING... IT'S...!!

Page 127: Gold and Black Sparks

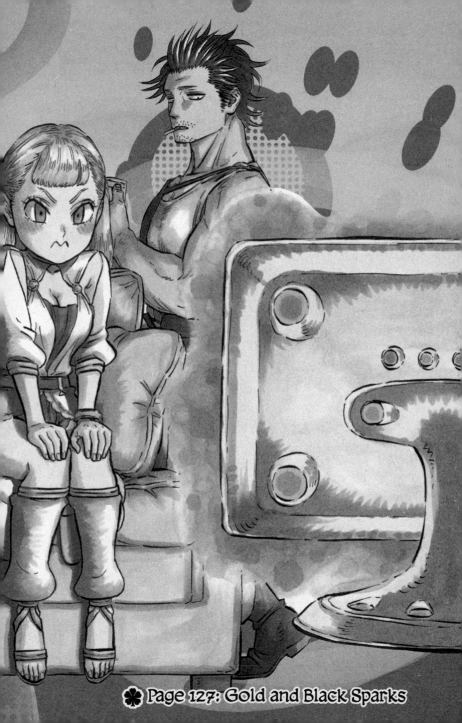

✿ Page 127: Gold and Black Sparks

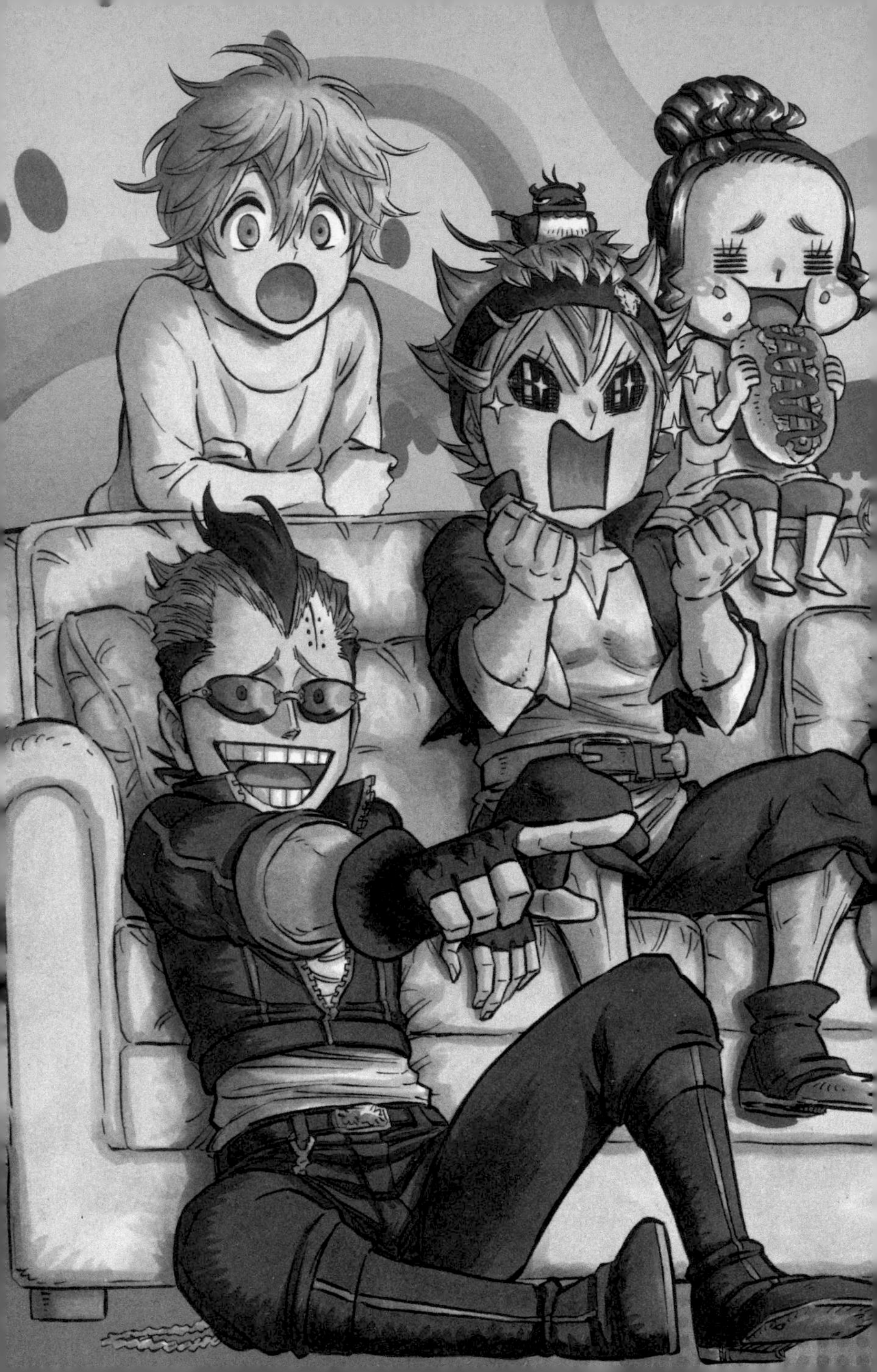

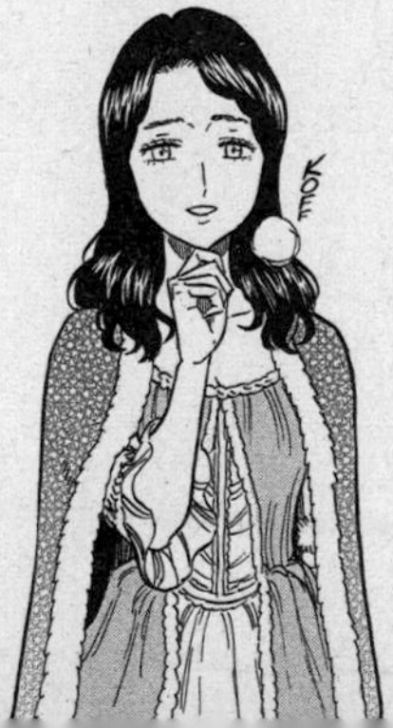
KOFF

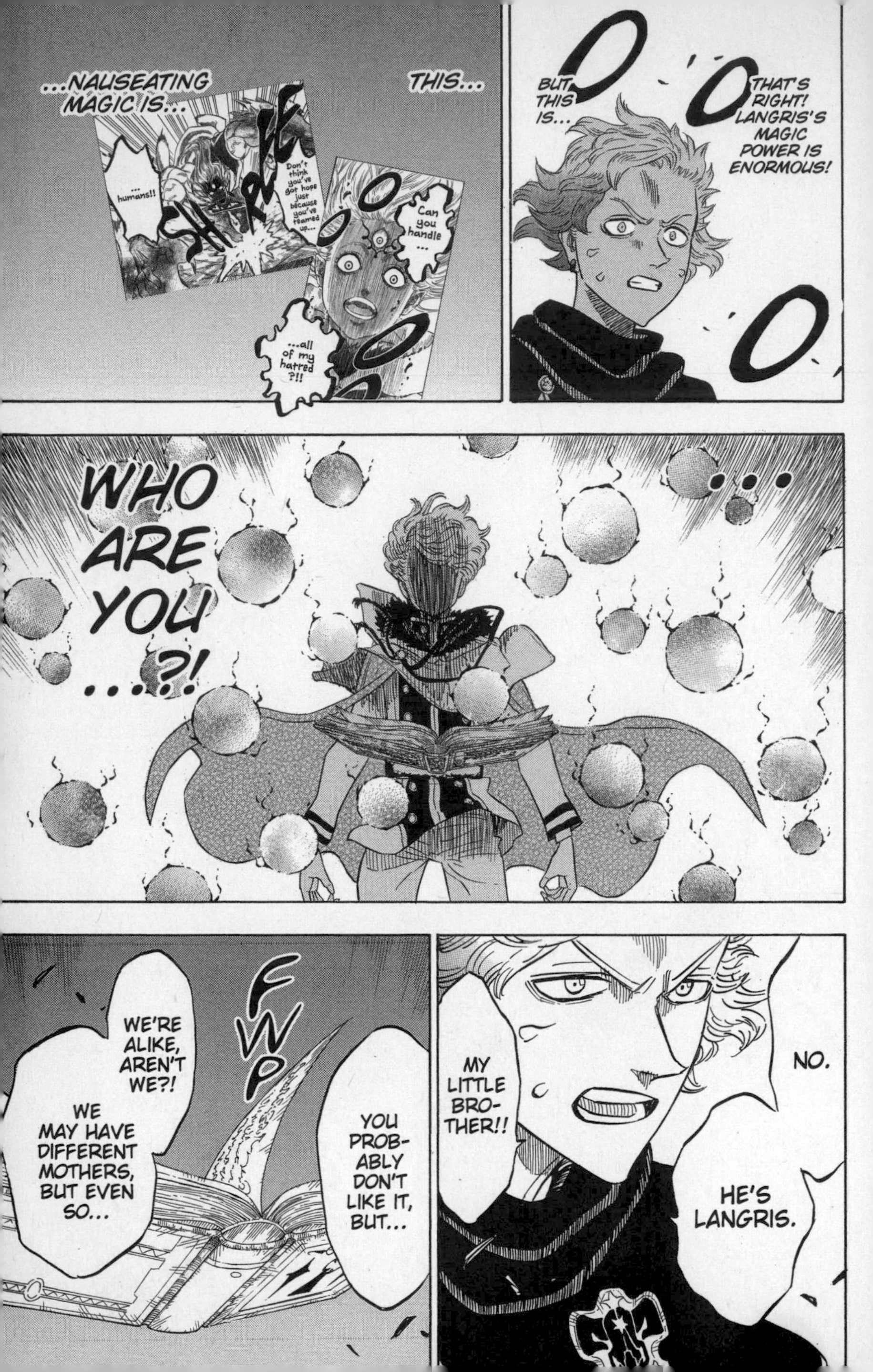
THAT'S RIGHT! LANGRIS'S MAGIC POWER IS ENORMOUS!
BUT THIS IS...
THIS...
...NAUSEATING MAGIC IS...
Don't think you've got hope just because you've teamed up...
...humans!!
Can you handle...
...all of my hatred?!!
WHO ARE YOU ...?!
...
NO.
HE'S LANGRIS.
MY LITTLE BROTHER!!
YOU PROBABLY DON'T LIKE IT, BUT...
WE'RE ALIKE, AREN'T WE?!
WE MAY HAVE DIFFERENT MOTHERS, BUT EVEN SO...
FWP

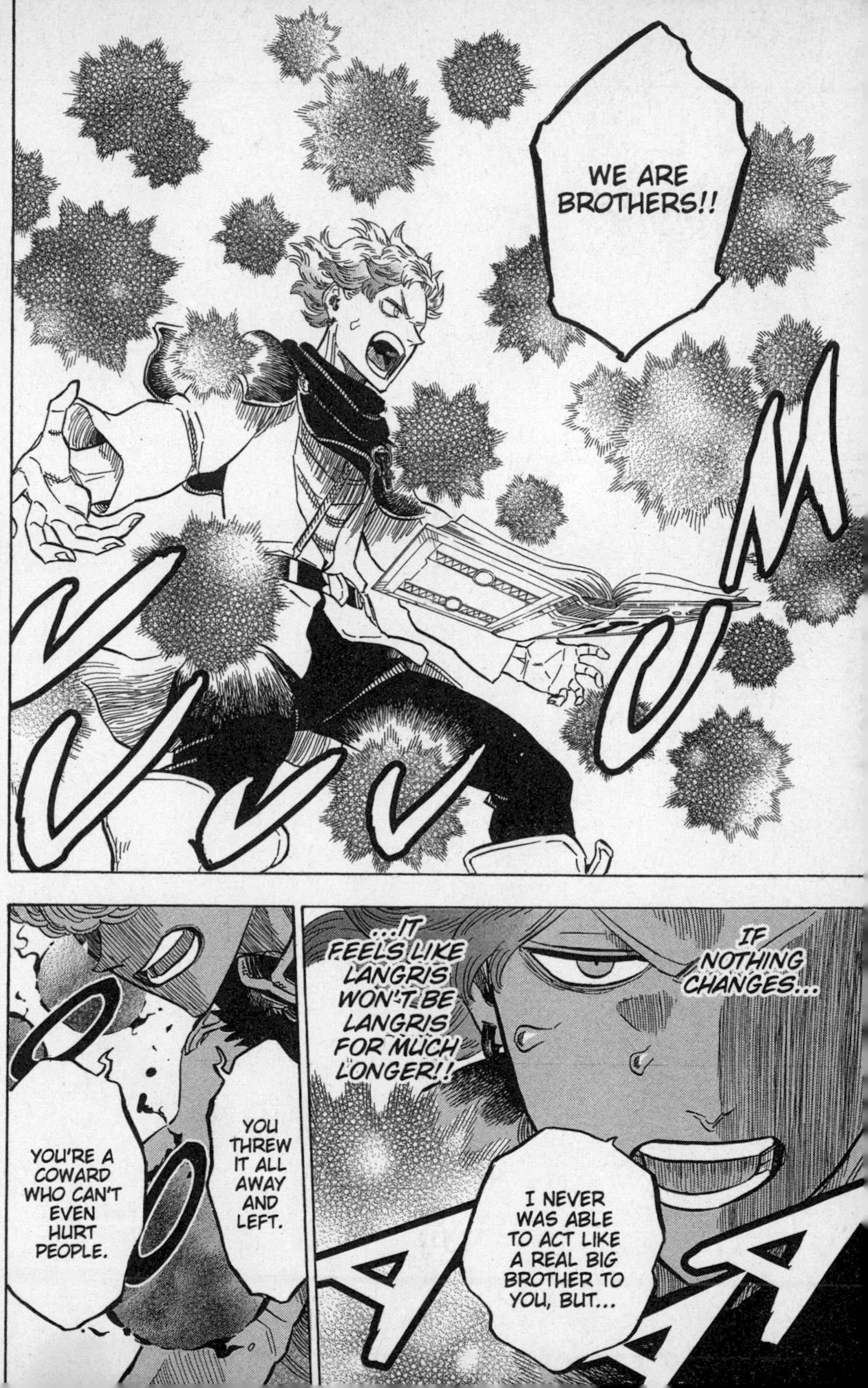
WE ARE BROTHERS!!
IF NOTHING CHANGES...
...IT FEELS LIKE LANGRIS WON'T BE LANGRIS FOR MUCH LONGER!!
I NEVER WAS ABLE TO ACT LIKE A REAL BIG BROTHER TO YOU, BUT...
YOU THREW IT ALL AWAY AND LEFT.
YOU'RE A COWARD WHO CAN'T EVEN HURT PEOPLE.

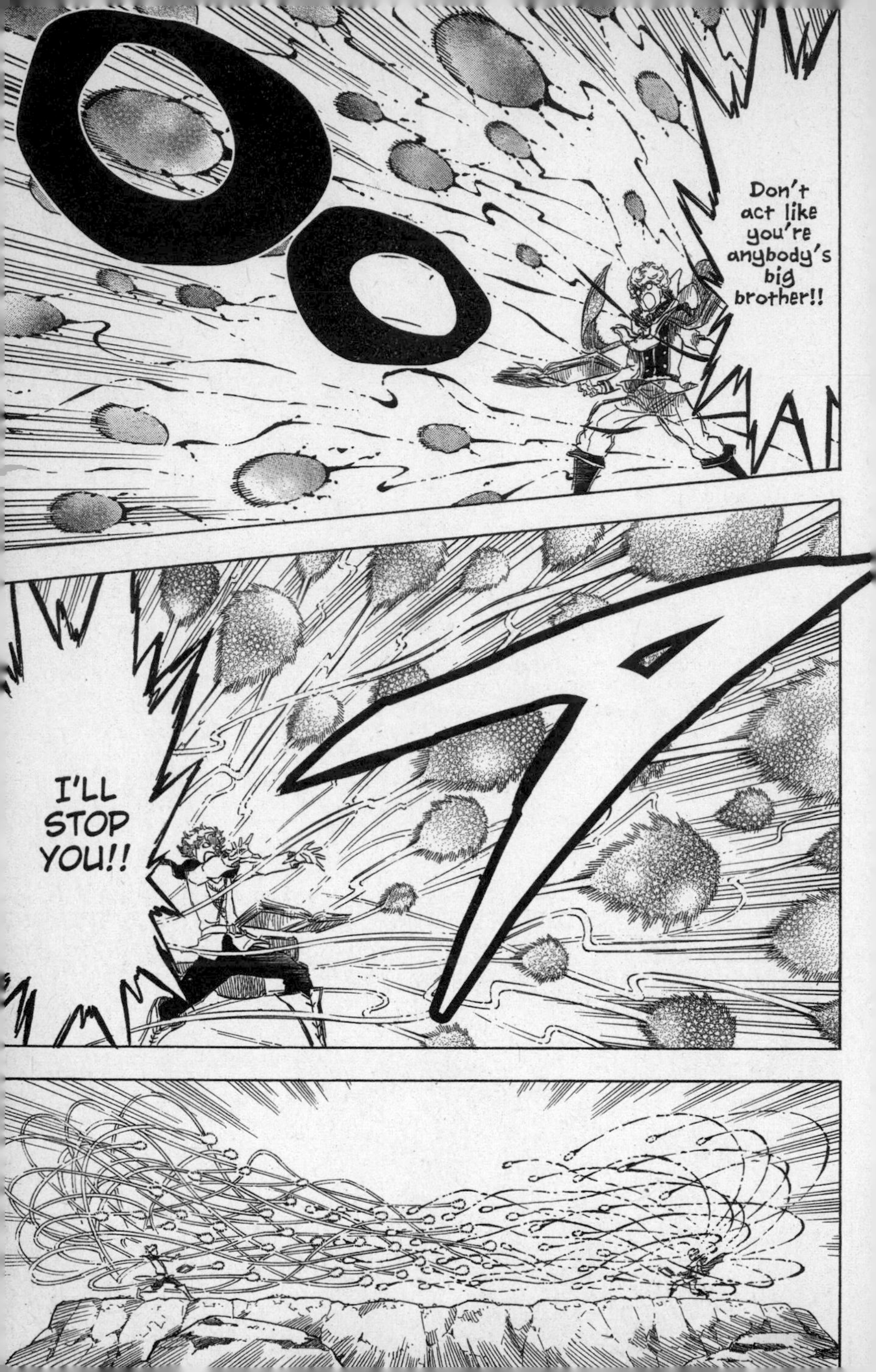
Don't act like you're anybody's big brother!!
I'LL STOP YOU!!

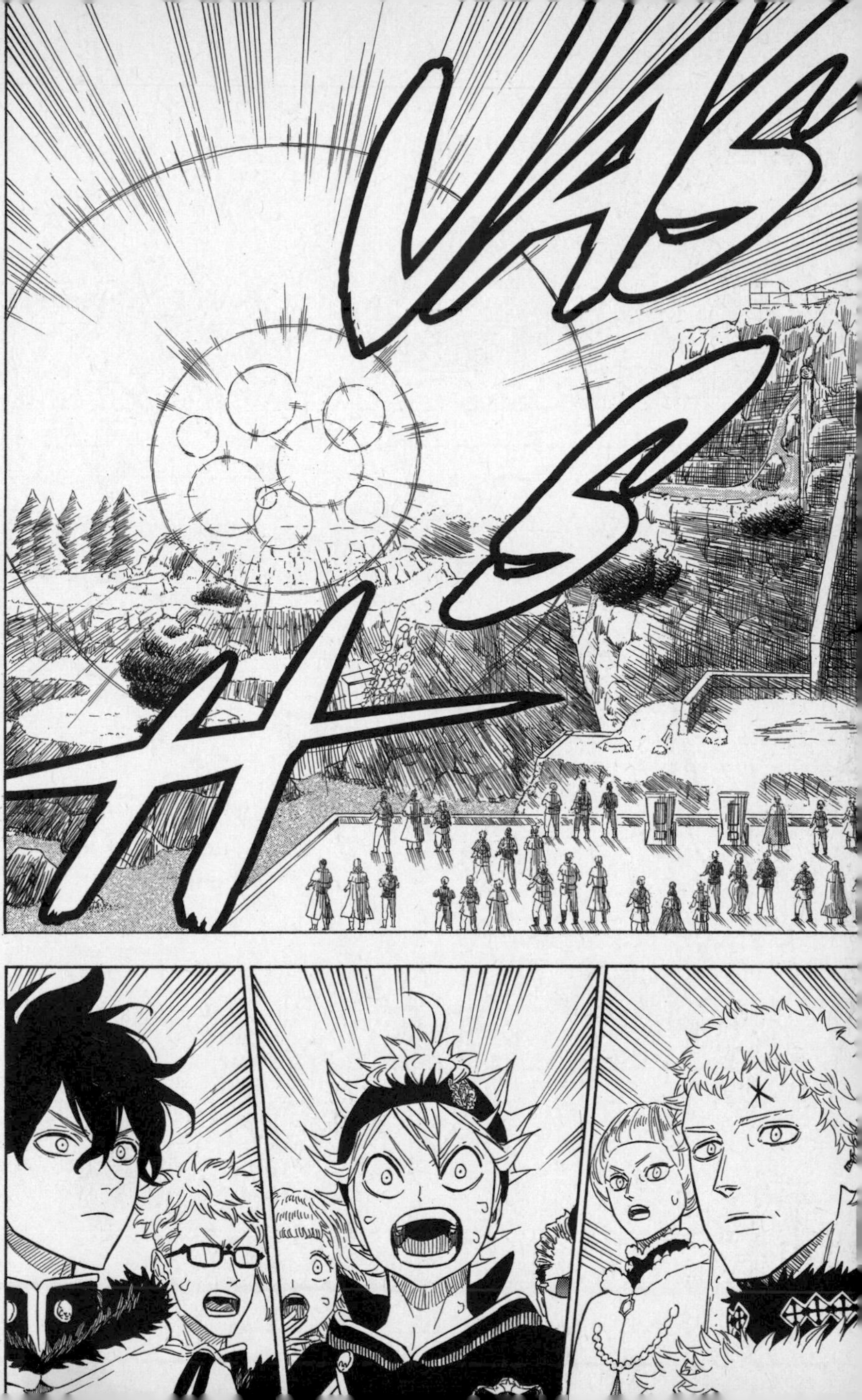

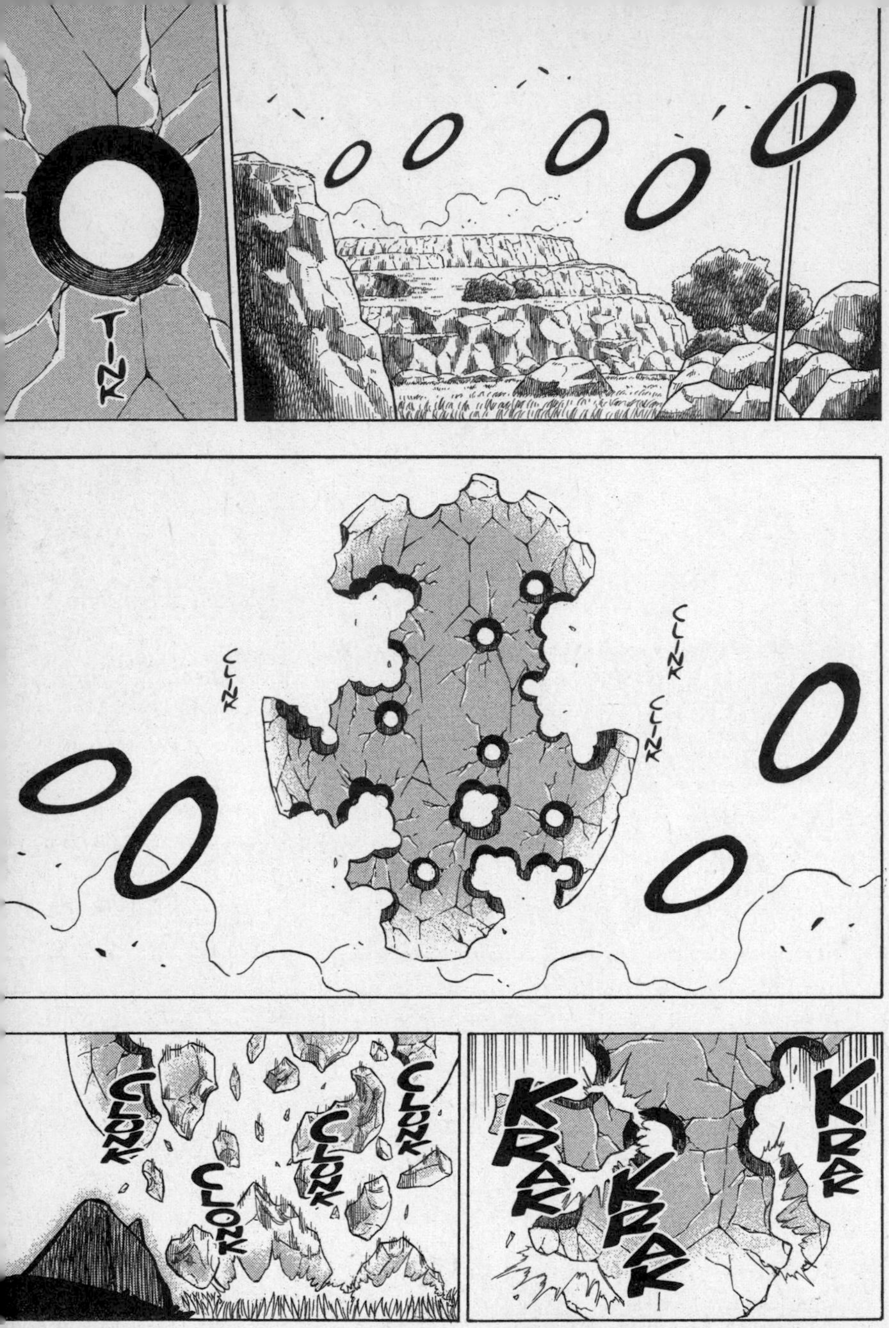
TINK
CLINK
CLINK
CLINK
KRAK
KRAK
KRAK
CLUNK
CLUNK
CLUNK
CLUNK

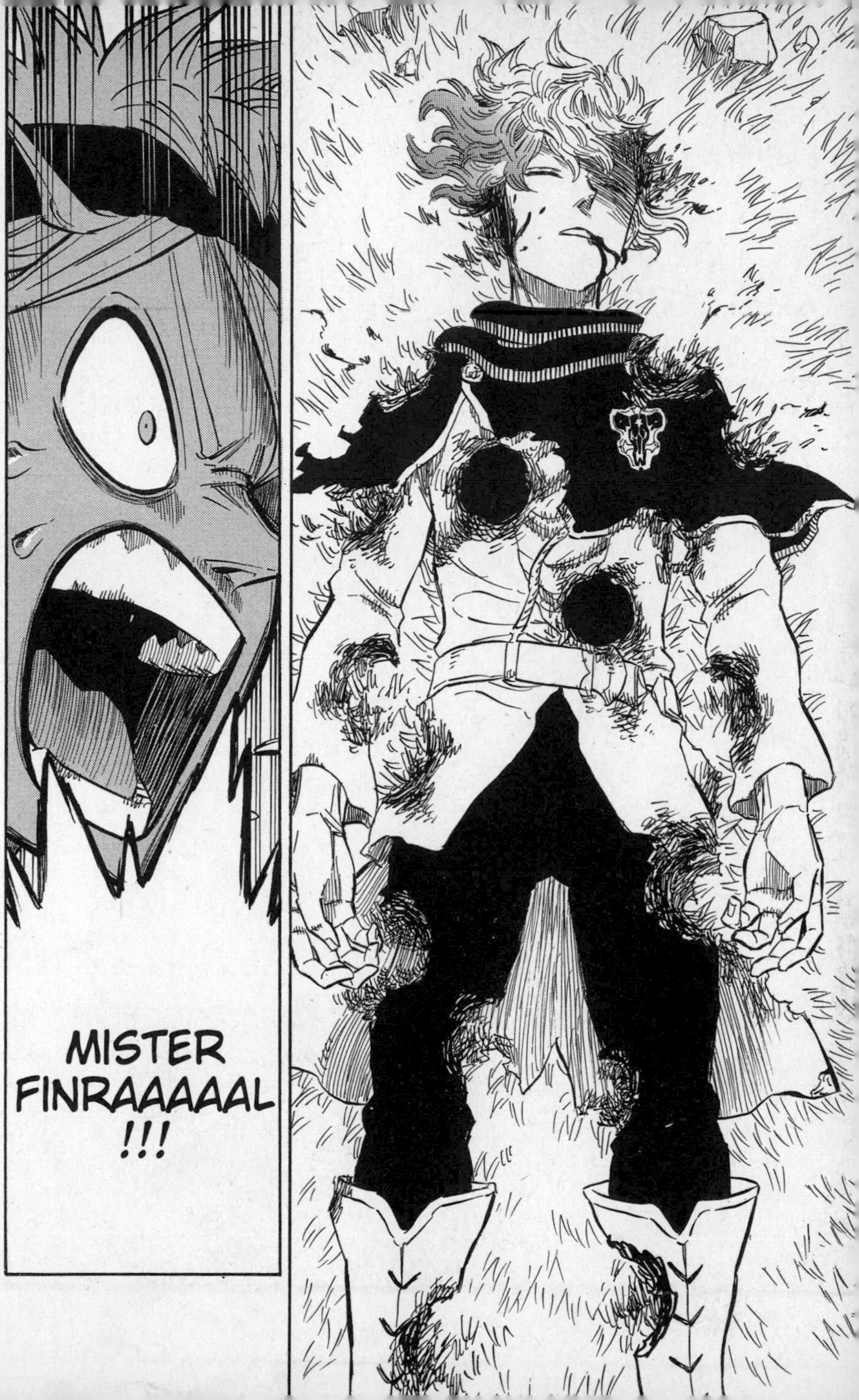
MISTER FINRAAAAAL !!!

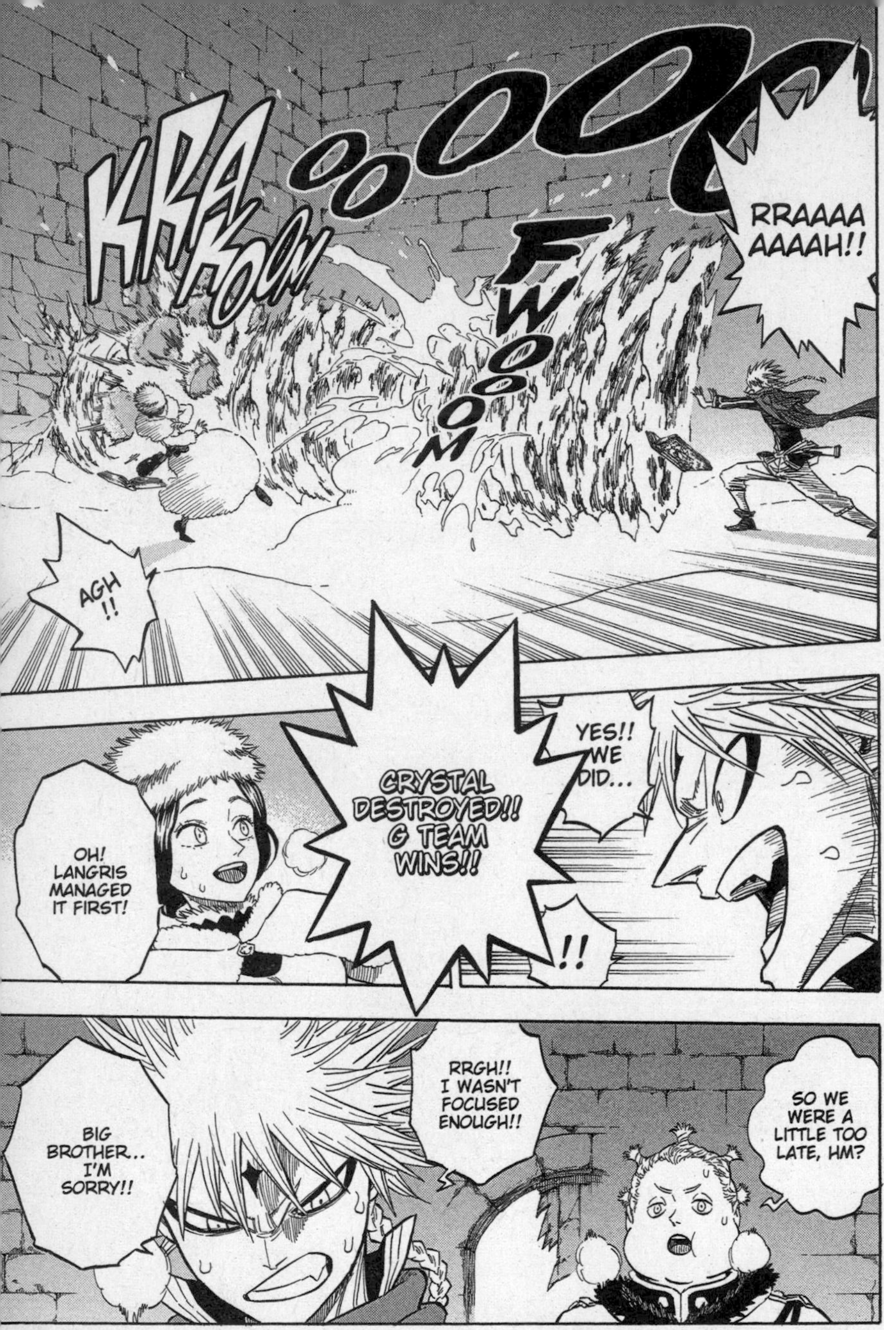
RRAAAAAAAAH!!
FWOOOOM
KRAKOOOOOOOM
AGH!!
YES!! WE DID...
!!
CRYSTAL DESTROYED!! G TEAM WINS!!
OH! LANGRIS MANAGED IT FIRST!
SO WE WERE A LITTLE TOO LATE, HM?
RRGH!! I WASN'T FOCUSED ENOUGH!!
BIG BROTHER... I'M SORRY!!

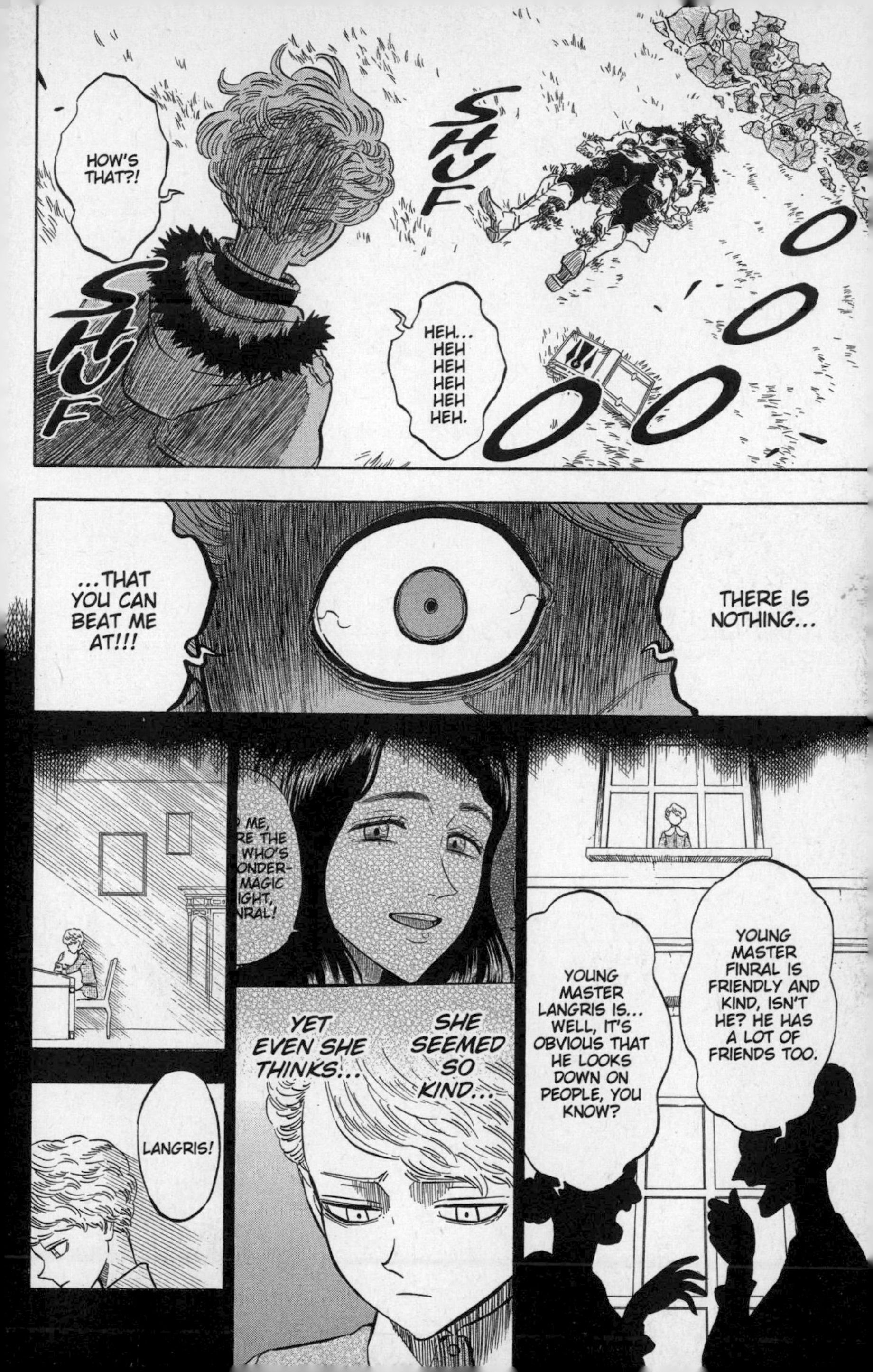
SHUF
HEH... HEH HEH HEH HEH HEH.
HOW'S THAT?!
SHUF
THERE IS NOTHING...
...THAT YOU CAN BEAT ME AT!!!
YOUNG MASTER FINRAL IS FRIENDLY AND KIND, ISN'T HE? HE HAS A LOT OF FRIENDS TOO.
YOUNG MASTER LANGRIS IS... WELL, IT'S OBVIOUS THAT HE LOOKS DOWN ON PEOPLE, YOU KNOW?
SHE SEEMED SO KIND...
YET EVEN SHE THINKS...
LANGRIS!

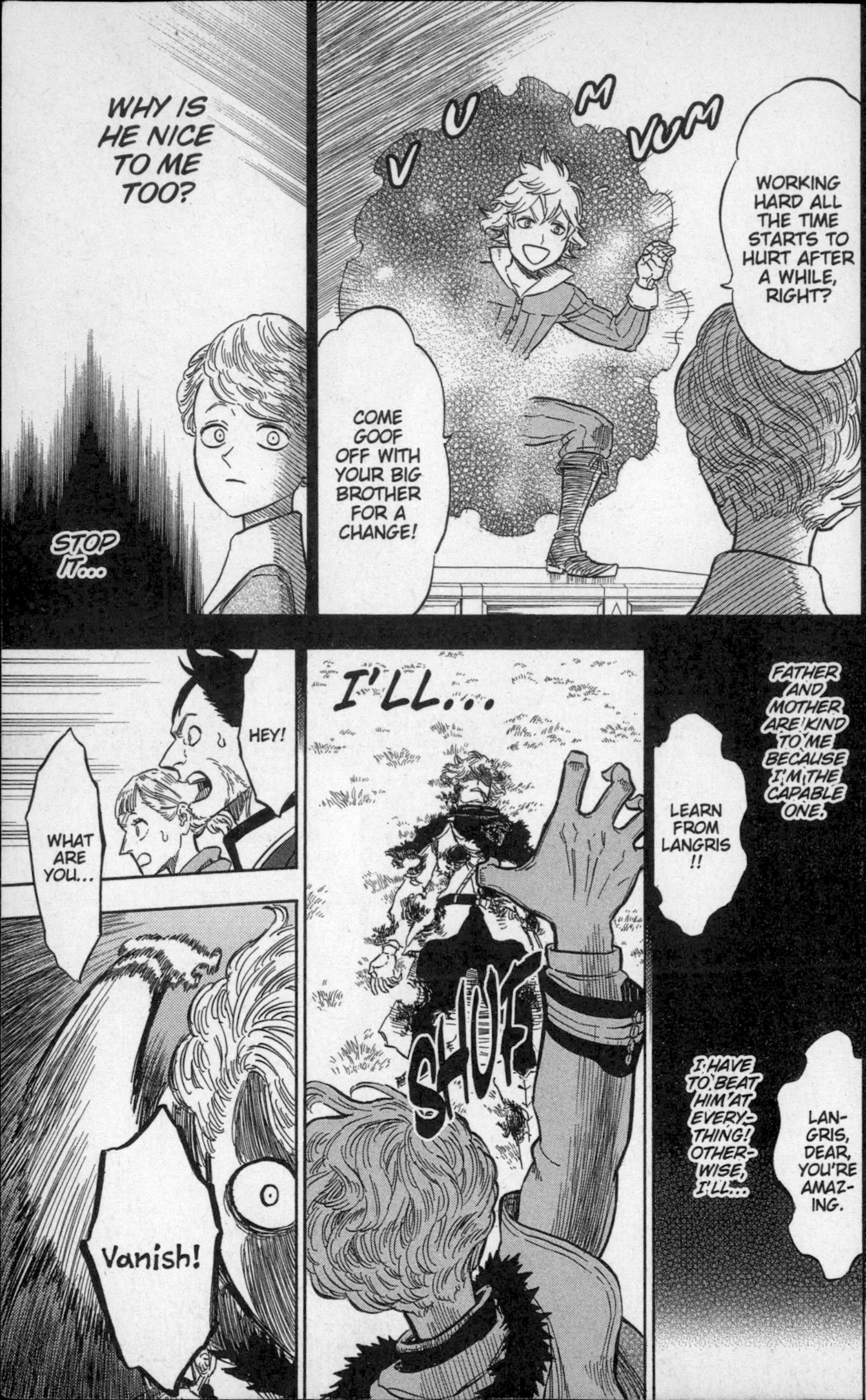
V U M
VUM
WORKING HARD ALL THE TIME STARTS TO HURT AFTER A WHILE, RIGHT?
COME GOOF OFF WITH YOUR BIG BROTHER FOR A CHANGE!
WHY IS HE NICE TO ME TOO?
STOP IT...
FATHER AND MOTHER ARE KIND TO ME BECAUSE I'M THE CAPABLE ONE.
LEARN FROM LANGRIS !!
LAN-GRIS, DEAR, YOU'RE AMAZ-ING.
I HAVE TO BEAT HIM AT EVERY-THING! OTHER-WISE, I'LL...
I'LL...
HEY!
WHAT ARE YOU...
Vanish!

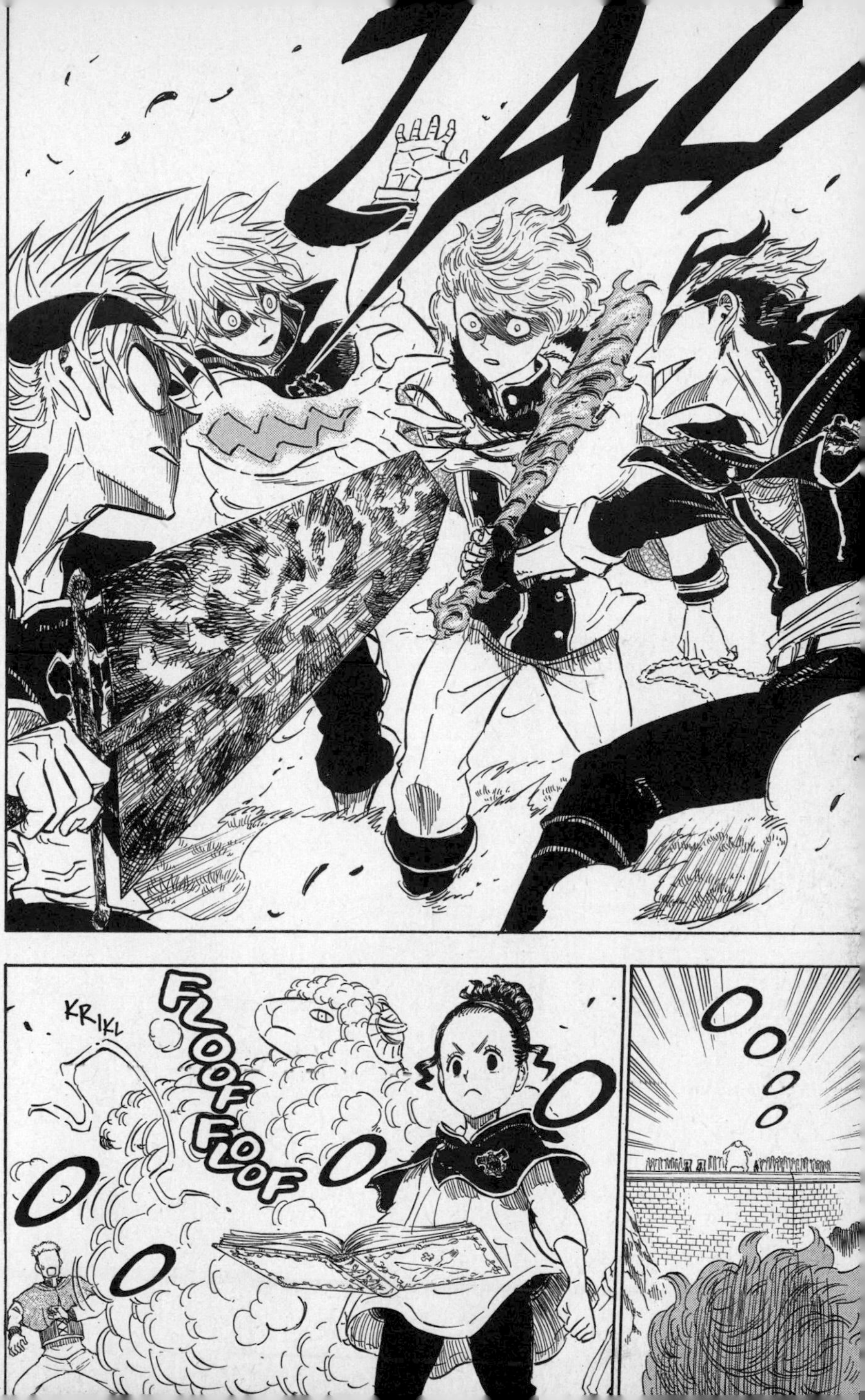
ZAH
OOOO
KRIKL
FLOOF FLOOF
OOOOO

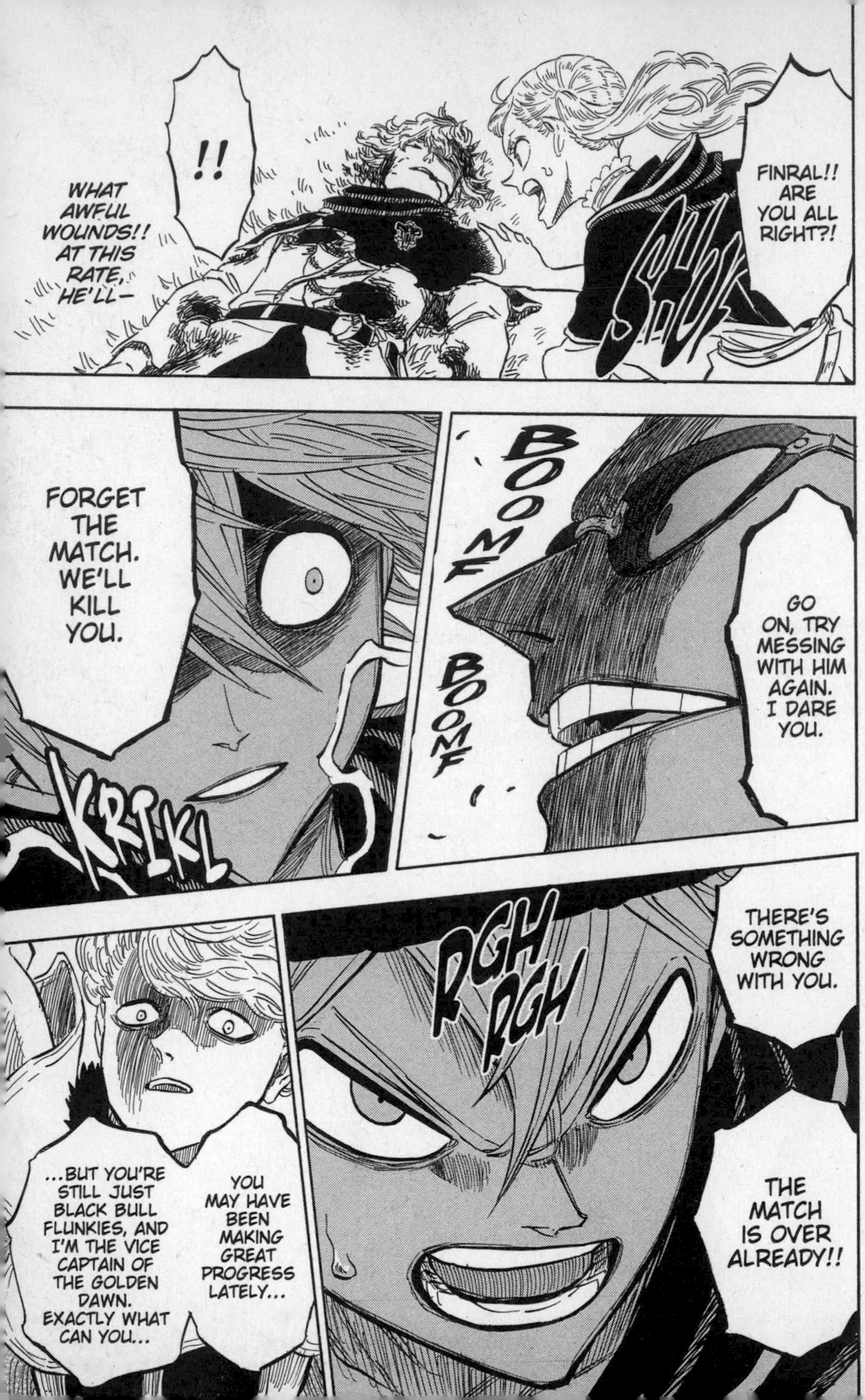
FINRAL!! ARE YOU ALL RIGHT?!
SHUK
!!
WHAT AWFUL WOUNDS!! AT THIS RATE, HE'LL—
BOOOMF
BOOOMF
GO ON, TRY MESSING WITH HIM AGAIN. I DARE YOU.
FORGET THE MATCH. WE'LL KILL YOU.
KRIKL
THERE'S SOMETHING WRONG WITH YOU.
RGH RGH
THE MATCH IS OVER ALREADY!!
YOU MAY HAVE BEEN MAKING GREAT PROGRESS LATELY...
...BUT YOU'RE STILL JUST BLACK BULL FLUNKIES, AND I'M THE VICE CAPTAIN OF THE GOLDEN DAWN. EXACTLY WHAT CAN YOU...

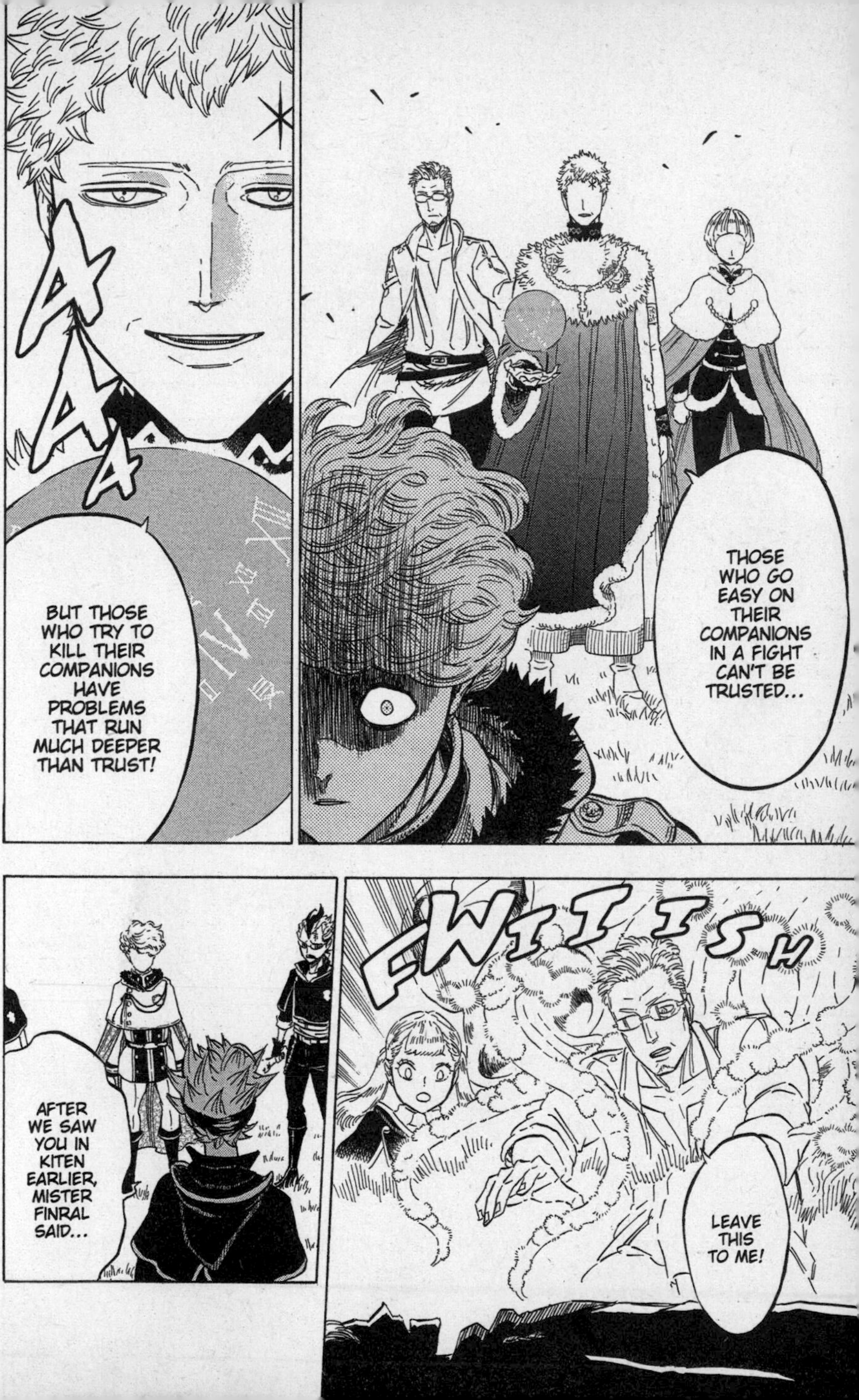
THOSE WHO GO EASY ON THEIR COMPANIONS IN A FIGHT CAN'T BE TRUSTED...
BUT THOSE WHO TRY TO KILL THEIR COMPANIONS HAVE PROBLEMS THAT RUN MUCH DEEPER THAN TRUST!
FWIIISH
LEAVE THIS TO ME!
AFTER WE SAW YOU IN KITEN EARLIER, MISTER FINRAL SAID...

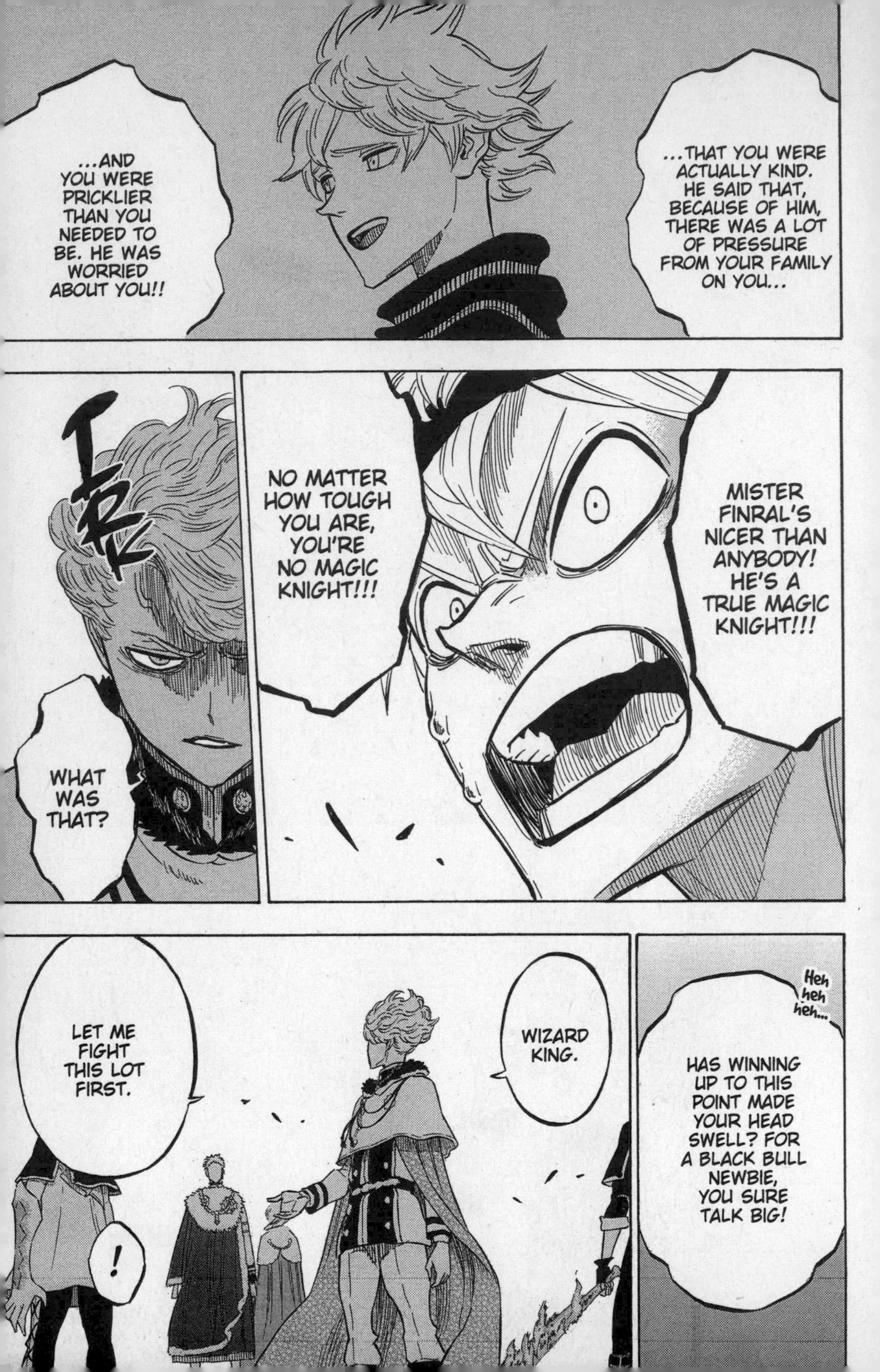
...THAT YOU WERE ACTUALLY KIND. HE SAID THAT, BECAUSE OF HIM, THERE WAS A LOT OF PRESSURE FROM YOUR FAMILY ON YOU...
...AND YOU WERE PRICKLIER THAN YOU NEEDED TO BE. HE WAS WORRIED ABOUT YOU!!
MISTER FINRAL'S NICER THAN ANYBODY! HE'S A TRUE MAGIC KNIGHT!!!
NO MATTER HOW TOUGH YOU ARE, YOU'RE NO MAGIC KNIGHT!!!
IRK
WHAT WAS THAT?
Heh heh heh...
HAS WINNING UP TO THIS POINT MADE YOUR HEAD SWELL? FOR A BLACK BULL NEWBIE, YOU SURE TALK BIG!
WIZARD KING.
LET ME FIGHT THIS LOT FIRST.
!

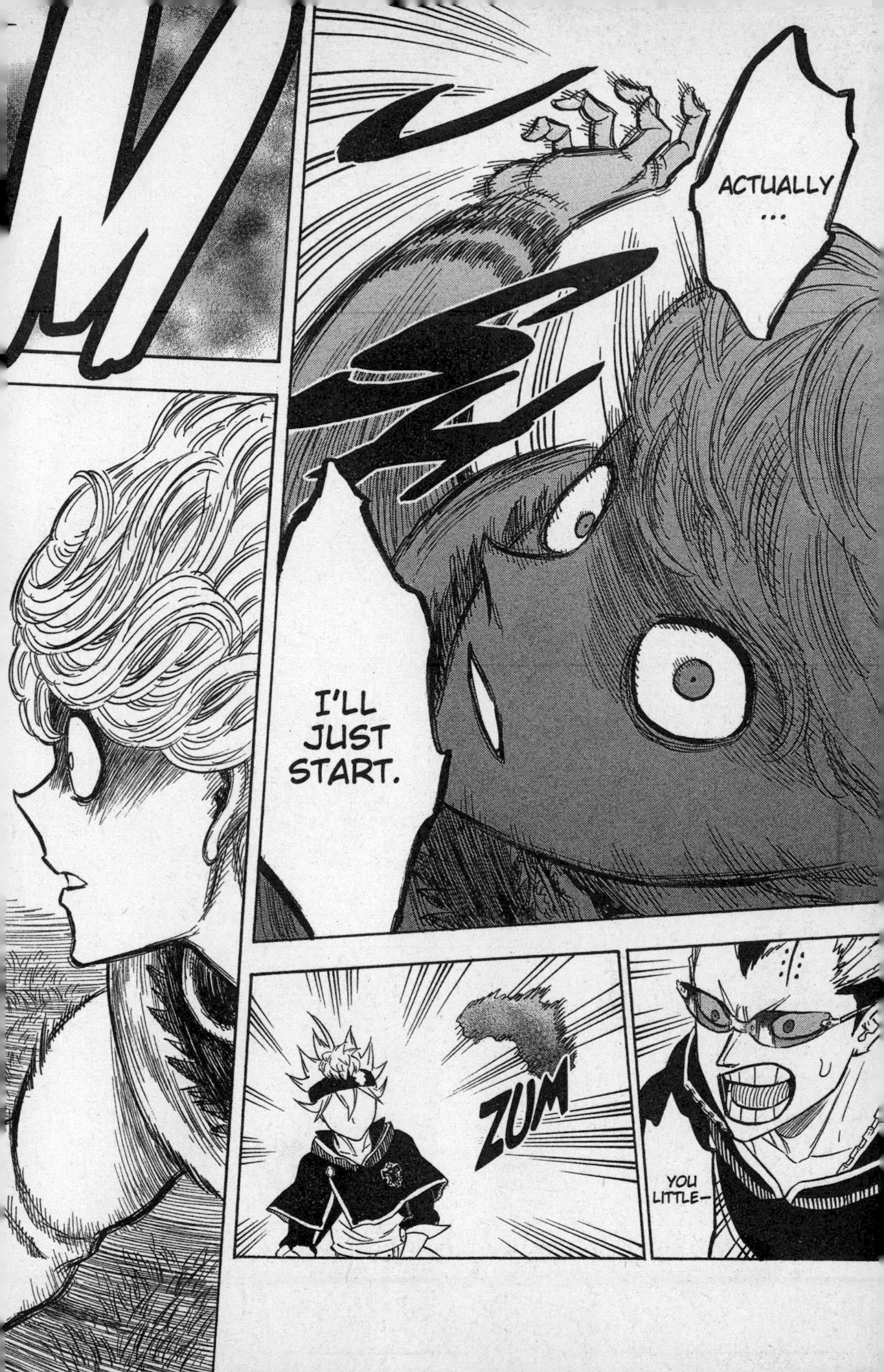
ACTUALLY ...
I'LL JUST START.
YOU LITTLE-
ZUM

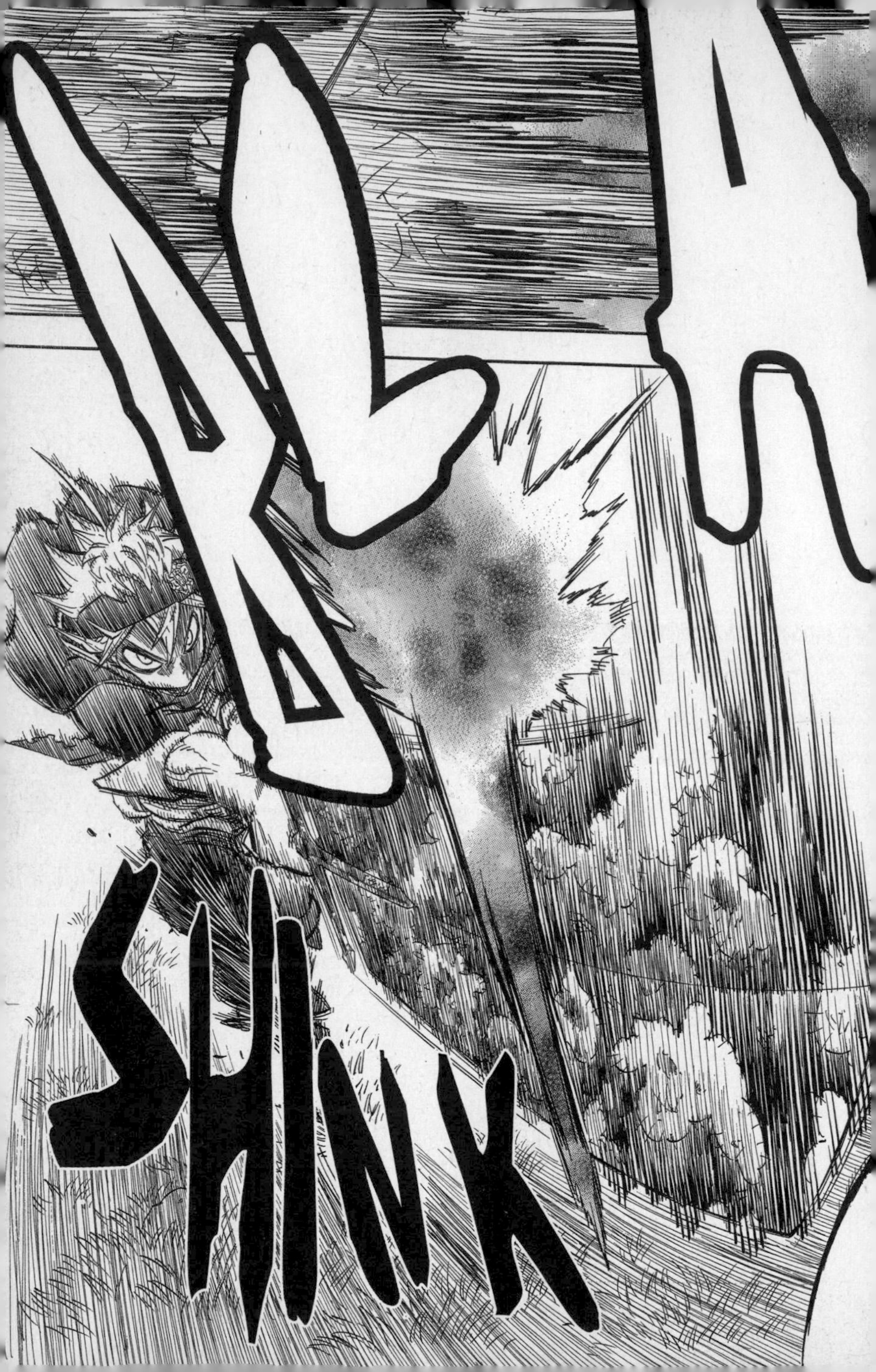
SHINK

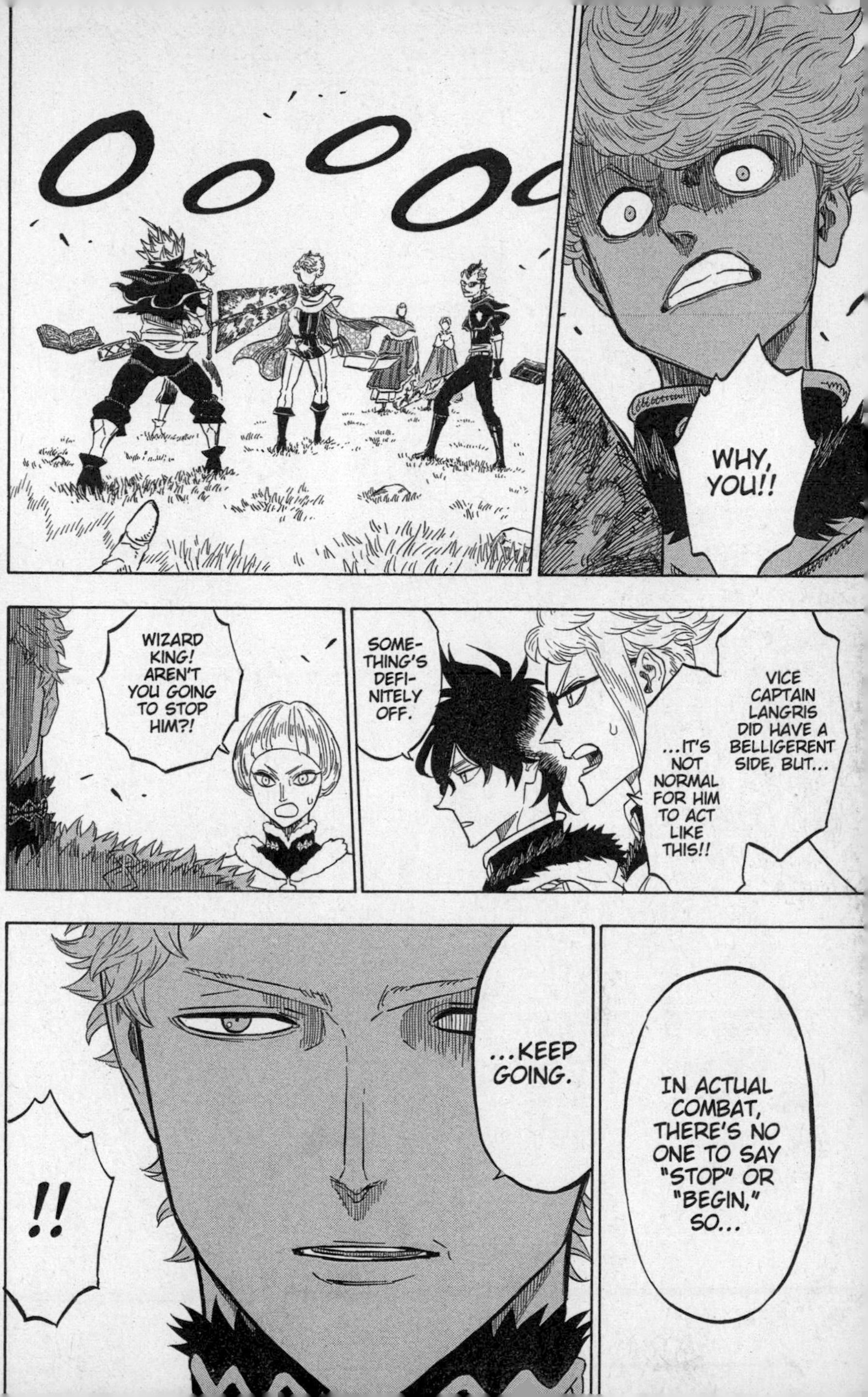
WHY, YOU!!
VICE CAPTAIN LANGRIS DID HAVE A BELLIGERENT SIDE, BUT...
...IT'S NOT NORMAL FOR HIM TO ACT LIKE THIS!!
SOME-THING'S DEFI-NITELY OFF.
WIZARD KING! AREN'T YOU GOING TO STOP HIM?!
IN ACTUAL COMBAT, THERE'S NO ONE TO SAY "STOP" OR "BEGIN," SO...
...KEEP GOING.
!!

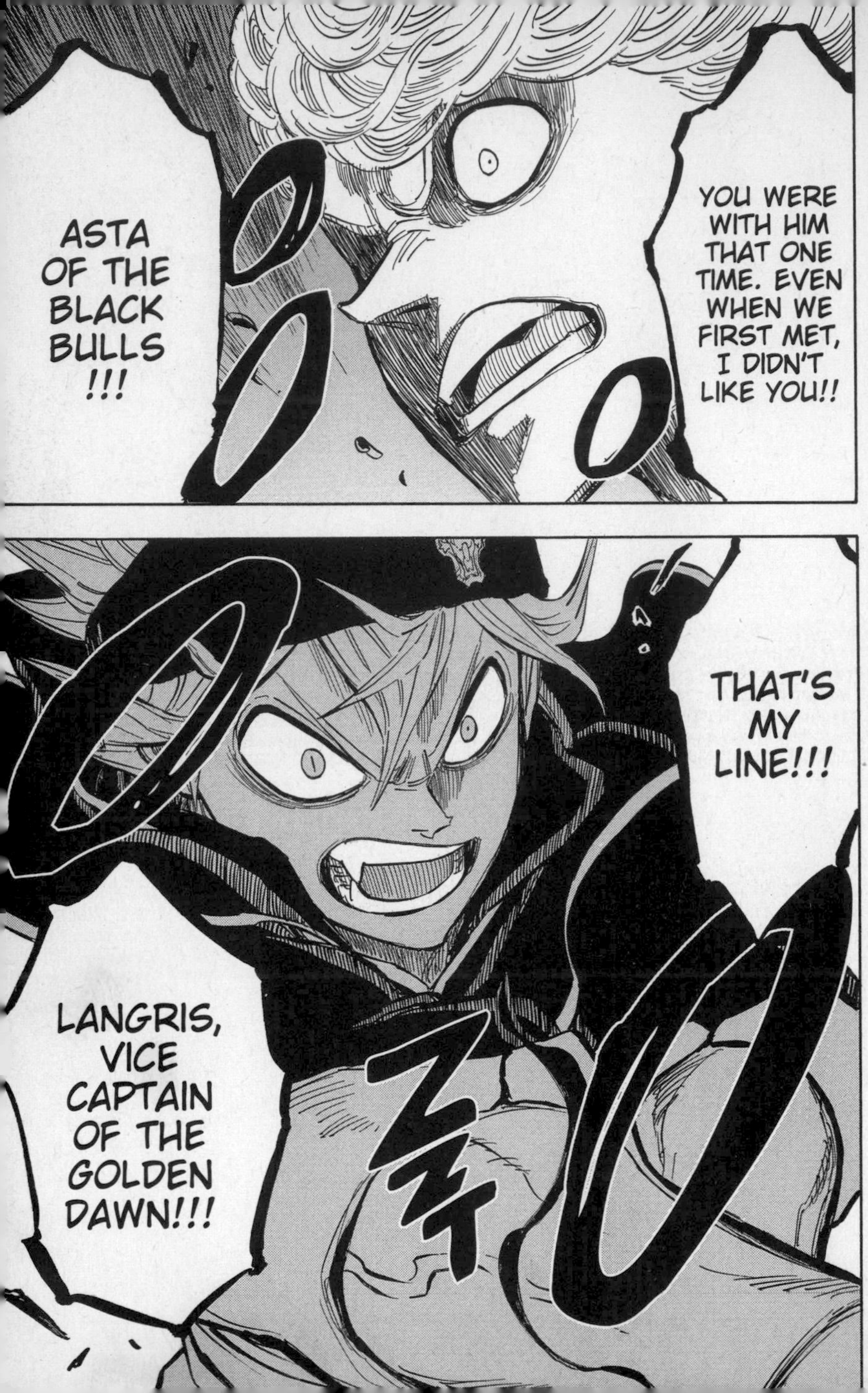
YOU WERE WITH HIM THAT ONE TIME. EVEN WHEN WE FIRST MET, I DIDN'T LIKE YOU!!
ASTA OF THE BLACK BULLS!!!
THAT'S MY LINE!!!
LANGRIS, VICE CAPTAIN OF THE GOLDEN DAWN!!!

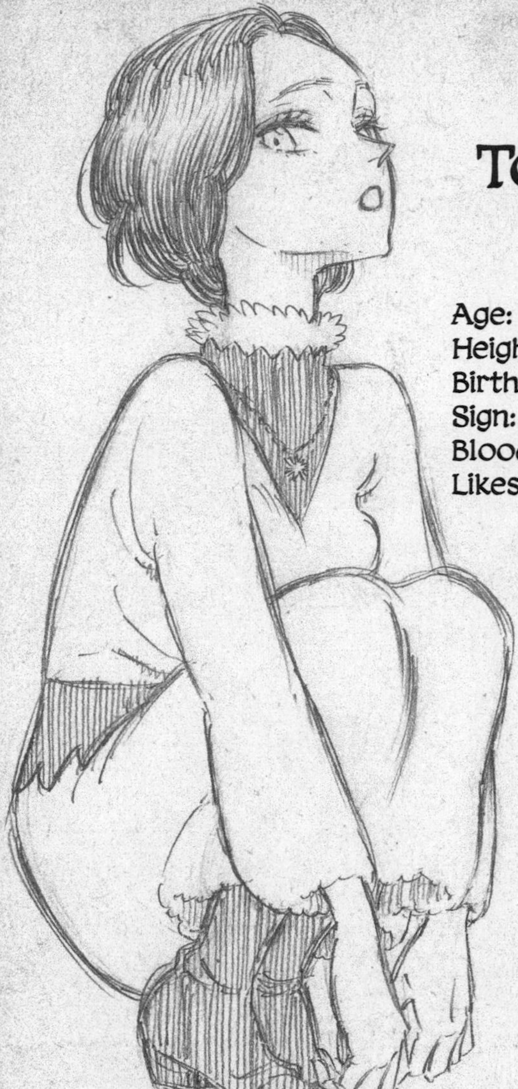

Fragil Tormenta

Age: 20
Height: 162 cm
Birthday: February 21
Sign: Pisces
Blood Type: A
Likes: Lemon sherbet, faithful people

C h a r a c t e r   P r o f i l e

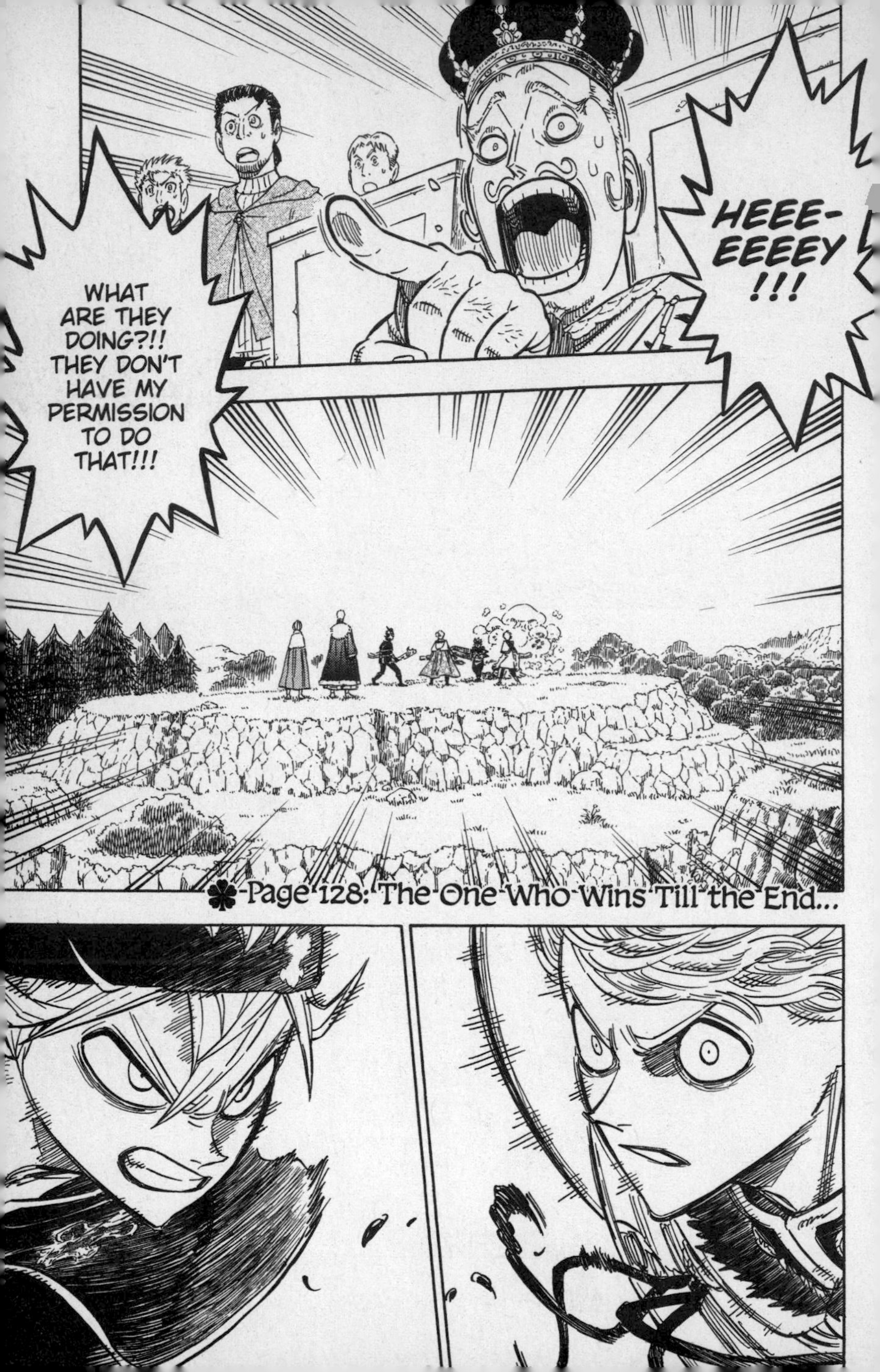
HEEEE-EEEEY!!!
WHAT ARE THEY DOING?!! THEY DON'T HAVE MY PERMISSION TO DO THAT!!!
Page 128: The One Who Wins Till the End...

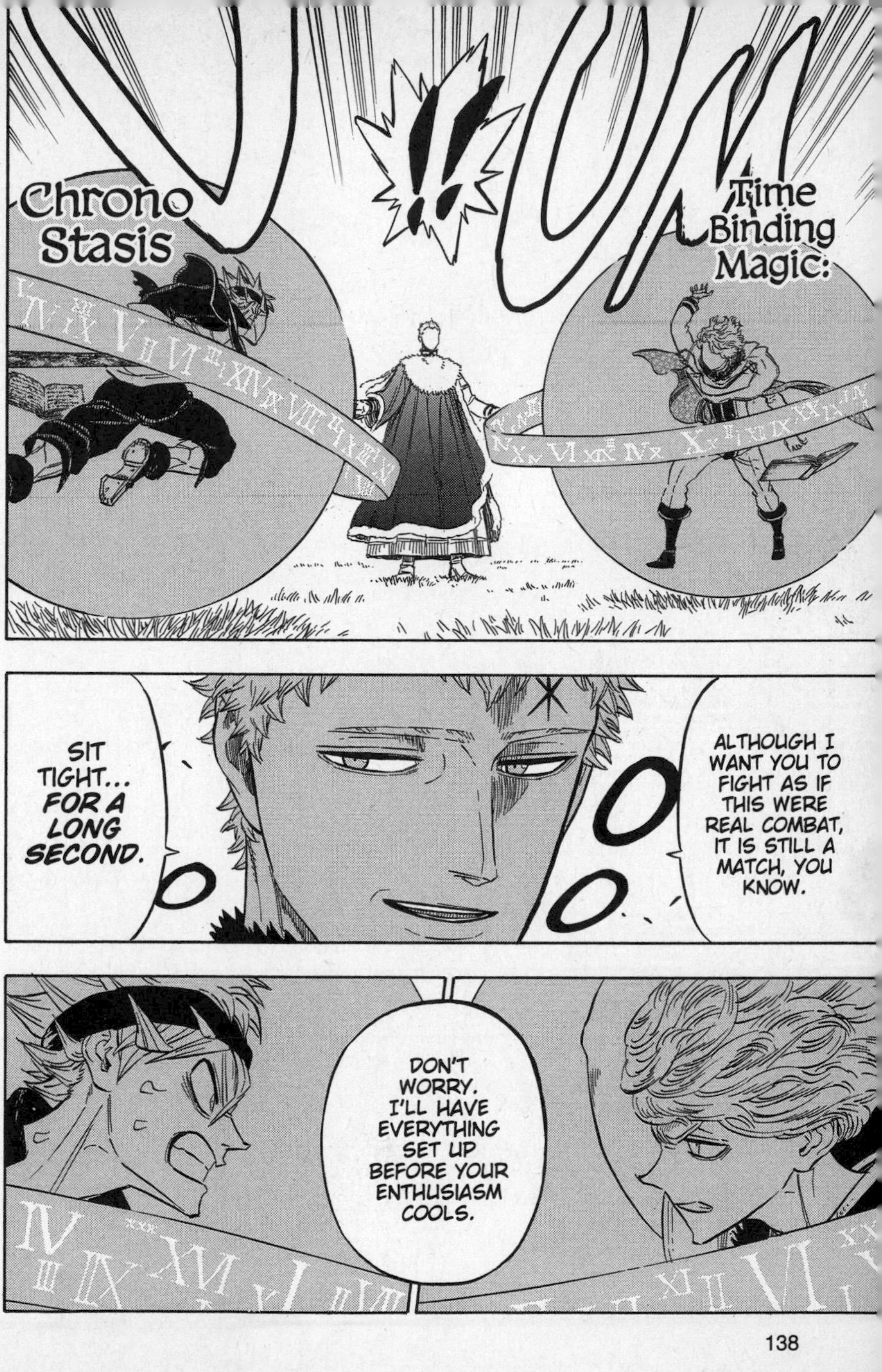
!!
Time Binding Magic:
Chrono Stasis
ALTHOUGH I WANT YOU TO FIGHT AS IF THIS WERE REAL COMBAT, IT IS STILL A MATCH, YOU KNOW.
SIT TIGHT... FOR A LONG SECOND.
DON'T WORRY. I'LL HAVE EVERYTHING SET UP BEFORE YOUR ENTHUSIASM COOLS.

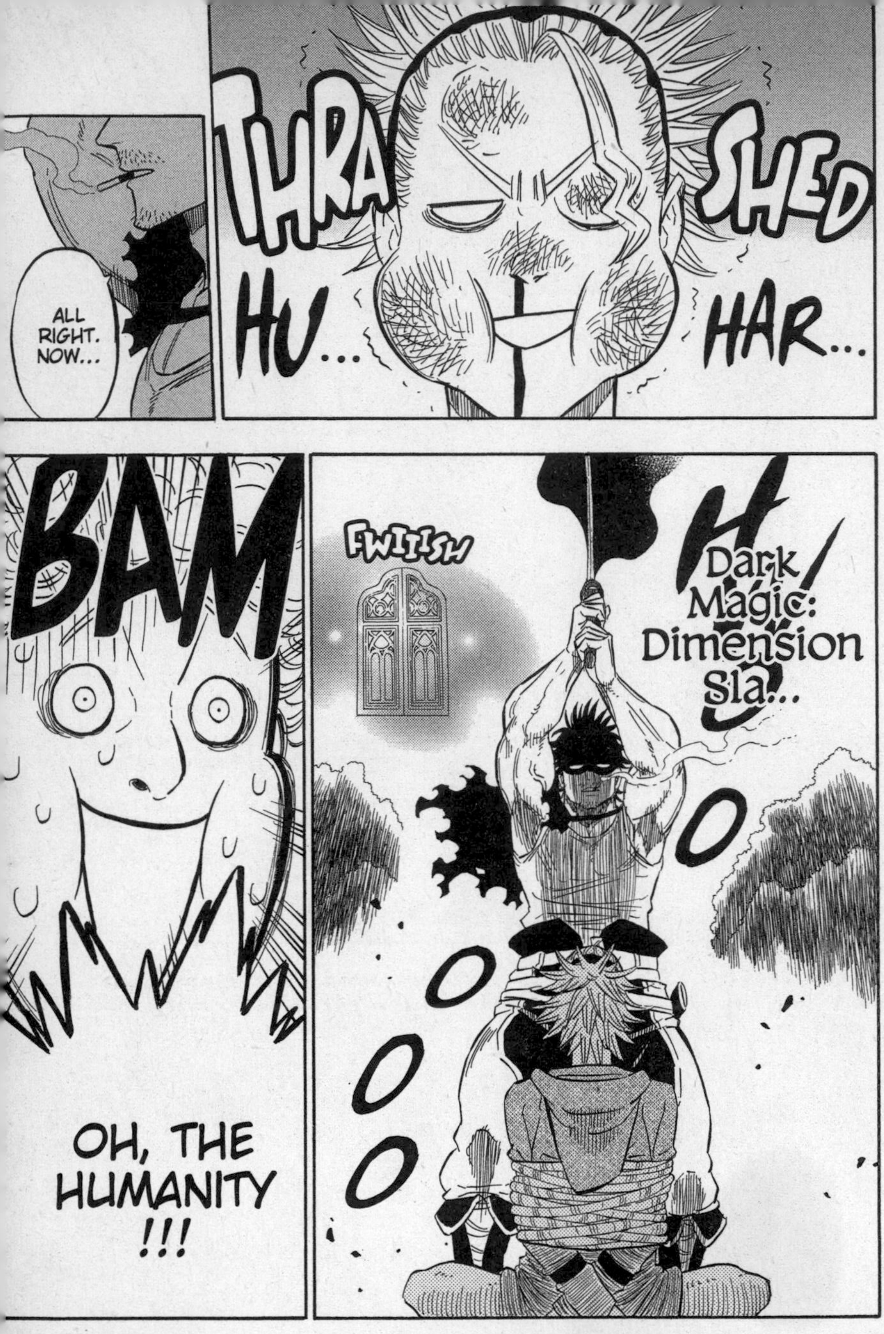
THRASHED
HU... HAR...
ALL RIGHT. NOW...
FWIISH
HOOOO!
Dark Magic: Dimension Sla...
BAM
OH, THE HUMANITY!!!

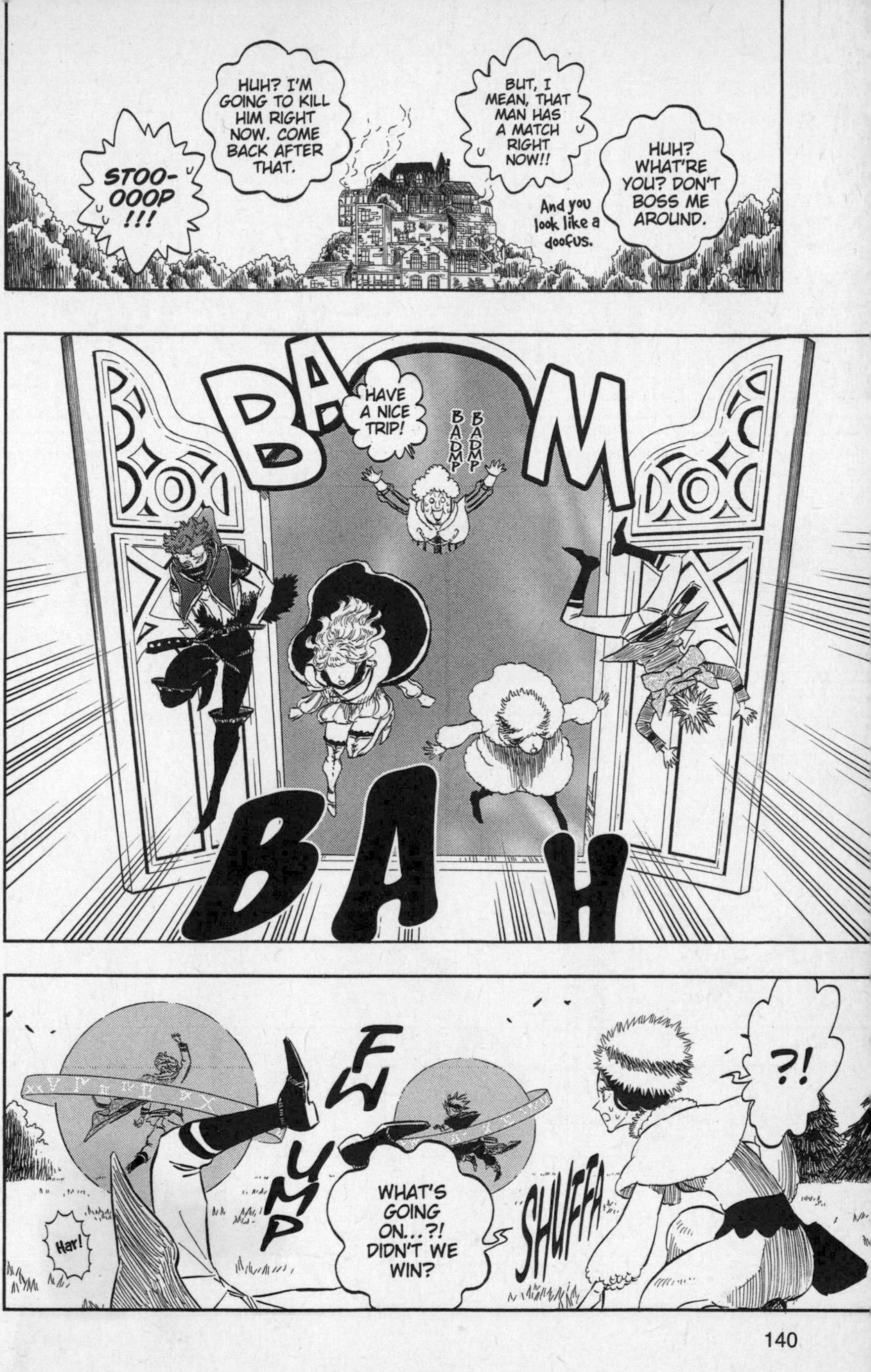
HUH? WHAT'RE YOU? DON'T BOSS ME AROUND.
BUT, I MEAN, THAT MAN HAS A MATCH RIGHT NOW!!
And you look like a doofus.
HUH? I'M GOING TO KILL HIM RIGHT NOW. COME BACK AFTER THAT.
STOO-OOOP!!!
BAM
BADMP BADMP
HAVE A NICE TRIP!
BAH
?!
SHUFFA
WHAT'S GOING ON...?! DIDN'T WE WIN?
FWUMP
Har!

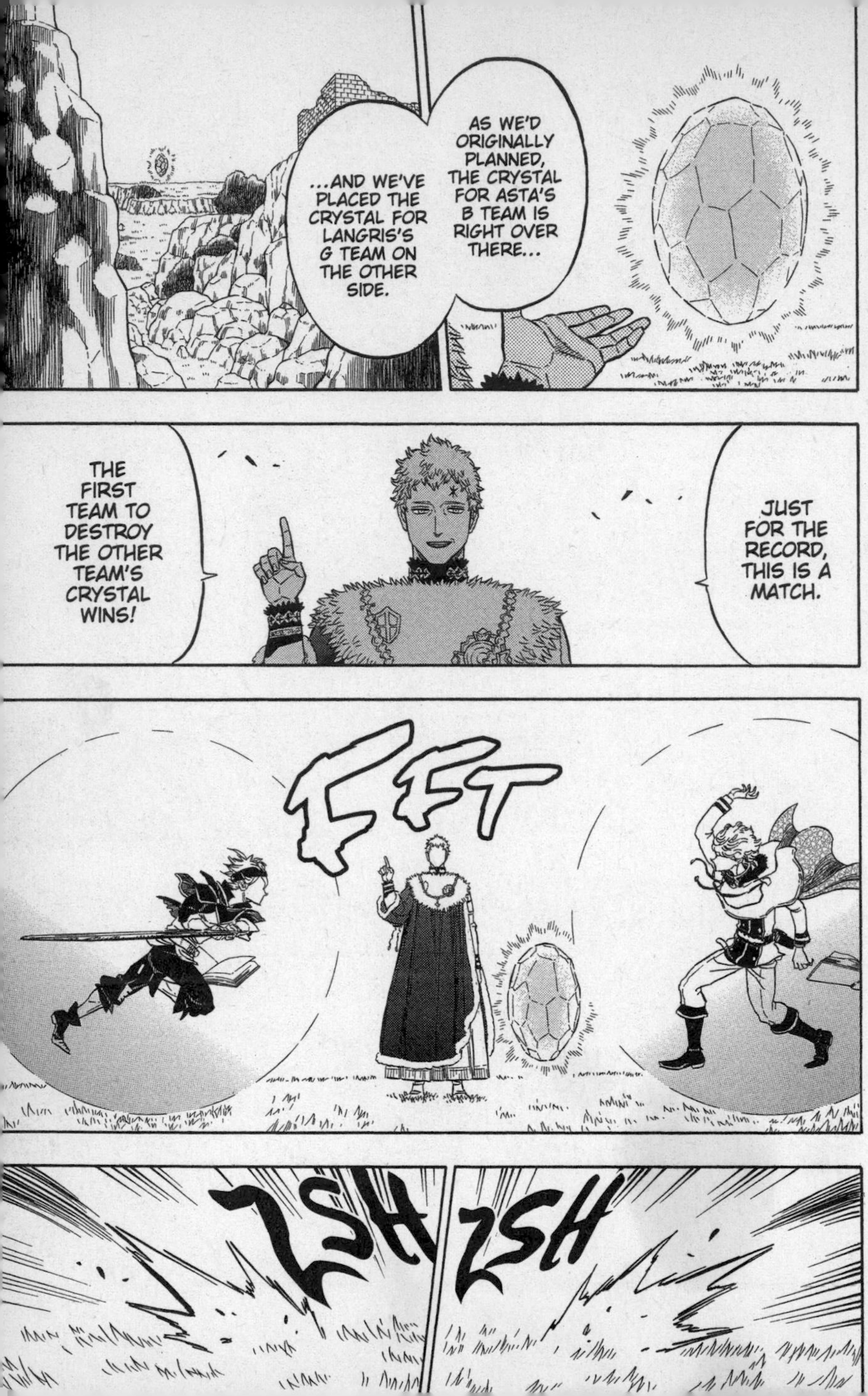
AS WE'D ORIGINALLY PLANNED, THE CRYSTAL FOR ASTA'S B TEAM IS RIGHT OVER THERE...
...AND WE'VE PLACED THE CRYSTAL FOR LANGRIS'S G TEAM ON THE OTHER SIDE.
JUST FOR THE RECORD, THIS IS A MATCH.
THE FIRST TEAM TO DESTROY THE OTHER TEAM'S CRYSTAL WINS!
FFT
ZSH
ZSH

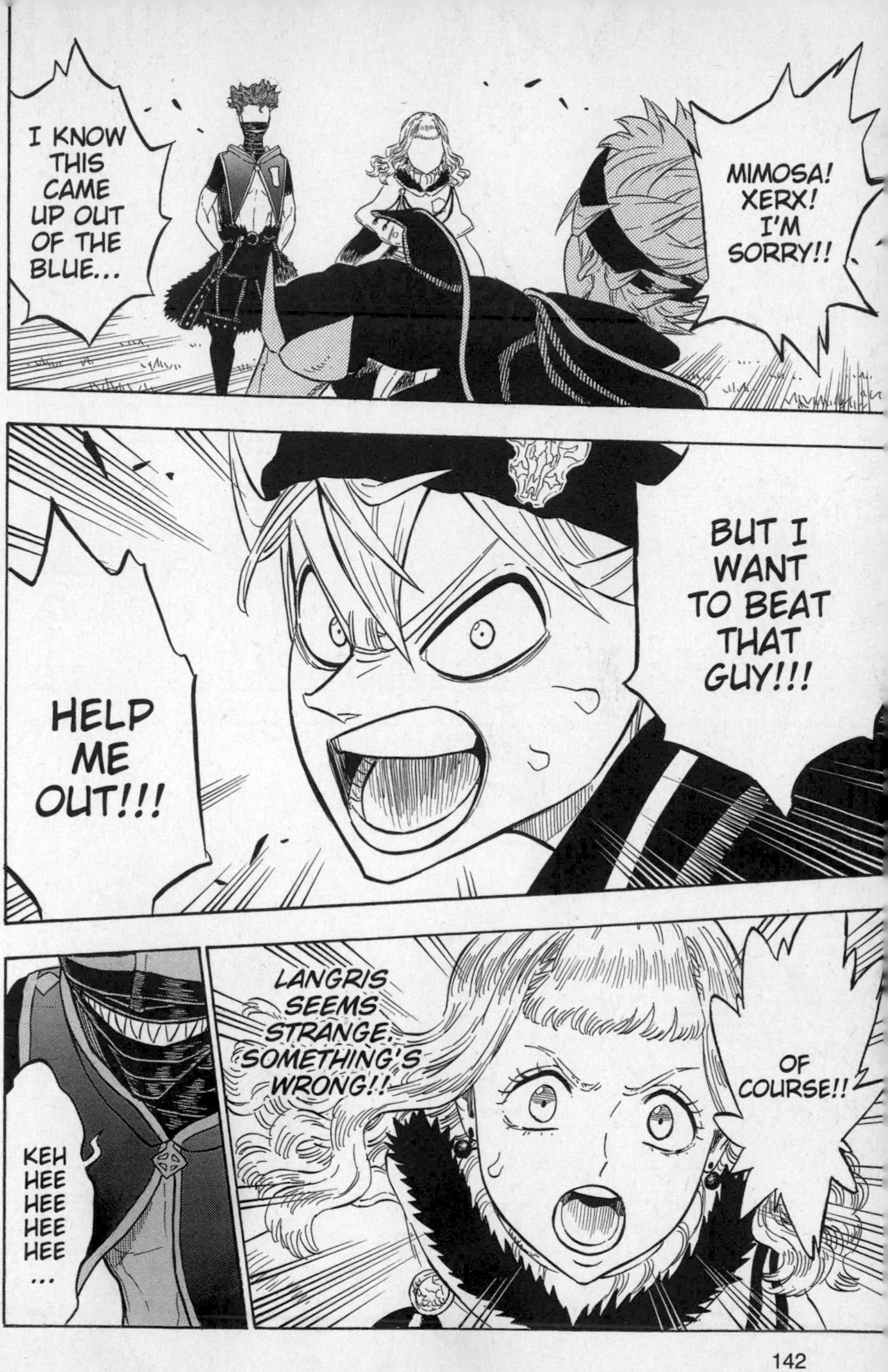
MIMOSA! XERX! I'M SORRY!!
I KNOW THIS CAME UP OUT OF THE BLUE...
BUT I WANT TO BEAT THAT GUY!!!
HELP ME OUT!!!
OF COURSE!!
LANGRIS SEEMS STRANGE. SOMETHING'S WRONG!!
KEH HEE HEE HEE HEE...

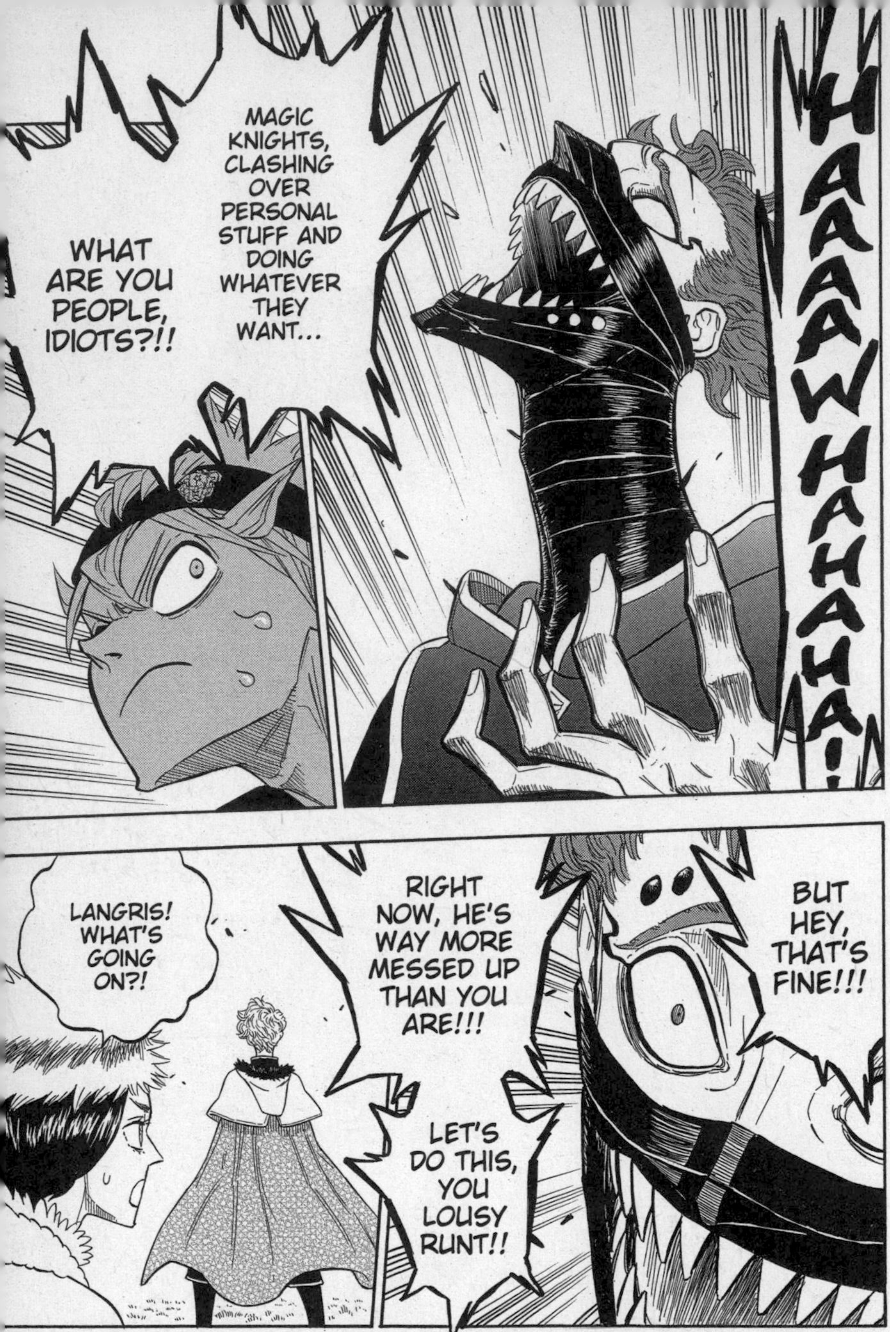
HAAAAWHAHAHAHA!
MAGIC KNIGHTS, CLASHING OVER PERSONAL STUFF AND DOING WHATEVER THEY WANT...
WHAT ARE YOU PEOPLE, IDIOTS?!!
BUT HEY, THAT'S FINE!!!
RIGHT NOW, HE'S WAY MORE MESSED UP THAN YOU ARE!!!
LET'S DO THIS, YOU LOUSY RUNT!!
LANGRIS! WHAT'S GOING ON?!

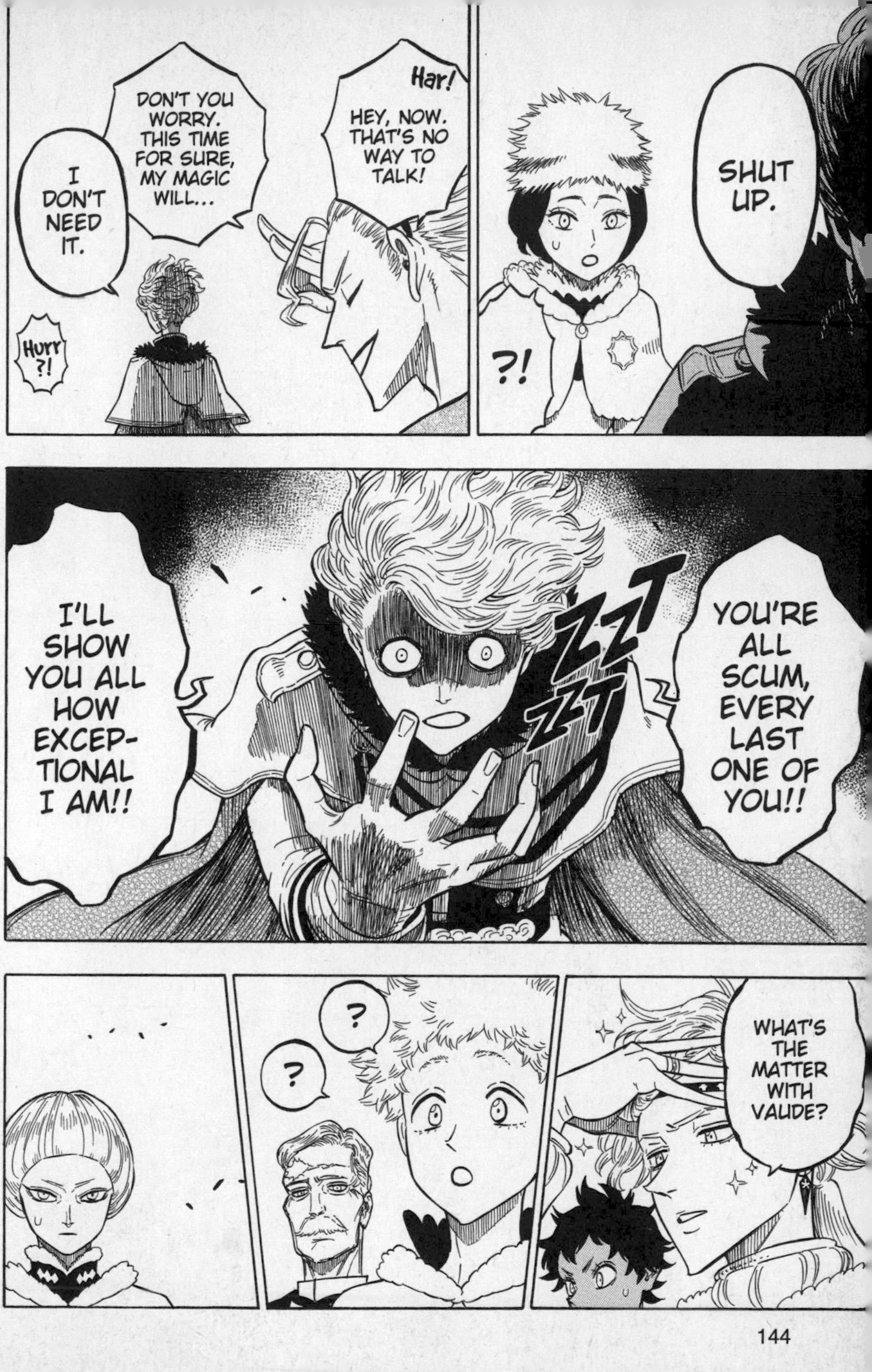
SHUT UP.
?!
Har!
HEY, NOW. THAT'S NO WAY TO TALK!
DON'T YOU WORRY. THIS TIME FOR SURE, MY MAGIC WILL...
I DON'T NEED IT.
Hurr ?!
YOU'RE ALL SCUM, EVERY LAST ONE OF YOU!!
ZZZT
ZZT
I'LL SHOW YOU ALL HOW EXCEP-TIONAL I AM!!
WHAT'S THE MATTER WITH VAUDE?
?
?
...
...

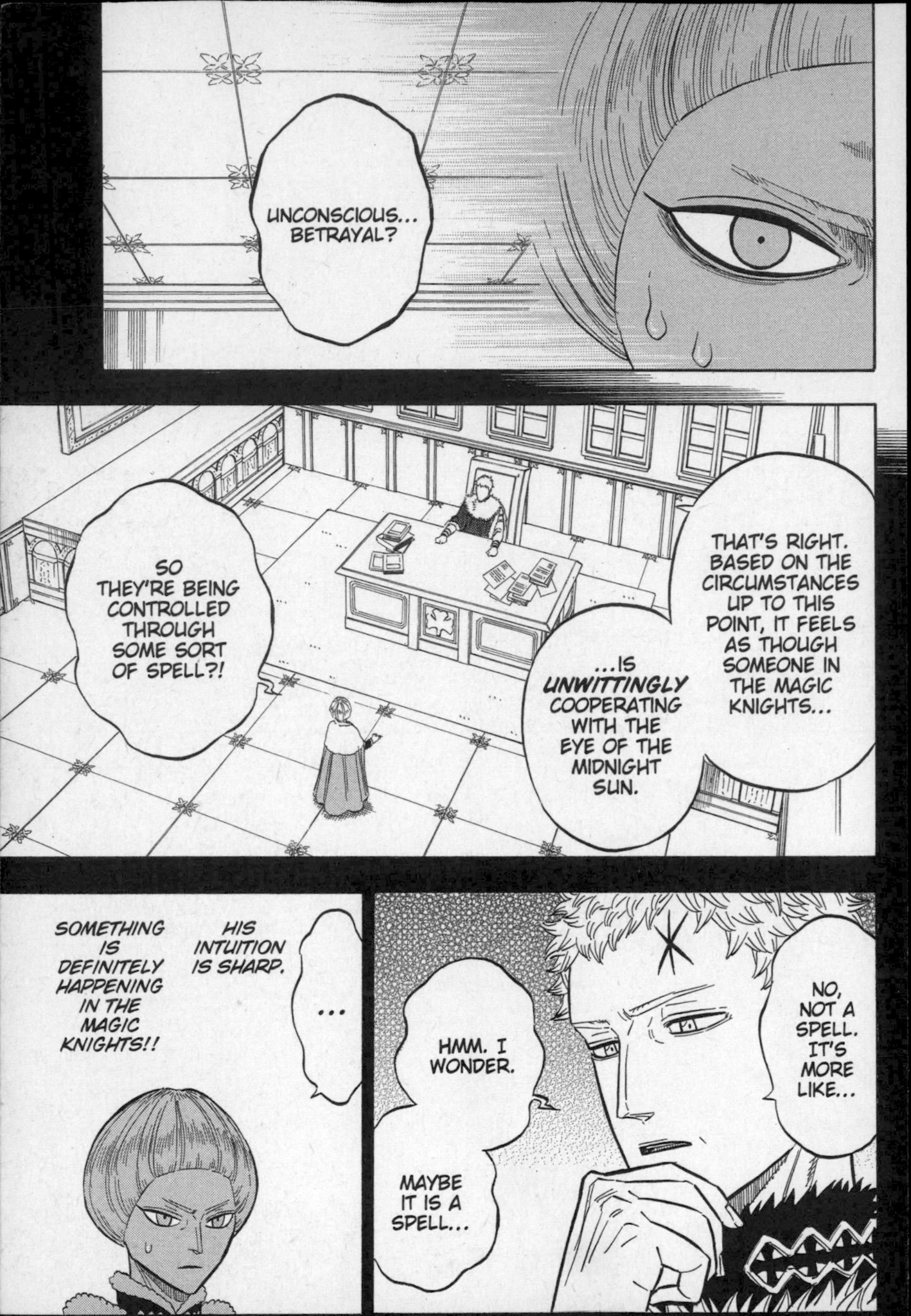
UNCONSCIOUS... BETRAYAL?
THAT'S RIGHT. BASED ON THE CIRCUMSTANCES UP TO THIS POINT, IT FEELS AS THOUGH SOMEONE IN THE MAGIC KNIGHTS...
...IS *UNWITTINGLY* COOPERATING WITH THE EYE OF THE MIDNIGHT SUN.
SO THEY'RE BEING CONTROLLED THROUGH SOME SORT OF SPELL?!
NO, NOT A SPELL. IT'S MORE LIKE...
HMM. I WONDER.
MAYBE IT IS A SPELL...
...
HIS INTUITION IS SHARP.
SOMETHING IS DEFINITELY HAPPENING IN THE MAGIC KNIGHTS!!

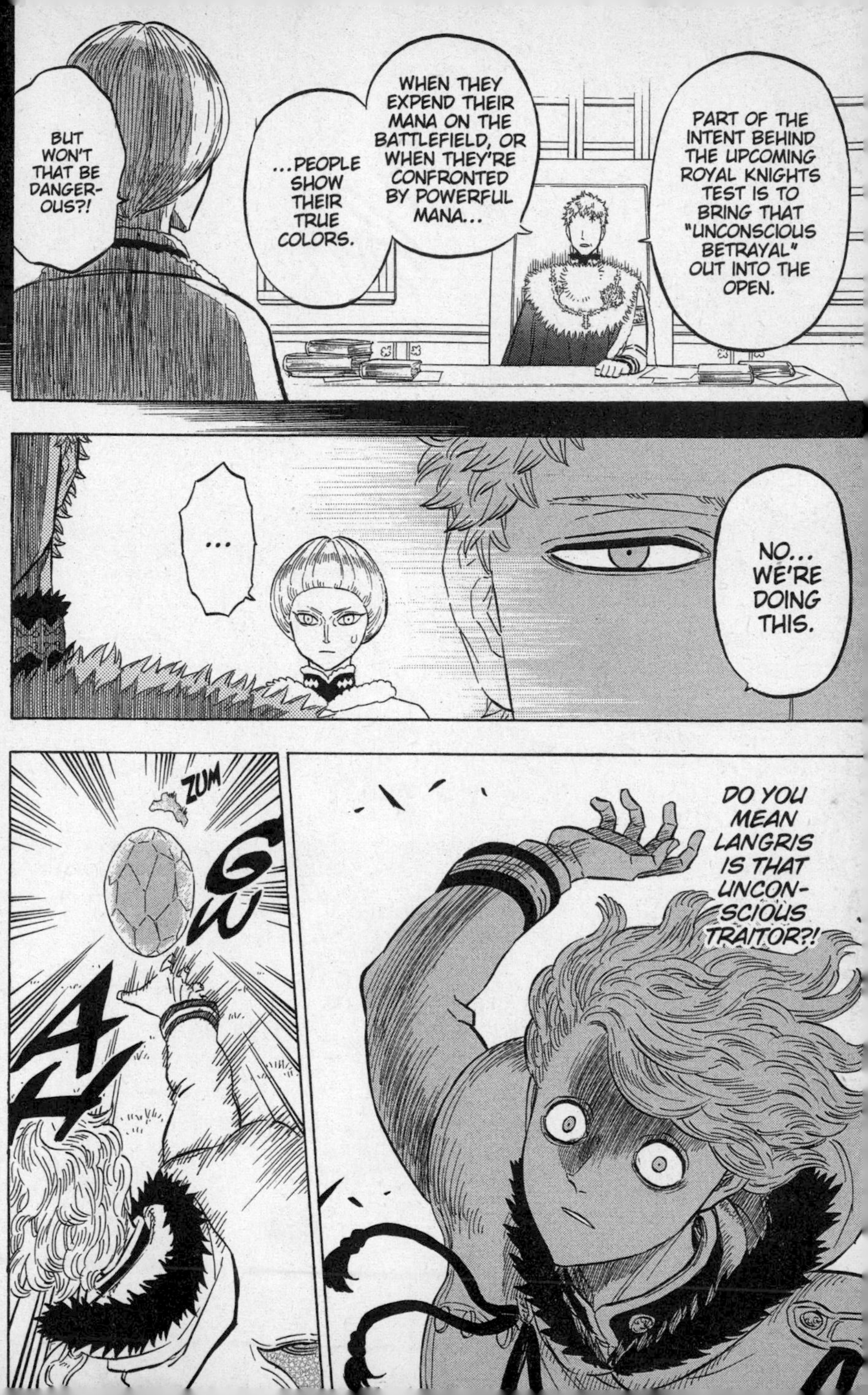
PART OF THE INTENT BEHIND THE UPCOMING ROYAL KNIGHTS TEST IS TO BRING THAT "UNCONSCIOUS BETRAYAL" OUT INTO THE OPEN.
WHEN THEY EXPEND THEIR MANA ON THE BATTLEFIELD, OR WHEN THEY'RE CONFRONTED BY POWERFUL MANA...
...PEOPLE SHOW THEIR TRUE COLORS.
BUT WON'T THAT BE DANGER-OUS?!
NO... WE'RE DOING THIS.
...
DO YOU MEAN LANGRIS IS THAT UNCON-SCIOUS TRAITOR?!
ZUM

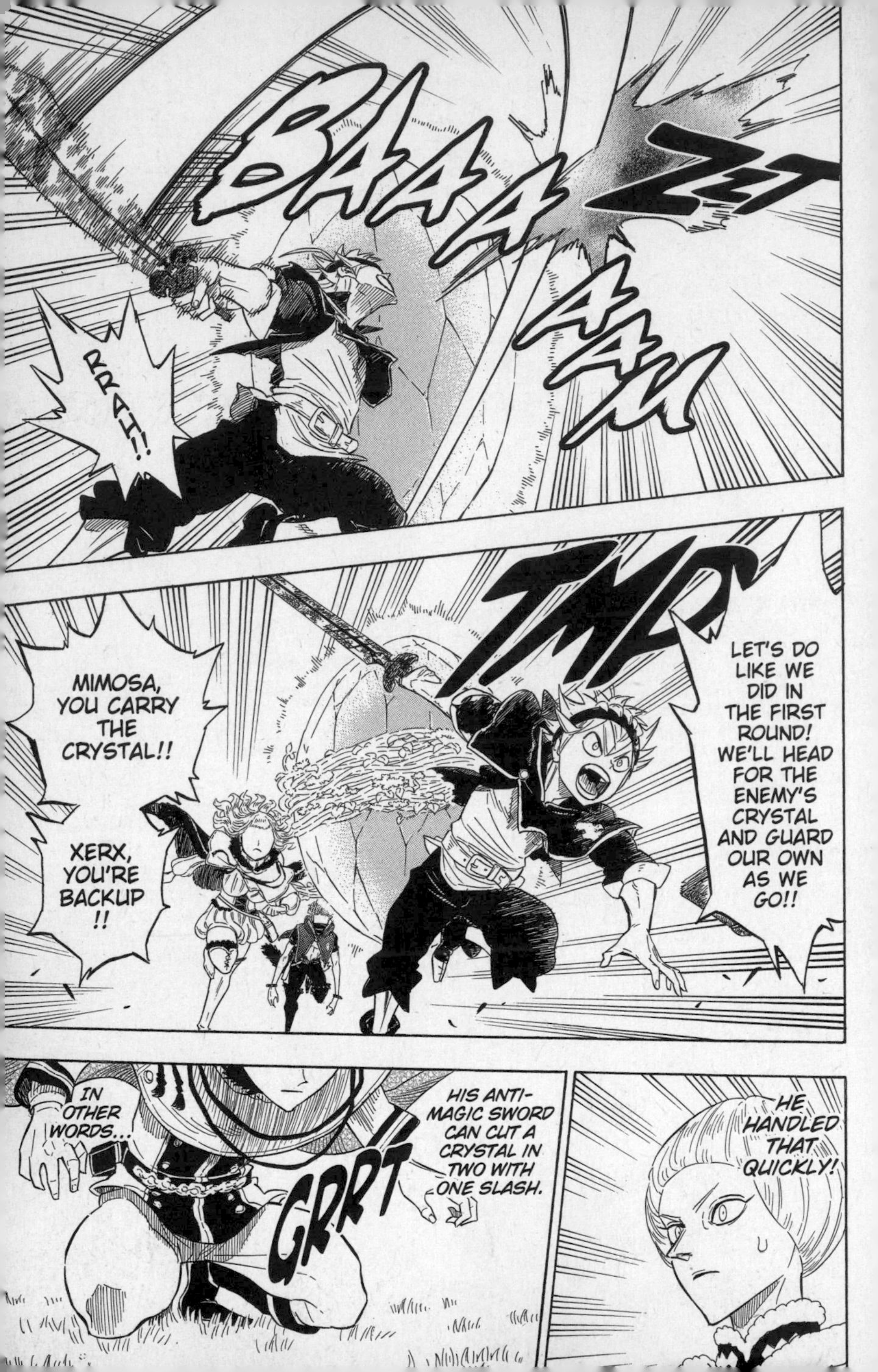
ZZT
BAAAAAAM
RRAH!!
LET'S DO LIKE WE DID IN THE FIRST ROUND! WE'LL HEAD FOR THE ENEMY'S CRYSTAL AND GUARD OUR OWN AS WE GO!!
TMP
MIMOSA, YOU CARRY THE CRYSTAL!!
XERX, YOU'RE BACKUP!!
HE HANDLED THAT QUICKLY!
IN OTHER WORDS...
HIS ANTI-MAGIC SWORD CAN CUT A CRYSTAL IN TWO WITH ONE SLASH.
GRRT

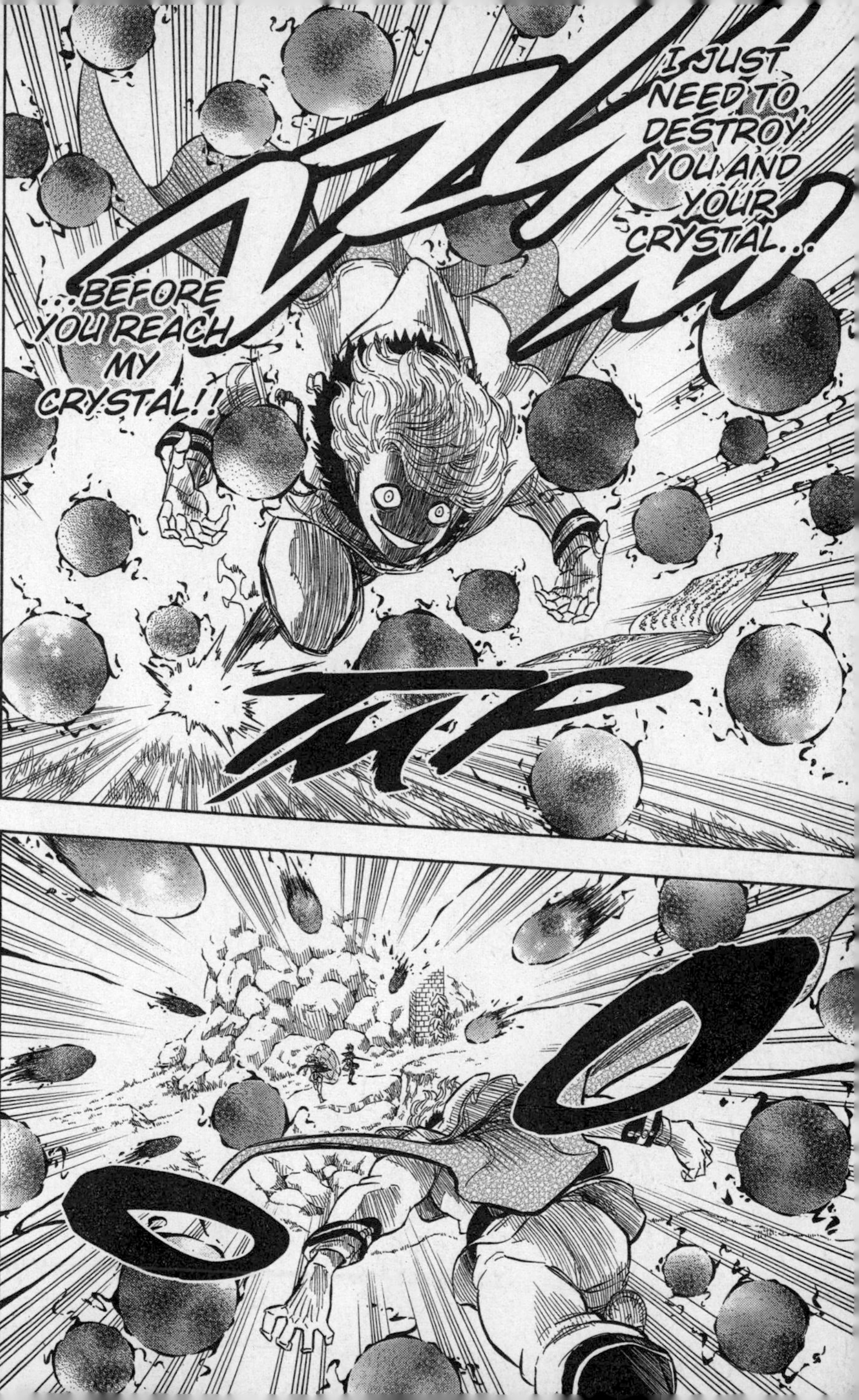
I JUST NEED TO DESTROY YOU AND YOUR CRYSTAL...
...BEFORE YOU REACH MY CRYSTAL!!
TAP

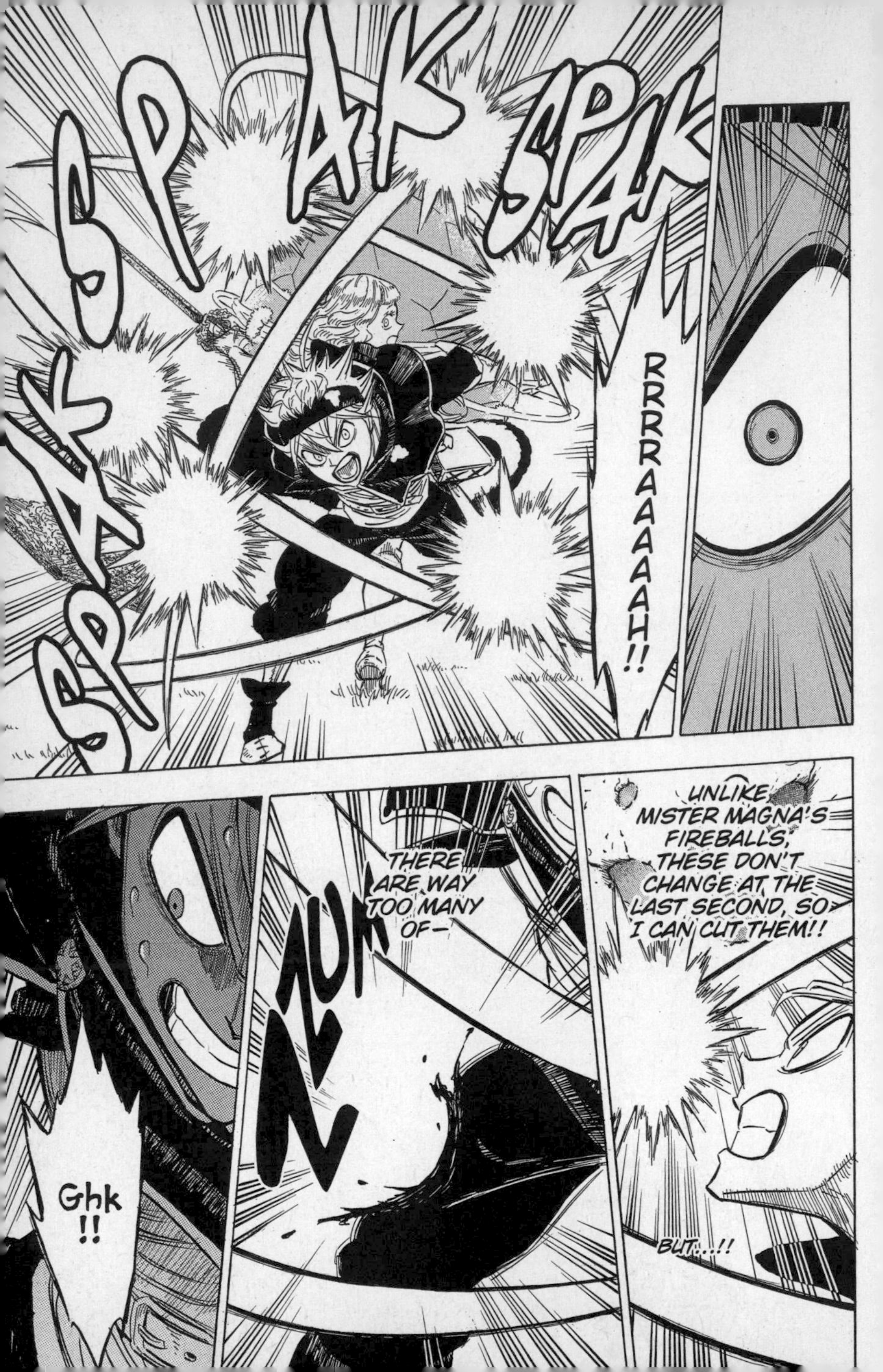
SPAK
SPAK
RRRRAAAAAAH!!
SPAK
UNLIKE MISTER MAGNA'S FIREBALLS, THESE DON'T CHANGE AT THE LAST SECOND, SO I CAN CUT THEM!!
BUT...!!
THERE ARE WAY TOO MANY OF—
ZUM
Ghk!!

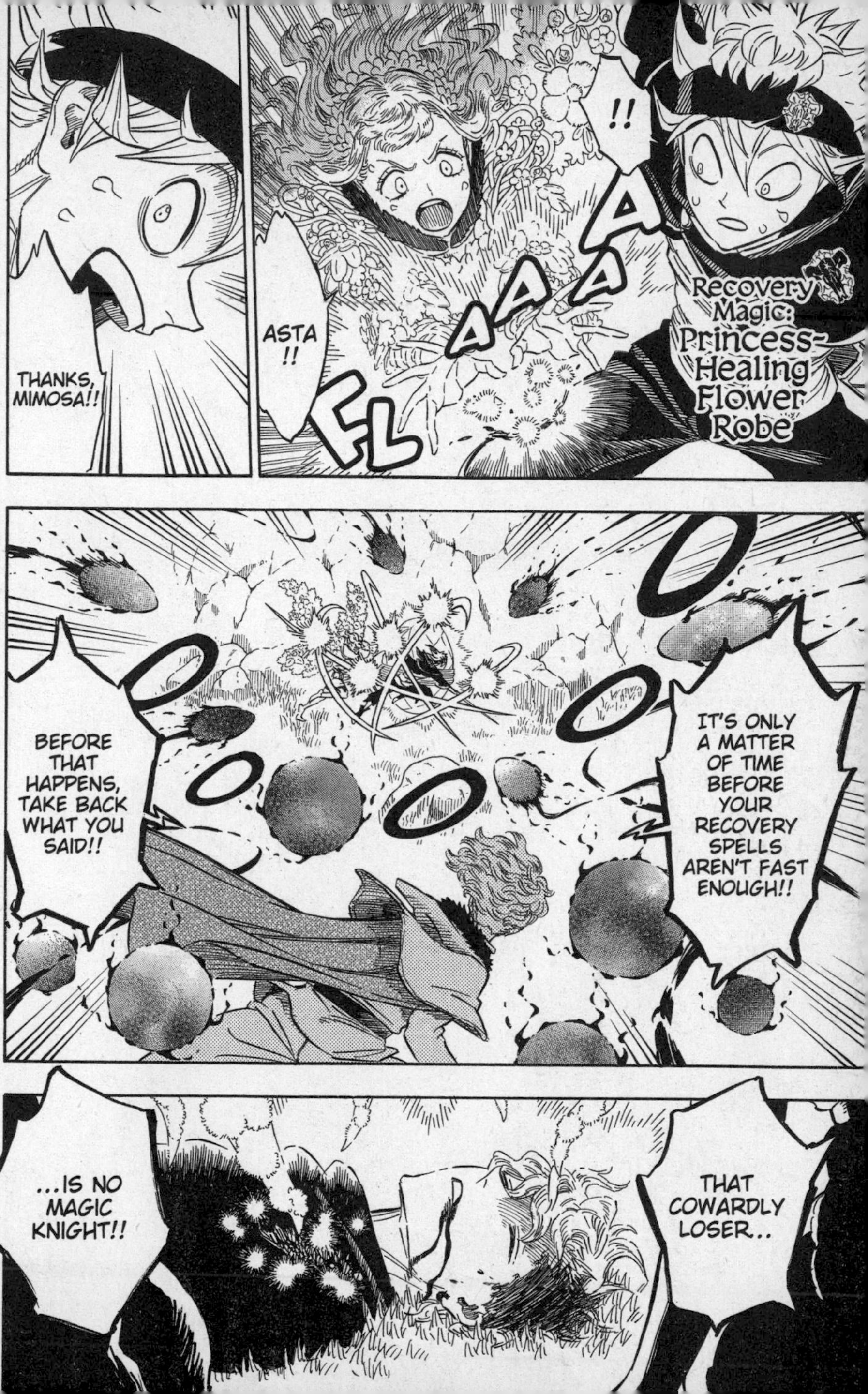
!!
Recovery Magic: Princess-Healing Flower Robe
FLAAAAA
ASTA !!
THANKS, MIMOSA!!
OOOOOO
IT'S ONLY A MATTER OF TIME BEFORE YOUR RECOVERY SPELLS AREN'T FAST ENOUGH!!
BEFORE THAT HAPPENS, TAKE BACK WHAT YOU SAID!!
THAT COWARDLY LOSER...
...IS NO MAGIC KNIGHT!!

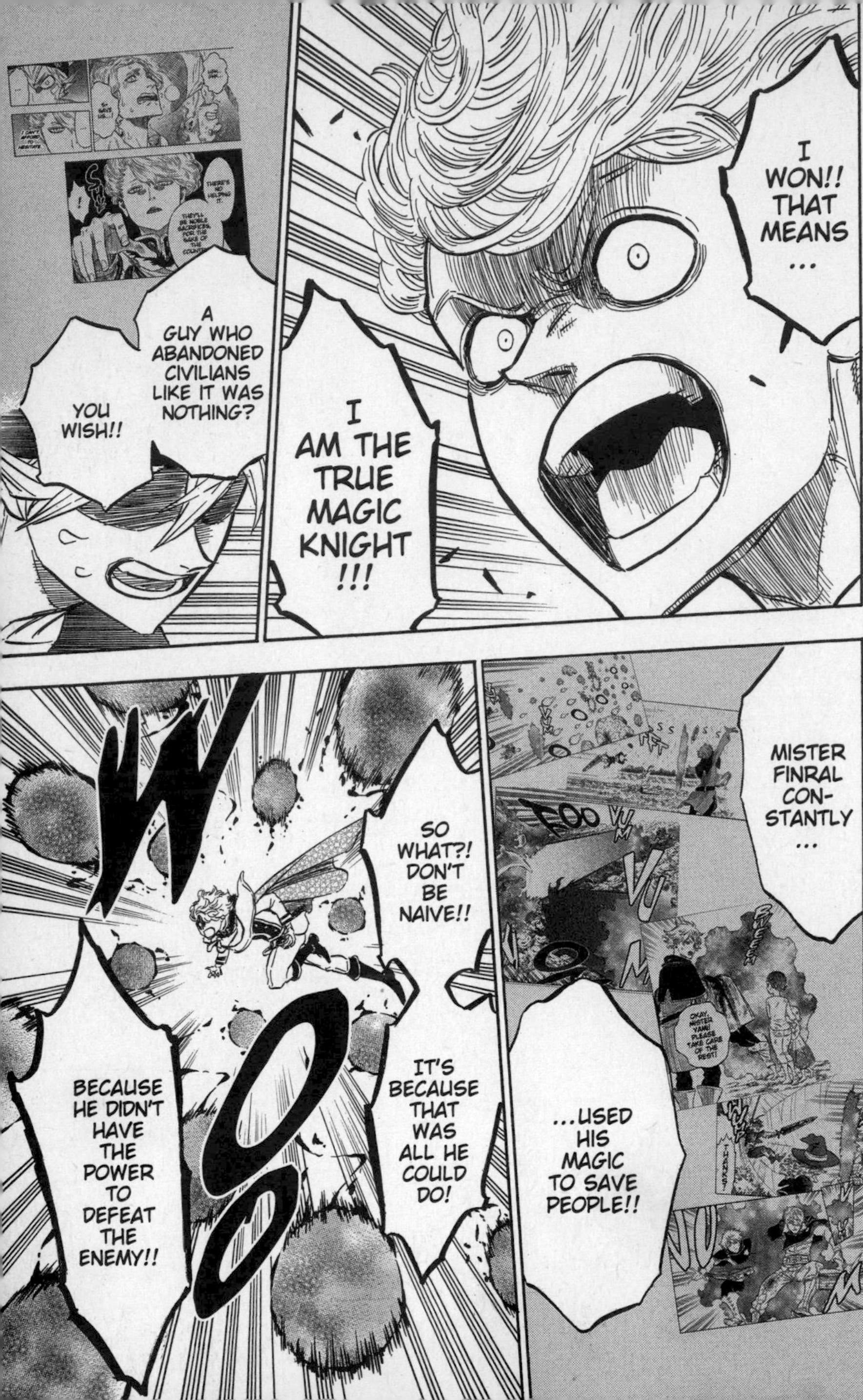
I WON!! THAT MEANS ...
I AM THE TRUE MAGIC KNIGHT !!!
A GUY WHO ABANDONED CIVILIANS LIKE IT WAS NOTHING?
YOU WISH!!
MISTER FINRAL CON-STANTLY ...
...USED HIS MAGIC TO SAVE PEOPLE!!
SO WHAT?! DON'T BE NAIVE!!
IT'S BECAUSE THAT WAS ALL HE COULD DO!
BECAUSE HE DIDN'T HAVE THE POWER TO DEFEAT THE ENEMY!!

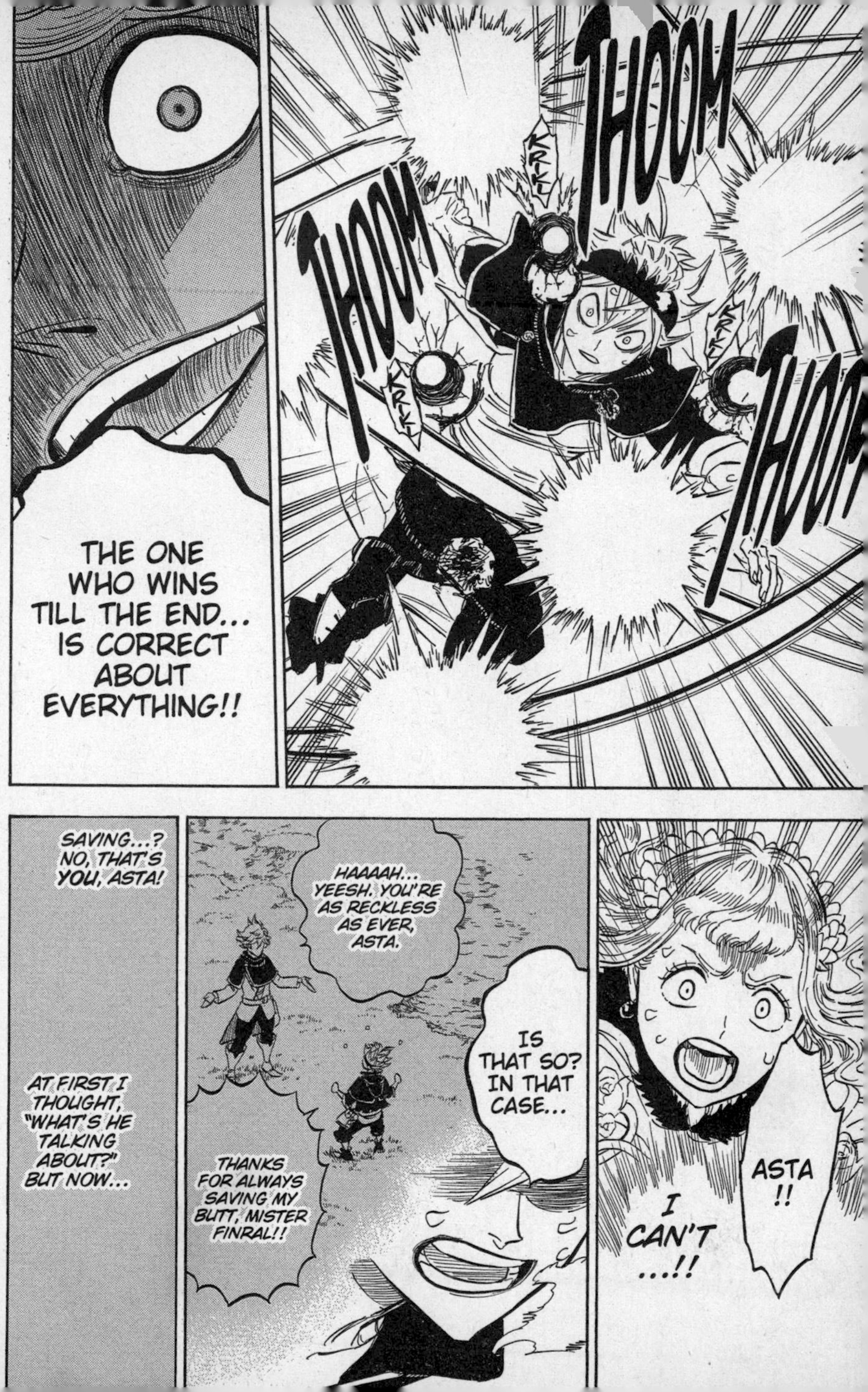
THOOM
KRIK
THOOM
KRIK
THOOM
KRIK
THOO
THE ONE WHO WINS TILL THE END... IS CORRECT ABOUT EVERYTHING!!
ASTA!!
I CAN'T...!!
HAAAAH... YEESH. YOU'RE AS RECKLESS AS EVER, ASTA.
THANKS FOR ALWAYS SAVING MY BUTT, MISTER FINRAL!!
IS THAT SO? IN THAT CASE...
SAVING...? NO, THAT'S YOU, ASTA!
AT FIRST I THOUGHT, "WHAT'S HE TALKING ABOUT?" BUT NOW...

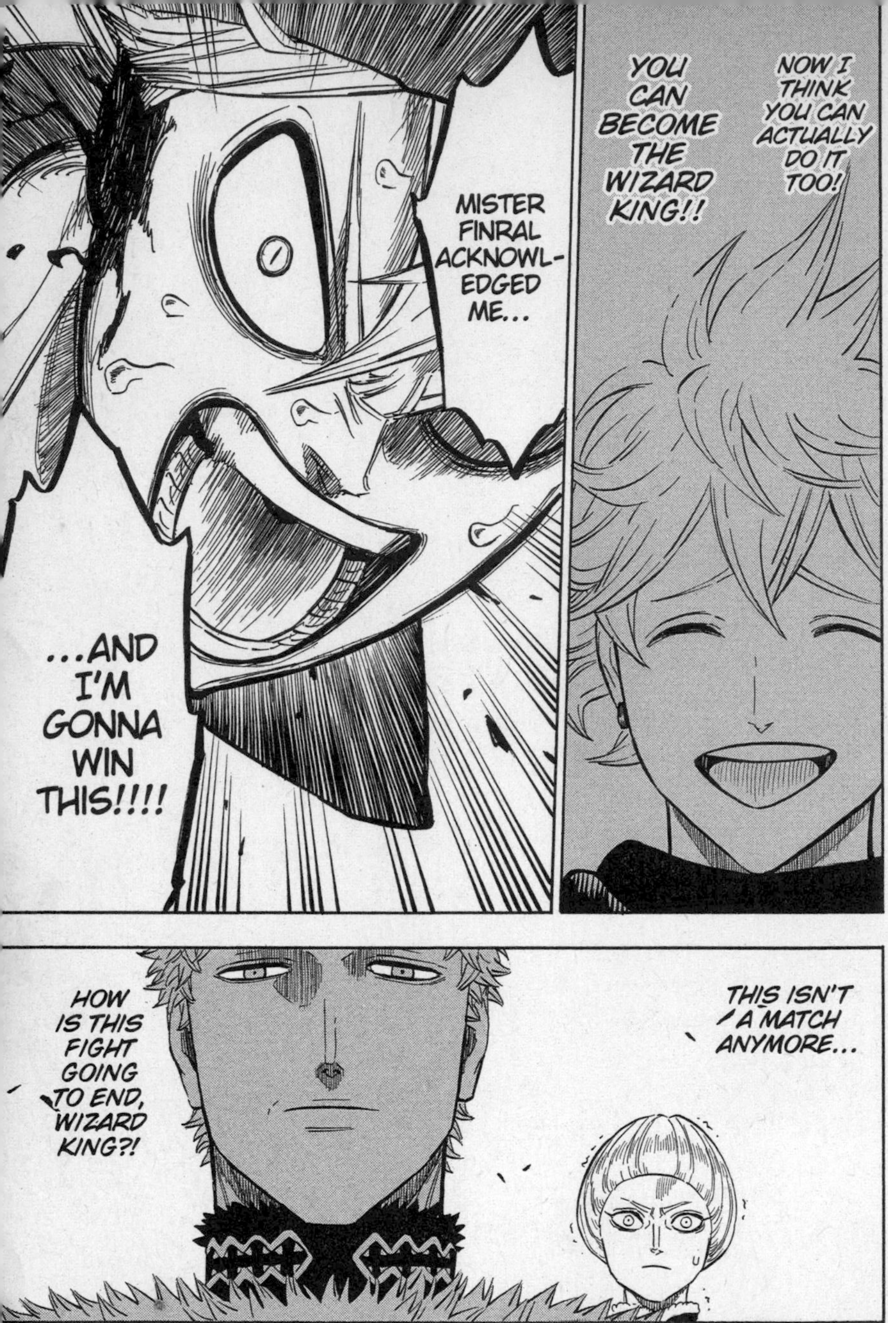
NOW I THINK YOU CAN ACTUALLY DO IT TOO!
YOU CAN BECOME THE WIZARD KING!!
MISTER FINRAL ACKNOWLEDGED ME...
...AND I'M GONNA WIN THIS!!!!
THIS ISN'T A MATCH ANYMORE...
HOW IS THIS FIGHT GOING TO END, WIZARD KING?!

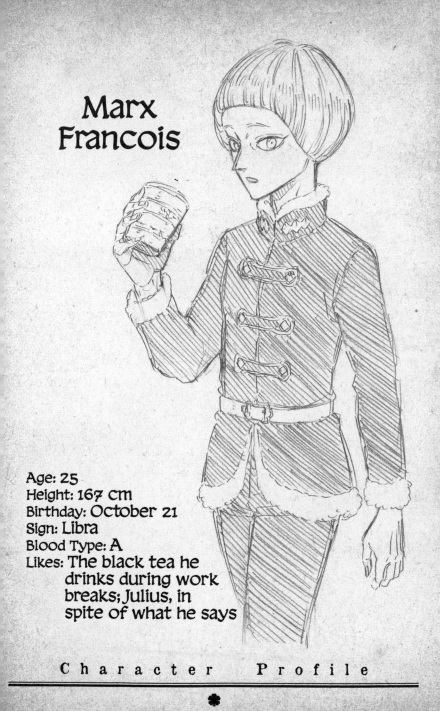

Marx Francois

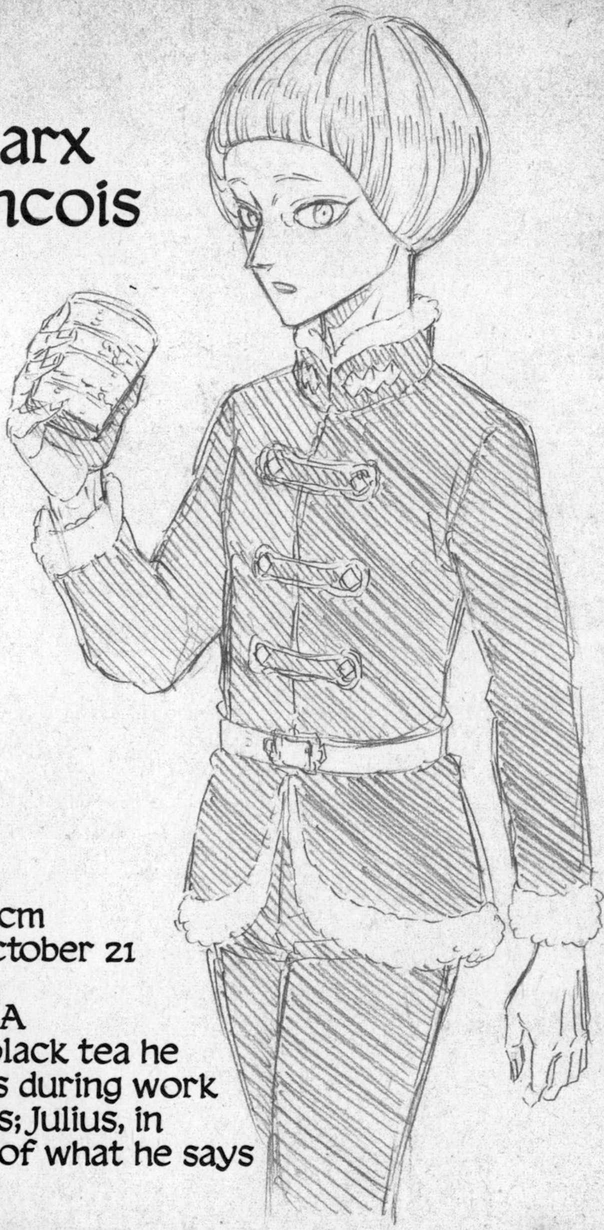

Age: 25
Height: 167 cm
Birthday: October 21
Sign: Libra
Blood Type: A
Likes: The black tea he drinks during work breaks; Julius, in spite of what he says

Character Profile

Page 129: The Life of a Certain Man

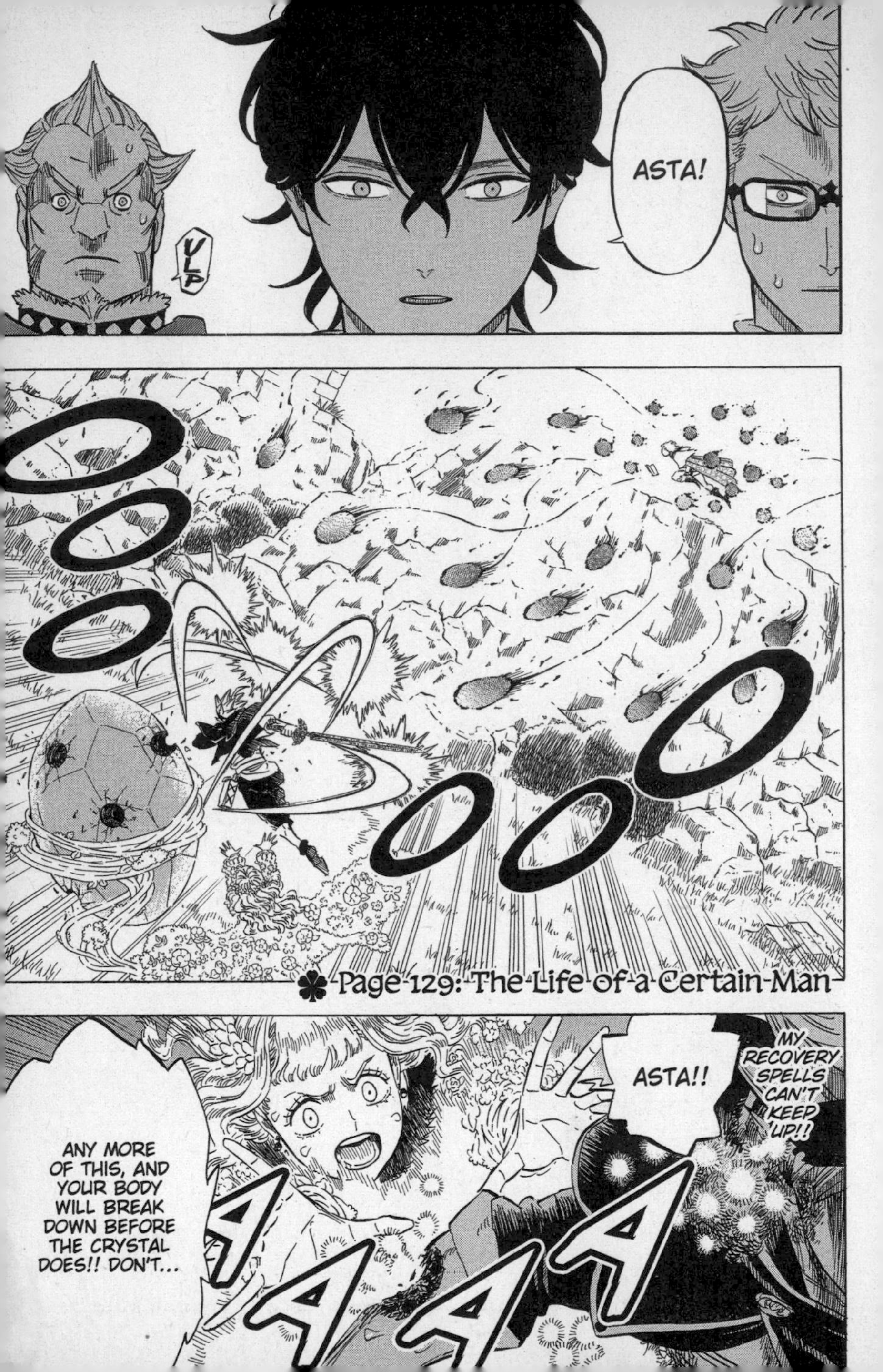
ASTA!
ULP
OOOOOOO
MY RECOVERY SPELLS CAN'T KEEP UP!!
ASTA!!
AAAA
ANY MORE OF THIS, AND YOUR BODY WILL BREAK DOWN BEFORE THE CRYSTAL DOES!! DON'T...

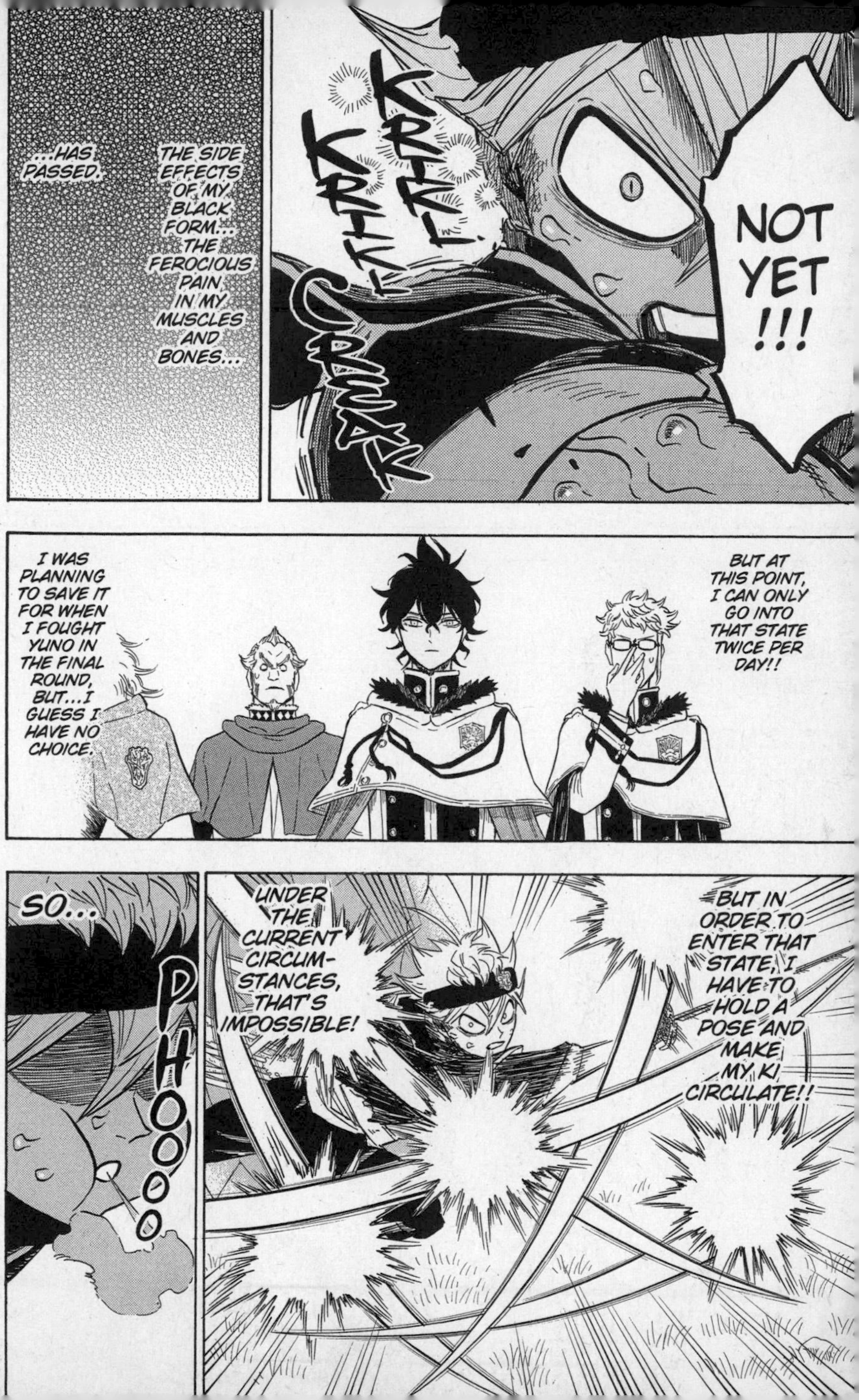
NOT YET!!!
KRIKL
KRIKL
CREAK
THE SIDE EFFECTS OF MY BLACK FORM... THE FEROCIOUS PAIN IN MY MUSCLES AND BONES...
...HAS PASSED.
BUT AT THIS POINT, I CAN ONLY GO INTO THAT STATE TWICE PER DAY!!
I WAS PLANNING TO SAVE IT FOR WHEN I FOUGHT YUNO IN THE FINAL ROUND, BUT...I GUESS I HAVE NO CHOICE.
BUT IN ORDER TO ENTER THAT STATE, I HAVE TO HOLD A POSE AND MAKE MY KI CIRCULATE!!
UNDER THE CURRENT CIRCUM-STANCES, THAT'S IMPOSSIBLE!
SO...
PHOOOOO

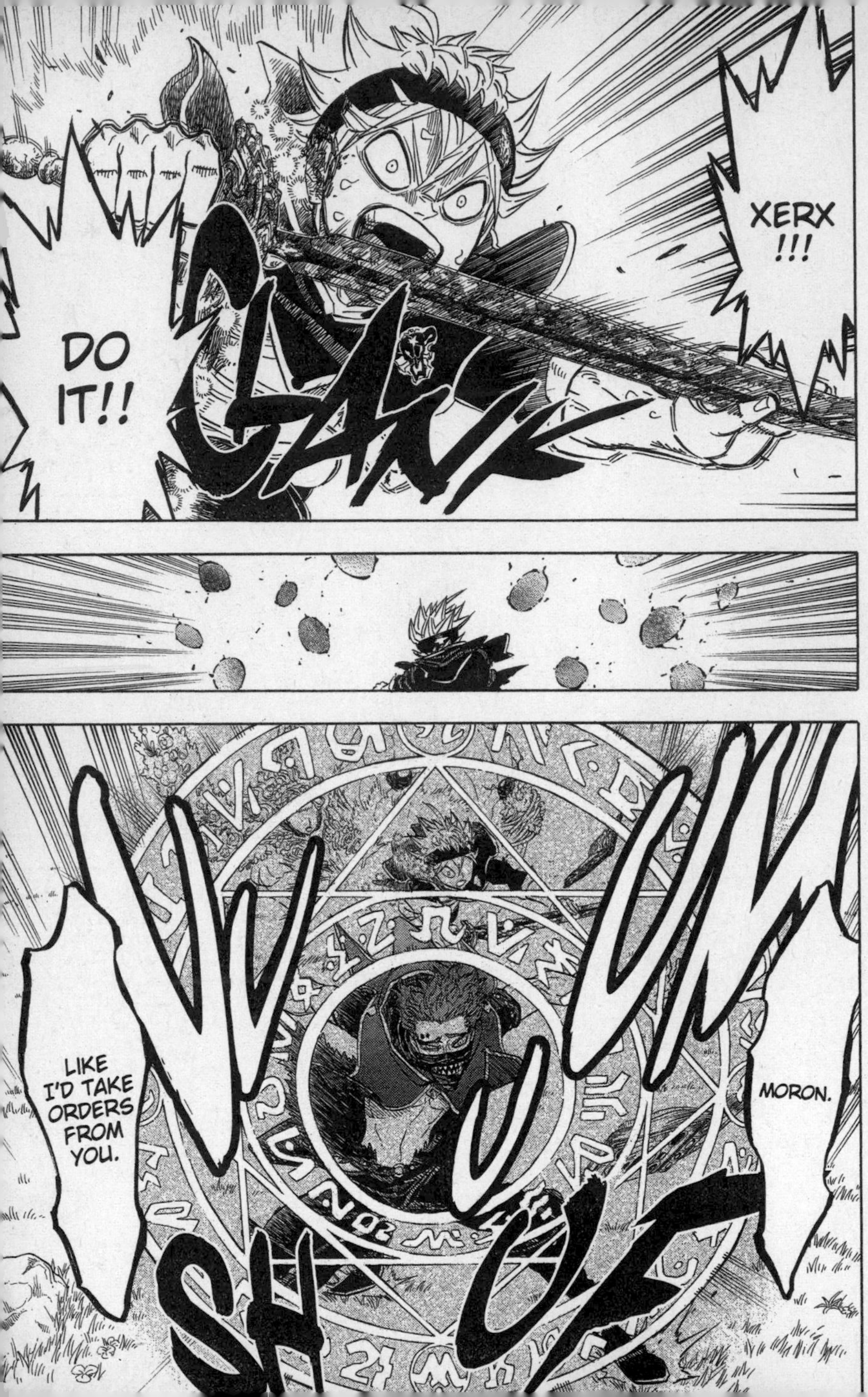
XERX!!!
DO IT!!
MORON.
LIKE I'D TAKE ORDERS FROM YOU.

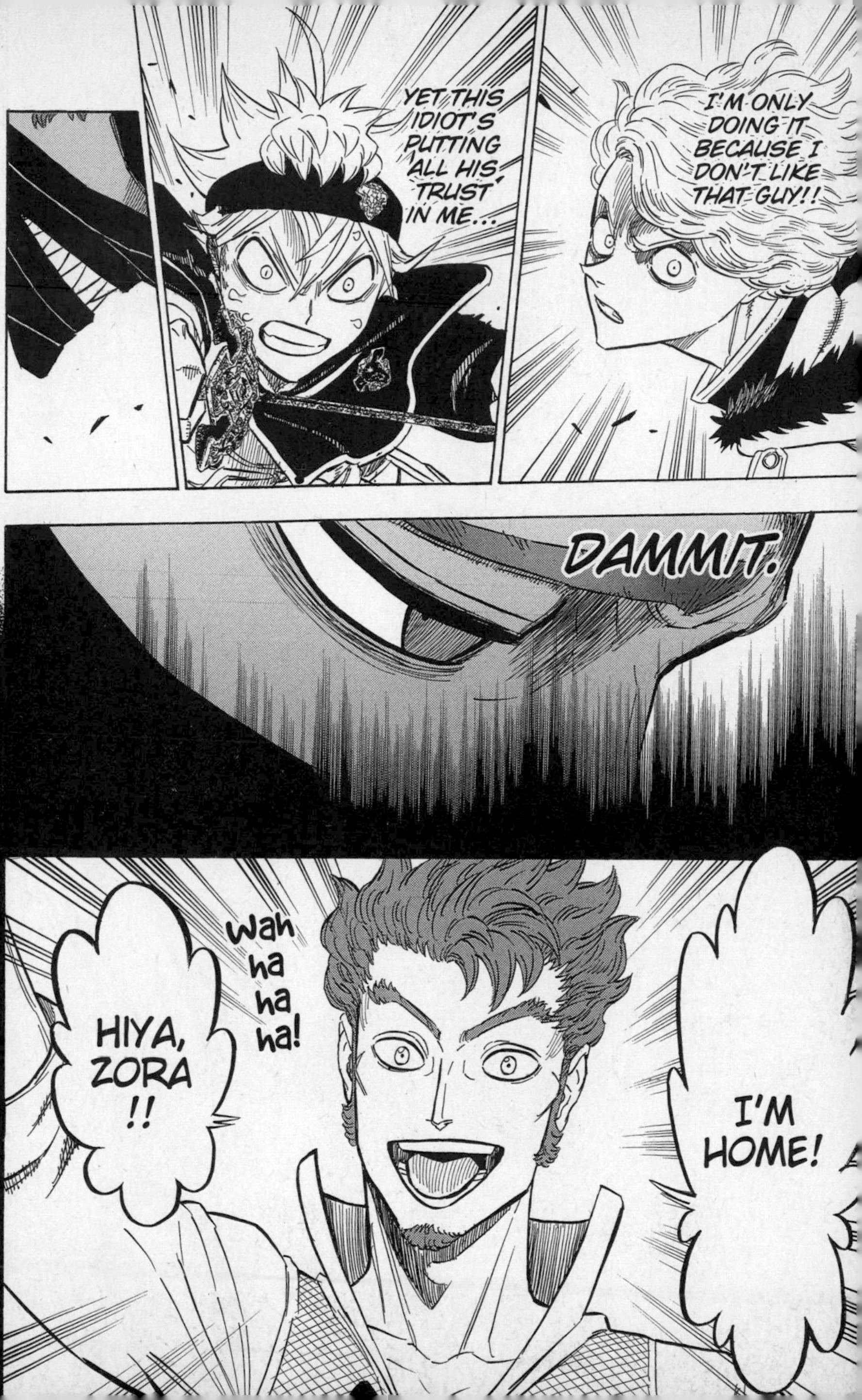
I'M ONLY DOING IT BECAUSE I DON'T LIKE THAT GUY!!
YET THIS IDIOT'S PUTTING ALL HIS TRUST IN ME...
DAMMIT.
I'M HOME!
Wah ha ha ha!
HIYA, ZORA!!

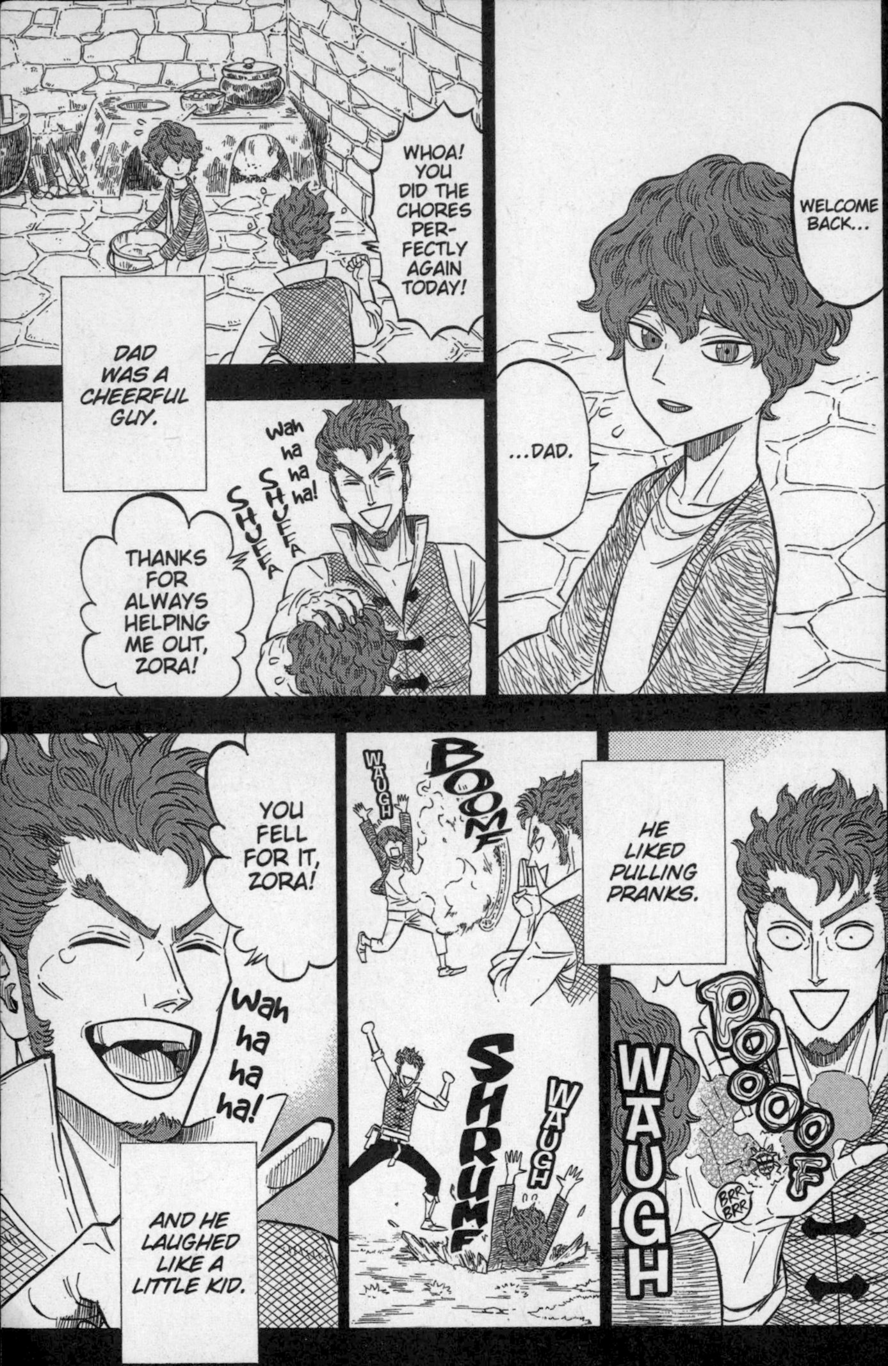
WELCOME BACK...
...DAD.
WHOA! YOU DID THE CHORES PER-FECTLY AGAIN TODAY!
DAD WAS A CHEERFUL GUY.
Wah ha ha ha!
SHUFFA SHUFFA
THANKS FOR ALWAYS HELPING ME OUT, ZORA!
HE LIKED PULLING PRANKS.
POOOOF
WAUGH
BRR BRR
WAUGH
BOOMF
SHRUMF
WAUGH
YOU FELL FOR IT, ZORA!
Wah ha ha ha!
AND HE LAUGHED LIKE A LITTLE KID.

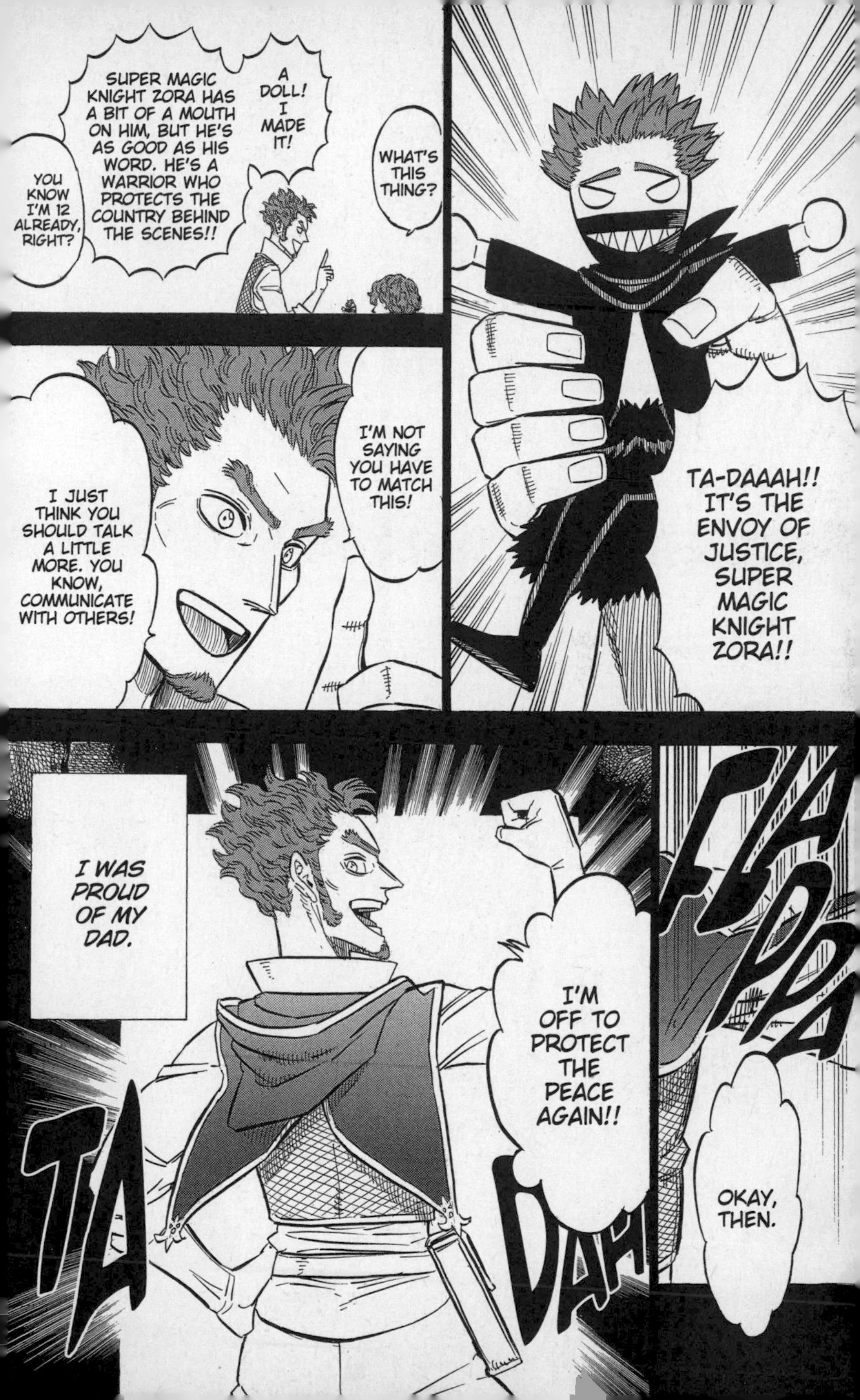
TA-DAAAH!! IT'S THE ENVOY OF JUSTICE, SUPER MAGIC KNIGHT ZORA!!
WHAT'S THIS THING?
A DOLL! I MADE IT!
SUPER MAGIC KNIGHT ZORA HAS A BIT OF A MOUTH ON HIM, BUT HE'S AS GOOD AS HIS WORD. HE'S A WARRIOR WHO PROTECTS THE COUNTRY BEHIND THE SCENES!!
YOU KNOW I'M 12 ALREADY, RIGHT?
I'M NOT SAYING YOU HAVE TO MATCH THIS!
I JUST THINK YOU SHOULD TALK A LITTLE MORE. YOU KNOW, COMMUNICATE WITH OTHERS!
OKAY, THEN.
I'M OFF TO PROTECT THE PEACE AGAIN!!
I WAS PROUD OF MY DAD.
DAH
TA

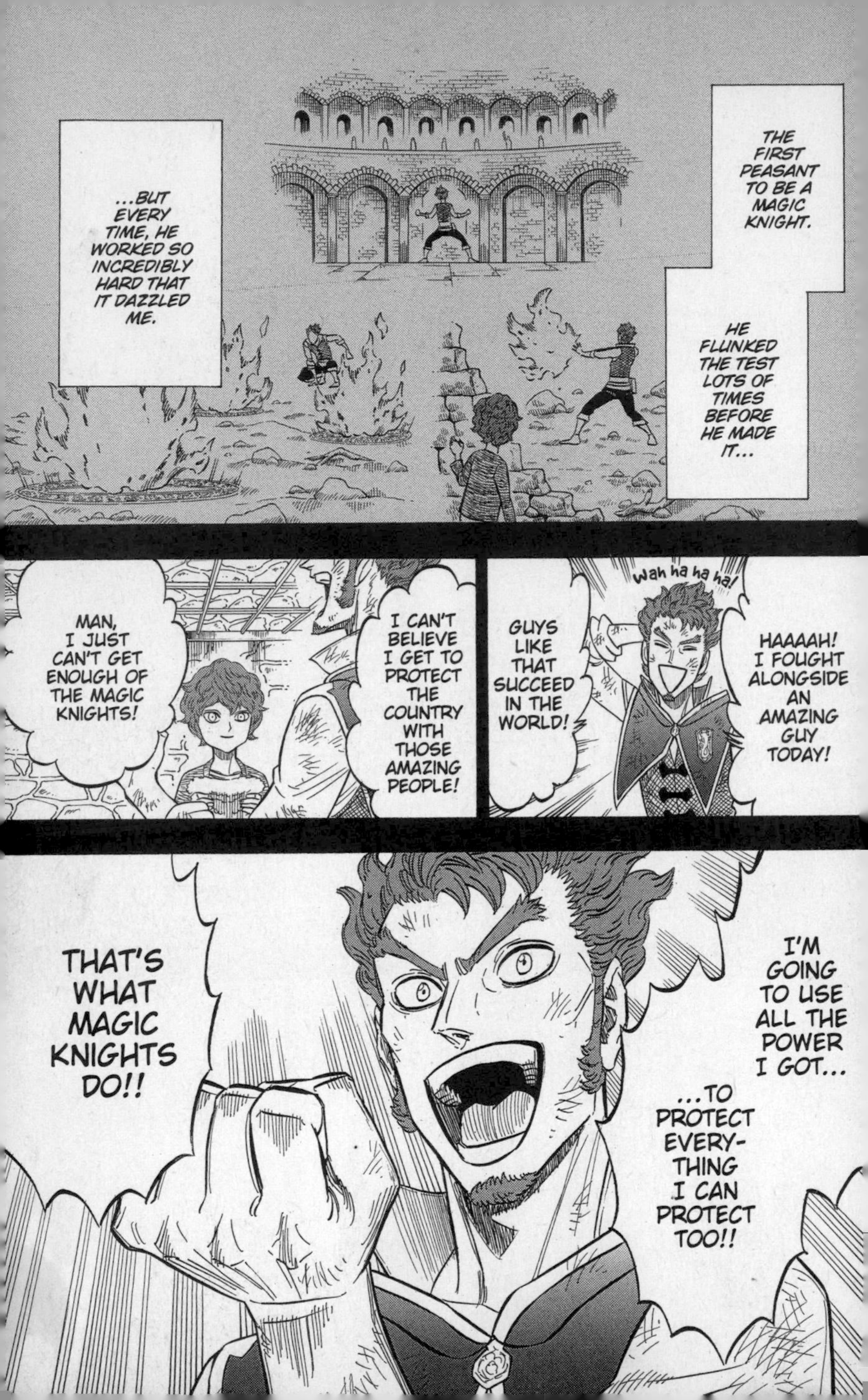
THE FIRST PEASANT TO BE A MAGIC KNIGHT.
HE FLUNKED THE TEST LOTS OF TIMES BEFORE HE MADE IT...
...BUT EVERY TIME, HE WORKED SO INCREDIBLY HARD THAT IT DAZZLED ME.
Wah ha ha ha!
HAAAAH! I FOUGHT ALONGSIDE AN AMAZING GUY TODAY!
GUYS LIKE THAT SUCCEED IN THE WORLD!
I CAN'T BELIEVE I GET TO PROTECT THE COUNTRY WITH THOSE AMAZING PEOPLE!
MAN, I JUST CAN'T GET ENOUGH OF THE MAGIC KNIGHTS!
I'M GOING TO USE ALL THE POWER I GOT...
...TO PROTECT EVERY-THING I CAN PROTECT TOO!!
THAT'S WHAT MAGIC KNIGHTS DO!!

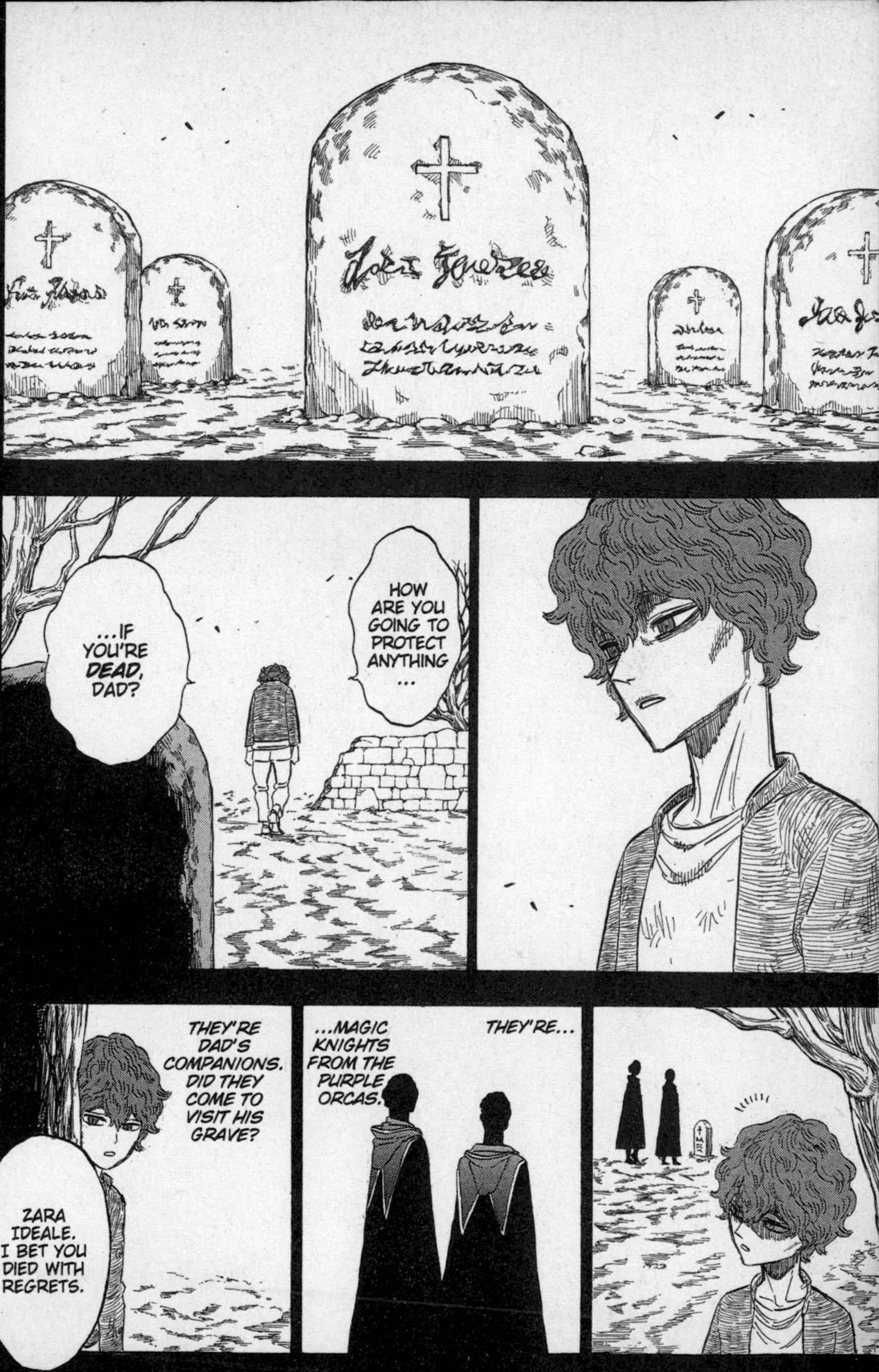
HOW ARE YOU GOING TO PROTECT ANYTHING ...
...IF YOU'RE DEAD, DAD?
THEY'RE...
...MAGIC KNIGHTS FROM THE PURPLE ORCAS.
THEY'RE DAD'S COMPANIONS. DID THEY COME TO VISIT HIS GRAVE?
ZARA IDEALE. I BET YOU DIED WITH REGRETS.

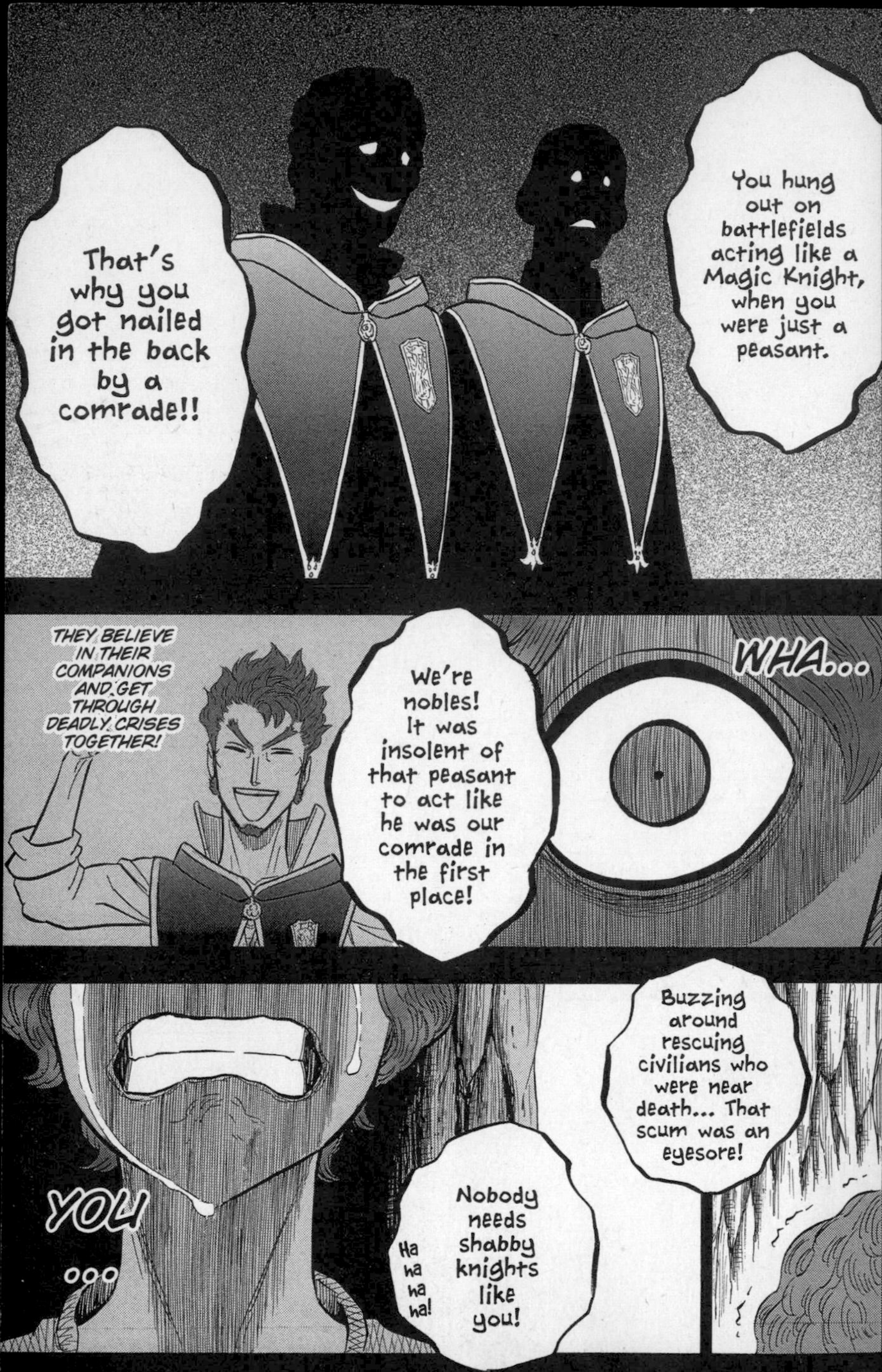
You hung out on battlefields acting like a Magic Knight, when you were just a peasant.
That's why you got nailed in the back by a comrade!!
WHA...
We're nobles! It was insolent of that peasant to act like he was our comrade in the first place!
THEY BELIEVE IN THEIR COMPANIONS AND GET THROUGH DEADLY CRISES TOGETHER!
Buzzing around rescuing civilians who were near death... That scum was an eyesore!
Nobody needs shabby knights like you!
Ha ha ha ha!
YOU...

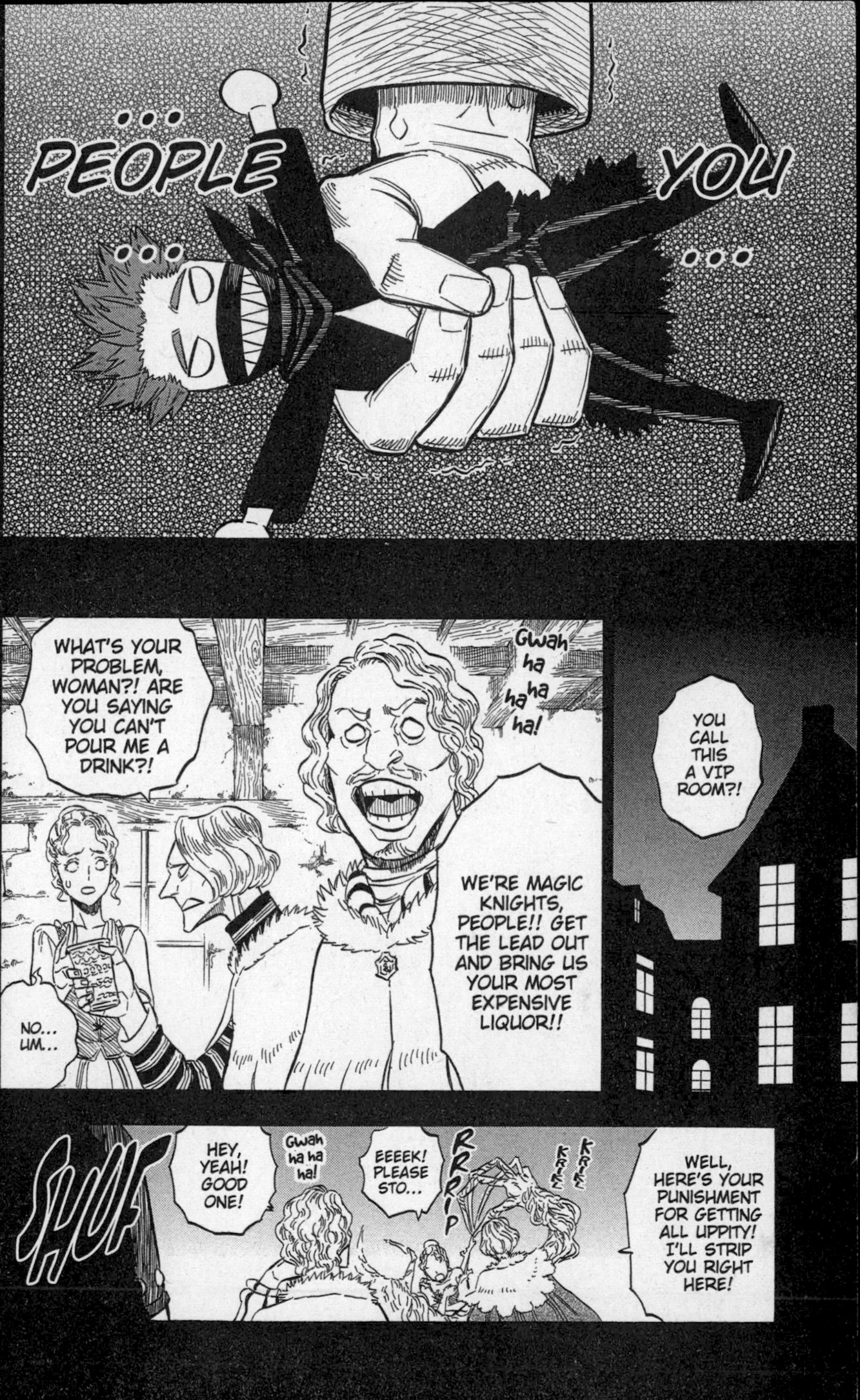
YOU
...
...
PEOPLE
...
YOU CALL THIS A VIP ROOM?!
Gwah ha ha ha ha!
WE'RE MAGIC KNIGHTS, PEOPLE!! GET THE LEAD OUT AND BRING US YOUR MOST EXPENSIVE LIQUOR!!
WHAT'S YOUR PROBLEM, WOMAN?! ARE YOU SAYING YOU CAN'T POUR ME A DRINK?!
NO... UM...
WELL, HERE'S YOUR PUNISHMENT FOR GETTING ALL UPPITY! I'LL STRIP YOU RIGHT HERE!
RRRIP
EEEEK! PLEASE STO...
Gwah ha ha ha!
HEY, YEAH! GOOD ONE!

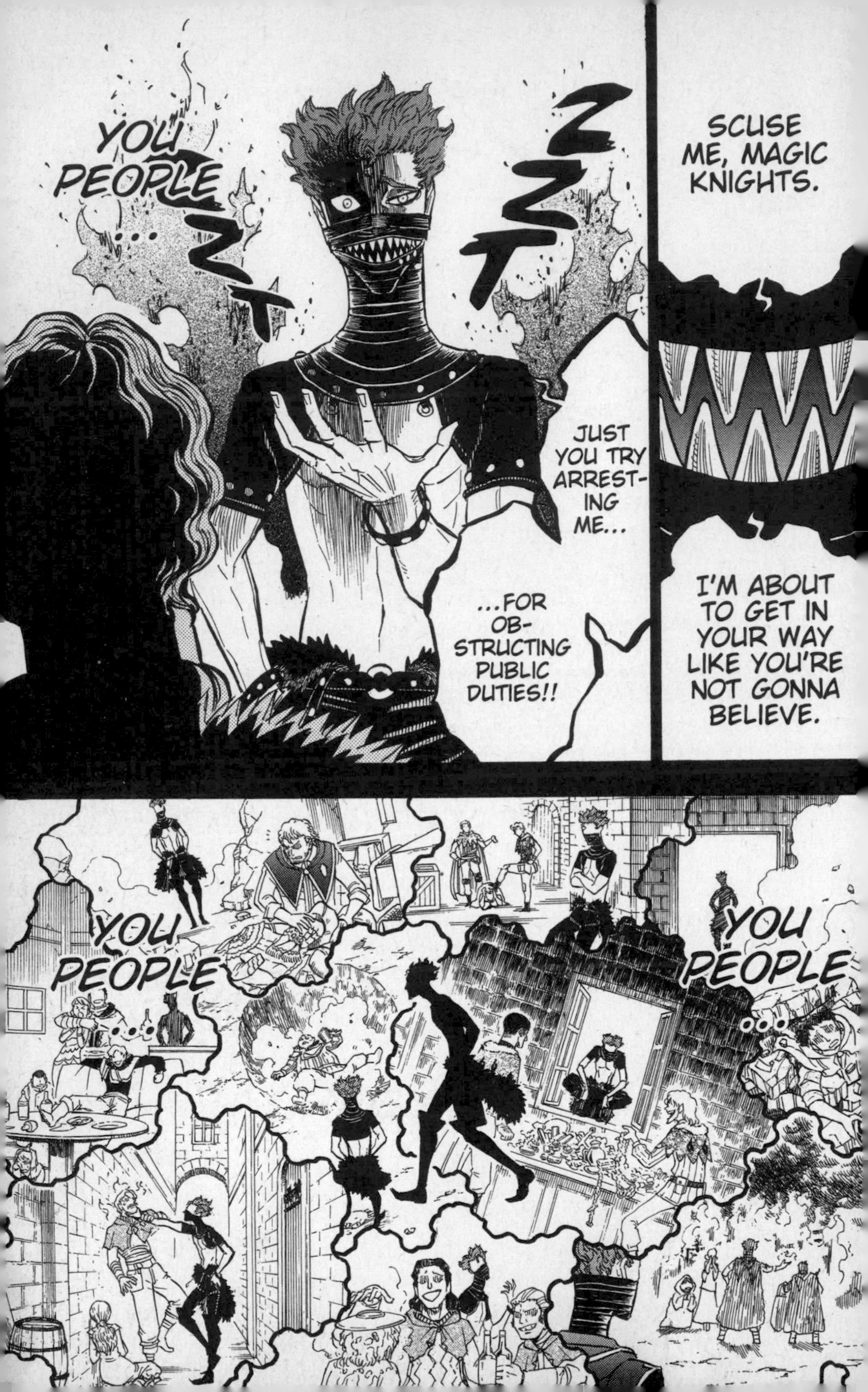
SCUSE ME, MAGIC KNIGHTS.
I'M ABOUT TO GET IN YOUR WAY LIKE YOU'RE NOT GONNA BELIEVE.
ZZT
JUST YOU TRY ARREST-ING ME...
...FOR OB-STRUCTING PUBLIC DUTIES!!
YOU PEOPLE ...
ZZT
YOU PEOPLE ...
YOU PEOPLE ...

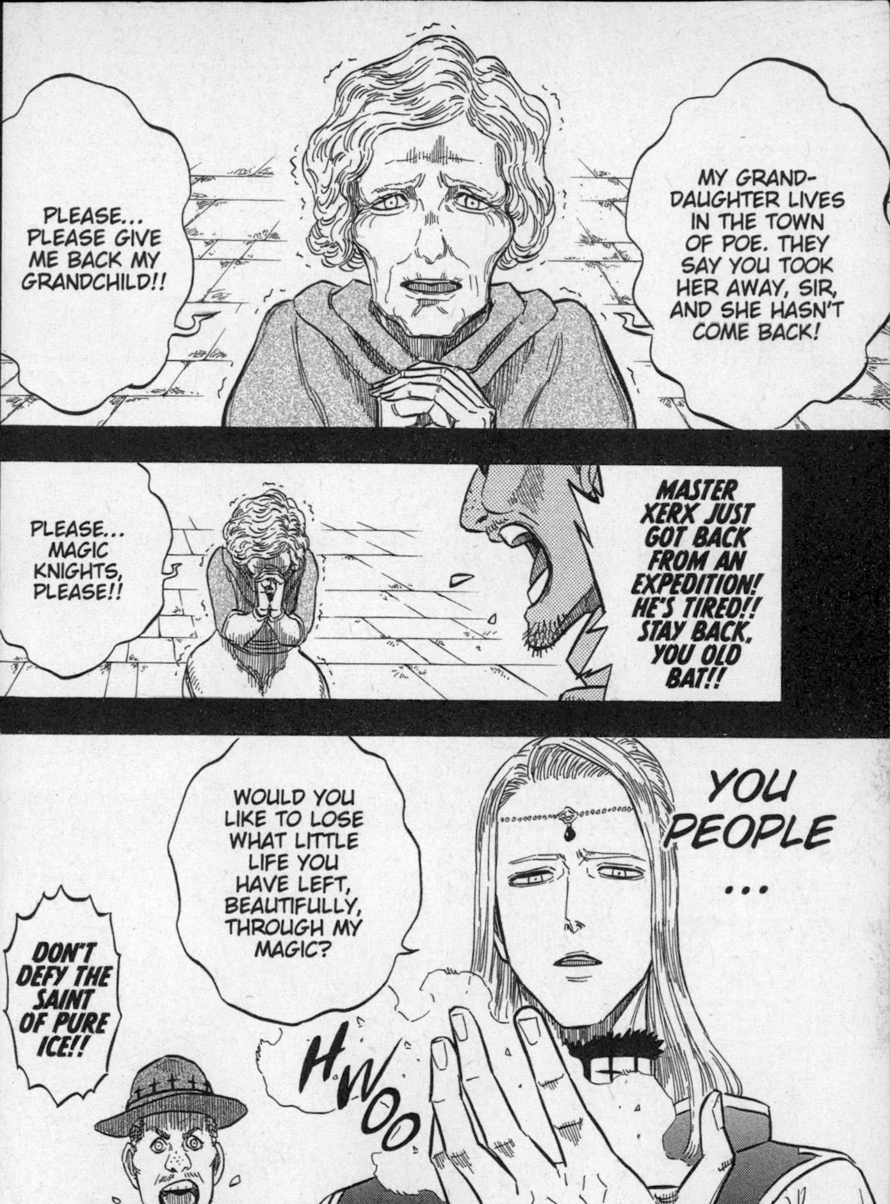
MY GRAND-DAUGHTER LIVES IN THE TOWN OF POE. THEY SAY YOU TOOK HER AWAY, SIR, AND SHE HASN'T COME BACK!
PLEASE... PLEASE GIVE ME BACK MY GRANDCHILD!!
MASTER XERX JUST GOT BACK FROM AN EXPEDITION! HE'S TIRED!! STAY BACK, YOU OLD BAT!!
PLEASE... MAGIC KNIGHTS, PLEASE!!
YOU PEOPLE ...
WOULD YOU LIKE TO LOSE WHAT LITTLE LIFE YOU HAVE LEFT, BEAUTIFULLY, THROUGH MY MAGIC?
DON'T DEFY THE SAINT OF PURE ICE!!
HWOO

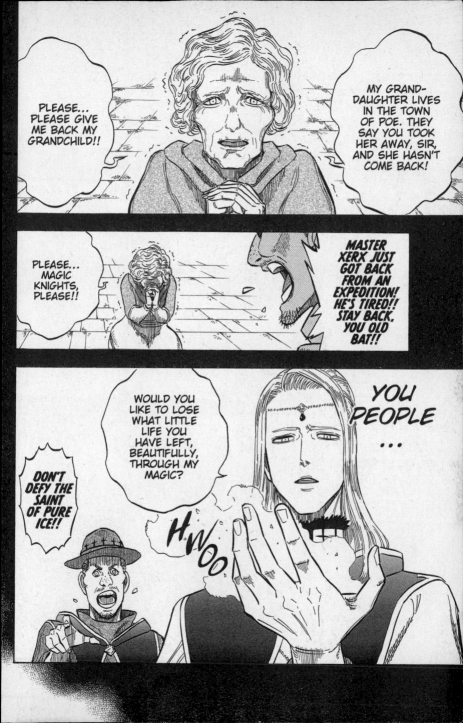

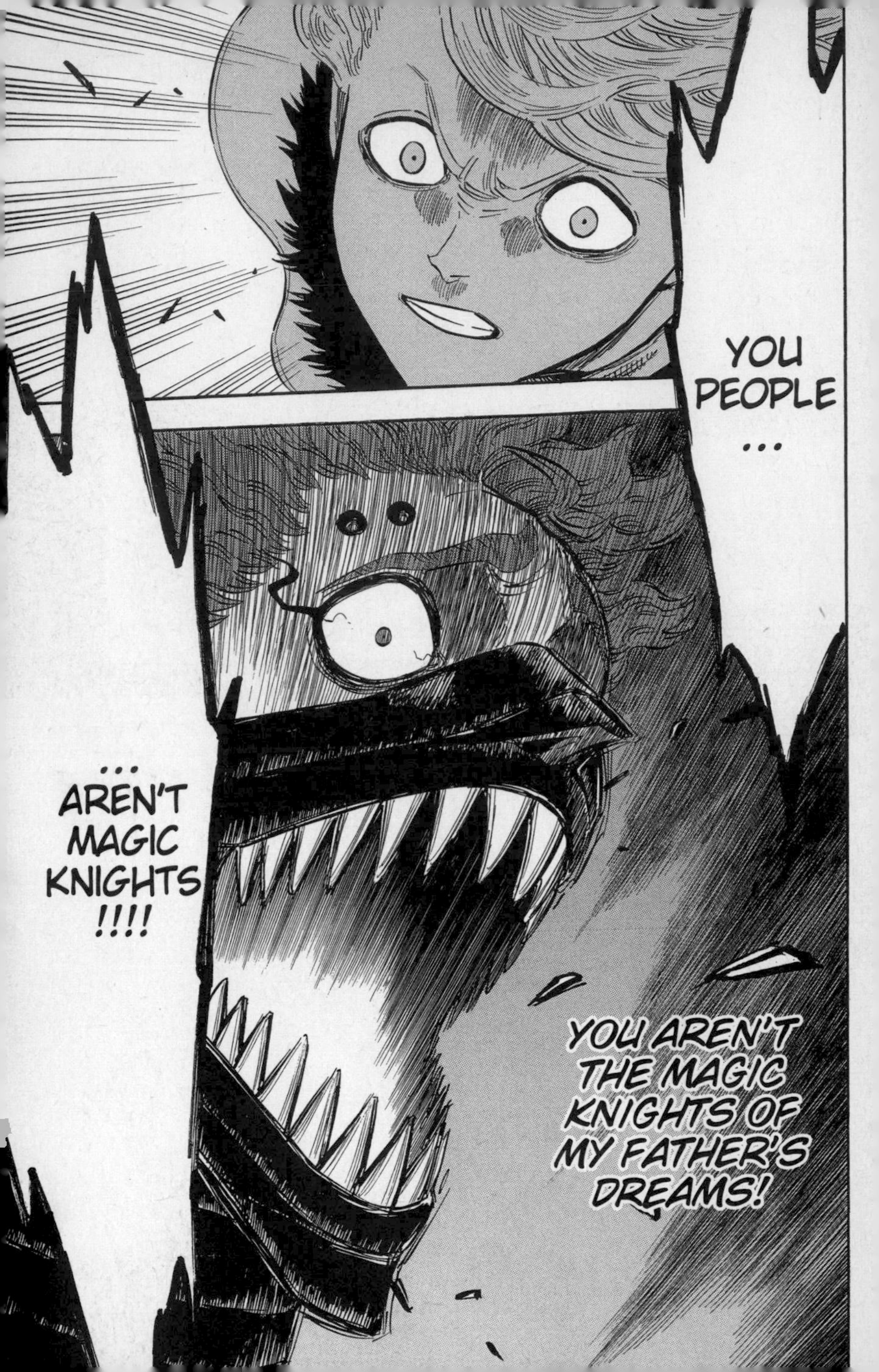
YOU PEOPLE ...
... AREN'T MAGIC KNIGHTS !!!!
YOU AREN'T THE MAGIC KNIGHTS OF MY FATHER'S DREAMS!

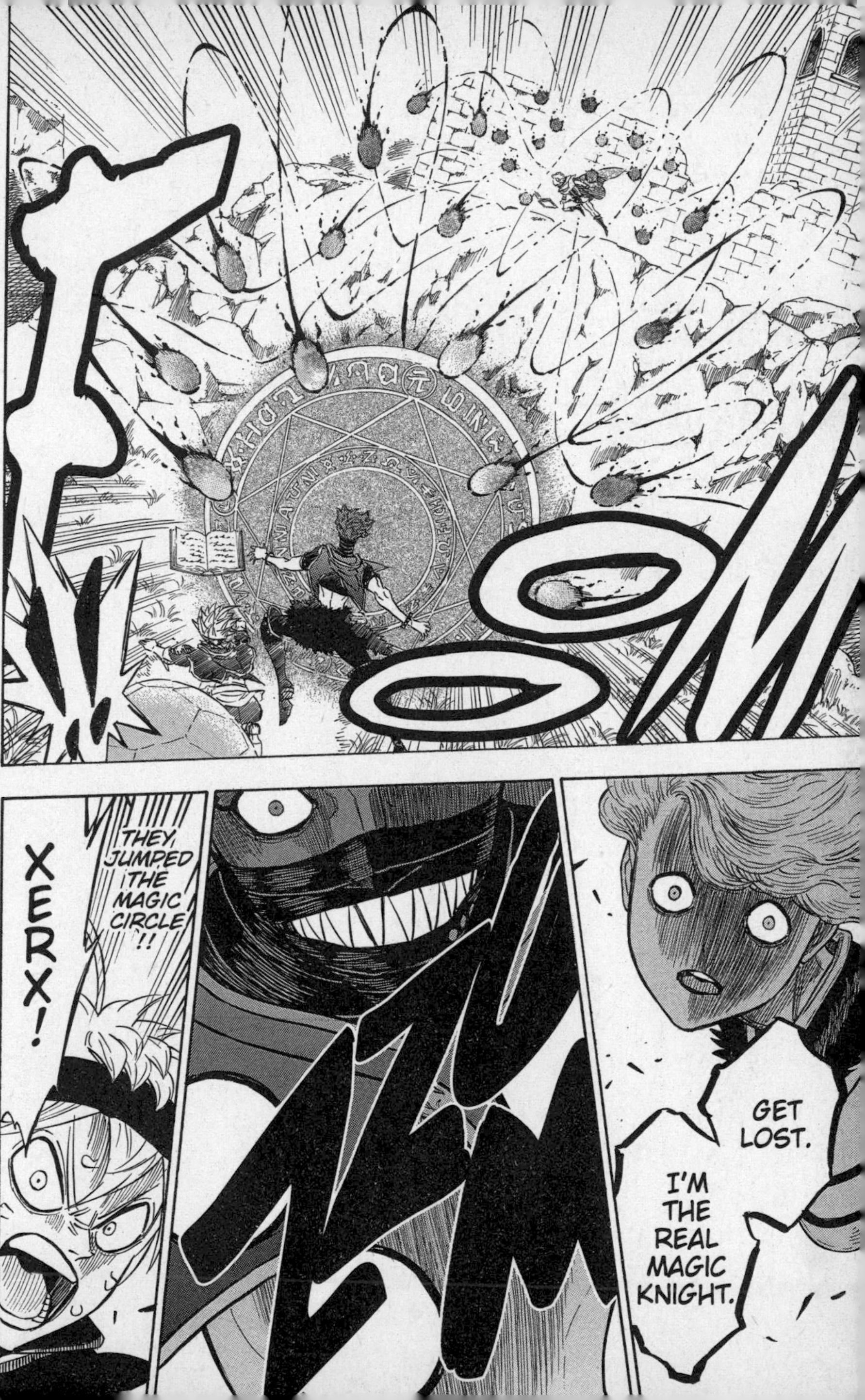
GET LOST.
I'M THE REAL MAGIC KNIGHT.
THEY JUMPED THE MAGIC CIRCLE!!
XERX!

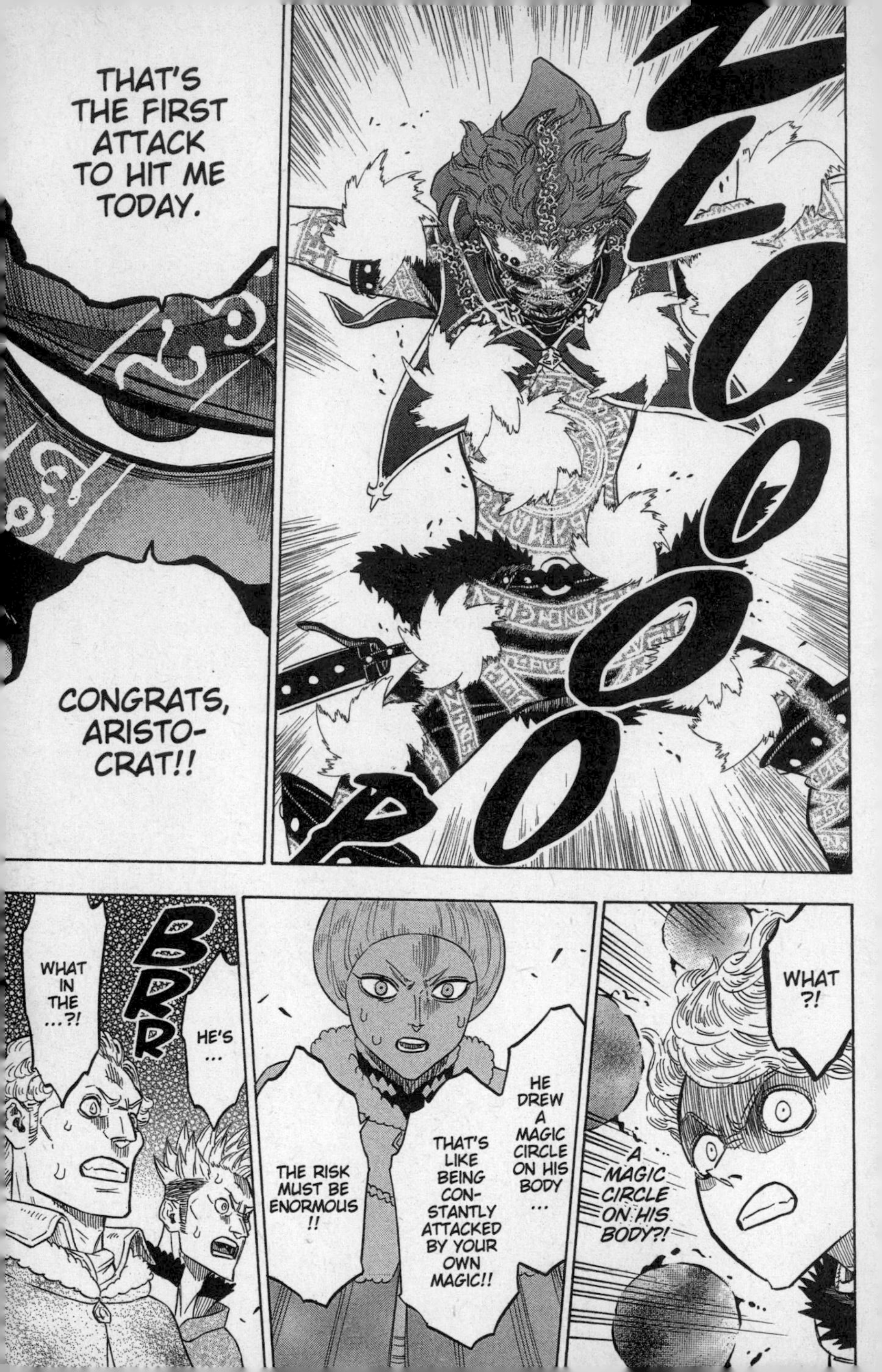
THAT'S THE FIRST ATTACK TO HIT ME TODAY.
CONGRATS, ARISTO-CRAT!!
WHAT ?!
A MAGIC CIRCLE ON HIS BODY?!
HE DREW A MAGIC CIRCLE ON HIS BODY ...
THAT'S LIKE BEING CON-STANTLY ATTACKED BY YOUR OWN MAGIC!!
THE RISK MUST BE ENORMOUS !!
BRR
WHAT IN THE ...?!
HE'S ...

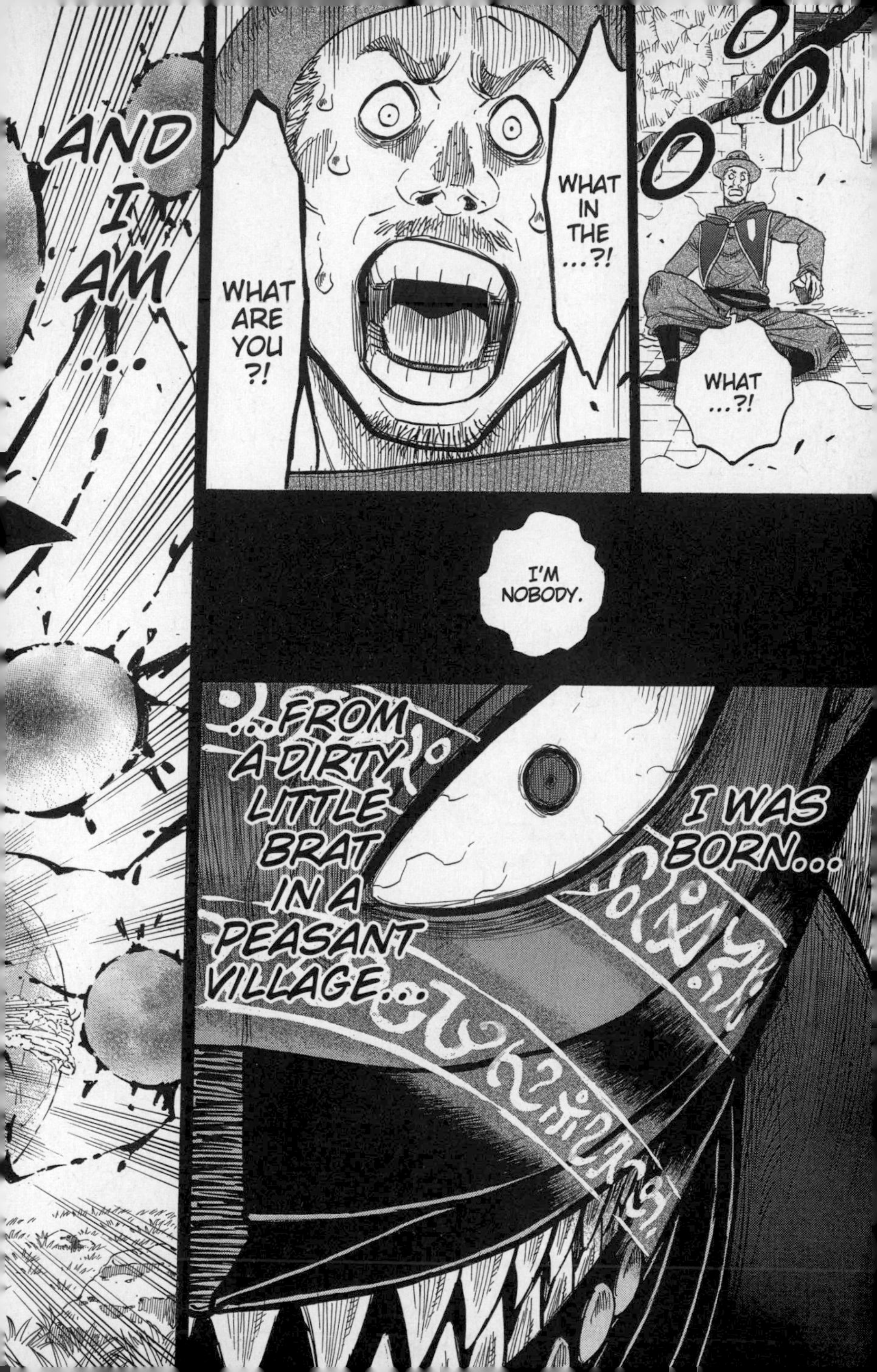
WHAT ...?!
WHAT IN THE ...?!
WHAT ARE YOU ?!
I'M NOBODY.
I WAS BORN...
...FROM A DIRTY LITTLE BRAT IN A PEASANT VILLAGE...
AND I AM...

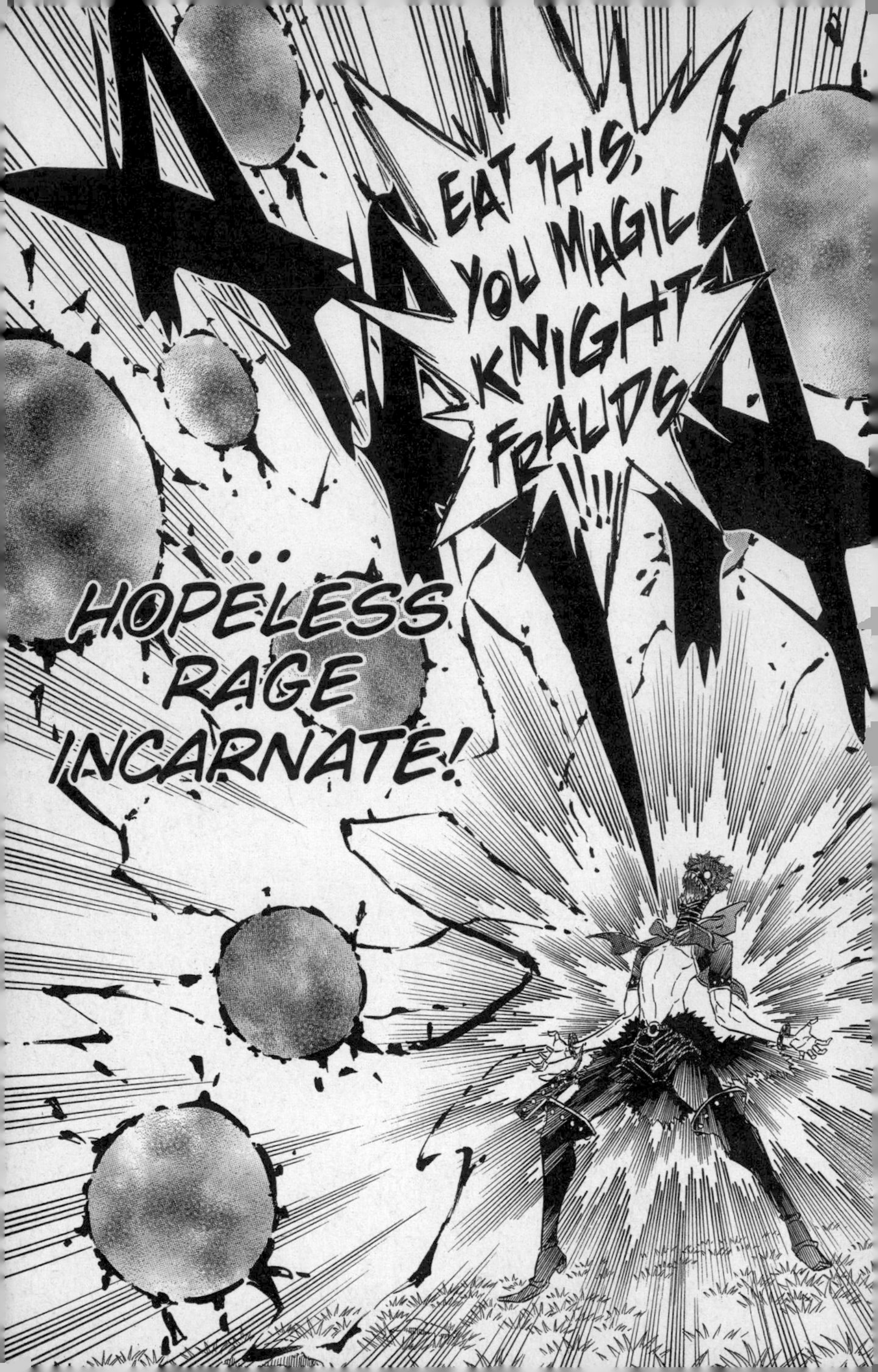
EAT THIS, YOU MAGIC KNIGHT FRAUDS!!!!
... HOPELESS RAGE INCARNATE!

Page 130: Burn It into You

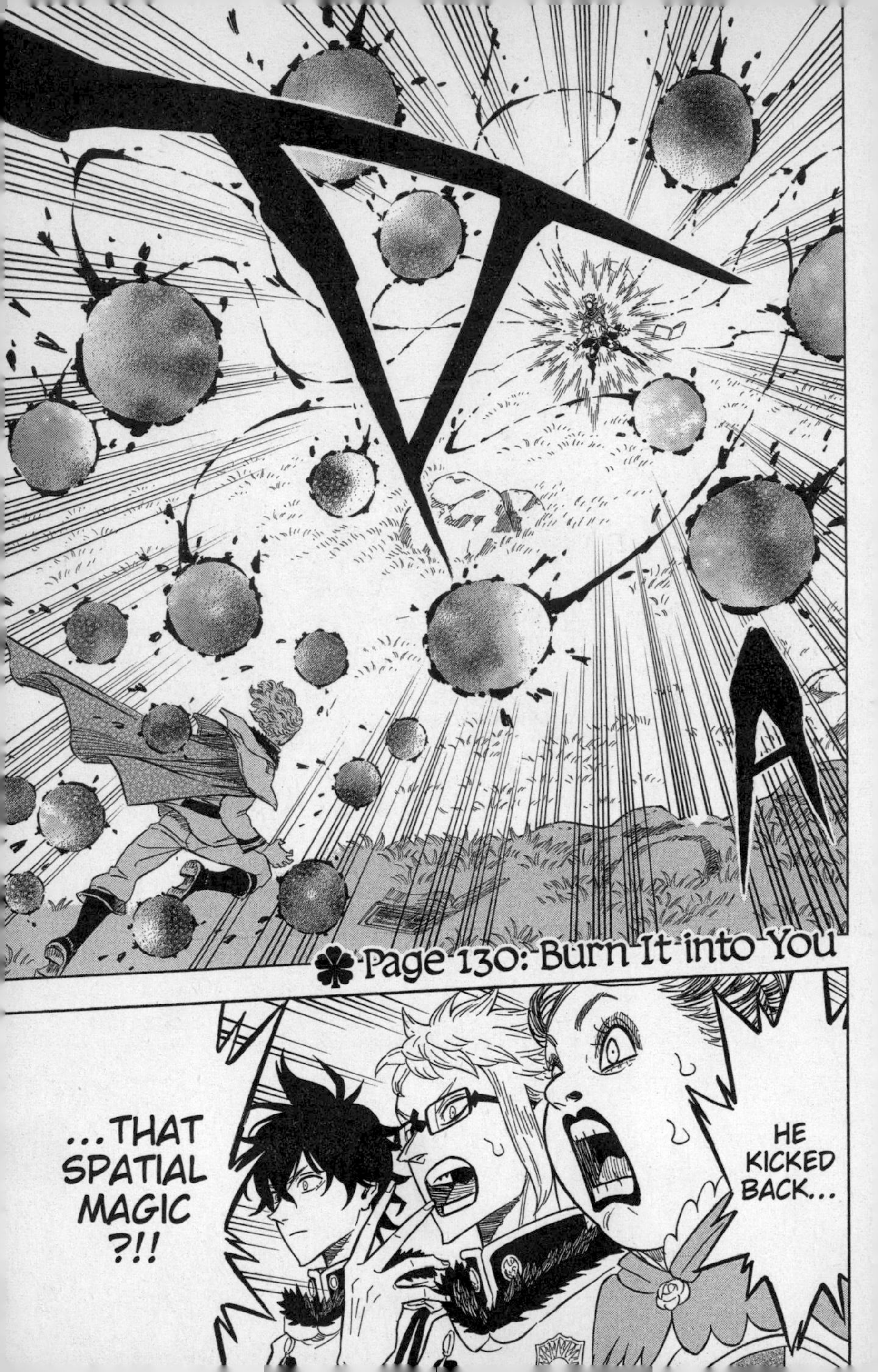
HE KICKED BACK...
...THAT SPATIAL MAGIC?!!

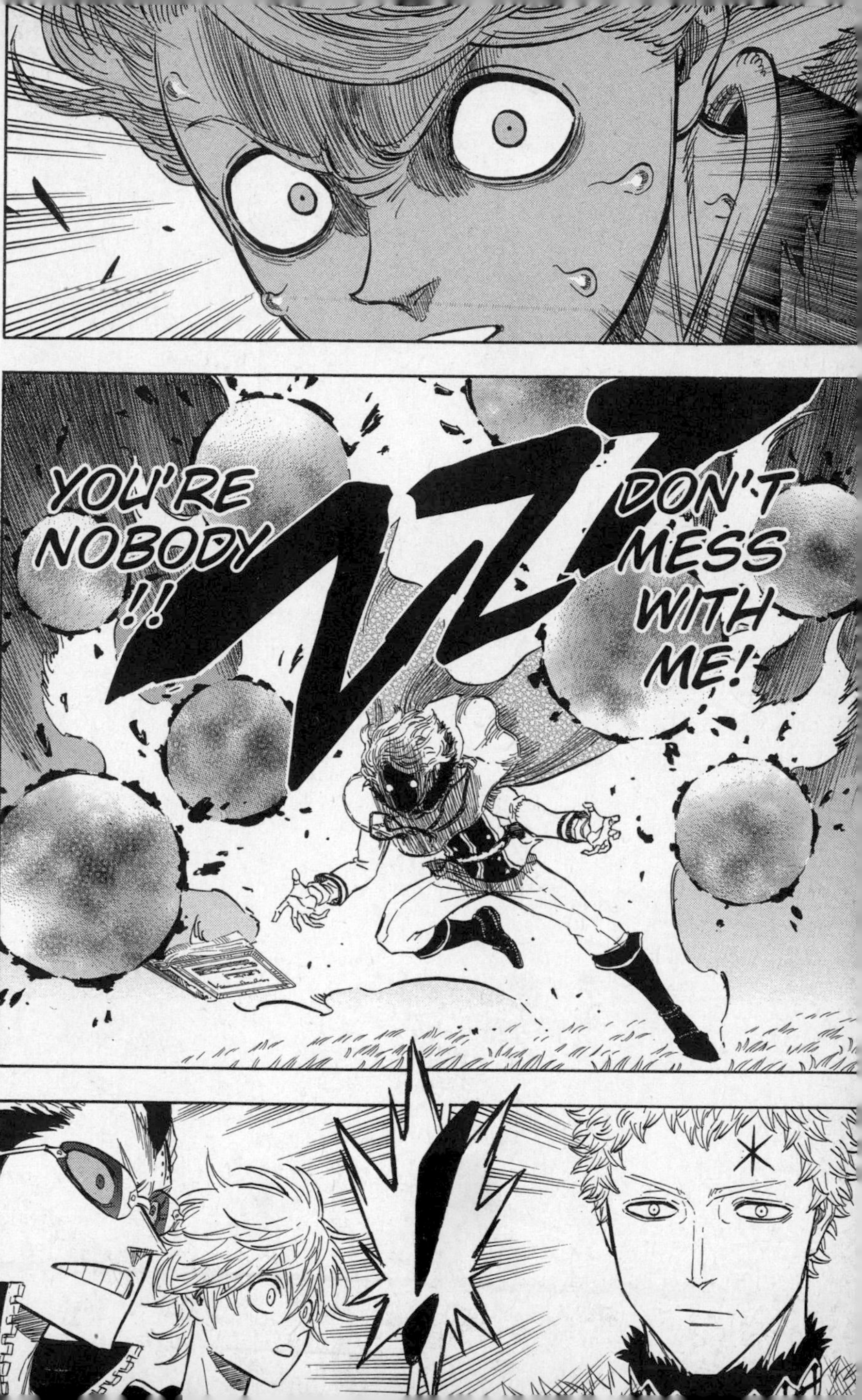
DON'T MESS WITH ME!
YOU'RE NOBODY!!

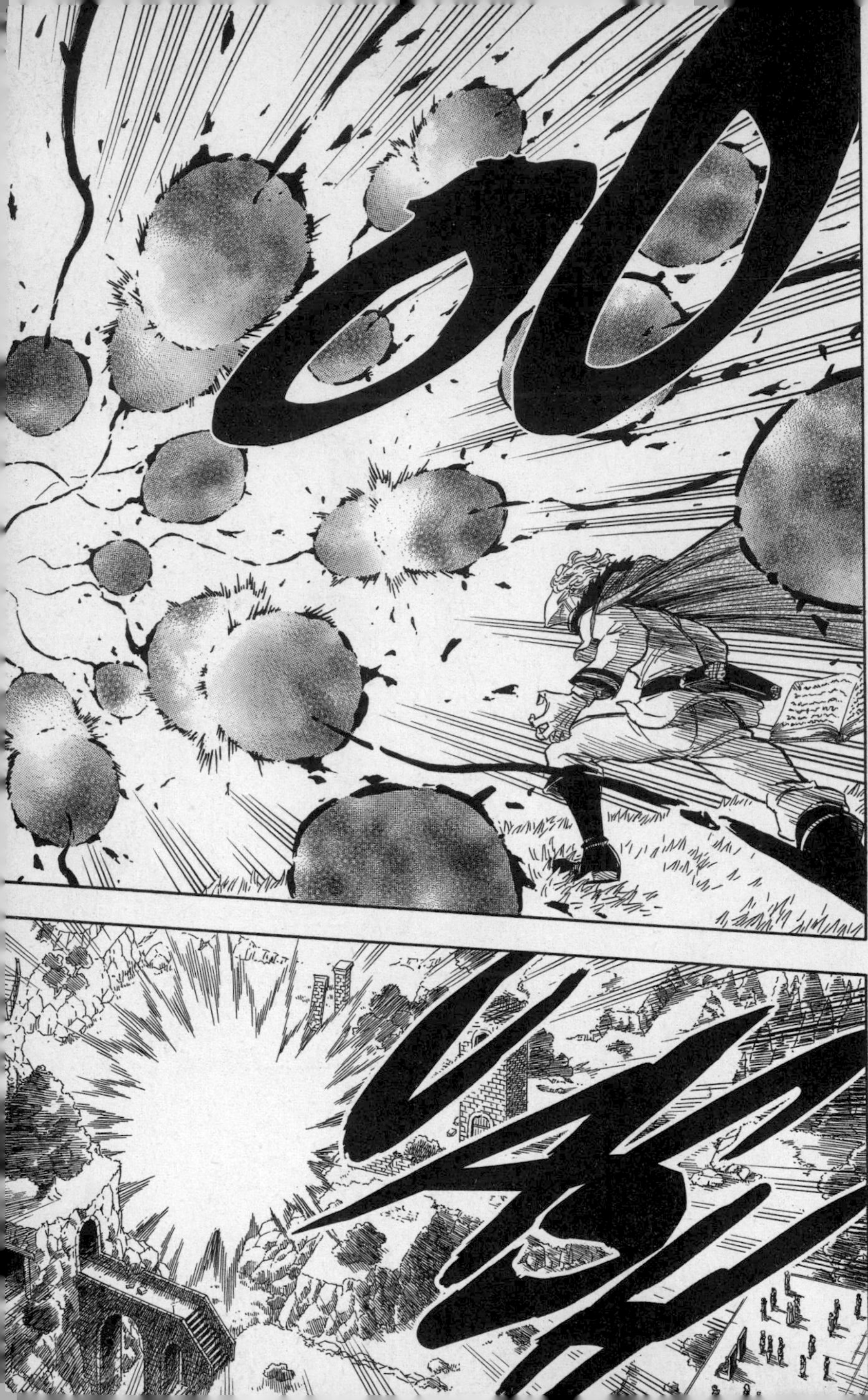

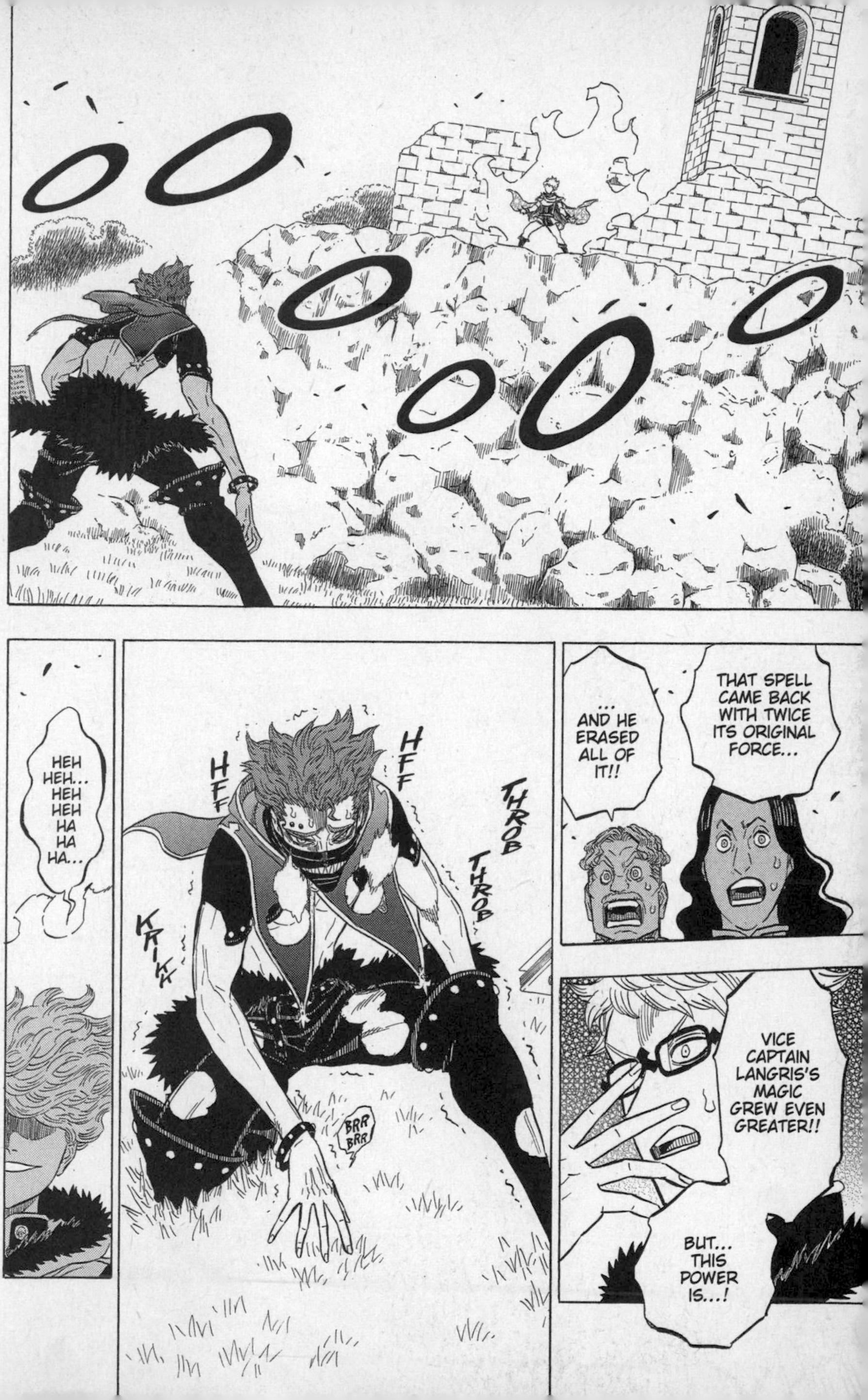
THAT SPELL CAME BACK WITH TWICE ITS ORIGINAL FORCE...
...AND HE ERASED ALL OF IT!!
VICE CAPTAIN LANGRIS'S MAGIC GREW EVEN GREATER!!
BUT... THIS POWER IS...!
HFF
HFF
THROB
THROB
KRIKK
BRR BRR
HEH HEH... HEH HEH HA HA HA...

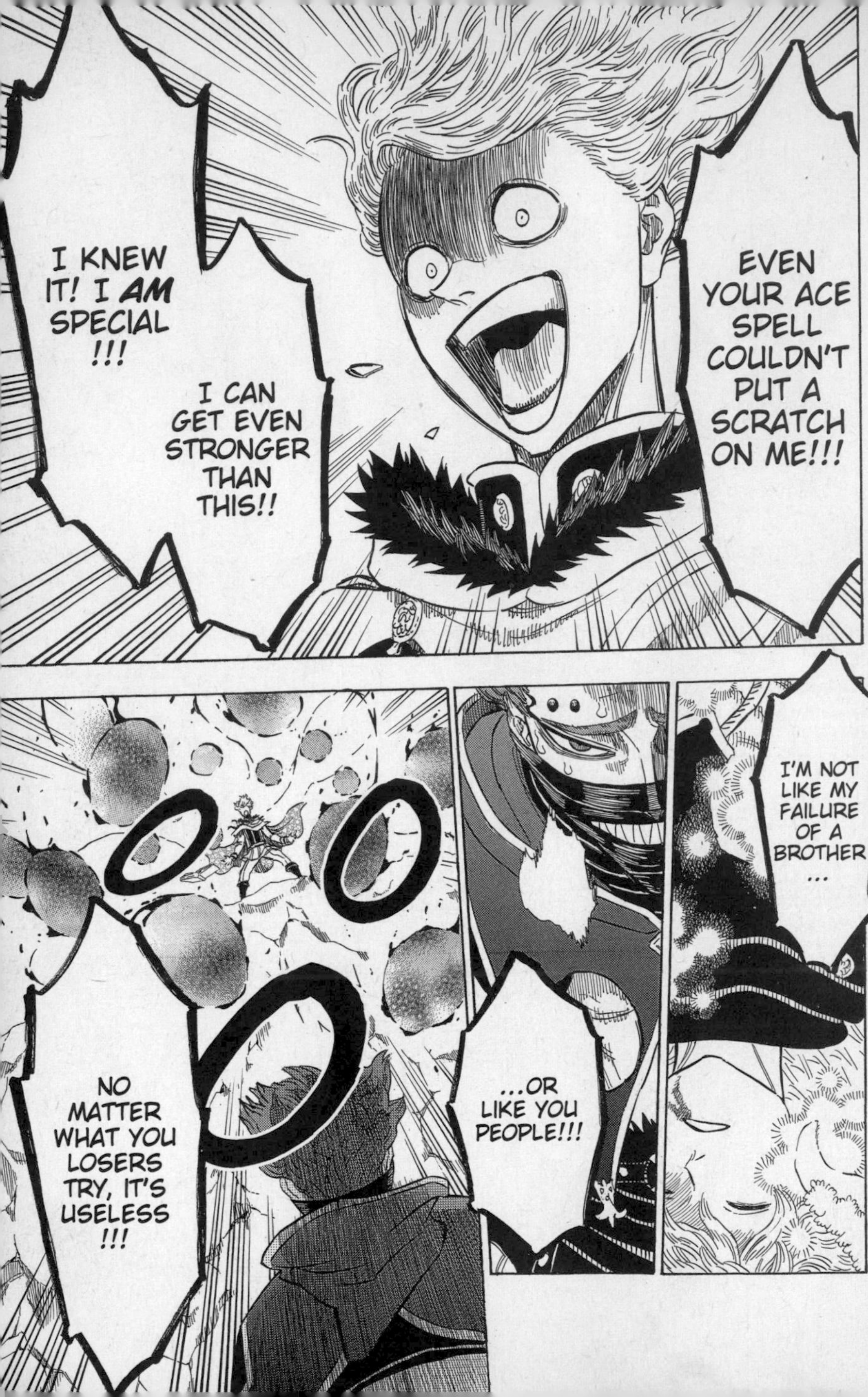
EVEN YOUR ACE SPELL COULDN'T PUT A SCRATCH ON ME!!!
I KNEW IT! I ***AM*** SPECIAL!!!
I CAN GET EVEN STRONGER THAN THIS!!
I'M NOT LIKE MY FAILURE OF A BROTHER...
...OR LIKE YOU PEOPLE!!!
NO MATTER WHAT YOU LOSERS TRY, IT'S USELESS!!!

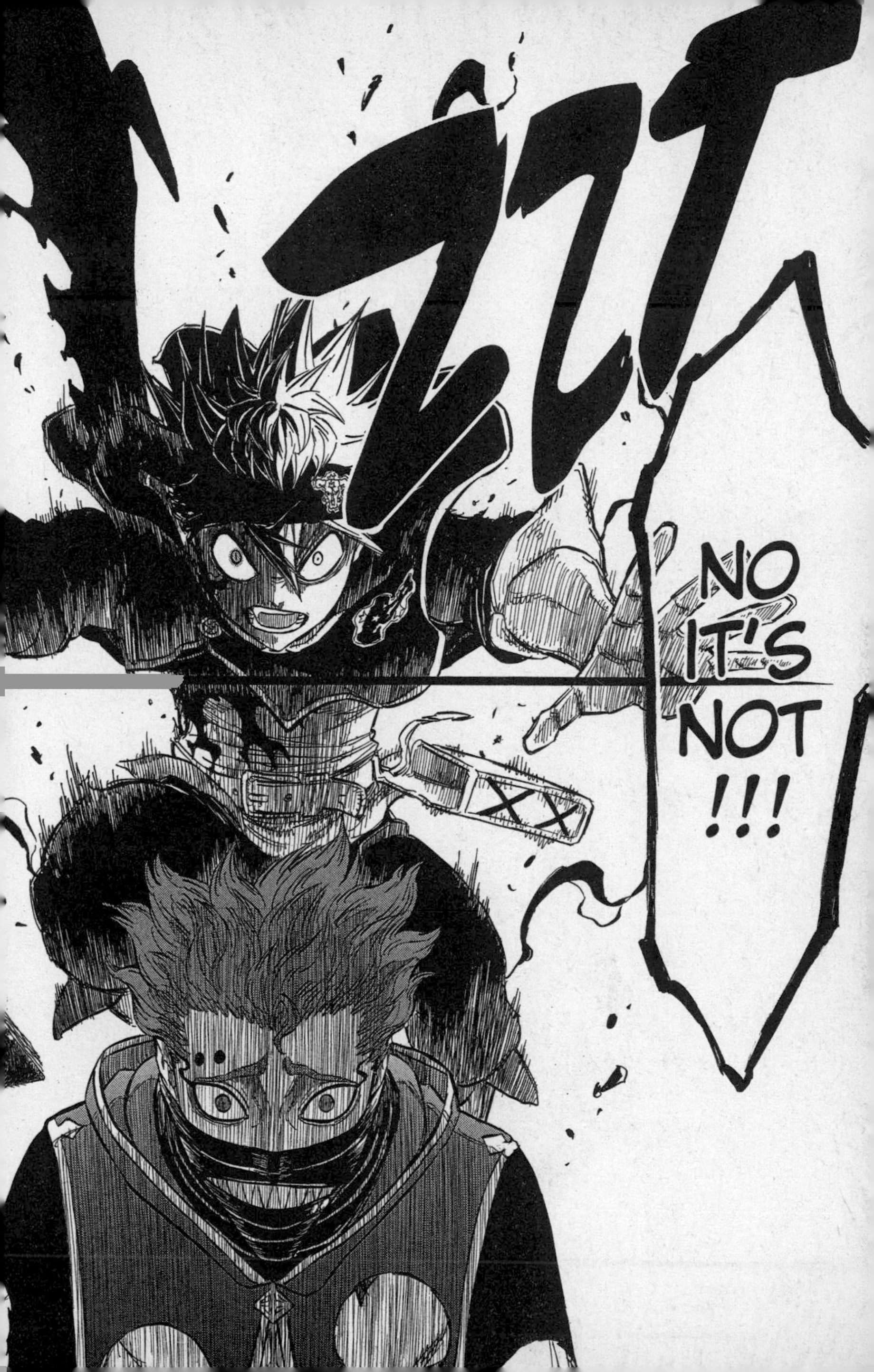
NO IT'S NOT!!!

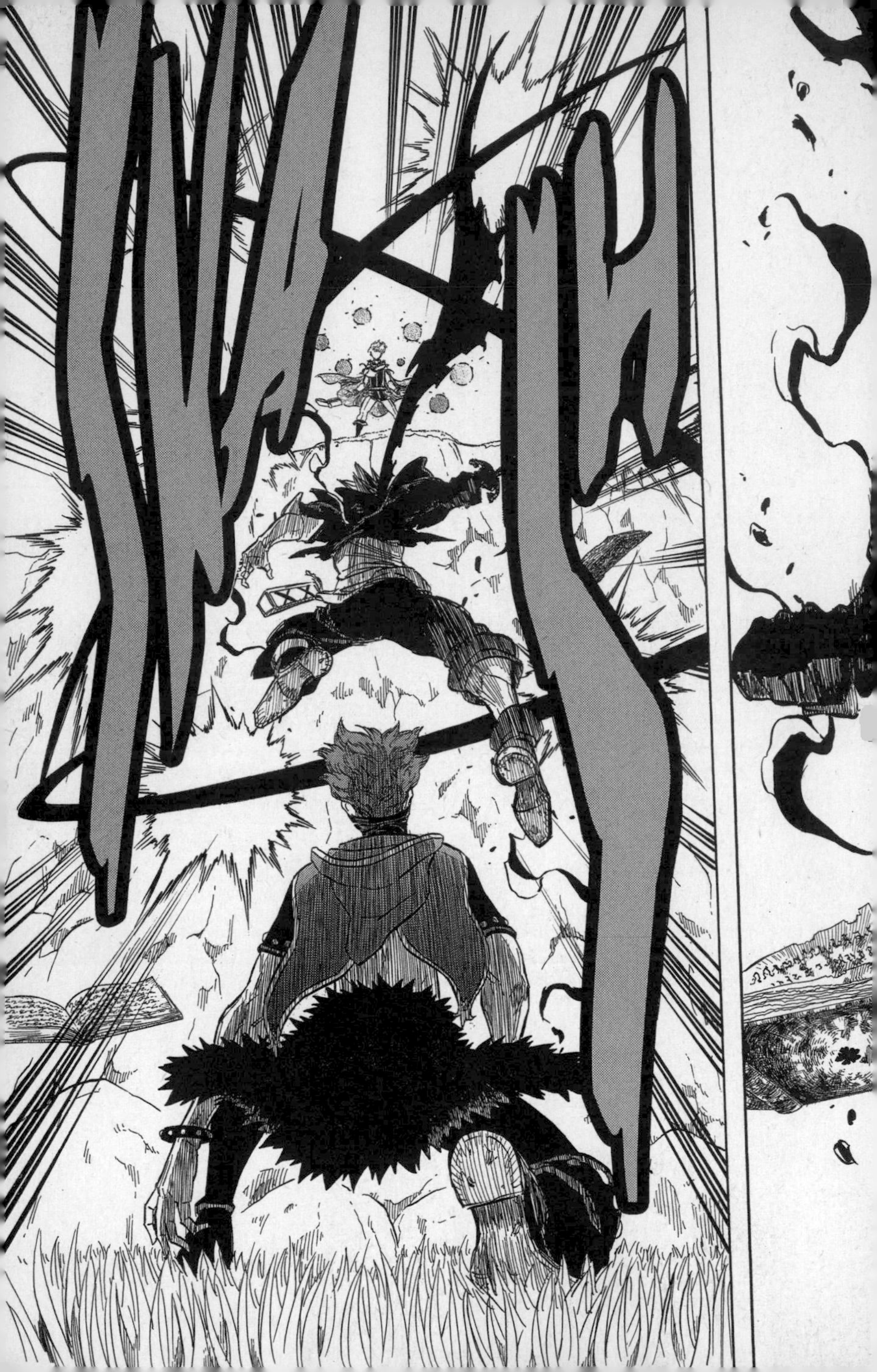

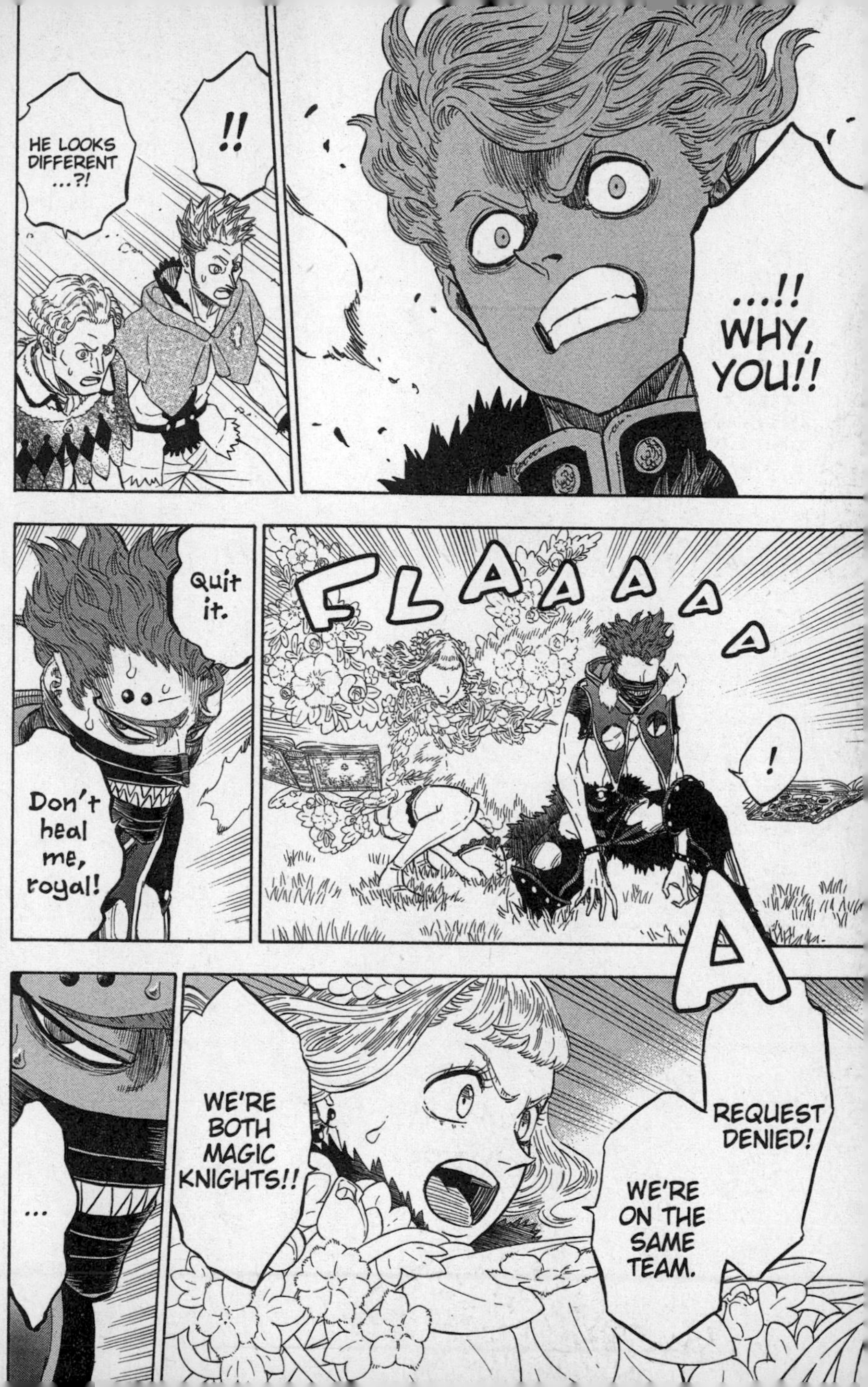
...!! WHY, YOU!!
!!
HE LOOKS DIFFERENT ...?!
FLAAAAAA
!
Quit it.
Don't heal me, royal!
REQUEST DENIED!
WE'RE ON THE SAME TEAM.
WE'RE BOTH MAGIC KNIGHTS!!
...

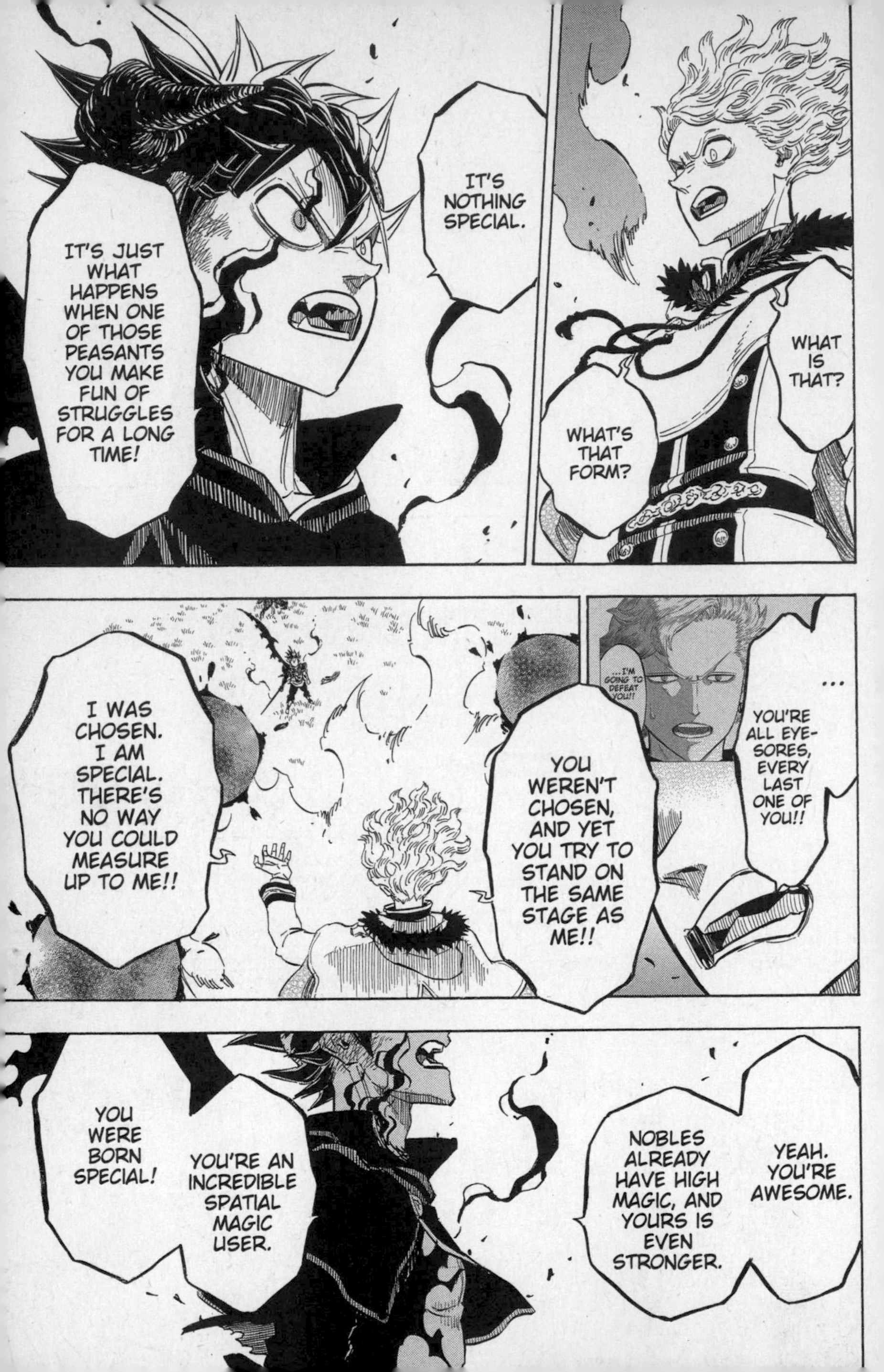

WHAT IS THAT?
WHAT'S THAT FORM?
IT'S NOTHING SPECIAL.
IT'S JUST WHAT HAPPENS WHEN ONE OF THOSE PEASANTS YOU MAKE FUN OF STRUGGLES FOR A LONG TIME!
...
YOU'RE ALL EYE-SORES, EVERY LAST ONE OF YOU!!
...I'M GOING TO DEFEAT YOU!!
YOU WEREN'T CHOSEN, AND YET YOU TRY TO STAND ON THE SAME STAGE AS ME!!
I WAS CHOSEN. I AM SPECIAL. THERE'S NO WAY YOU COULD MEASURE UP TO ME!!
YEAH. YOU'RE AWESOME.
NOBLES ALREADY HAVE HIGH MAGIC, AND YOURS IS EVEN STRONGER.
YOU'RE AN INCREDIBLE SPATIAL MAGIC USER.
YOU WERE BORN SPECIAL!

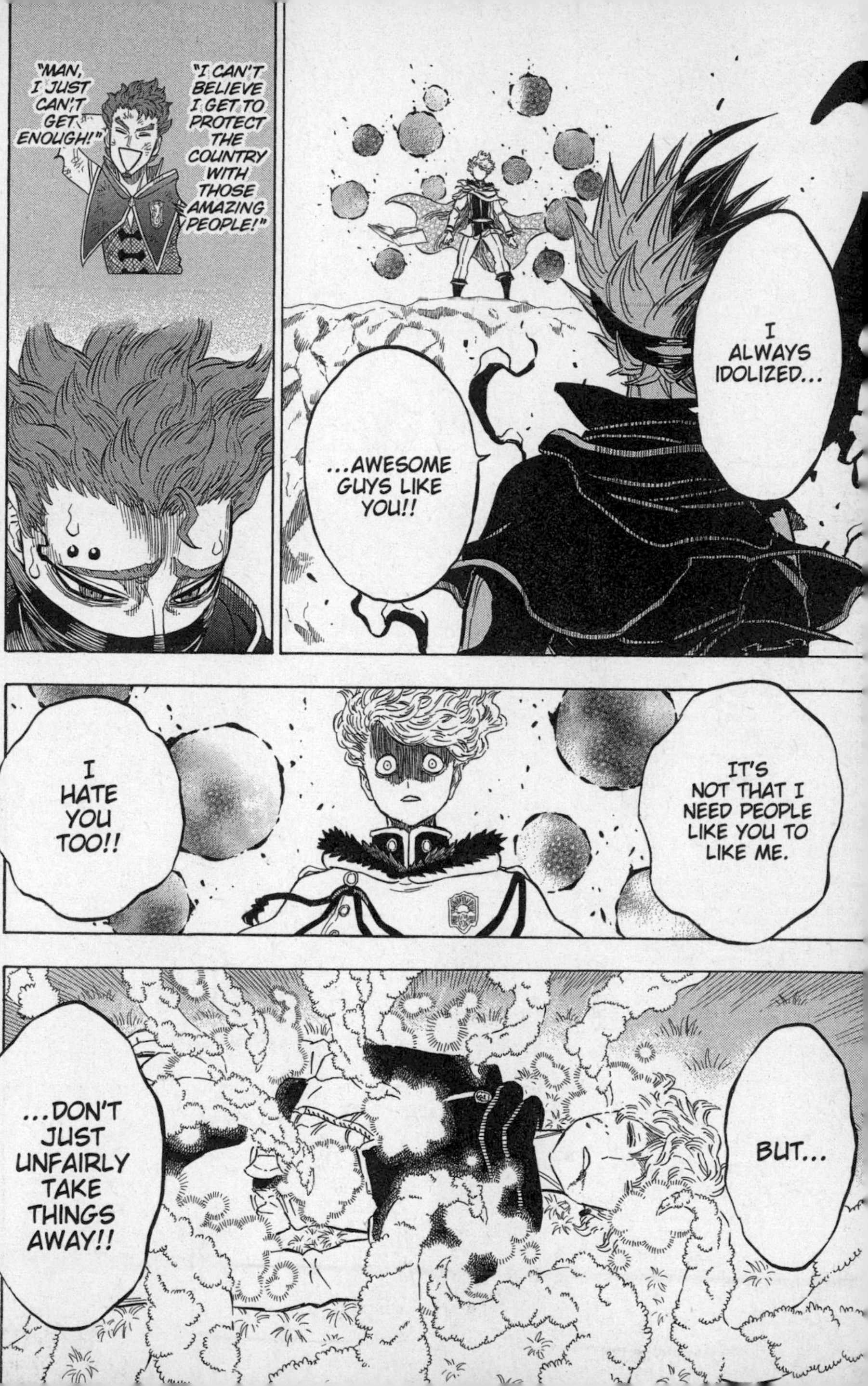
I ALWAYS IDOLIZED...
...AWESOME GUYS LIKE YOU!!
"I CAN'T BELIEVE I GET TO PROTECT THE COUNTRY WITH THOSE AMAZING PEOPLE!"
"MAN, I JUST CAN'T GET ENOUGH!"
IT'S NOT THAT I NEED PEOPLE LIKE YOU TO LIKE ME.
I HATE YOU TOO!!
BUT...
...DON'T JUST UNFAIRLY TAKE THINGS AWAY!!

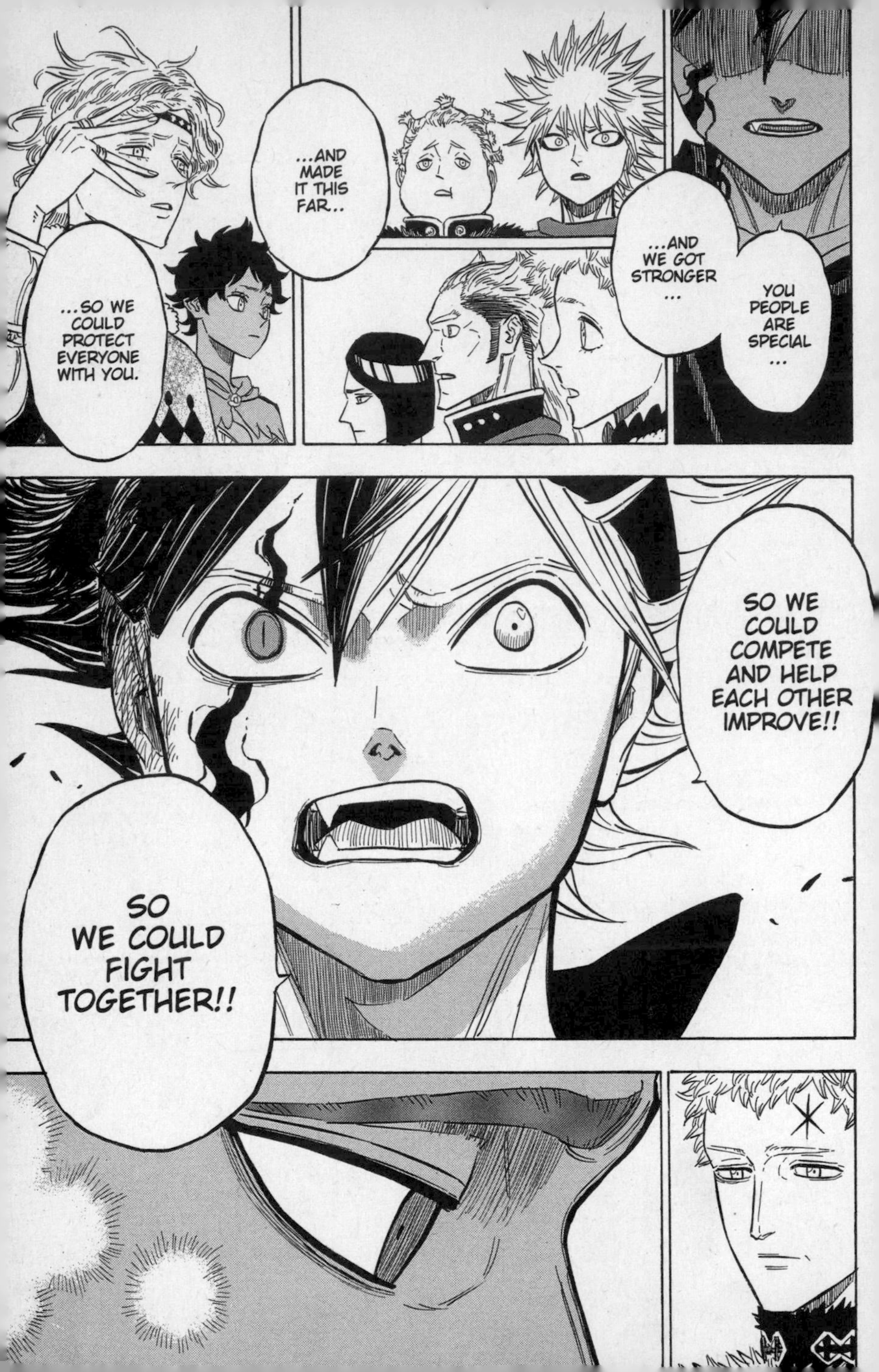
YOU PEOPLE ARE SPECIAL ...
...AND WE GOT STRONGER ...
...AND MADE IT THIS FAR...
...SO WE COULD PROTECT EVERYONE WITH YOU.
SO WE COULD COMPETE AND HELP EACH OTHER IMPROVE!!
SO WE COULD FIGHT TOGETHER!!

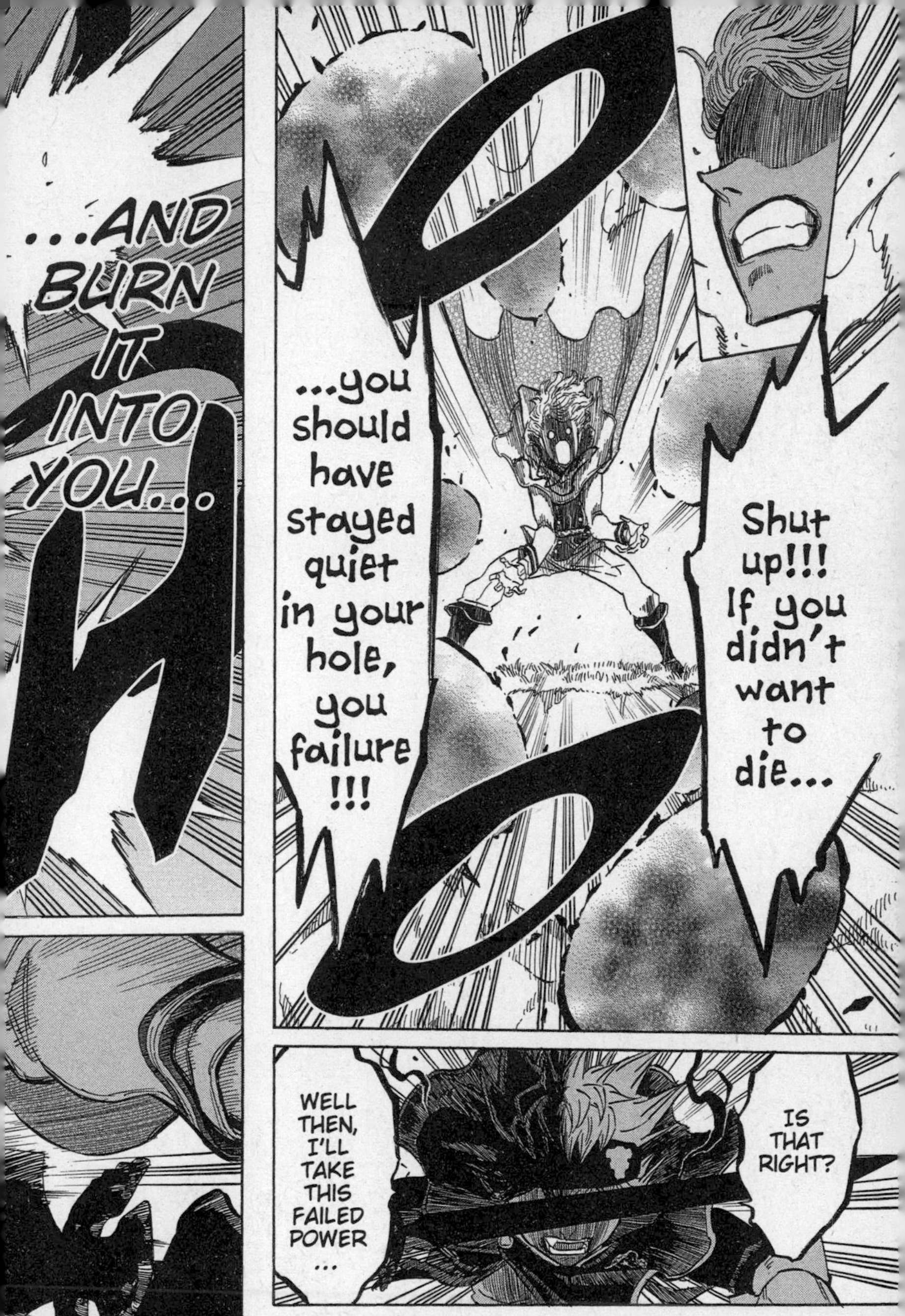

Shut up!!! If you didn't want to die...
...you should have stayed quiet in your hole, you failure!!!
IS THAT RIGHT?
WELL THEN, I'LL TAKE THIS FAILED POWER...
...AND BURN IT INTO YOU...

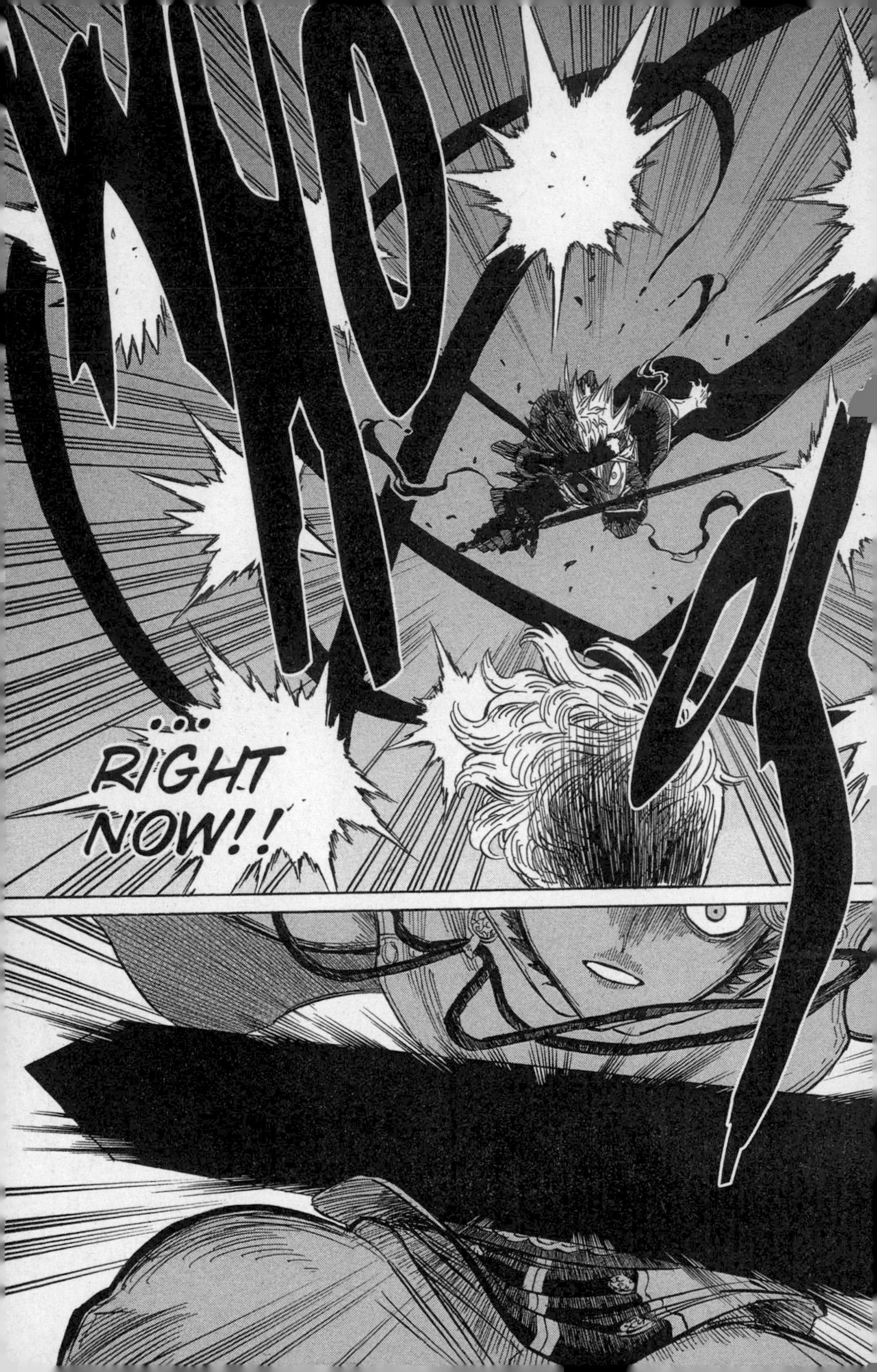
...RIGHT NOW!!

GWAH-
OOM

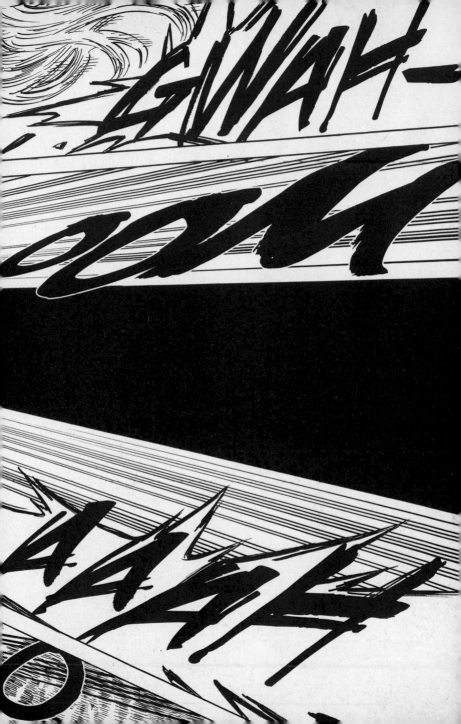

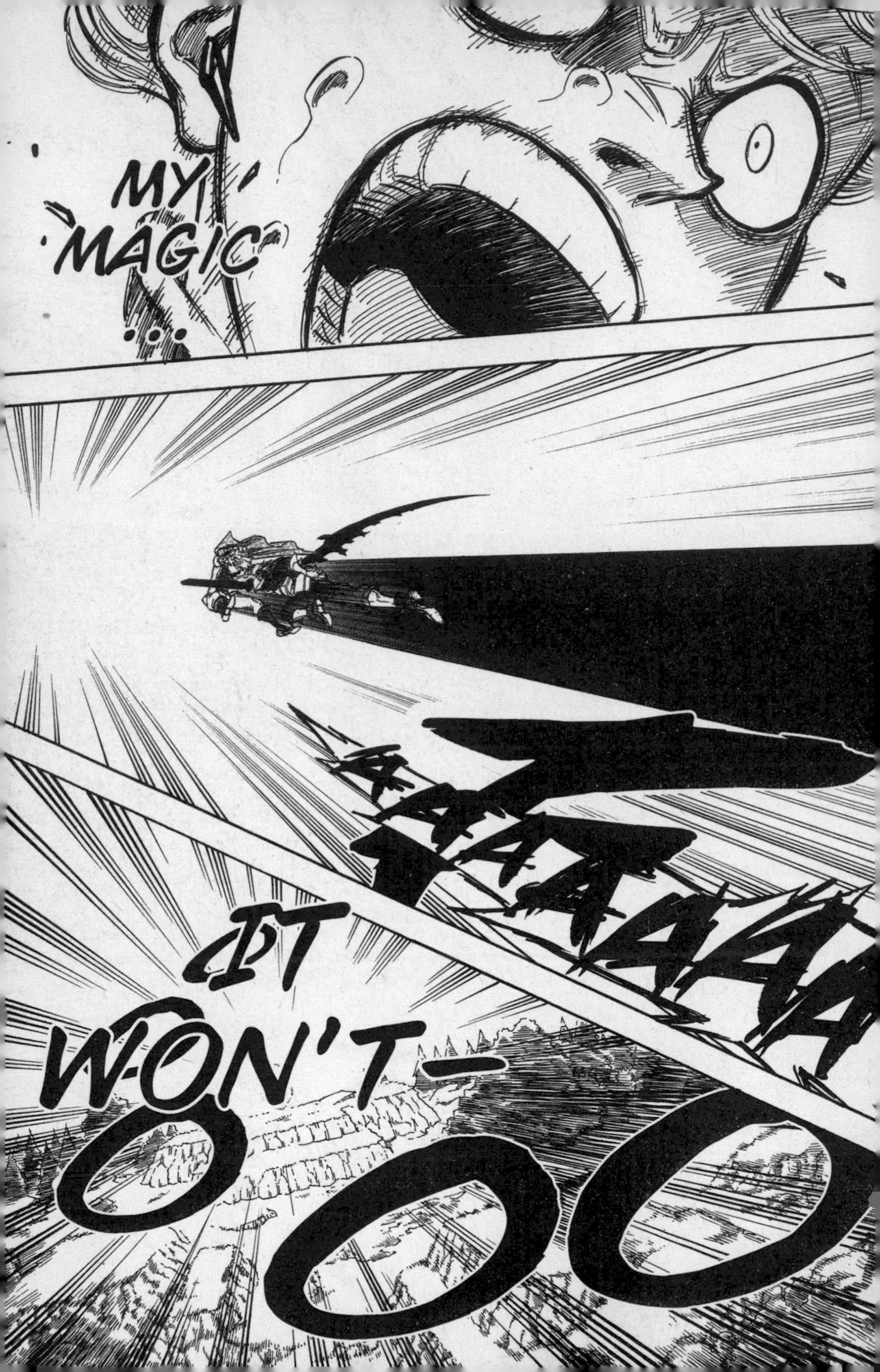
MY MAGIC ...
ZAAAAAAA
IT WON'T-
OOO

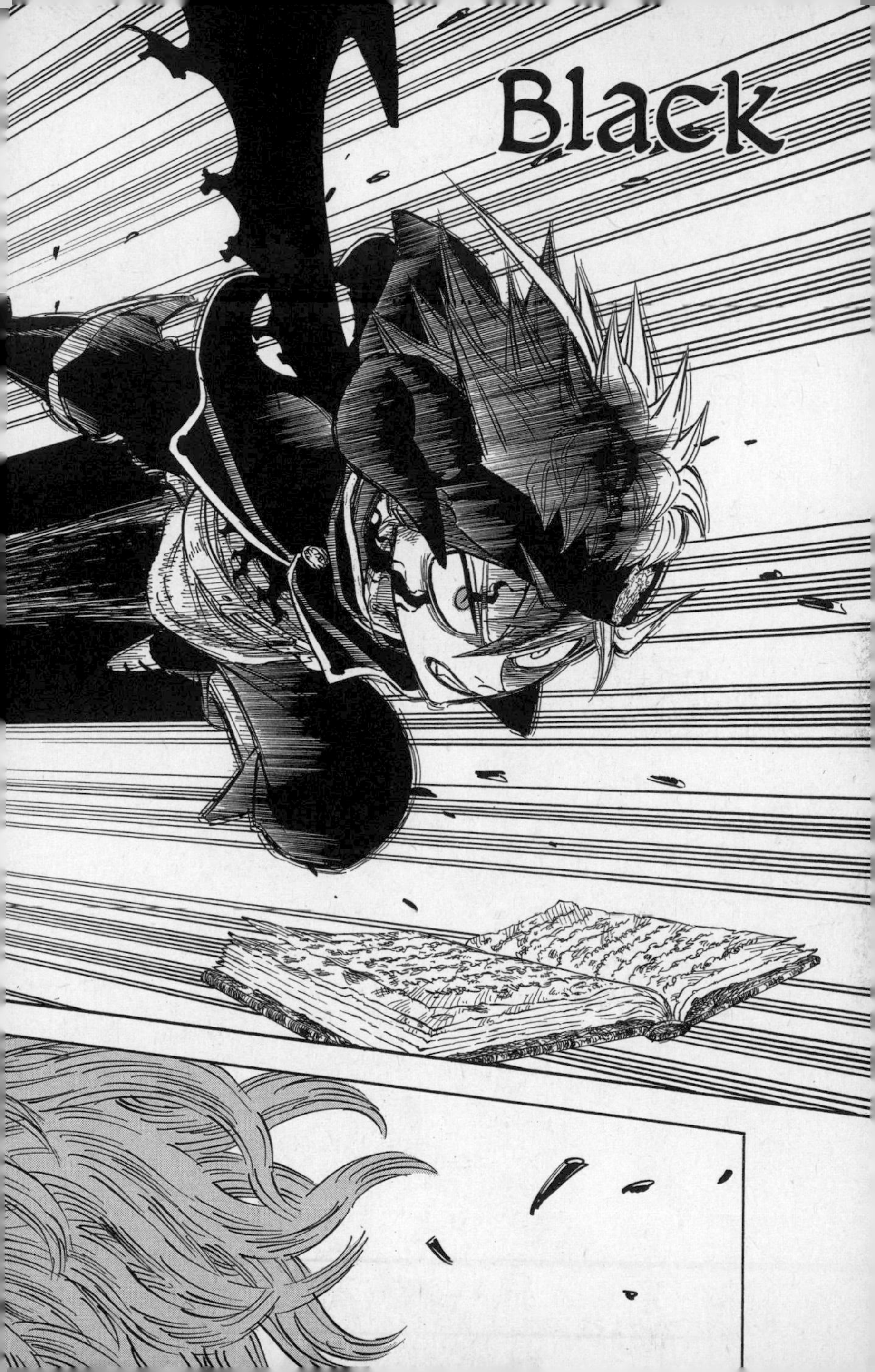
Black

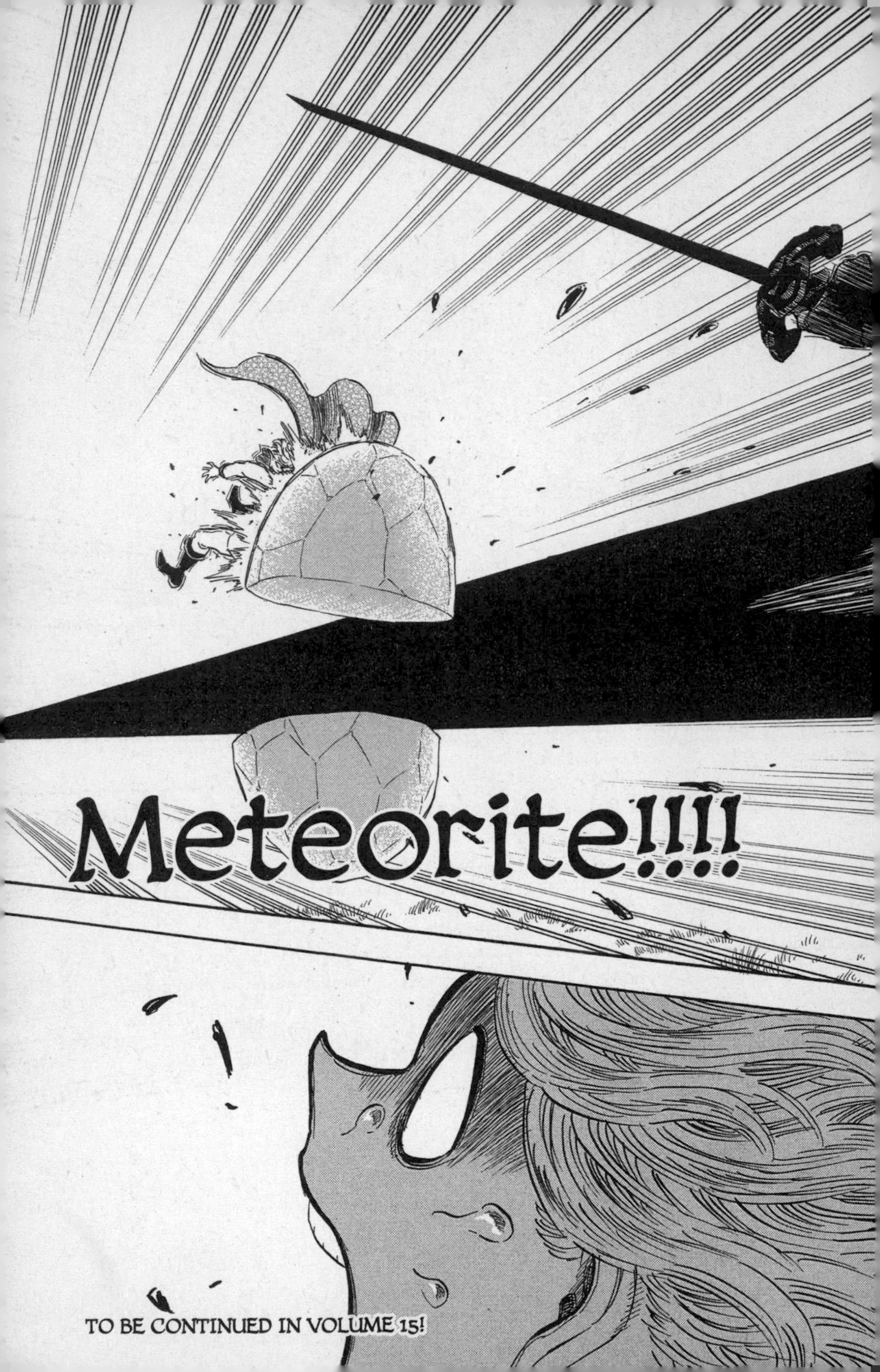
Meteorite!!!!
TO BE CONTINUED IN VOLUME 15!

The Blank Page Brigade

This volume's topic:
What food do you hate, even though you've never tried it?

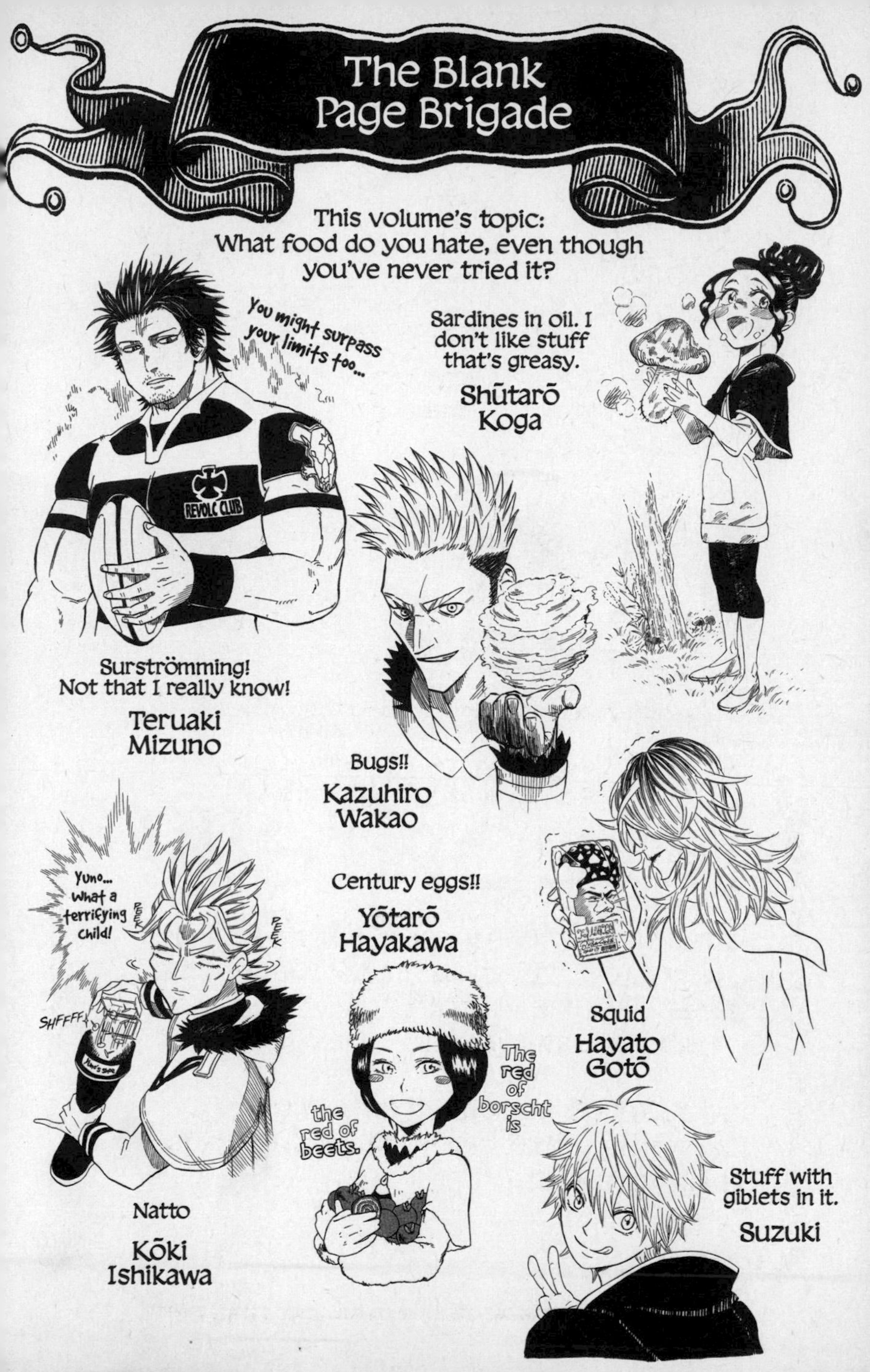

Sardines in oil. I don't like stuff that's greasy.
Shūtarō Koga
You might surpass your limits too...
REVOLC CLUB
Surströmming! Not that I really know!
Teruaki Mizuno
Bugs!!
Kazuhiro Wakao
Squid
Hayato Gotō
Century eggs!!
Yōtarō Hayakawa
The red of borscht is the red of beets.
Yuno... what a terrifying child!
PEEK
PEEK
SHFFFF
Natto
Kōki Ishikawa
Stuff with giblets in it.
Suzuki

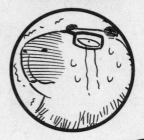

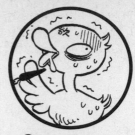

Oysters.

©

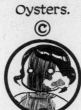

Green curry, although I love curry.

Captain Tabata

I have no dislikes! I've even eaten insects for a magazine project.

Editor Katayama

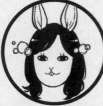

Mantis shrimp.

Designer Iwai

Green peas and rice.

Comics Editor Koshimura

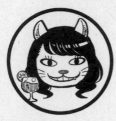

AFTERWORD

❀

One day, my mom called me up and she kept saying "Black is amazing!" I had no idea what she was talking about, but she meant this manga.

I felt terribly grateful to be drawing something that my mom could get that excited about.

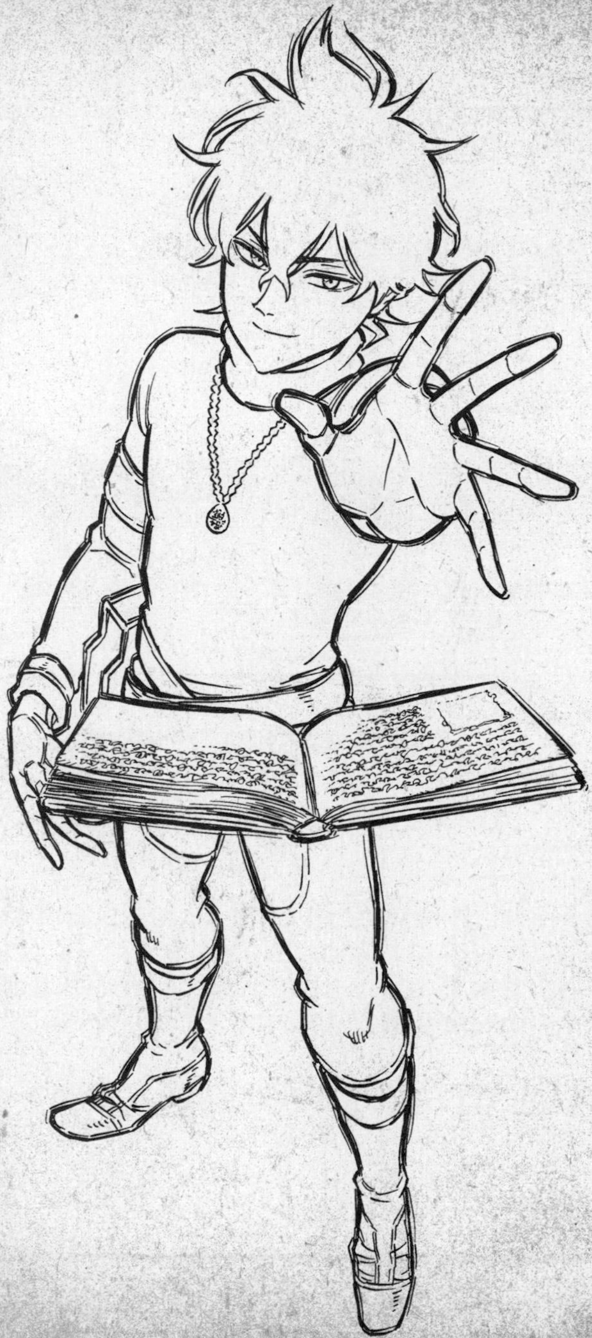

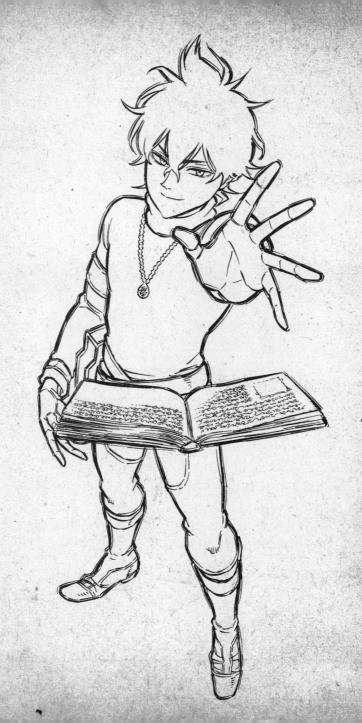

Special Bonus Materials

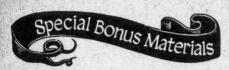

The cover illustrations for *Weekly Jump* Issue 44, 2017! Presenting the full-body shots of Asta and Yuno!!

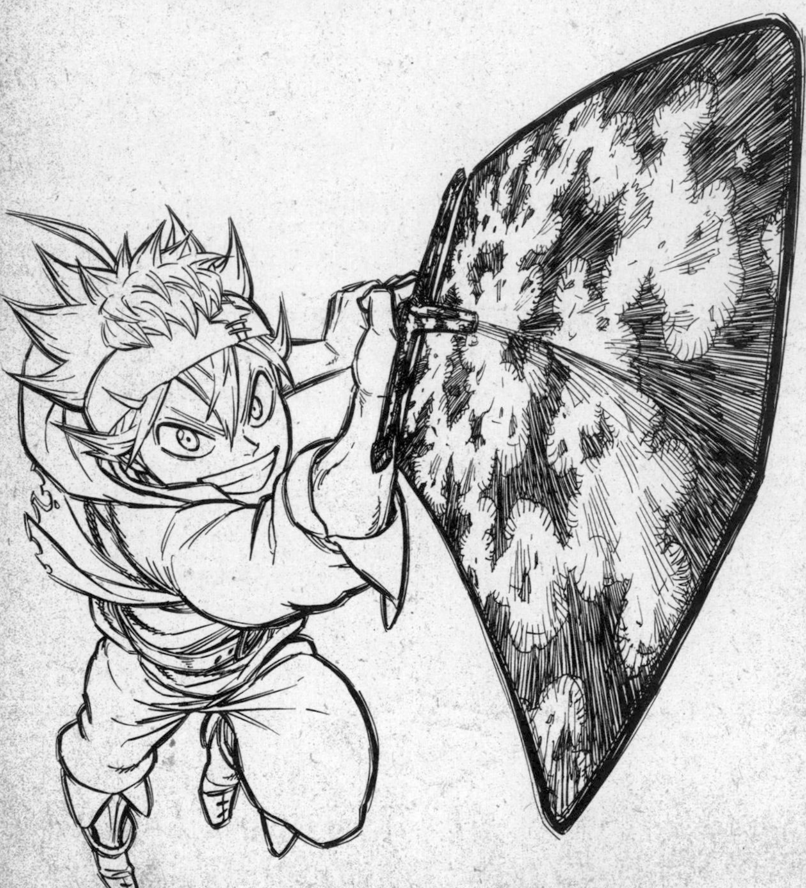

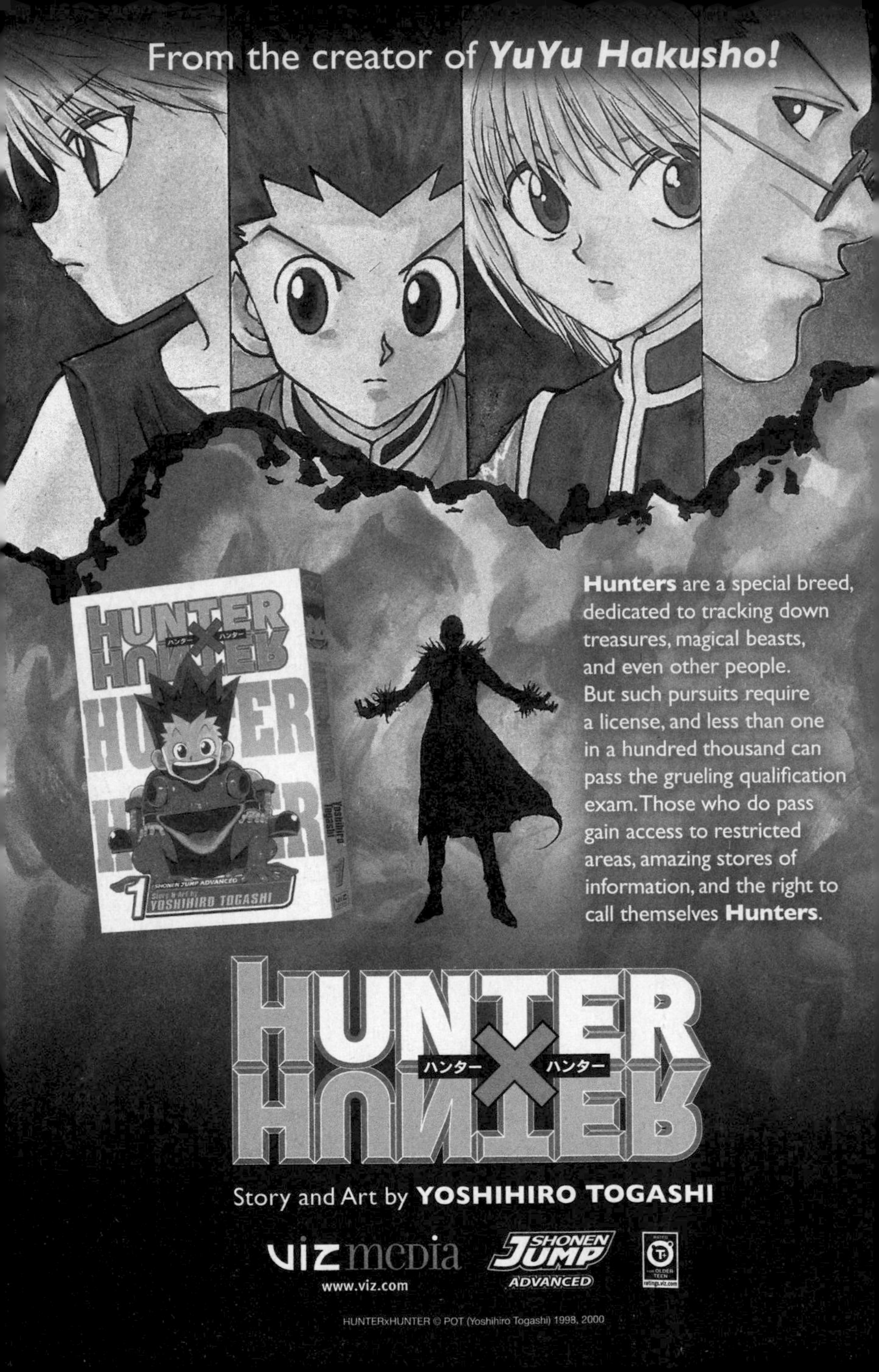
From the creator of *YuYu Hakusho!*
Hunters are a special breed, dedicated to tracking down treasures, magical beasts, and even other people. But such pursuits require a license, and less than one in a hundred thousand can pass the grueling qualification exam. Those who do pass gain access to restricted areas, amazing stores of information, and the right to call themselves **Hunters**.
HUNTER ハンター × ハンター HUNTER
Story and Art by YOSHIHIRO TOGASHI
viz media
www.viz.com
SHONEN JUMP ADVANCED
HUNTERxHUNTER © POT (Yoshihiro Togashi) 1998, 2000

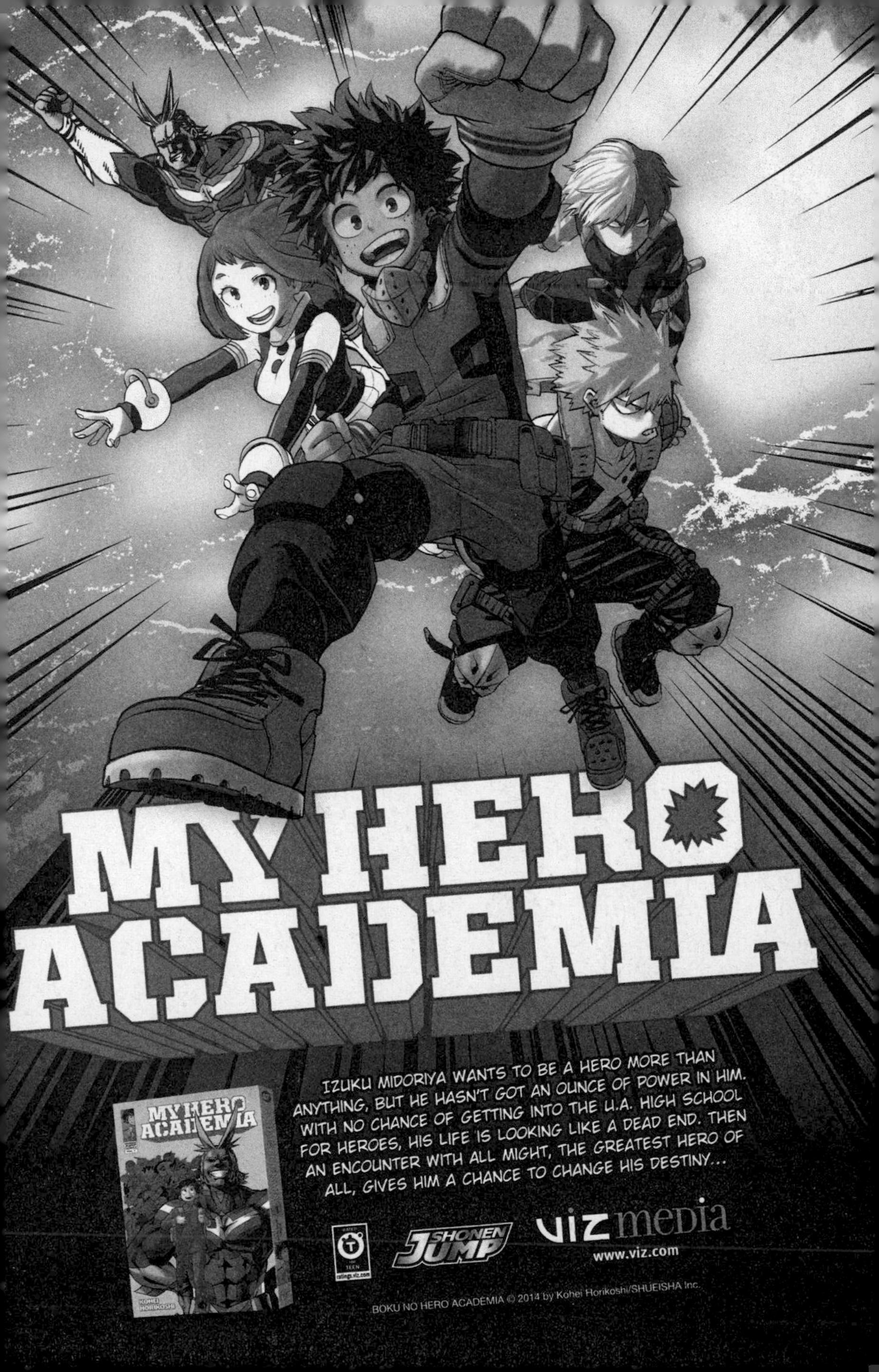
MY HERO ACADEMIA
IZUKU MIDORIYA WANTS TO BE A HERO MORE THAN ANYTHING, BUT HE HASN'T GOT AN OUNCE OF POWER IN HIM. WITH NO CHANCE OF GETTING INTO THE U.A. HIGH SCHOOL FOR HEROES, HIS LIFE IS LOOKING LIKE A DEAD END. THEN AN ENCOUNTER WITH ALL MIGHT, THE GREATEST HERO OF ALL, GIVES HIM A CHANCE TO CHANGE HIS DESTINY...
MY HERO ACADEMIA
KOHEI HORIKOSHI
SHONEN JUMP
viz media
www.viz.com
BOKU NO HERO ACADEMIA © 2014 by Kohei Horikoshi/SHUEISHA Inc.

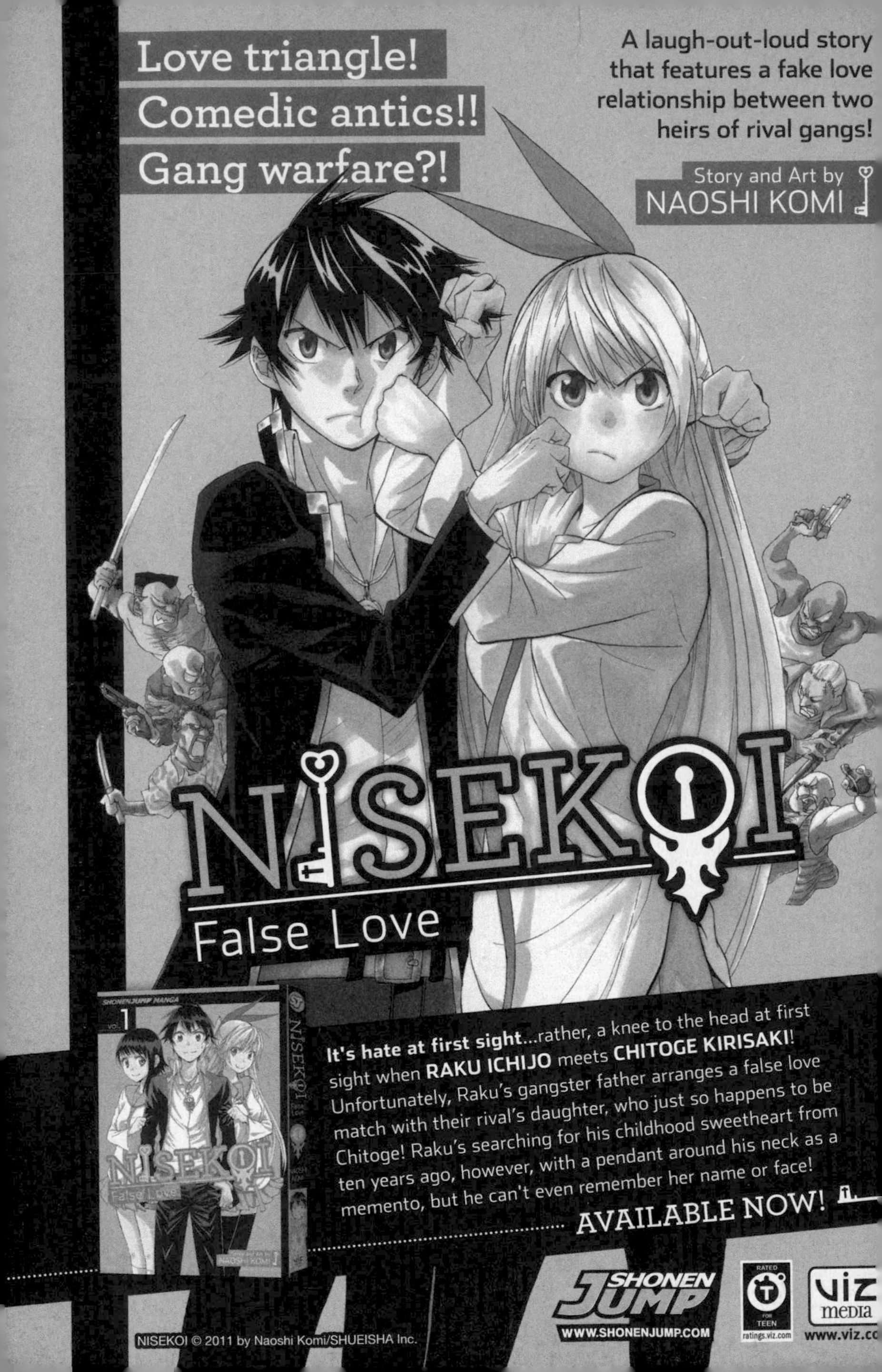
Love triangle!
Comedic antics!!
Gang warfare?!
A laugh-out-loud story that features a fake love relationship between two heirs of rival gangs!
Story and Art by
NAOSHI KOMI
NISEKOI
False Love
SHONENJUMP MANGA
vol. 1
NISEKOI
False Love
It's hate at first sight...rather, a knee to the head at first sight when RAKU ICHIJO meets CHITOGE KIRISAKI! Unfortunately, Raku's gangster father arranges a false love match with their rival's daughter, who just so happens to be Chitoge! Raku's searching for his childhood sweetheart from ten years ago, however, with a pendant around his neck as a memento, but he can't even remember her name or face!
AVAILABLE NOW!
SHONEN JUMP
WWW.SHONENJUMP.COM
RATED T FOR TEEN
ratings.viz.com
VIZ media
www.viz.co
NISEKOI © 2011 by Naoshi Komi/SHUEISHA Inc.

ASTRA
LOST IN SPACE

CAN EIGHT TEENAGERS FIND THEIR WAY HOME FROM 5,000 LIGHT-YEARS AWAY?

It's the year 2063, and interstellar space travel has become the norm. Eight students from Caird High School and one child set out on a routine planet camp excursion. While there, the students are mysteriously transported 5,000 light-years away to the middle of nowhere! Will they ever make it back home?!

ASTRA
LOST IN SPACE

Story and Art by KENTA SHINOHARA

VIZ

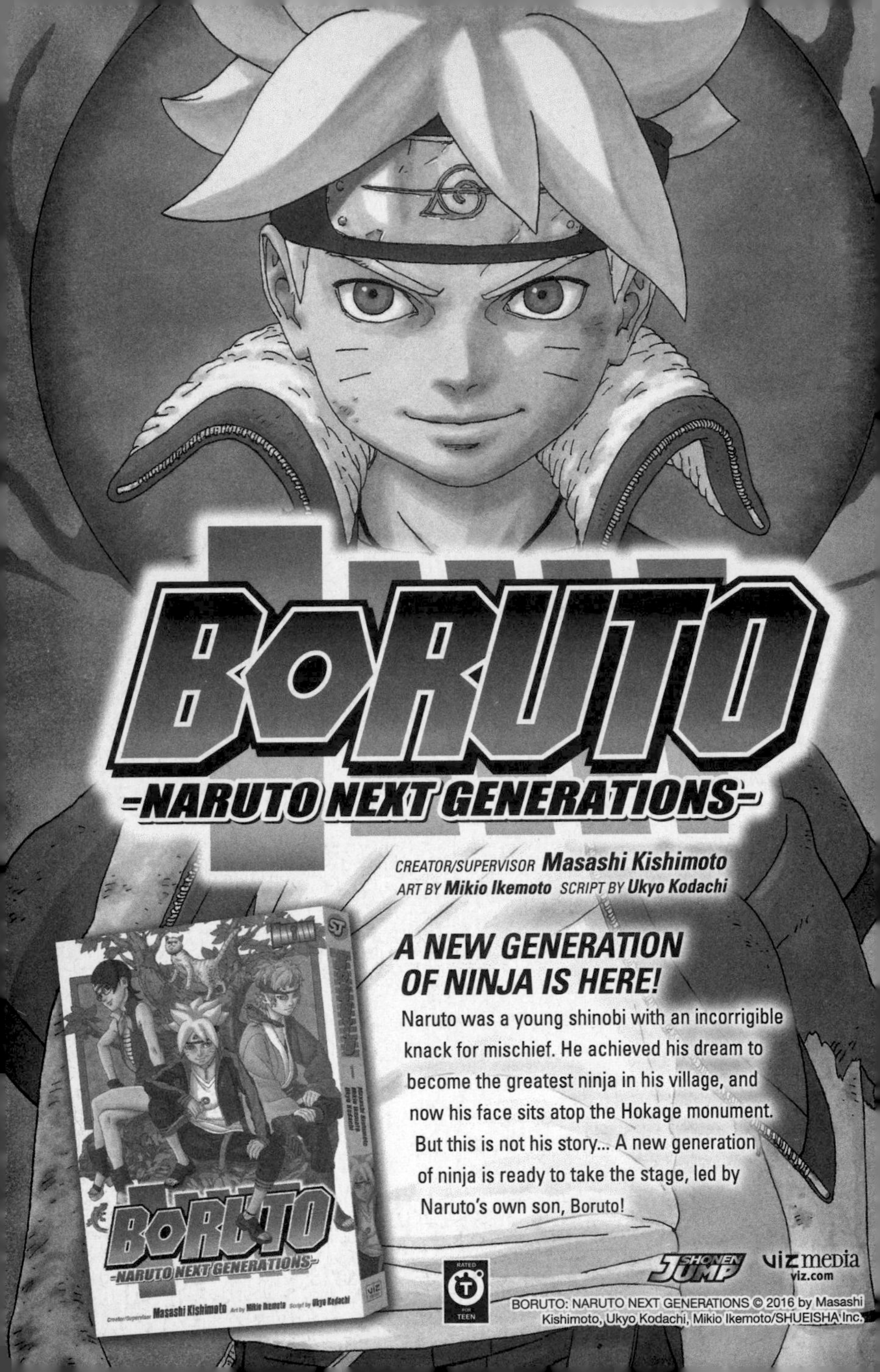
BORUTO
-NARUTO NEXT GENERATIONS-
CREATOR/SUPERVISOR Masashi Kishimoto
ART BY Mikio Ikemoto SCRIPT BY Ukyo Kodachi
A NEW GENERATION OF NINJA IS HERE!
Naruto was a young shinobi with an incorrigible knack for mischief. He achieved his dream to become the greatest ninja in his village, and now his face sits atop the Hokage monument. But this is not his story... A new generation of ninja is ready to take the stage, led by Naruto's own son, Boruto!
BORUTO
-NARUTO NEXT GENERATIONS-
Creator/Supervisor Masashi Kishimoto Art by Mikio Ikemoto Script by Ukyo Kodachi
RATED T FOR TEEN
SHONEN JUMP
viz media
viz.com
BORUTO: NARUTO NEXT GENERATIONS © 2016 by Masashi Kishimoto, Ukyo Kodachi, Mikio Ikemoto/SHUEISHA Inc.

Stop

YOU'RE READING THE WRONG WAY!

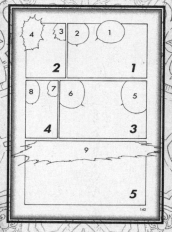

BLACK CLOVER

reads from right to left, starting in the upper-right corner. Japanese is read from right to left, meaning that action, sound effects, and word-balloon order are completely reversed from English order.